Genealogical Abstracts from Palmyra

Wayne County, New York

Newspapers
1810-1854

Originally Transcribed by

S. D. Van Alstine

with
Additions by
Harriet Evretts Wiles

Edited by
Mary Keysor Meyer

HERITAGE BOOKS
2019

HERITAGE BOOKS
AN IMPRINT OF HERITAGE BOOKS, INC.

Books, CDs, and more—Worldwide

For our listing of thousands of titles see our website
at
www.HeritageBooks.com

Published 2019 by
HERITAGE BOOKS, INC.
Publishing Division
5810 Ruatan Street
Berwyn Heights, Md. 20740

Originally published by Pipe Creek Publications, 1996

Heritage Books by the authors:

Genealogical Abstracts from Palmyra, Wayne County, New York, Newspapers 1810–1854
Originally Transcribed by S. D. Van Alstine, with Additions by Harriet Evretts Wiles; Edited by Mary Keysor Meyer

Marriage and Death Notices from the Newark [New York] Weekly Courier, 1869–1873
Harriet Wiles

Heritage Books by Mary Keysor Meyer:

Cemetery Inscriptions of Madison County, New York, Volume 1
Mary K. Meyer and Joyce C. Scott

*Deaths, Births, Marriages from Newspapers Published in
Hamilton, Madison County, New York, 1818–1886*
Mrs. E. P. Smith, Joyce C. Scott and Mary K. Meyer

*A Directory of Cayuga County Residents Who Supported
Publication of the History of Cayuga County, New York*

*Abstracts from Madison County, New York Newspapers
in the Cazenovia Public Library*

Baltimore City Birth Records, 1865–1894

*Divorces and Names Changed in Maryland
by Act of the Legislature, 1634–1867*

*Free Blacks in Harford, Somerset and
Talbot Counties, Maryland 1832*

*Meyer's Directory of Genealogical Societies in the U.S.A.
and Canada: 1998–2000, 12th Edition*
Family of Mary K. Meyer

*Westward of Fort Cumberland: Military Lots Set Off for
Maryland's Revolutionary Soldiers*

Who's Who in Genealogy and Heraldry 1990
Mary Keysor Meyer and P. William Filby

All rights reserved. No part of this book may be reproduced or transmitted in any form or by any means, electronic or mechanical, including photocopying, recording or by any information storage and retrieval system without written permission from the author, except for the inclusion of brief quotations in a review.

International Standard Book Numbers
Paperbound: 978-1-58549-836-9
Clothbound: 978-0-7884-6016-6

DEDICATION

GAVE ALL HE HAD - COULD ANYONE DO MORE THAN ESTY?

PASTOR EMERITUS OF NATURE AND PHILOSOPHER PHRENOLOGIST
PHENOMENAL MAKES VALUABLE GIFT TO
FREE LIBRARY

"Doc" Jason Esty, 86 years older than when he first saw the the light of day in this vicinity in 1822, shook the dust of Palmyra from his feet this week and retired to the privacy of home life near C. H. Latting's farm in Farmington, where "far from the madding throng" he will pass the remainder of his allotted 116 years in peace and quiet. Pastor Emeritus of Nature's school and herb-doctor extraordinary, the "doctor" has been a picturesque figure here, one that will be greatly missed on our streets and in his customary haunts.

Besides a number of handsome and roomy castles which the "doctor" had spent considerable time in erecting upon beautiful slopes in Spain, he had little else to give the village here where he had lived so long, save one thing. This is a bound volume of the files of the Wayne Sentinel from 1825-1830, containing among many interesting items, an advertisement of Joseph Smith's, "Book of Mormon".

With the assistance of the snake editor of the Journal, Doc has made these papers into a suitable gift, which as soon as it can be properly inscribed, will be presented to the Kings Daughters Free Library in fee simple, absolute with all the donor's dower rights surrendered. A valuable historical reference it is too.

It was all he had to give and he gives it freely. Could anyone do more?

PREFACE

The records presented here were abstracted in 1913 by the late S. D. Van Alstine and Harriet Wiles, a native of Newark, New York at a much later date, from The Wayne Sentinel which was published in Palmyra, NY.

Both used copies of the Sentinel held in the King's Daughter's Library in Palmyra, NY. Mr. Van Alstine also used other copies housed at the Masonic Hall in Palmyra.

Although for the most part, both used the same newspapers from which to abstract information - at times one would abstract a personal item which seemed to have escaped the other. Mrs. Wiles seemed to have found earlier editions of the paper than Mr. Van Alstine. This was undoubtedly due to the accession of additional copies by the Library between the years 1913 and 1933 when Mrs. Wiles was working.

Each abstracter had his/her own peculiarity in copying entries. While Mrs. Wiles copied the name of the officiating minister at a marriage, Mr. Van Alstine evidently thought that bit of information was unimportant. But Mr. Van Alstine seems to have gleaned more data - that is a larger number of marriages and deaths than Mrs. Wiles.

In addition to just vital statistics, Mr. Van Alstine copied other news items concerning accidents, social life and business advertisements,; crimes, fires, education, and even a little humor along the way.

As a result this work is more than an important genealogical tool; it tells the story of Palmyra and the surrounding area; its growth from the early days of the old Erie Canal to the coming of the railroad and Macadam roads. It looks at religion from Lorenzo Dow to Joseph Smith and the birth of Mormonism. It notes the original publication of the first Book of Mormon.

It reflects the history of medicine at any early age, the cholera epidemics - rife along the route of the canal; the inability to save lives as the result of severe injuries; it gives us a peek into a world where there were more men than women and when women were rarely mentioned by name publicly - even in death or as the parent of a child.

This is the story of one small area of Central New York as it grew up alongside the Erie Canal.

INTRODUCTION

Events transcribed from the these newspapers published in Wayne County, NY are entered here chronologically - the date of the newspaper in boldface type preceding the entry of the items which appeared in that particular issue.

Standard abbreviations are used throughout the work. Remarks in parenthesis are those made by either Van Alstine or by Wiles while those in brackets were made by the present editor.

The editor copied names and other words - as they were spelled. These words may not be spelled correctly and certainly a number of names were not spelled as they are spelled today. We must bear in mind that by the time a name or a date or a place name was given verbally to the editor; the editor wrote it in longhand, then he or a typesetter set the type - a word or name could become rather garbled.

As he got into his work, Mr. Van Alstine adopted a system of abbreviations for the names of villages, towns, etc. The present editor after devoting some thought to his (unexplained) system of abbreviations solved most of the mysteries. One abbreviation which he used, "P.G." was never solved. It could have referred to Port Gibson or to Port Glasgow. I have chosen, however arbitrarily, to assume the abbreviation referred to Port Glasgow as it is in Wayne Co. and Port Gibson is in Ontario County. However, if it creates a problem for any researcher, I would advise searching in the other area.

Also, part way through his massive undertaking, Mr. Van Alstine adopted a habit of saying a couple were married or an individual died in "Town". The users of this work should be aware that throughout the United States the word "town" generally denotes a village or perhaps even a city. However, in New York State although a "town" can also be a village but - when used as "in the town of" it denotes what is called a township in other states.

Mary K. Meyer, Editor

GENEALOGICAL NOTES FROM VARIOUS WAYNE COUNTY NEWSPAPERS

JUNE 26, 1810

John Smith and William H. Cuyler offer town lots for sale formerly owned by Daniel Sawyer. OR

MAY 12, 1812 OR&WA

LIST OF TOWNS IN ONTARIO COUNTY

Canandaigua	Williamson	Ontario
Bristol	Palmyra*	Honeoye
Gorham	Seneca	Farmington
Geneseo	Bloomfield	Boyle
Penfield	Middlesex	Sparta
Benton	Jerusalem	Naples
Phelps	Sodus*	Livonia
Lyons*	Avon	Lima

[* These towns later became part of Wayne Co. at its formation. mkm]

Asa R. Swift of Palmyra is m. to Miss Fanny Cole, a dau. of Mr. Southard Cole. OR&WA

MAY 26, 1812

George Durfee and Miss Pamilla Starkes are m. in Palmyra. OR&WA

SEPTEMBER 22, 1812

Court martial of Samuel Jennings. OR&WA

JANUARY 12, 1813

Lorenzo Clark of Naples and Laura Turner were m. at Palmyra. OR&WA

MARCH 2, 1813

Benjamin Cole d. in Palmyra, ae 55 yrs. OR&WA

JANUARY 4, 1813

Henry S. Crone of Palmyra: deserter, (fined?) $10.00. OR

JUNE 18, 1823

J. D. Everingham adv. for books; John Fleming, Jr. adv. 30,000 acres of land for sale in PA.; S. Ledyard of Pultneyvlle, J. Colt and J. Grandin of Palmyra adv. lumber; A. McIntyre - drug store; Wells Anderson adv. hides etc.; T. P. Baldwin adv. for someone to build a post and rail fence.

Canal Navigation: A line of elegant Packet Boats is preparing and will be ready to run between Utica and Schenectady on the first opening of the canal which it is supposed will take place in one or two weeks. PH&CA

MAY 26, 1812

William Howe Cuyler, as Sec. & Treas. of the Ontario Mfgr. Co., adv. lots for sale, making up the village of Manchester. OM

MAY 5, 1819

J. & O. White - dry goods; M. M. Dox & Co. of Sodus will pay cash for wheat; S. Scovell & Co. - dry goods; T. C. Strong wants wheat in payment of the Register.

John Russell adv. 1c reward for a runaway indentured servant boy named Daniel Butts ae 18 yrs. PR

Moses Padley of Ontario adv. 1 mill reward for a runaway apprentice, Francis Reed, May 5, 1819.

E. Shepardson, postmaster notifies O. P. Sheldon that a letter he sent to Abraham C. Sheldon at Albany is returned to Palmyra from the Dead Letter office; J. L. Thayer - dry goods; Alexander McIntyre - adv. snuff. PR

J. R. Robson - tailor; Ten Eyck & Fondey, Geneva - groceries; Abner Cole, attorney, formerly of Cole & Baldwin; Miss Durand - Milliner; Joel Coe, Jr. of Auburn - card factory; Asa Lilly, Capt. of the Light Dragoons calls a meeting at his house. PR

Mortgage Sales: Colt & Ledyard, Pultney Ville - Harbour ware-houses etc; George Tucker & John Smith, Williamson - lime; Thomas P. Baldwin, attorney. PR

OCTOBER 4, 1820

Married: in Palmyra, the 26th ult by F. Smith, Esq., Nehemiah Dodge and Miss Fannie Beebe, both of Pompey, Onondaga Co., NY.

Adv.: Lasher & Cande - stone - under T. C. Strong's printing office; Seymour Scovel wants to buy cattle also oats; Hart Hammond - postrider; T. C. Strong - books; Marshall Johnson - blacksmith; J. O. White - dry goods; Seymour Scovell want ashes; J. D. Hayward wants two coopers; T. C. Strong - wants accounts paid.

OM* - Ontario Messinger; OR* - Ontario Register; PR* - Palmyra Register
OR & WA* - Ontario Register & Wayne Advertiser
PH & CA* - Palmyra Herald & Canal Advertiser

GENEALOGICAL NOTES FROM THE WESTERN SPECTATOR & WAYNE ADVERTISER

Press not received, delayed the first issue a few days... Type came from Bruce's foundry in New York; press is Rust's Improved Patent and the paper is from Brown's Mill in Manchester.

Zion Church gets a new organ from New York City and Rev. Burton H. Hickox becomes the new Pastor.

Married: May 12, 1830 in Groton, CT, Albert G. Smith and Julia A. Burrows.

Died: June 8, 1830, Ann Sophia Foster, dau. of Jeter Foster.

Died: May 16, 1830, in Lyons, Emery Hewlet.

Died: May 17, 1830, in Canandaigua, [Livingston Co.], Margaret O'Hara, wife of Capt. William O'Hara.

Died: May 21, 1830, Rebecca Hall, ae 30 yrs., wife of Bailey Hall.

Died: May 27, 1830, in Geneva, [Ontario Co.], Mrs. Susannah Loncost, ae 37 years.

Died: May 27, 1830, in Macedon, Electa Rand, wife of Samuel Rand, ae 23 years.

Died: May 27, 1830, in Rochester, [Monroe Co., NY], Harriet Ward, wife of Levi A. Ward.

Died: May 27, 1830, in Fishkill, [Dutchess Co.], Jacob VanBenschoten, ae 77 years.

Died: May 27, 1830, in Poughkeepsie, Catherine G. Livingston, ae 85 yrs., widow of Gilbert Livingston.

Died: May 27, 1830, in Wheeler, [Steuben Co.], William Homes, ae 52 years.

Died: May 27, 1830, William Vial North, age 18 months, son of Norris North.

PALMYRA SENTINEL NEW ITEMS

OCTOBER 1, 1823:

Married at Vernon, Oneida Co., NY, on the 25th ult., Mr. Leonard Westcott, merchant of his village, to Miss Eliza Carpenter of the former place.

Married: in Macedon, on the 28th by the Rev. E. M. Spencer, Mr. William Tolford of this village to Miss Mary Spear of the former place.

Died: in this town on the 21st ult., Major Edward Durfee, aged 51 years, one of the first settlers.

Died: on the 21st ult., Jonathan S., son of William T. Hussey of this village, aged 15 months.

Died: on the 27th [ult.?], Ann Chase, an adopted child of Doctor Durfee Chase, aged 4 years.

Died: on the 27th [ult.], Margaret P., dau. of Mr. Samuel Allen, aged 14 months.

Died: on the 29th [ult.?], Mrs. ---Tague, aged 17 years.

OCTOBER 8, 1823:

Married in Williamson, on the first inst., by the Rev. Mr. True, Mr. WilliamWashington Cary to Miss Jane Potter.

Married: in this village on the 8th inst., Col. James A. Stoddard of Macedon, to Miss Hannah Hall of the former place.

OCTOBER 15, 1823 - No items copied or issue unavailable.

OCTOBER 22, 1823

Erie Canal Navigation Co. adds two new boats to their line: the Chancellor Kent and the Benjamin Wright, making eight between Utica & Rochester in 48 hrs. or less.

New Article for Transportation: A boat arrived here last evening from Rochester having on board 300 live hogs on their way to Connecticut, on a peddling voyage. Report of a celebration in Albany on the opening of the Canal.

Married: in Windsor, CT, on the --inst., Mr. Joel Thayer, of Vienna [Oneida Co.] to Miss Nancy Belden [or Selden], of the former place.

Married: in Vienna on the 21st inst., by Rev. Mr. Brace, Mr. Cromwell Lloyd, to Miss Delia Boughton, all of Vienna, [Oneida Co.].

Died: in this town last evening, Mrs, Sarah Gregg, aged 58 years.

Adv.: Smith & Champion - Palmyra S. St. John - wants to buy 20 tons of hay (Herd's grass or red clover).

Calvin Perkins - carriage factory near west end of village.

William A. McLean adv. uncalled for letters.

J. D. Everingham & Co. - dry goods.

Williams & Co, near Jessup & Palmer's basin, has dry goods.

Israel J. Richardson, Wayne Co. Clerk has office in Palmyra.

Eagle Hotel - S. St. John, on south side of Main St., opp. Rogers basin and the Collectors office where the boats land.

L. B. Barnum, Canandaigua - cabinet maker.

S. Allen - mail stage, Palmyra to Canandaigua.

James D. Everingham - storage and forwarding.

Dr. Luther Cowan - drugstore lately occupied by D. K. Jones.

P. Tucker has a set of military equipments for sale.

M. Toohey - for sale the Weekly Shamrock published at P. Tucker's.

Andrew G. Low - fulling business.

Jonah Howell- dressing cloth - closes out business. Samuel D. Huntington continues Howell's business.

Williams & Co. continues Jessup & Palmer.

J. D. Everingham - books.

P. West & Co. - boots, shoes & saddles, having bought out J. Foster & Co.

Jacob A. Dana - carriage making opp. J. Benson's.

S. Ledyard of Pultney Ville, J. Colt and P. Grandin of Palmyra - lumber & supplies;

Thomas Patterson of Macedon, adv. he will not be responsible for debts contracted by others.

Bushnell & Stevens move to Leroy and D. Hendee, collects for them.

A. Randolph & Co. hats.

Burr Butler, tailor, one door west of A. McIntyre's drug store.

David Benham, tailor, takes J. Foster's location - wants an apprentice.

T. J. Stimson - sign painting.

T. C. Strong wants to settle his accounts with others.

Vincent G. Barney & Kingsley Miller - dissolve.

Manson Sherman - stone cutting, Pultneyville.

William Wadsworth-Geneseo has Merino sheep for sale.

B. B. Brown of Manchester - wool carding.

W. L. Marcy, Comptroller - notice concerning quit rents.

Andrew G. Low - wants three journeyman.

OCTOBER 29, 1823

Thanksgiving proclamation for December 18, 1823.

Adv.: R. W. Smith & T. P. Baldiwn will conduct a public singing school at the Academy.

Vincent G. Barney succeeds Barney & Miller - wheat wanted.

P. Grandin - distillery near Boyle's Mill in Macedon - for sale or rent.

B. & C. Palmer, Macedon - lime for sale.

N. Thayer wants settlements for L. Thayer & Co. A. McIntyre - drugs;

A. R. Galloway, South Williamson adv. a stray horse.

NOVEMBER 5, 1823 - No items copied.
NOVEMBER 12, 1823 - No items copied
NOVEMBER 19, 1823
Died: in this village on the 15th inst., John H. Tice, age 21 months.

NOVEMBER 26, 1823 - no items copied.
DECEMBER 3, 1823
Married in Macedon on the 26th ult., by the Rev. Mr. Stockton, Mr. William Porter to Miss Marina White.

Married: in Manchester, Mr. Garrett Vandroof to Miss Cornelia Woodward.

Died: in Birdstown, KY, of yellow fever, on the 16th of Sept., Mr. Silas Hulbert, formerly of this village, aged 30 years. He left a wife and one child.

DECEMBER 10. 1823 - No items copied.
DECEMBER 17, 1823
Married: in this town last evening by A. R. Tiffany, Esq., Mr. Hiram Rhude to Miss Laura Smith.

Died: in this town on the 15th inst., Mr. William Wilcox, aged 54 years - one of the early settlers.

Died: at Kinderhook, on the 25th ult., Mrs. Christina Cantine, relict of the late Moses I. Cantine, Esq., formerly one of the Editors of the Albany Argus.

Died: at his residence near Georgetown, DC, the 1st inst., Baron Frederick Graham, Minister from the Prussian Government to the United States.

Died: in Farmington, Moses Aldrich, son of Dr. Stephen Aldrich, aged 16 years.

Died: in Dublin [Ireland?], on the 25th ult., Mrs. Mary Goff, in the 75th year of her age. She was born in the room she died in, was married and had 20 children -in the same room, yet had not a single relative living to attend her funeral.

DECEMBER 24, 1823
Died: at Frankfort, Germany, on October 20th, his Royal Highness, Prince Louis of Hesse-Darmstadt.

Married: in this village on the 28th inst., by F. Smith, Esq., Mr. Gordon Buck to Miss Percis Drake.

DECEMBER 31, 1823
Married: in Macedon, the 16th inst., by the Rev. Mr. Stockton, Mr. William P. Ward to Miss Mary Ann Stoddard.

JANUARY 7, 1824 - No items copied

JANUARY 14, 1824 - No items copied

JANUARY 21, 1824

Married in this village on the 15th inst., by Rev. Mr. Stockton, James Field, Esq., to Miss Cynthia Hathaway.

Married: at Lockport, [Niagara Co.], on the 4th inst., Mr. Joseph Coe of Mt. Morris, [Livingston Co.], to Miss Sophia Harwood of Macedon.

Married: in Macedon, on the 22nd by A. Spear, Esq., Mr. Bennett Bates, Jun., to Miss Rosamond Brown.

JANUARY 28, 1824

Married: in Macedon on the 18th, Mr. Robert Lewis to Miss Nancy Champlain.

Married: in this town on the 17th by F. Smith, Esq., Mr. Hiram H. Tooker to Miss Mary Taft.

Died: in Auburn [Cayuga Co.] on the 25th, Thompson Pease, son of Mr. James Pease of this village.

FEBRUARY 4, 1824

Died: in Manchester, on the 25th ult., Miss Fanny Beach, aged 18 years.

FEBRUARY 11, 1824 - List of advertisers:

North & Pierson - stove pipe factory - one door west of S. Noble's Mansion House.
S. McDonald - furniture for sale.
Mrs. St. John - wants borrowed books returned.
Hiram K. Jerome - attorney, one door east of Eagle Hotel.
Dr. Luther Cowan - druggist.
Manson Sherman - Pultneyvile - stone cutting.
S. St. John - wants to buy hay.
Henry M. Meade - Canadaigua - Farmer's exchange
L. B. Barnum - Canandaigua - cabinet maker.
William A. McLean - adv. hours at Post Office.
Simeon T. Kibbe - Canandaigua - insurance.
T. J. Stimpson - painter.
O. Hartwell - Ontario - lottery.
J. & L. Thayer - dry goods.
A. Randolph & Co. - hats.
A. McIntyre - druggist.
J. S. Eggleston - has Gain Robinson's bills to collect.
T. Beale & Co. - Canandaigua - Dutch Bolting cloth.
P. Tucker - wants to buy wood.
W. A. Corwin - lost a pocket book.
Dorastus Cole - has house for rent.
David Benham - tailor.
Job Albro - adv. a stray cow.
S. Drown - mail stage.

Horace Meech - forwarding; formerly with DeGraff, Walton, & Co.
P. Tucker - Palmyra Lottery Office.
A. R. Galloway - adv. a stray horse
James Field - will pay cash for wheat.
Jacob A. Dana - carriage maker.
J. D. Everingham & Co. - storage.
Burr Butler - tailor.
Plain Truth, Canandaigua - $1.00 per yr.
J. & S. Colt - wants to buy pork and flax seed.
H. Niles - Baltimore Weekly Register.
County Clerk - opens an office in Palmyra.
T. P. Baldwin - wants books returned.

FEBRUARY 18, 1824
The subscribers intend to petition the next Legislature for the passage of a law to half-shire the county, so that the courts may be held alternately at the villages of Palmyra and Lyons.
Rev. Benjamin Stockton will be installed this day at the Presbyterian Meeting house in this village.
Married at Moravia [Cayuga Co.] the 11th inst., by Rev. Mr. Smith, Mr. Vincent G. Barney of Rushville, of this village to Miss Nancy Connet of the former place.
Married: in this town on the 10th inst., by James White, Esq., Mr. Nathaniel Davenport of Williamson to Miss Lydia Harris of this town.

FEBRUARY 25, 1824
Married: in Manchester, on the 15th inst., by S. Hamilton, Esq., Mr. John D. Nottingham to Hannah Wells.

MARCH 2, 9, 17, 1824 - No items copied.
MARCH 24, 1824
Married: in East Bloomfield, on the 18th inst., by Rev. Mr. Steele, Alfred Barrett, Esq., of Lockport, Niagara Co. to Miss Sophronia Benjamin of the former place.
Married: in Farmington, Mr. Elisha Hayward to Miss. Lucinda Brace.
Died: in this town on the 21st inst., Mrs. Mary Benham, aged 70 years.

MARCH 31, 1824
Married: in this town on the 29th inst., by Frederick Smith Esq., Mr. Ruell W. Robinson to Miss Rhoda Thayer.
Committed suicide: Mr. Robert Adams, an old inhabitant of this town, on Sunday last. Deceased was a native of Ireland. He left a will devising his property to a brother and sister there. He was a bachelor about 50 years old and had no relatives in this country.

APRIL 7, 1824

Married: in this town on Thursday last, by Rev. Mr. Stockton, Dr. Durfee Chase to Lucinda C. Gregg.

APRIL 14, 1824 - No items copied or issue missing.

APRIL 21, 1824

Married: in this town on the 15th inst., by Rev. Mr. Stockton, Mr. John G. Gregg and Miss Ann Wilcox.

Died: in Macedon on the 13th inst. at the house of Mr. John F. Packard, Dr. J. Steinmetz Aru--, lately from the city of New York, aged about 50 years. His body was brought to this village and interred in Masonic form on Thursday last.

Died: in this town on the 10th inst., Mrs. Sally Franklin.

APRIL 28, 1824

Married: at Oak Orchard, [Orleans Co.], on the 21st inst., by Rev. David Pratt, Mr. James Tisdale of this place, to Miss Sophia Brown of the former place.

MAY 5, 1824 - no items copied.

MAY 12, 1824 - no items copied.

MAY 19, 1824

Married: in Farmington, on Sunday last, Mr. Daniel Bidwell to Miss Maria Howland.

Died: on the 5th inst. in Philadelphia where she was visiting, Mrs. Susan DeWitt, wife of Simeon DeWitt, Esq., of Albany, late Miss Linn of this city, 2nd dau. of the late, Dr. Linn (New York Evening Post).

MAY 22, 1824 - No items copied or issue unavailable.

JUNE 2, 1824

Married in this village on the 27th ult., by Rev. Mr. Stockton, Mr. Robert W. Smith, to Miss Miranda Jessup.

Married: at Rome [Oneida Co.], on the 24th [ult] Mr. George N. Williams of this place to Miss Mary Olmstead of the former place.

JUNE 9, 1824 - no items copied or issue missing.

JUNE 16, 1824

Married: at New Hartford [Onedia Co.], on the 8th inst., by Rev. Mr. Aikin, Mr. L. W. Sibley, publisher of the Monroe Republican, at Rochester, to Miss Nancy Remington of the former place.

Married: in Howard, Stueben Co., on the 3rd inst., by Rev. Mr. Higgins, Mr. B. Franklin Smead, Editor of The Farmer's Advocate [Bath] to Miss Eliza Demick of this place.

Married: in Phelps on the 20th ult., by Rev. M. Rowe, Dr. Joshua M. Terry of this town to Miss Nancy J. Van Duesen of the former place.

Married: in this town on the 17th ult., Mr. Stephen Rowley to Miss Phebe Wood.

Married: at Bath, Mr. Thomas J. Dudley of Rushville, [Yates Co.], to Miss Caroline Bull.

Married: in Hopewell, by elder Sha[w?], Mr. Luther Dean, of Canandaigua to Miss Ruth Brundage of Hopewell, [Ontario Co.].

Married: by the Rev. J. Merril, Mr. Lyman Babcock to Miss Nancy Birdsey.

Married: Capt. Joel S. Hart to Miss Lydia Cook. June 23, 1824.

JUNE 23, 1824

Married: in Dayton, OH, Mr. Conrad Reed to Miss Catharine Weaver. "Nothing more fit indeed, Since we all do know: A WEAVER must have a REED before the loom can go."

Died: in Baltimore, [MD or NY?] after a long illness, Mrs. Anne Niles, wife of H. Niles, Esq., editor of the Register, aged 44 years.

JUNE 30, 1824

Drowned in Macedon on the 26th inst., George Crane, son of Mr. Turner Crane, aged about 11 years.

JULY 7, 1824 - No items copied or issue unavailable.

JULY 14, 1824

Married: in Farmington, on Monday last by Nathan Pierce, Esq., Mr. Isaac Mead to Miss Bathsheba Eddy.

JULY 21, 1824

Died: in Lyons on the 14th inst., Mr. John R. Holmes, son of Robert Holmes, formerly of New Hampshire, aged 24 years.

JULY, 28, 1824

Married in Batavia, on the 18th, Mr. Nathan Follett to Miss Clarinda Miller.

Died: in Farmington on the 17th inst., Mrs. Julian Aldrich, wife of Mr. Mowry Aldrich, aged 24 years.

Died: at West Bloomfield on the 17th inst., Mrs. Clarissa, wife of Samuel Nichols, Esq., and daughter of Mr. Reuben Lee, aged 29 years.

Died: in Phelps, on the 15th inst., Mr. Thaddeus Oaks, and old and respectable inhabitant of that town. He left a wife and two small children. He was one of the first settlers.

AUGUST 11, 1824

Died in this town on the 5th inst., Mrs. Cynthia Hulburt, aged 23 years.

Died: at Warsaw [Wyoming Co.] on the 13th ult., Col. Jabez G. Fitch, a Revolutionary patriot, in the 61st year of his age.

AUGUST 18, 1824

Died in this town on the 19th inst., Mrs. Susanna Curtis, aged 44 years.

Died on the 10th inst., Mrs --- Howell, the widow of Jonah Howell, deceased.

Died: on the 15th inst., Mrs. Lucy Harris, aged 74 years.
Died: on the 23rd ult., Chloe Thayer, aged 1 year.

AUGUST 25, 1824
Married: in Macedon, on the 22nd inst. by Jonathan Boynton, Esq., Thomas Bancroft, Esq., of Ontario to Miss Patience Palmer of Macedon.
Died: at South Williamson, on the 18th inst., Miss Philena Hanks, late of Madison, Vermont.

SEPTEMBER 15, 1824
Married: in Benton on the 7th inst., Mr. Isaac Kedder to Miss Betsey Haxton.
Married: in Richmond [Ontario Co.], on the 1st inst. by Rev. Mr. Horton, Mr. Robert L. Rose, of Fayette [Seneca Co.] to Miss Almira Allen, dau. of Nathaniel Allert [sic], Esq.
Married: in Farmington on the 5th inst., by Rev. James Boyle, Dr. Rand White of Shortsville, [Ontario Co.]. to Miss Lydia Wyborn of the former place.
Died: in Farmington on the 7th inst., Job H. Eddy, aged 3 years.

SEPTEMBER 22, 1824
Died: in Rochester, on the 9th inst., Mrs. Sally Ensworth, wife of Dr. Azel Ensworth, aged 56 years.

SEPTEMBER 29, 1824:
Married: in this town on the 12th inst., Mr. Daniel Wood, a Revolutionary pensioner, aged 61, to the widow Ann Terry, aged 41.

OCTOBER 6. 1824
Married: in this town on the 29th ult., Mr. Linden Knapp to Miss Susan McCollum.

OCTOBER 13, 1824
Married: in the town on the 6th inst., Mr. Hiram Wilcox to Miss Lucy Stoddard.
Died: in Canandaigua on Sunday, Oct. 1, Mr. O. Seymour, cashier of the Utica Branch Bank.
Died: on the same day [as above], Luther Cole, Esq., the father of Adrian Cole, deceased.
Married: in Palmyra, on the 31st ult., by S. Sabins, Esq., Mr. Hiram Parks to Miss Hannah Sutton.

OCTOBER 20, 1824 - List of advertisers.
A. Pierson - dry goods for sale
T. P. Baldwin - Commissioner to take acknowledgments.
P. Sexton - Patent cooking stoves.
J. D. Bemis - Canandaigua - Book store.
J. L. Ransom - bricks for sale, 2 mi. east of the village.
P. Tucker - wants a post rider to distribute the Wayne Sentinel in Williamson, Ontario, Macedon, and Penfield.

Mrs. DuBois - millinery.
E. C. Kingsley et al - post coaches Palmyra to Canandaigua.
Smith & Mason - hat store.

OCTOBER 27, 1824
Died in this town, on the 21st inst., Miss Achsa Pomeroy, late of Buckland, MA, age 22 years.

NOVEMBER 3, 1824
Died: in this town on the lst inst., Mrs. Lucy Wilcox, aged 19 years.
Died: on the 28th ult., Mr. David Johnson, aged 1 (?) year.

NOVEMBER 10, 1824 - no items copied or unavailable.

NOVEMBER 17, 1824
Married: in this town on Thursday last, Mr. George Smith of Farmington to Miss Lucina Durfee, of Palmyra
Married: in Williamson by John Barber, Jr., Esq., Mr. Dennis Cory to Miss Dorcas Hedsall.
Married in Ontario, by Seth Eddy., Esq., Mr. John Wheeler to Miss Margaret Church.
Married: in Palmyra, by Asher Doolittle, Esq., Mr. David Steele, to Miss ---Butts.
Married: Mr. Nathan M'Vie to Miss Esther Jefford.
Married: in Farmington Mr. Ira Parver to Miss Amy Lapham.
Married: Mr. George Culver to Miss Olive Smith.
Died: in Macedon on Monday, Mrs. Lucinda Warner, aged 32 years.

NOVEMBER 24, 1824 - No items copied or unavailable.

DECEMBER 1, 1830
Married: in Williamson on the 25th ult., Mr. Sheldon Beach to Miss Ann Beam.
Married: in Lyons, on the 18th ult., by Rev. Oliver True, Mr. John A. Davenport to Miss Almira Simmons.
Died: in this town on the 26th ult., Mr. Gideon Sherman, aged 31 years.

DECEMBER 8, 1824
Died: in this village last Monday morning, William A. McLean, Esq., aged 25 years.

DECEMBER 15, 1824 - List of Advertisers:
Tucker & Gilbert - book store.
L. Westcott - storage & forwarding.
Flower & Leach - tailoring.
Independent school in upper room of the Academy -Tobias Ostrander, Superintendant.
P. West - buys out Jessup & Palmer's share in store.
William Parke - dry goods.
D. I. Smith - will put in fireplaces.
Frances Olmstead - milliner.

DECEMBER 22, 1824 - No items copied or issue unavailable.

DECEMBER 29, 1824

Married: on the 23rd inst., by Frederick Smith, Esq., Mr. Robert Curtis to Miss Ann Williams, both of Palmyra; also by the same on the 28th, Mr. Thomas Hill to Miss Elizabeth Blanchard of the town of Manchester, in Ontario County.

JANUARY 12, 1825

Married: on the 5th inst., by Frederick Smith, Esq., Mr. Wrolin K. Metcalf to Miss Ann Ance Ande [sic] Bennett, both of Macedon; also by the same on the 6th inst. Mr. Allen Durfee to Miss Sally Thayer of Palmyra.

Married: in Ontario, on Wednesday evening [Jan. 5] by Jonathan Boynton, Esq., Mr. Lovewell Hurd of this village to Miss Sally Smith, daughter of Mr. George Smith of the former place.

JANUARY 19, 1825

Married: in Farmington on the 13th, by Rev. Mr. Stockton, Mr. Joseph Johnston to Miss Sarah Homes.

JANUARY 26, 1825 - no items copied or unavailable.

FEBRUARY 2, 1825

Died: at Canandaigua on the 21st ult., Simeon T. Kibbe, Esq., aged 30 years.

FEBRUARY 9, 1825

Married: at Oak Orchard [Orleans Co.] on the 6th inst., Maj. William Willcox of this town, to Miss Wealthy Brown of the former place.

Died: in Albany on the 30th ult., Mrs. John A. Lansing, aged 76 years.

FEBRUARY 16, 1825

Married in Newark on the 6th inst., by Rev. S. Pomeroy, Mr. Lynn Corbin, to Miss Lydia Bryant, dau. of Mr. Simeon Bryant.

Married: in Manchester on the 9th inst., by Rev. Mr. Benham, Mr. Silas Bustell to Miss Alsady Aldrich.

Married: in Penn Yan, by Hon. William H. Oliver, Doct. James Hermans of Middlesex, [Yates Co.], to Miss Eliza Hart of the same place.

FEBRUARY 23, 1825

Married: in Macedon on the 16th inst., Mr. Justus Hill to Miss Mariah Arnold.

Died: in this town on the 17th inst, Miss Caroline Lakey.

Died: in Macedon on the 12th inst., Mr. Artemus Ward.

Died: on the 9th inst., Mr. Winslow.

MARCH 2, 1825 - no items copied or unavailable

MARCH 9, 1825 - no items copied or unavailable

MARCH 16, 1825

Married: in Williamson, on the 24th [ult.?], Mr. Peter Leighton to Miss Salome Shurtliff.

MARCH 23, 1825

Married: in Pompey, Onondaga Co., on the 15th ult., John Fleming, Jr.. Esq., Attorney-at-law, of Manlius and late of this village to Miss Louisa Wheaton, daughter of Augustus Wheaton, Esq. of the former place.

MARCH 30, 1825

Died in this village on the 26th inst., William D., infant son of Mr. J. D. Hayward.

APRIL 6, 1825

Married: in Michigan on the 2nd inst., Mr. William Harwood to Miss Abigail Albro, both formerly of this place.

Married: in Williamson, on the 23rd ult., by Rev. Linus North, Mr. Edward Pooley to Miss Margaret Caldwell.

Married: in Macedon on the 3rd inst., by Rev. Mr. Smith, Mr. Durfee Osband of this town to Miss Marietta Ward of the former place.

Married: Mr. Nathan Estlow to Miss Mary Leach.

Married: Mr. Ford Packard to Miss Chloe Lapham.

Married: Mr. Orin Chase to Miss Sophia Dillingham.

Died: at Newark on the 30th ult., Mary Elizabeth, infant daughter of Dr. Artemus Doane, age 4 mos., 25 days.

APRIL 13, 1825 - no items copied or unavailable.
APRIL 20, 1825 -   do
APRIL 27, 1825

Married: in Williamson, on the 21st inst., by Rev. Joseph Wilkins, Mr. Henry Warner to Miss Betsey Whitcomb.

Married: on the 9th inst., Mr. Thomas J. Streeter to Miss Minerva Phelps.

MAY 4, 1825 - no items copied or unavailable
MAY 11, 1825   do
MAY 18, 1825

Married: in Macedon on the 4th inst., by F. Smith, Esq., Mr. Benjamin Nichols of Pultneyville to Miss Mary Ann Miner of the former place.

Married: in Ontario on the same day, by Rev. Mr. Strong, Mr. Alva W. Turner to Miss Caroline Boynton, both of Ontario; likewise, Dr. --- Frisbee of Vienna to Miss Sophronia Boynton of Ontario.

Died: in Phelps on Friday last, General William Burnett, aged 61 years.

MAY 25, 1825
Married: in Durham, [Greene Co], NY on the 17th inst., by Rev. Mr. Williston, Mr. Charles Thayer of this village to Miss Mary Ann Hart of the former place.

JUNE 1, 1825 - no items copied or unavailable.
JUNE 8, 1825   do
JUNE 15, 1825
Died: in Macedon on the 1st inst., Col. John Bradish, aged 75 years, one of the first settlers of the town.

JUNE 22 1825 - no items copied or not available.
JUNE 28, 1825
Died: in New Orleans on Feb. 2nd last, Mr. Jared C. Selby, late of this place.
Died: at Sodus very suddenly on the 15th inst., Dr. Morris T. Jewell.
Died: in this village on the 23rd inst., Phebe Maria, daughter of Mr. William T. Hussey, aged 2 years.

JULY 5, 1825 - list of advertisers.
Tucker & Gilbert - printing, books etc. Wayne Co. Book Store.
Williams & Co. - hardware.
Caius Robinson - drugs.
J. D. Nottingham - Manchester - sulphur springs.
L. Hurd - Public House Palmyra - lately occupied by S. Hathaway.
Miss Van Winkle - milliner - in house occupied by Mr. McDonald, 3 doors west of Eagle Hotel.
J. D. and J. Everingham - take in Giles S. Ely - becomes J. D. Everingham & Co.
S. St. John - insurance.
Zenas Foster - hemp seed.
S. W. Arnett - adv. a mahogany bureau for sale.
M. Kingman - livery.
T. P. Baldwin - Commissioner of Deeds.
James Davis of Macedon adv. land for sale.
John Belote - adv. a stray mare.
Wooster & Gilbert - cabinet makers.
Trustees for creditors of Jacob Occarina.
[E. C.] Kingsley & [R. P.] Lazell - stage line.
O. Heartwell - Canandaigua - lottery.
D. S. Jackways - adv. farm for sale.
Charles Hudson - adv. land 2 mi. east of Palmyra for sale.
Peter Freer of Macedon adv. his wife, Rachel Freer.
Thomas Rogers - adv. a stray horse.
Asa Smith - adv. a stray horse.

The first boats passed from the west and the north through the Erie Canal, into the tide waters of the Hudson River at Albany amidst the celebration of thousands.

JULY 12, 1825
Married: in Arcadia on the 30th ult., by Rev. William Bow, Mr. Mills H. Bosworth of PA to Miss Adelia E. Biollet of the former place.
Married: in Caswell Co., NC on the 10th ult., Mr. William Bean to Miss Sarah E. Greenfield.
Died: in New York, on the 3rd inst., Col. Charles G. Haynes, late Adj. General of the militia for this state.

JULY 19, 1825
Died: in Gorham, [Ontario Co.], on the 16th inst., Mr. Southworth Cole, Sr., Esq., aged 63 yrs., father of Abner Cole of this village.
Died: in this village on the 16th inst., Mr. Jacob A. Dunn, aged 42 years.

JULY 26, 1825
Died: in this village Monday, the 1st inst., Miss Prudence C. Fairbanks, aged 23 years.

AUGUST 2, 1825 -no items copied or not available.
AUGUST 9, 1825
Died: in Auburn on the 29th ult., Mrs. Sarah H. Stockton, mother of Rev. B. B. Stockton of this village.

AUGUST 16, 1835 - no items copied or not available.
AUGUST 23, 1825
Died: in Ontario on the 23rd ult., Mrs. Azuba Barber, wife of Mr. John Barber, aged 61 years.

AUGUST 30, 1825
Married: in Manchester on the 28th inst., by Elder Sha [sic], Mr. Benjamin Mosier to Miss Ruth Butts.
Died: in Wolcott, on the 24th inst., Rev. Jonathan Hovey, aged 72 years.
Died: in New York on the 14th inst., Arthur Breese, Esq., aged 53 years, Clerk of the Supreme Court at Utica.

SEPTEMBER 6, 1825
Married: in Middlesex by Rev. Mr. Merrill, Mr. Button M. Williams, to Miss Eliza Williams, dau. of R. M. Williams, Esq.

SEPTEMBER 13, 1825
Married: in Ontario on the 28th ult., Rev. James Boyle to Miss Laura Putnam, both of the same place.
Died: in this town on the 7th inst., Mrs. Charlotte Lakey, consort of Mr. James Lakey, age 63 years.

Died: in Williamson on the 8th inst, Mr. Elisha Cowan.

Died: in Canandaigua on the 2nd inst., Mrs. Phoebe B. Stevens, aged 39 years, wife of Mr. John A. Stevens and daughter of Mr. Phineas Bates.

SEPTEMBER 20, 1825 - no items copied or inaccessible
SEPTEMBER 27, 1825 -   do
OCTOBER 4, 1825
WAYNE COUNTY BANK: The following will petition the Legislature for the incorporation of a bank to be called "Wayne County Bank"; $100,000 capital and priveleged to raise $250.000: Ambrose Hall, Z. Williams, Joel Thayer, David Eddy, David White, Jonathaan Boynton, Henry Jessup, N. H. Beckwith, Leonard Westcott, Levi Thayer, G. N. Williams, Luther Filmore, George Palmer, and Abraham Spear.

ADVERTISERS:
Drs. McIntyre & Peckham - physicians.
Randolph (Albert Randolph & Azel Van Druver) dissolve. Van Druver continues the business.

OCTOBER 11, 1825
Died: in this village on the 26th ult., Elizabeth, an infant dau. of Alexander R. Tiffany, Esq., ae 1 yr. 4 months.

Married: in Macedon on the 29th ult., Mr. David B. Bates of this village to Miss Amanda Barnes of Macedon.

Married: in this town on the 4th inst., Mr. House, Mr. Daniel Smith to Miss Mary Barnhart.

Married: in Canandaigua on the 29th ult., by the Rev. B. H. Hickox, Mr. Earl D. King to Miss Mary Bunnell.

OCTOBER 18, 1825
Died: in Palmyra, on the 10th inst., Mr. Enoch Saunders, ae 53 years.

Died: in Macedon, on the 9th inst., Gardner Hale.

Married: in Vienna on Sunday evening last, Dr. J. S. Eggleston of this village to Miss Hannah Ann Payne of the former place.

Died: in Palmyra on the 10th inst. Mr. Enoch Saunders, aged 53 years.

OCTOBER 25, 1825
Married: in Cunningham, MA on the 12th inst., Mr. Caius C. Robinson of this village to Miss Eliza Warner of the former place.

Died: at his residence in Lyons, on the 17th inst., John S. Tallmadge, Esq., late 1st Judge of this county, aged 27 years; leaves a wife an infant son.

Died: in Macedon on the 18th inst., Mrs. Mary Simpson, aged 50 years.

NOVEMBER 1, 1825
Married: in Groton, CT, on the 18th ult., by Rev. J. C. Wightman, Mr. Luther Tucker of Ontarioville, to Miss Frances A. Smith, dau. of Mr. Dennison Smith of the former place.

NOVEMBER 8, 1825 - no items copied or inaccessible.
NOVEMBER 18, 1825
Died: in this village on the 5th inst., Mr. Andrew G. Low, aged 28 years.

NOVEMBER 22, 1825 - no items copied or inaccessible
NOVEMBER 29, 1825
Died: in this village on the 22nd inst., Mr. Zebulon Williams, in his 59th year, a wealthy and useful citizen.

DECEMBER 6, 1825
Married: at Sodus on the 12th inst., by Rev. J. Townsend, Mr. Chauncey Newell to Miss Tammson A. Stone, daughter of Rev. William Stone. [The foregoing is Mrs. Wiles copied version; Mr. Van Alstine's version did not give issue of paper except to state it was No. 125 - which would equal 6 Dec. However, he gives a marriage date of Sept. 28th, 1825. The editor cannot make the decision for the the reader as to which is the correct version.]

ADVERTISERS;
Mrs. Lawrence opens a grammar school Nov. 28th.
S. St. John removes his business to the new brick hotel at the intersection of Main St. and the Canandaigua Road.
Stephen Willcox - has brick for sale.
W. J. & J. O. Teller - tailors.

The public is cautioned to beware of William H. Utter and Reuben Jones formerly Utter & Jones who gave "leg bail" and left debts behind.

DECEMBER 13, 1825
Died: in this village, Saturday last, Mr. Alanson Smith, aged 23 years.
Died: in Buffalo, Mr. Patrick O'Rourke, formerly of this village, age 50 years.
Died: in Batavia, Mr. Franklin G. Miller, in the 20th year of his age, eldest son of D. C. Miller, Esq., Editor of the Republican Advocate.

JANUARY 3, 1826
Married; in Macedon on the 22nd ult., Dr. Dexter Kingman to Miss Mahala Van Duzer.
Married: on the 1st inst., Mr. Azariah Mallary to Miss Azuba White.
Married in this town on the 29th ult., Mr. James Barns of Manchester, to Sophia Stacy of Palmyra.
Died: in Macedon, on the 27th ult., Mr. Willis Kelley, an old resident.
Died: in Manchester, on the 29th ult., Mr. Nathaniel Taylor, aged 91 years.

JANUARY 10, 1826 - no items copied or inaccessible
JANUARY 17, 1826 do
JANUARY 24, 1826
Adv.: Tucker & Gilbert (publishers of the Wayne Sentinel) removed to first door in the new block, corner of Main & Clinton Sreets.
The Wayne Co. Medical Society held its semi-annual meeting at Solomon St. John's, Jan. 2, 1826.

ADVERTISEMENTS
J. & L. Thayer - dry goods.
Dr. Gain Robinson wants bills paid.
Robinson & Eggelston - wants bills paid;
J. D. Everingham - dry goods.
Smith & Mason want bills paid.
A. R. Galloway - wants bills paid.
L. Cowan - wants bills paid.
Apartment in Brick Block, one door east of P. Sexton's
Jewelry offered for sale.
Joseph Winship - bakery.
Dr. D. Chase; James Field - grain bought.
L. Hurd, hotel keeper where S. Hathaway was located.
Solomon St. John - insurance.
W. J. & J. C. Teller - tailors.

JANUARY 31, 1826
Married: in Pittsford on the 22nd inst., Mr. William Ross of Palmyra to Miss Bloomy C. Nelson of the former place.
Married: in Macedon on the 26th inst., Mr. Caleb Van Duzer to Miss Abigail Mallary.
Died: suddenly in Farmington, Ontario Co., on Wednesday last, Mr. Gideon Clark, 57 years of age.
Lyman I. Daniels - attorney (lst ad is dated Sept. 20, 1826).

FEBRUARY 7, 1826
Married: at Oak Orchard, Orleans Co., on the lst inst., Mr. William Winslow of Macedon to Widow Thomas of the former place.
Died: at Auburn, [Cayuga Co.], Wed., last, Maj. Richard Goodell, Keeper of the State Prison.
Died: in Utica, [Oneida Co.], on the 25th ult., Mr. Andrew Merrill, one of the publishers of The Western Recorder, aged 35 years.
Died: in Palmyra, on the 1st inst., Mrs. Lucina Smith, wife of George Smith, of Farmington and dau. of Mr. Lemuel Durfee of this town, aged 20 years.

FEBRUARY 14, 1826
Married in Ontario on the 1st inst., Mr. Henry Farnham of this village to Miss Betsey Smith of the former place.

Married: in this village on the 12th inst., Mr. Robert Walker to Miss Mary Harris.
Died: in Wolcott on the 5th inst., Mr. Andrew Chapin, formerly of Salisbury, CT, aged 86 years.
Died: in Canandaigua, on the 7th inst., Sarah, daughter of P. P. Bates, aged 17 years.
Adv.: S. McDonald - shoe cobbler.

FEBRUARY 21, 1826
Married: in Vienna [Oneida Co.] on the 15th inst., Mr. Addison J. Comstock of Lockport, [Niagara Co.], to Miss Sarah Dean of the former place.

FEBRUARY 26, 1826 - no items copied or inaccessible.
MARCH 3, 1826 - no items copied or inaccessible.
MARCH 10, 1826
Married: March 5, 1826, Ralph Fisk and Nancy Roby.
Died: in this village on the 6th inst., Mr. Daniel G. Moss of Lockport, [Ontario Co.], aged 34 years.
Died: the 4th inst., Mr. Augustus Calkins, age 33 years.
Died: in Ontarioville, on the 8th inst., Mr. Harry S. Moore, aged 32 years.

MARCH 17, 1826
Married: in Macedon, by the Rev. Mr. Bakesley on the 23rd (ult), Mr. Job Fish to Miss Maria Brown.

MARCH 24, 1826
Died: in this town on the 17th inst., John Swift, Jr., youngest son of the late Gen. John Swift, aged about 12 years.
Married: March 23, 1826, in Macedon, Job Fish and Maria Brown.

MARCH 31, 1826
Married: in Arcadia by Rev. Mr. Stevens, on the 29th inst., Mr. William Chittenden to Miss Amanda Melvina Wheaton.

APRIL 7, 1826
Married: in Palmyra by the Rev. Mr. House, on the 19th ult., Mr. John H. Haddock of Rochester to Miss Abigail A. Wells of this village.
Died: in Parkman, OH, on the 22nd ult., Hon. Seth Phelps, aged about 75 years.

APRIL 14, 1826
Married in this village by the Rev. Mr. Stockton on the 8th inst., Dr. Azel Ensworth of Rochester to Miss Betsey Johnson of this place.
Married: in Leroy, [Genesee Co.], on the 6th inst., by the Rev. Mr. Myers, Mr. Horatio Stevens to Miss Harriet Ganson, dau. of Major James Ganson.
Married: in Binghamton on the 6th inst., Ralph Lester, Esq., of Canandaigua to Miss Rhoda Ann Whiting.

Died: in Macedon on the 9th inst., Mrs. Gitty M. Hallett, consort of Jacob W. Hallett.
Died: in Macedon, on the 11th inst., Mrs. Keziah Hill, wife of David Hill.

APRIL 21, 1826
Married: in the village by F. Smith, Esq., on the 18th inst., George Liscom to Miss Sarah M. Dow (Low?).
Married: at Cornwall, CT, on the 28th ult., by Rev. Mr. Chase, Mr. Elias Boudinot of the Cherokee Nation of Indians to Miss Harriet R. Gold, dau. of Col. Deacon Benjamin R. Gold of Cornwall.

APRIL 28, 1826
Married at Utica on the 10th inst., by Rev. Mr. Anthony, George B. Throop, Esq. of Auburn to Miss Frances Hunt, eldest daughter of Montgomery Hunt of the former place.
Died: in Macedon on the 26th inst., Mr. Estelow, one of the oldest settlers.
Death: Aaron C. Nottingham of Manchester, committed suicide.

MAY 12, 1826
Died: in Livonia [Livingston Co.], on the 2nd inst., Thaddeus B. Wilcox, son of Mr. R. Wilcox, in the 16th year of his age.

MAY 19, 1826
Married: in Macedon by the Rev. Mr. Blakesley on the 10th inst., Mr. Norton Porter to Miss Bathsheba Sheffield.

MAY 26, 1826
Married in this town on the 24th inst., by Rev. Mr. House, Mr. Joshua Driscoll to Mrs. Maria Van Duser.
Married in Williamson, by Rev. Mr. Blakesly on the 21st inst., Mr. Benjamin Hill, Jr. of Macedon to Miss Nancy Skinner of Williamson.
Married in Macedon on the same day [as above] by Rev. Mr. Blakesly, Mr. James Mellen to Widow M'Knight.
Died: in New Orleans in February last., Mr. William B. Low, formerly of the village, aged 25 years.
Died: in Batavia, on the 25th ult., Dr. Elisha Warner of Canandaigua, aged 31 years.

MAY 2, 1826 - no items copied or inaccessible.
MAY 9, 1826 - no items copied or inaccessible.
MAY 16, 1826   do
MAY 23, 1826   do
MAY 30, 1826   do
JUNE 6, 1826   do
JUNE 13, 1826   do
JUNE 20, 1826   do

JUNE 25, 1826

Married at Pultneyville, by Rev. Mr. B. B. Stockton on the 22nd inst., the Rev. Mr. Hurlburt of Natchez, MS to Miss Jane Eliza Rees of the former place.

Died: in Richmond, Ontario Co., on the 9th inst., Mrs. Betsey Allen, wife of Nathaniel Allen, Esq., aged 29 (59?).

JULY 1, 1826 - no items copied or inaccessible.

JULY 7, 1826

Died: in Geneva on the 2nd inst., Mr. James Ireland of Williamson, Wayne Co., late of Edinburgh, Scotland, aged about 25 years.

Died: in Pultneyville, on the 4th inst., Mrs. Sarah Selby, age 87 years.

JULY 14, 1826

Married: in Ontario on the 9th inst., by Rev. Daniel Lyons, Mr. Edwin Tiffany to Miss Eunice Green.

Died: in this town on the 11th inst., Mrs. Catharine Durfee, aged about 22 years.

Died: in Arcadia on the 7th inst., James Thompson, Esq., aged 68 years.

JULY, 21, 1826 - no items copied or unavailable

JULY 28, 1826

Married: in Ontario by J. Boynton, Esq., on the 16th inst., Mr. David Hill of Macedon, ae 56 yrs. to Miss Elizabeth Hill of Hudson, ae 45 yrs.

Married: on the 29th ult., Mr. Elnathan Bentley to Miss Diantha Willcox, both of this town.

AUGUST 4, 1826

Died: in Auburn on July 19th, Stephen W. Hughs, Esq., Sheriff of Cayuga Co., aged 33 years.

Died on the 29th ult., Maj. William Ray [or Roy], aged 54 years.

Died in Clarendon, Orleans Co., on the 25th of July, William Lewis, Esq., Sheriff of Orleans Co., age 35 years.

AUGUST 11, 1826

Married: in Ontario, on the 3rd inst., Mr. James T. Taft of Wayne Co., MI to Miss Almina Blanchard of the former place.

Married: on the 2nd inst., Mr. Chester Williams to Miss Margaret Teachout, both of Manchester.

Married in Canandaigua, by Rev. Mr. Hickox on the 10th inst., Mr. Hiram S. Bancker to Miss Maria Sibley.

Married in Batavia, on the 2nd inst., by Rev. Mr. Smith, Mr. Married in Batavia, on the 2nd inst., Frederick Follett, Editor of the Times, to Miss Sarah Sutherland, daughter of Major Isaac Sutherland.

Died: in this village on the 9th inst., Mr. John Kennedy, late, we believe from Rochester. He was a stranger in this place.

Died: in Johnstown, Montgomery Co., on the evening of the 25th ult., Henry Cunningham, in the 36th year of his age.

AUGUST 18, 1826
Alvah Waters committed suicide. Inquest held in Farmington on the 14th inst.
Died: in this place on the 15th inst., Mr. Benjamin Miller, aged 52 years.
Died: in Canandaigua, the same day (15th inst.), Miss Lydia A. Gooding, daughter of Mr. William Gooding, aged 20 years.
Died: on the 10th inst., Mr. Jacob Stoudinger, late of New York City, aged 23 years.
Married: in Stafford Street on the 2nd inst., Mr. William Stafford to Miss Ruth Butts.

AUGUST 25, 1826
Died in Lyons on the 16th inst., Hiram T. Day, late Editor and Publisher of the Lyons Advertiser, aged about 30 years. Masonic funeral.

ADVERTISERS: James F. Barker - jeweller in Abner Cole's shop, corner of Main & Chapel St., one door east of St. John's Hotel.
Franklin House, D. Hendee, lately occupied by L. Hurd.
Lyman I. Daniels moves his law office.
Canal Packet Boat fare on whole route from Schenectady to Buffalo is reduced from 4c to 3c per mile, inc. board and 2c exclusive of board.

SEPTEMBER 1, 1826
Married: in Ontario on the 16th ult., by Rev. Joseph Wilkins, Mr. William Town to Miss Maria Renyon.
Married: in Marion, by Rev. Mr. Kirry (?), Mr. Epinetus Ketchum to Miss Ann Payne.
Married: on the 24th [ult.], by Rev. J. Wilkins, Joseph W. Gates to Miss Harriet Levens

SEPTEMBER 9, 1826:
Married: in this village, Sept. 2nd, by Rev. Benjamin B. Stockton, Lorin B. Towsley and Miss Ann Maria Robson.
Married: at the same time as above, Mahlon (?) Kingman of Palmyra to Miss Susan Thayer of Vienna.
Died: Sept. 1, in Palmyra, Dr. Luther Cowan, aged 29 yrs.
Died: in Canandaigua, Sept. 5th, George Clarke, aged 36 years.
Died: in Albany, Aug. 29th, Thomas Bridgen, Esq.

ADVERTISERS: Arba Wood advertises to collect back bills.
James Hitchcock advertises his wife, Sarah Hitchcock (June 12, 1826).
Daniel Buck advertises his wife, Hepsibath T. Buck. (July 14, 1826)

SEPTEMBER 15, 1826

Married: in Arcadia on the 7th inst., by Rev. Mr. Pomeroy, Mr. Bella Franklin of this town, to the Widow Hyde of the former place.

Died: at Ovid, the 2nd inst., General Charles Thompson.

SEPTEMBER 22, 1826

Married: in this village on Sunday last (17th), by F. Smith, Esq., General Walter Grieve of Geneva to Miss Ann Scott of this village.

Married: Sept. 13th, at Canandaigua by Rev. B. H. Hickox, John A. Stevens, Editor of the Ontario Messenger, to Amelia Ackley of Montreal.

Married: Sept. 21st, by Rev. B. H. Hickox, John A. Stevens, to Miss Aurelia Ackley.

Married: by the same, Sept. 21st, Thomas B. Barnum, Editor of The Syracuse Advertiser and Miss Clarissa Atwater.

Adv.: Daniel Comstock adv. a stray cow.

SEPTEMBER 29, 1826- No items copied.

OCTOBER 20, 1826

Married: in Farmington, on the 28th ult., Mr. Nathan Stoddard of Macedon and Miss Rhoda Payne of the former place.

OCTOBER 13, 1826 - No items copied.

OCTOBER 20, 1826

Married: in Macedon on the 17th inst., Mr. Frederick U. Sheffield to Miss Lucy N. Stoddard.

Married: in this town on the 12th inst., Mr. Ezekiel Kellogg of MI to Miss Naomi Harris of this town.

OCTOBER 27, 1826

Married: in this town on the 25th inst., Mr. Benjamin Hibbard to Miss Sally Lobdell.

Died: in Canandaigua on Sunday morning last, Nathaniel Gorham, aged 63 years, son of Nathaniel Gorham, Esq., of Charlestown, MA, who was a president of the Congress of the United States under the Articles of Confederation, and who with Oliver Phelps was the original purchaser from the Commonwealth of Massachusetts, of the whole of the western part of New York State. He purchased his father's interest in Ontario County and removed to this place in 1789 (From the Ontario Repository)

Died: in this town on the 20th inst., Mr. Nathan Bently.

Died: Oct. 24, 1826, on the 24th inst., Mrs. __ Snow, lately arrived in this place.

Married: in St. Lukes Church, Rochester, on the 26th ult., Mr. Edward Scranton of the Monroe Republican, to Miss Mary Ann Sibley.

NOVEMBER 3, 1826 - No items copied.

NOVEMBER 10, 1826

Married in this town on the 6th inst., Mr. George Smith to Miss Ann Letts.

Died: in this village on the morning of the 7th inst., Mrs. Bernice Stone, aged 28 years.
Died: at Philadelphia, Seleck Osborn, Esq., poet, formerly editor of the Delaware Watchman.
Died: at Cooperstown, Farrand Stranahan, late a Senator from Otsego County.
Died: in Batavia, Hon. John J. Ross, 1st Judge of Genesee County.

NOVEMBER 17, 1826 - no items copied or inaccessible.
NOVEMBER 24, 1826
Married: in Manchester, Mr. Wert (Wort) to Miss Elizabeth House.
Married: Mr. Cornelius Holoday to Miss Charlotte Bigelow.
Married: Mr. Hiram Smith to Miss Jerusha Barden.
Married: Died: in this village on the 19th inst., of consumption, Mr. Rollin Hammond, aged 34 years.

DECEMBER 1, 1826 - no items copied
DECEMBER 8, 1826   do
DECEMBER 15, 1826   do
DECEMBER 22, 1826   do
DECEMBER 29, 1826
Died: in Auburn, Cayuga Co., on the 9th inst., Hon. Jedidiah Morgan, late Senator from this district.

JANUARY 5. 1827
Died: in Phelps on Friday evening last, Mr. Lemon Hotchkiss, aged about 45 years.
Died: in Geneva on the 21st ult., Walter Grieve, Esq., Brig. General of the 4th Brigade, NY State Artillery, aged 55 yrs.

JANUARY 12, 1827 - no items copied or inaccessible.
JANUARY 19, 1827 -   do
JANUARY 26, 1827
Married: in Scipio [Cayuga Co.], on the 10th inst., Mr. Barton Durfee of this town to Miss Phebe Bowen of the former place.
Married: in Macedon on the 11th [inst] by F. Smith, Esq., Mr. Thomas Raineer of this town to Miss Deborah Tabor of the former place.
Married: in Arcadia on the 22nd inst., by Rev. Mr. Bailey, Mr. Josiah Stanbro to the widow Ruth Culver.

FEBRUARY 2, 1827
Married: in Macedon on the 25th ult., by Rev. Mr. Stockton, Mr. Franklin Hurlbut to Miss Jane Robinson.
Married: last evening, Mr. Ira Parker of MI, to Miss Mary Horton of this town.
Died: in Macedon suddenly, on the 12th ult., Mr. Webb Harwood, aged about 70 years; he migrated to this town from Hampshire Co., MA in 1790.

FEBRUARY 9, 1827

Married in this town by Rev. Mr. Wright, M. Bidwell of Orleans Co., to Miss Ann Barnhart of this town.

FEBRUARY 16, 1827 - no items copied or inaccessible

FEBRUARY 23, 1827

Married: in Penfield, [Monroe Co.] on the 9th inst., Mr. Moses C. Baker of Macedon to Miss Mariah Hare of the former place.

Married: in Manchester, Mr. Jenks Wells to Miss Mehitable Wells.

Married: Mr. James Thompson to Miss Mary Babcock.

Married: Mr. Gardner Bird to Miss Eliza Johnson.

Married: Mr. Moses Salsbury to Miss Sally Sage.

Married: Mr. Henry Cox to Miss Mary Fish.

Married: Mr. Calvin Winslow to Miss Ella M'Umber.

Married Mr. William Clark to Miss Margaret Whitney.

MARCH 2, 1827 - no items copied or inaccessible

MARCH 9, 1827

Jessup & Palmer announce dissolution of partnership, Jan. 1, 1827; S. Leonard announced he has opened a select school, in the upper room of the Academy.

MARCH 19, 1827 - James Overnight is settling the affairs of J. E. & Co. Jan. 18, 1827.

Pomeroy Tucker has severed his connection with The Wayne County Sentinel: J. H. Gilbert continues.

Married: April 1, 1827 in Palmyra, Paul S. Brown and Rebecca Lobdell.

Solomon St. John prints cards advising that he is leaving Palmyra soon and expects to move to Geneva; A. R. Tiffany and T. R. Strong have become partners; J. Dunning opens a school in the Academy; J. Linnel opens a school over H. H. Beckwith's store. Tucker & Gilbert have dissolved their partnership.

MARCH 16, 1827

Died at Penn Yan on the evening of the 1st inst., Abraham P. Vosburg, Esq., Attorney and Counsellor at Law.

Died: in this town suddenly on the 10th inst., Mr. James Lakey, aged 70 years.

Died: in Williamson, on the 10th inst., Mr. Stephen Fish, aged 80 years.

Died: in Sodus on the 10th inst., Major Alfred James Deming, aged 34 years.

Died: in Philadelphia on the 2nd inst., Miss Mary Naftel of this village.

MARCH 23, 1827

Married: in Palmyra on Friday, the 15th inst., by F. Smith, Esq., Mr. Roderick M'Donald to Miss Eliza Coon.

Married: in this village last evening, by Rev. Mr. Stockton, Mr. James F. Barker to Miss Henrietta Selby.

MARCH 30, 1827
Married: in Macedon on the 29th inst., by F. Smith, Esq., Mr. George Brown to Miss Lucina Harris.

APRIL 6, 1827 - no items copied or inaccessible
APRIL 13, 1827   do
APRIL 20, 1827   do
APRIL 18, 1827
Announcement: To the Publick: A sale and transfer of this paper, and of the Printing & Book selling establishment connected with it has been made to Egbert B. Grandin. s/J. H. Gilbert.

APRIL 27, 1827
Died: in Newark, on the 6th inst., Mrs. Polly Showers, aged 32 years, wife of Capt. James S. Showers, late of Cairo, Greene Co.

MAY 4, 1827
Married: in Geneva, by the Rev. Dr. Axtell, on the 2nd inst., Mr. Delamater, merchant of the city of Hudson to Miss Cathalina Bogert, daughter of H. H. Bogert, Esq.
Died: in Butler, Wayne Co., on the 22nd ult., Ransom Ward, son of Mr. John Ward of Auburn, in his 39th year.
Died: in New Hampshire, Francis Brown, aged 72 years; he was in the Lexington battle and served in the Revolution.
The new and elegant freight boat, Benjamin Franklin will be launched this morning at 10 o'clock.

MAY 10, 1827
Married in this town, the 13th inst., by F. Smith, Esq., Mr. Milton Hill to Miss Mary Bartlett; also Mr. Constant Terry to Miss Lucy Brown.
Married: in Port Byron [Cayuga Co.], on the 13th inst., Mr. Hiram L. Ripley of Rochester to Miss Lucia Wells of the former place.

MAY 17, 1827 - No items copied.
MAY 25, 1827
Died: at Rowley, MA, on the 7th inst., Mr. Robert S. Coffin of the "Boston Bard", son of the late Ebenezer Coffin, A. M.
Died: lately in Sharon, [Scoharie Co.], Mrs. Deborah Gannett who served three years as a soldier in the ranks during the Revolutionary War, aged 97 years.
[sic]

JUNE 1, 1827

Married: in Vernon [Oneida Co.], on the 17th ult., Dr. J. S. Douglas of Oswego [Oswego Co.] late of this village, to Miss Martha Pierson of the former place.

JUNE 8, 1827

Notice: The building Committee is now ready to receive proposals for erecting an Episcopal Church in this village, ... s/Thomas Rogers 2nd and Levi Thayer.

June 1, 1827; E. W. Burnall was keeper of the Bunker Hill Hotel: Fuller & Smith have a dry goods store in the Brick Block, #4.

JUNE 15, 1827

Married: in Macedon on the 7th inst., by the Rev. Mr. Blakesley, Mr. Erastus Spear to Miss Rebecca Hill.

Married: in Utica [Oneida Co.], on the 30th ult., John M. Holly, Esq, of Lyons [Wayne Co], to Miss Mary Kirkland, eldest daughter of Gen. Joseph Kirkland of the former place.

JUNE 22, 1827

Married: in Williamson, [Wayne Co], on the 31st ult., Mr. John M. Harlow of Newark [Wayne Co], to Miss Phebe Ann Jerolds of the former place.

Died: in this town on Wednesday, the 6th inst., Miss Laura Beers, aged about 33 years.

JUNE 29, 1827 - no items copied or inaccessible

JULY 6, 1827

Died: in Manchester, Ontario Co., on the 1st inst., Mr. John Young, a soldier in the Revolution, aged 68 years.

JULY 13, 1827 - no items copied or inaccessible.

JULY 20, 1827   do

JULY 27, 1827   do

AUGUST 3, 1827

Married: in Marion, [Wayne Co.] on the 12th inst. [ult.?], by Isaac R. Sanford, Esq., Mr. Hiram Harris to Miss Lucinda Harris.

Married: in Newark, on the 9th inst. [ult.?], Mr,. Orrin Errickson of Rochester, to Miss Hannah Bockhoven, of L;yons {Wayne Co.].

Died: July 29, 1827, in Manchester, Leonard Short, son of Theodore Short aged 27; left a wife and one child.

Died: July 18th, in Clyde, Henry Southard, merchant.

AUGUST 10, 1827

Truman Hemingway pledges to give the head of every family in Palmyra, unable to procure the same, a free copy of the Holy Bible.

AUGUST 17, 1827

Rev. John A. Clark of Palmyra has received his A. M. degree from Union College.

Married: Aug. 12th, in Marion, by Isaac R. Sanford, Hiram Harris to Lucinda Harris.

Died: while going from N. O.[New Orleans] to New York by boat, Rev. Horace Holley, brother of Byron Holley.

Died: at Montezuma, Aug. 6th, Col. Comfort Tyler, ae 63 years.

AUGUST 23, 1827

Died: on his passage from Orleans to New York, The Rev. Horace Holley, aged 46 years, late President of Transylvania University and brother of Myron Holley, Esq.

Married: in Albany, this month, Mr. Thomas S. Ranny, printer, formerly of Ithaca, [Tompkins Co.], to Miss Maria Gager, of Albany.

Died: at Montezuma, Cayuga Co., on August 6th, Col. Comfort Tyler, aged 63 yrs.

Married: in Jamesville, [Onondaga Co.], on the 17th of last month, by Black Prince, Esq., Mr. David Wilson, ae 42 to Miss Mary Ann Shepherd, a young and sprightly lass of 13 years.

Married: in Newark on the 9th inst., by Rev. Mr. Campbell, Mr. Aaron Errickson, of Rochester, to Miss Hannah Bockhoven, of Lyons, [Wayne Co.].

AUGUST 31, 1827

Marcus Tuttle and Amasa Williston were drowned in Lake Ontario, off Sodus, Aug. 21st; Capt. H. N. Troop on the boat was saved.

Married: at the Friends Meeting House in Macedon, On the 29th ult., Elihu Durfee of Palmyra and Mrs. Sarah F. Shove.

Married: Aug. 9th, Aaron Errickson of Rochester and Hannah Bockhoven of Lyons.

Married: Aug. 9th, Thomas S. Ranney, printer, and Maria Gage, of Albany.

Married: on the 4th inst., by the Rev. Mr. Clark, Mr. John H. Gilbert, formerly one of the editors of this paper, to Miss Chloe P. Thayer, dau. of Mr. Joel Thayer, all of this village.

Married: in this village, Wed. last, by Rev. Mr. Porter, Mr. Henry Wells to Miss Sarah Daggett.

Married: in Marion, Tues, last, Mr. Sylvanis Wing to Miss Margaret Sickles.

Married: in Rochester on the 1st inst., Elihu Minshall, editor of The Album, to Miss Mary May.

Married: in Manchester, [Ontario Co.], on the 8th inst., by P. Mitchell, Esq., Peter P. R. Hayden to Miss Cynthia Stewart.

Died: in Farmington, Ontario Co., Mon., Sept. 3, Mrs. Mary Gardner.

SEPTEMBER 20, 1827

Married in the Friends Meeting house in Macedon, the 29th ult., Mr. Elihu Durfee of this village to Mrs. Sarah Shove, of the former place.

Married: on the 4th inst., by Rev. Mr. Clark, Mr. John H. Gilbert,, formerly one of the editors of this paper, to Miss Chloe P. Thayer, dau. of Mr. Joel Thayer, all of this village.

Married: in this village Wed. last, by Rev. Mr. Porter, , Mr. Henry Wells to Miss Sarah Daggett.

Married: in Marion, Tues. last, Mr. Sylvanis Wing to Miss Margaret Sickles.

Married: In Rochester on the 1st inst., Elihu Minshall, editor of The Album, to Miss Mary May.

Died: in Farmington, Ontario Co., Mon., Sept. 3rd, Mrs. Mary Gardner.

SEPTEMBER 20, 1827

Died: in this village, on Tues., Sept. 11, 1827, Maria Smith, ae 13 mos., dau. of Frederick Smith, Esq.

Died: in Farmington, Ontario Co., on Mon., the 3rd inst., Mrs. Mary Gardner, ae abt. 21 yrs., wife of Sunderland P. Gardner.

Died: in Hopewell, Mr. John S. Whitney, ae 28 years.

Died: in Manchester, Ontario Co., Aug. 28th, William Cogswell, ae abt. 19 yrs., son of Daniel Cogswell, formerly of Hopewell. At the time of his death he resided with Harvey Harmon. Relatives unknown.

SEPTEMBER 28, 1827

Married: in this town, , Tues., the 25th inst., by Rev. Mr. Wright, Mr. Jacob Sherman and Miss Sarah Lawton, formerly of Hamilton, Madison Co, NY.

OCTOBER 12, 1827

Married: in this village, the 4th inst., by Rev. Mr. Clark, Chad Southwick, of Cayuga Co., to Mrs. Margaret Jennings of this village.

NOVEMBER 16, 1827

Married: in the town of Macedon, on the 14th inst., Mr. Paul Jagger, of Williamson, and Miss Sarah Bradish of the former place.

DECEMBER 7, 1827

Married in Manchester, the 22nd ult., by Stephen Alling, Esq., Hiram Langdon and Miss Betsey Barden.

Married: in Rochester, VT, on the 12th ult., by Rev. Mr. Hurlburt, Luther Tucker, one of the editors of the Rochester Daily Advertiser, to Miss Naomi Sparhawk, dau. of H. [?] Sparhawk, Esq., of the former place.

Married: in Farmington, the 27th ult., by W. Smith, Esq., Seth W. Bosworth and Miss Catharine Pound.

Married: in Ontario, Sun., the 25th ult., Amos Loop, formerly of Mentz, Cayuga Co., to Miss Cynthia Peck.

Married: in Vienna [Oneida Co.], Dec. 3rd, John M. Bell, of Geneva to Miss Giraud, of Manchester.

Married: in New York, M. M. Noah, Esq., editor of The Enquirer, to Miss Rebecca Jackson.

DECEMBER 28, 1827

Married: at Vienna, [Oneida Co.], the 24th inst., by Rev. John A. Clark, Mr. Moses B. Whitmore, of Phelps, to Miss Dorothy Edmundson, dau. of Thomas Edmundson, of the former place.

Married: in Manchester, the 9th inst., George Stafford to Miss Sarah Warren.

Married: in Prattsburgh, Steuben Co., the 24th inst., by Rev. Mr. Hotchkiss, George E. Hayes, druggist, of Canandaigua village, to Miss Emily H. Hopkins, of the former place.

JANUARY 2, 1828

Among those attending the New Year Celebration at Hurd's Hotel were T. P. Baldwin, Joel Thayer and Ambrose Salisbury.

Married: In Marion, Dec. 24, 1827, by Rev. Seth Mattison, John Frankenberger of Geneva and Miss Mary Ann Hall, dau. of Amasa Hall, Jr. of Marion, NY.

Died: Dec. 31, 1828, in Ontario, William Hill.

Died: Dec. 31, 1828, at the home of his father, at East Ridge in this county, Thursday last, Edward G. Stone, son of the Rev. William Stone, and brother of one of the editors of the New York Commercial Advertiser, ae 26 years.

JANUARY 10, 1829 (EXTRA)

Died: at the Hermitage, Rachel Jackson, consort of General Andrew Jackson.

Adv. - J. Francis wants to engage an apprentice lad.

JANUARY 16, 1829

Accounts of James Field, payable to George N. Williams and Philip Grandin; another notice that accounts of same are payable to Charles Smyth, Jr.

Married: In this town, Jan. 7, 1829, by Rev. William Fowler, Philander B. Rice, of Williamson, to Miss Hannah Green of Palmyra.

Married: Jan. 8, 1829, in Palmyra, by F. Smith, Esq., David Bement and Miss Eliza Bird, also Jedidiah Dewey, Jr. and Miss Eleanor McUmber, all of Manchester.

Married: In this town, Jan. 15, 1829, by Rev. Mr. Chamberlain, Robert Homes to Miss Amanda Durfee, all of this town.

Died: in Arcadia, Dec. 31, 1828, Silas Cooper, age 83 years.

Died: In Manchester, Jan. 12, 1820, Miss Cephlanett Pratt, dau. of Elkanah Pratt, age 15 years.

JANUARY 23, 1829

Wells Anderson, Chairman and E. B. Grandin, Sec. of a meeting of "Mechanics".

Married: Jan. 18, 1829, in St. Johns Church in the town of Sodus, by Rev. Mr. Hubbard, Joseph August Phelps, of Williamson, and Ruth Ann Howard, of the same place.

Married: Jan. 7, 1829, in this town, by William Wilcox, Esq., John Soule and Miss Phebe Burden.

Adv.: Stephen Hopkins found 8 yds of cloth - no owner.

JANUARY 30, 1829

Messers David and Durfee, have taught a High School for more than a year past.

The Episcopal Church is now completed. It was built by Capt. Marvin of Romulus.

Meeting to consider "Palmyra High School"; the committee consists of George Beckwith, Chm., P. Tucker, Sec.; and....

George N. Williams   Thomas Rogers, 2nd

Ovid Lovell	W. M. Bayard
Truman Heminway	E. S. Townsend
George Beckwith	David Eddy
Thomas Lakey	Russell Whipple
F. U. Sheffield	Elijah Kent
Daniel Hendee	David White
Beckwith, George	E. S. Townsend
Gain Robinson	William Rogers, Jr.
William N. Lummis	James P. Bartle
Albert Alsop	Asa B. Smith
Luther Tucker	Truman Heminway
Thomas Rogers, 2nd	Abraham Spear
Ambrose Salisbury	Thomas Wickham
Maltby Clark	Artemus Matthewson

Married: In Macedon, Jan. 22, 1829, David Blackman and Miss Deborah Beals, dau. of B. Beals.
Died: In this village, Jan. 24, 1829, Mrs. Sally Hurd, wife of Lovell Hurd, ae 24 years.
Died: In Geneva, Jan. 24, 1829, Jarvis L. Smith, an old inhabitant and book seller.

Adv.: Jarvis L. Thayer will settle accounts of Lovwell Hurd.
Thomas L. Aker, of Rochester Adv. the Eagle Tavern for rent.

FEBRUARY 6, 1829
Married: In Farmington, Feb. 6th, by Rev. A. D. Eddy, Abiather Power and Susan Rapelye.
Died: In this town, Feb. 2nd, Joel Foster, Deacon of the Presbyterian Church, age 60 yrs.; he was b. in Southampton, L. I., Dec. 13, 1768 and came here in 1792, one of the first settlers.
Died: In Canandaigua, Jan. 29, Jeremiah Van Rensselaer, age 60 years.

FEBRUARY 13, 1829
Married; In this village, Feb. 12th, by Rev. Mr. Campbell, Erasmus D. Robinson and Miss Calista D. Peck, all of Palmyra.
Married: Feb. 10th, by F. Smith, Esq., Joseph Gleason and Miss Harriet Brown, both of Manchester.

FEBRUARY 20, 1829
Married: Feb. 17th, by Rev. Mr. Campbell, James P. Horton and Caroline M. Goldsmith, all of this town.
Married: On the 10th inst., by Frederick Smith, Esq., Mr. Joseph Gleason to Miss Harriet Brown, both of Manchester.
Married: In Port Gibson, [Ontario Co.], on the 5th inst., Mr. David Smith of this village, to Miss Eliza Howe, of the former place.

Married: In Marion, on the 16th inst., by Rev. E. Blakesley, Mr. William Palmer of Macedon, to Miss Matilda Skinner of the former place.

Died: In Geneva, Feb. 12th, Rev. Henry Axtell, D. D., Pastor of the Presbyterian Church; his older dau., Rebecca d. Feb. 14, 1829; both buried in one grave.

FEBRUARY 27, 1829

Married: Feb. 26th in Manchester, Uri Decker and Miss Experience M. Baker, both of Manchester.

William Campbell and Charles Durfee to be instructors in the Palmyra Classical School.

Philip Grandin turns over to Meech & Woodward his commission and forwarding business. [Horace Meech and Jabez Woodward]

Champion & Howell dissolve; Champion continues the business.

MARCH 6, 1829

Married: March 5, 1829, in Palmyra, by Rev. Mr. Campbell, Alpheus Martin of Canandaigua, to Miss Sarah Beebe of Palmyra.

Married: March 5th, in Phelps, by Rev. Mr. Strong, Joseph S. Beebe of Palmyra to Miss Mary Ann Crosby of Phelps.

Died: Feb. 20th near Auburn, George Whitfield Hatch, formerly of Wayne Co., age 59 years.

Adv.: The Palmyra House recently known as the St.John Hotel rented to F. W. Lee; Joseph Willcox adv. a stray colt.

MARCH 13, 1829:

Married: March 4th in Geneseo, LeGrand L. Morse, one of the editors of the Ontario Messenger, to Miss Mahala Pierce, dau. of John Pierce of Geneseo.

Married: in Lyons, Feb. 26th, by Rev. Mr. Rowe, Samuel Sheldon of Palmyra to Miss Elvira Brown of Newark.

Died: in this town, Stephen Sherman, age 40 years.

Died: in Manchester, March 7th, Selden Noyes, aged 20 yrs.; he had been sick five years.

Died: March 4, 1829, in Canandaigua, Mrs. Sybella Adeline VanRensselaer, widow of Jeremiah S. Van Rensselaer, age 54 years.

MARCH 20, 1829

A post office has been established in the village of Berlin to be called Lock Berlin with William H. Griswold as postmaster.

Married: in Macedon, Jun 21, 1828 [sic] [prob. a typographical error and should be Jan. 21, 1829], by the Hon. Jonathan Boynton, H. Worden and Miss P. Reeves.

adv.: Eggleston & Hotchkins, opposite J. Benson's cabinet shop.

MARCH 27, 1829

Married: March 25, 1829, in this village, Haskell Linnell and Melissa Morehouse.

Married: in Manchester, March 25th by Mr. Howland, Esq., James H. Johnson, Jr. to Miss Rachel Aldrich of Manchester.

Died: March 14th at Clyde, Eli Frink, age 45 yrs. Left ten children.
Died: March 21st, at Montezuma, [Cayuga Co.], Mrs. Hannah Fisher, at age 81 yrs., widow of George Fisher, an old Revolutionary soldier.
Died: March 9th, in Port Bay, Mrs. Margaret Sheldon, age 30 years.
Died: March 9th in Yates, Elder Jeremiah Irons, age 63 yrs., Pastor of the Baptist church, formerly of Palmyra.
Adv.: Samuel T. Horton - dry goods in the new Brick Building at the corner of Fayette and Main Sts.; Nathan Parshall adv. Archer Galloway's notes.

APRIL 3, 1829

Married: March 29th in the Presbyterian church in this village, by Rev. Mr. Campbell, Harvey Steele and Mrs. Anna Perkins.
Married: March 13, 1829 in Logan, MI, Curran Bradish, formerly of Macedon, and Ruby S. Comstock, dau. of Darius Comstock, of the former place.
Died: April 1st in this village, Daniel Buck, age 45 years.
Died: March 20th, in Penfield [Monroe Co.], John Johnson, ae 39 yrs., formerly of Wayne County.

APRIL 10, 1829

Daniel Hendee, Josiah Wright, and Truman Heminway appointed by the Governor and Senate as auctioneers.
Truman Heminway posts an objection to anothers giving out Bibles to those he prefers to supply. [A lengthy notice.]
Married: in Lyons, March 26th, Amos Woodruff and Eliza Potter.
Married: March 26th, George Martin and Sally Woodruff.
Married: April 3rd, James Hill, of the U. S. Army and Amanda Doyle, an Indian.
ADV.: H. H. Treat & Co., have taken over the warehouse occupied by James Field & Co. Mrs. Gough, dressmaker, opposite G. Beckwith's store:
Patrick Boyle offers the Yellow Mills for sale.

APRIL 17, 1829

NOTICE: A meeting of the Palmyra Library to be held at A. Hendee's - persons having library books are requested to return them.
Peter Redmond rents Patrick Boyle's mill.

APRIL 24, 1829

First packet boat of the season passed east; navigation opened between Montezuma and Buffalo.
The Town of Ontario has been divided. The north town retains the name of Ontario, the new town is to be called Walworth.
Horace Church is keeping the Eagle Hotel on Main St. in Palmyra; later known as the Powers Hotel although it is a new building.
Married: April 5, 1829 in Port Glasgow, David Smith of Palmyra and Miss Eliza Howe.

Married: in Marion, April 16th, by Rev. E. Blakesley, William Palmer of Macedon and Matilda Skinner, of the former place.

Married: in New York city, April 14th, by the Rt. Rev. Bishop Hobart, Hon., J. W. Hallett, late first judge of Wayne Co., to Margaret, youngest dau. of Alexander Macomb.

ADV: David Smith - painting;
Ruth Sherman, exec. to sell property of Stephen Sherman, deceased, May 9th; Jeremiah Notingham wants to buy oats.

MAY 1, 1829

Married: April 20th, in Lyons, by Rev. L. Hubbell, William Griffith, of Rochester and Elizabeth McClary of the former place.

Married: in Canandaigua, April 23rd, by Rev. A. D. Eddy., John A. Granger and Miss Harriet Jackson, dau. of the late Amasa Jackson of New York.

MAY 8, 1829

Wayne Co. Bank stock offered for sale - books to be kept by Horace Church at the Eagle Hotel; Committee: Joel Thayer, Philip Grandin, Henry Jessup, James P. Bartle, and Thomas Rogers, 2nd.

Adv.: Joel McCollum wants to sell 50 village lots.

MAY 15, 1829

Married: in Sodus, May 15th, William H. Dennison and Miss Caroline Turner, dau. of Enoch Turner.

Died: May 6th, Isaac Blossom, ae 47 years.

Died: in this village, May 11, 1829, Sylvester Birdsall, son of Sutton Birdsall, age 21 months.

Adv.: Thomas P. Baldwin, attorney, over the Palmyra Book Store.

MAY 22, 1829

Married: in Auburn, May 13th, Rev. E. G. Gear, Pastor of Zion church, Palmyra, to Miss Mary Y. Howe, of Auburn.

Married: My 12th, in New York, by the Mayor, William R. Brewster of Canandaigua, to Elizabeth, dau. of Samuel Mott, of New York.

Died: May 18 in Williamson, Amaziah Chappell, a Revolutionnary soldier, ae 76 yrs. On the same day, his wife, Jerusha died, ae 71 years.

MAY 29, 1829

Died: in this village, Ann Maria Lovell, infant dau. of Ovid Lovell.

Adv: Milo Galloway adv. a lady's camlet mantle lost;

Weed & Niles - drugs, etc.

JUNE 5, 1829

Married: in this village, June 4th, by Rev. Mr. Gear, James Sumner and Alma Parker, of Palmyra.

JUNE 12, 1829

The Editor of the Sentinel reports that the verdict of the jury in his libel suit brought by Israel D. Richardson, was "Not Guilty."

Married: in Pittsford [Monroe Co.], May 20th, Dr. Abner Barnard, of Lockport [Ontario Co.], and Miss Harriet Jane Hepburn of Perrinton.

Married; in New York City, May 20, 1829, John N. Rose of Geneva and Jane Eliza, youngest dau. of John Navarre Macomb of New York.

Died: May 30, 1829, an infant child of Thomas P. Barnum.

JUNE 19, 1829

News: A stranger was drowned in attempting to swim the Tonawanda Creek near its mouth on the 25th ult. He had called his name, Samuel Wolcott, and said he had two children living in Palmyra; the letters, "S. W." appeared in Indian ink on his left arm. (From the Buffalo Journal).

Died: in Marion, June 7th, Miss Catherine Shaw, ae 23 years.

Died: in Rochester, June 3rd, Joseph Henry Roberts, ae 4 years, son of E. J. Roberts.

Adv.: George Culver, of East Palmyra lost his spectacles.

JUNE 26, 1829

Editorial on the Golden Bible".(First mention of Mormonism). Title page is given in this issue of the Sentinel in full.

Committee for the Ju ly 4th parade: T. R. Strong, M. Bayard, W. W. Willcox, P. Tucker, R. S. Williams, C. E. Thayer, and George W. Cuyler.

Married: June 18th in Waterloo, E. P. Moon, editor, and Elizabeth G. Sholes, oldest dau.of John Sholes.

Married: in Penn Yan, June 4th, John Newell of Phelps and Mary Elizabeth, dau. of P. P. Underhill, of Phelps.

Died: in Pittsburgh, June 14th, Ira Selby, Jr., oldest son of Ira Selby, ae 25 yrs.; formerly of Phelps.

Adv.: Oren Warner adv. a stray mare.

JULY 3, 1829

ADV: C. Robinson & H. N. Loomis - drugs, in brick row, 4 doors east of the Eagle Hotel.

JULY 10, 1829

Married: in Macedon, July 6th, Benjamin Greig of Rochester to Miss Fuilealema Carpenter of Macedon.

Married: in Manchester, July 4th, by David Holland, Esq., Abraham Duesler and Miss Lusina Aldrich.

Married: in Palmyra, July 4th, John Ayres and Miss Kazia Clark.

Died: in this town, on the 30th ult., Mr. Francis Horton, aged 26 years.

JULY 17, 1829
Died: July 13th in Macedon Daniel Miles aged 30 years.
Died: in Manchester, July 5th, John Shekell, aged 54 years.
Died: in Canandaigua, July 1st, Ezra S. Squires, aged 23 years.

ADVERTISERS: F. Dike adv. a house and lot for sale, west end of Main St.; W. G. Rodney, a teacher, opens a school July 15th, one door east of Dr. Eggleston's house opposite Ovid Lovell's store.

JULY 24, 1829
Rev. John A. Clark of New York, late rector of Zion Church, will preach in the new Episcopal Church in this village on Sunday.

JULY 23, 1829
Died: suddenly, July 28th, Abner Hill, one of Macedon's first settlers, ae 54 years.

JULY 31, 1829
Died: July 22nd in Galen, Mrs. Anna Hinman, wife of Harris Hinman.
Died: July 27th in Canandaigua, Miss Mary Antis, dau. of William Antis, ae 20 years.
Died: July 17th, in Phelps, Mrs. Ann Shekell, widow of Capt. Samuel S. Shekell, ae 80 years.
Married: in Palmyra, June 23rd, by William Wilcox, Nathaniel Piper and Harriet Johnson.
Married: June 27th in Phelps, Silas Hemingway, of Geneva and Miss Mary Ottley, dau. of Capt. Ottley.
H. Nelson, butcher, to be found at K. Miller's, the keeper of the Franklin House.

AUGUST 7, 1829
Rev. Lorenzo Dow will preach in this village Aug. 2nd; Elijah Linnell and Alvah Scott have dissolved their shoe business - Linnell will continue.
Married: in Sodus, July 30th, Jeremiah Storms and Mariah Peeler, both of Sodus.
Married: July 8th in Poughkeepsie, by Rev. Dr. Cuyler, J. Nelson of Newark, toMiss Cornelia Low of the former place.
Died: July 27th, in Ontario, Mrs. Charlotte Randolph, ae 62 years.

AUGUST 14, 1829
Notice: The Galen post office now becomes the Clyde post office and the Clyde post office in Monroe Co. now becomes North Rochester.
Married: Aug. 10th, in this town, by Rev. Pomeroy, Edwin Hopkins and Elizabeth Ann Porter.
Married: Aug. 8th, in Williamson, Elias B. Bassy and Lucinthia Wilber.
Married: in Marion, Aug. 11th, by Mr. Marvin, Esq., Eli Cobb and Sarah Dexter.
Died: Aug. 8th, in this town, Lemuel Durfee, ae 70 years.
Died: July 28th, in Freedom, Cattaraugus Co., Dr. Dyer Cowdrey.

ADV.: James White has milk for sale; Charles T. Payne - groceries;
Payne & Gilbert dissolve their partnership - C. T. Payne continues.

AUGUST 21, 1829
Mr. Lorenzo Dow will preach in the Methodist Chapel tomorrow.
Marlin W. Willcox has been appointed postmaster in place of Joseph S. Colt who has been removed.
Died: Aug. 15th, in this village, Samuel D. Robinson, formerly of Pittsburgh, at the age of 28 years.

AUGUST 28, 1829
The celebrated itinerant preacher, Lorenzo Dow, delivered a discourse in a field adjacent to the Methodist Chapel in this village, Sat. p. m. last, to an audience of at least 3000 people.
Rev. Jason Allen will be in charge of Palmyra High School.
Married: in Palmyra, Aug. 10th, by Rev. Pomeroy, Edmond Hopkins and Elizabeth N., dau. of Nathaniel J. Potter.
Married: Aug. 23rd, in Lyons, A. L. Beaumont and Clarissa G. Holley, 2nd dau. of Myron Holley.
Married: Aug. 15th, in Arcadia, Nathan Newkirk and Emma Parmalee.
Married: July 5th in Lewiston, Il, Joel Wright and Emily Phelps, dau. of Stephen Phelps, formerly of Palmyra.

SEPTEMBER 4, 1829
Married: in Lyons, Sept. 4th, George C. Cole, of Palmyra to Maria Waters.

ADV: Drs. Gain and Caius C. Robinson, ask settlement [of debts].

SEPTEMBER 11, 1829
Luther Howard buys out E. B. Grandin bindery and library.
Died: in Clyde, Sept. 3rd, George Reitz of the firm T. & G. Reitz age 31 yrs.

SEPTEMBER 18, 1829
Married: in this town, Sept. 16th, by Rev. Mr. Gear, Horace Birdsall of Ovid and Dorcas Flagler.
Died: in Lockville, Sept. 9th, Mrs. Mary Ann Hendee, wife of Col. Daniel Hendee, formerly of Palmyra.
Died: in this village, Sept. 16th, Mrs. Washington Linnell.
Died: in this town, Sept. 14th, Mrs. Sarah Durfee, wife of Stephen Durfee, ae 46 years.
Died: Aug. 2nd, at the Bay of St. Louis, L. N. Wooster, formerly of Rochester.
Died: in Cummington, MA, Sept. 21st, Clark Packard, son of Philander Packard, ae 21 years.
ADV: Palmyra Brewery (Woodward & Co.); Hiram Niles succeeds Weed & Niles.

SEPTEMBER 25, 1829
Married: at Rose, Sept. 16th, Charles B. Sherman and Lucina Allen, all of Rose.
Died: in this town, Sept. 21st, Mrs. Lucy Lakey, wife of Abner F. Lakey, ae 35 years.

ADV: Joseph Colt adv. a lost servant, Naomi M. Evans;
>Pendergast & Tucker adv. village lots on Fayette, Chapel and Jackson St.; Joseph Naftel is about to leave Palmyra on Sept. 24th.

OCTOBER 2, 1829
Died: Oct 2nd 1829, at New Orleans, Burrage Smith, formerly of Rochester.

OCTOBER 9, 1829
Died: Sept. 28, 1829, in Lockport, Nathan Comstock, ae 55 yrs., formerly of Macedon.
ADV: Miss Southworth, milliner in the new brick block nearly opposite J. & J. S. Colt and one door east of N. H. Beckwith's store.

OCTOBER 16, 1829
George Beckwith takes in Richard L. Clark and moves to the new Brick Block opposite J. & J. S. Colt, two door west of the Eagle Hotel.
Married: Sept. 30th, in Leroy, Henry F. Palmer and Emma E. Beckwith.
Died: Oct. 11th in this town, Seth Harris, ae about 14 years.
ADV: Stephen Archer adv. for stray colts; George Beckwith & Co. - broadcloths; Stillman Jackson, gunsmith, two doors west of Bunker Hill Hotel; D. Holmes, tailor at the corner of Church and Main St.

OCTOBER 23, 1829
ADV: [Nathaniel H.] Beckwith & [Gurdon C.] Leech - clothing;
Executors in Ambrose Hall estate, James S. Stoddard, William Wilcox, and Abner F. Lakey; William Whitely adv. for claims.

OCTOBER 30, 1829
Alexander R. Tiffany is a candidate for Justice of the Peace in town of Palmyra; Inspectors of Election for this town have given notice that the poll will be held the first day at Ambrose Salisbury's dwelling house; on the second day at schoolhouse near Paul Goldsmith's in the forenoon and in the afternoon at William P. Nottingham's Bunker Hill House and on the 3rd day at Asa Lilly's Inn.
ADV: A. C. Sunderland adv. sand at the Brewery pit.

NOVEMBER 6, 1829
Luther Tucker appointed postmaster at Walworth, v. Yoemans removed.
Died in Geneva, on Monday, the 26th ult., Mr. Andrew McNab, aged 45 years.
Died: in New York, on the 20th ult., Mr. James Dunn, of the firm of Douglass & Dunn, Albany, aged 32 years and 21 days.
Adv.: Miss Stanley - dressmaker over Miss Southworth's store; E. D. Robinson adv. a stray cow.

NOVEMBER 13, 1829

The body of Benjamin D. Goldsmith of this town, who was drowned in Lake Erie sometime in September last, has recently drifted ashore at Long Point, Upper Canada.

NOVEMBER 20, 1829

The first Assembly will be held at Horace Church's Assembly Room, Fri. evening, 27 Nov. at 7:00 p.m. - Carriages will call for the ladies.

Married: Nov. 17th, in this village, by Rev. A. E. Campbell, Dr. Waterman Hanks of Marion and Mary Jane Cramer.

NOVEMBER 27, 1829

Married: Nov. 15th in Palmyra, Abraham I. VanCamp and Almira Rawson.

Married: Nov. 1, 1829 in Sodus, Riley Baldwin to Miss Louisa Pullman, dau. of Joseph Pullman.

Married: Nov. 1st, in Williamson, Mr. Davis and Louisa Perry.

Died: Nov. 18th, in Williamson, Mrs. Charity Selby.

DECEMBER 4, 1829

Died at Savannah, GA on the 15th ult., Mr. Alonzo W. Kinsley, of the firm of A. W. Kinsley & Co., type-founders, Albany [NY]

Adv.: Administrator of Samuel Elmendorf, adv. for claims.

DECEMBER 11, 1829

We have received the first number of the Newark Republican.

Married: Dec. 6, 1829, in Manchester, Henry E. Perry and Angelia B. Stillman, both of Palmyra.

Died: Nov. 28, 1829, at Newark, Hubbard Pond.

ADV.: J. & L. Thayer - Dry Goods take in H. & C. Thayer; Haskell Linnell wants a boy to help make chairs.

DECEMBER 18, 1829 - "this issue seems to be missing."

DECEMBER 25, 1829

Married: Dec. 2nd, in Manchester, Hiram Bement and Harriet Persons.

Married Dec. 2nd, in Manchester, Matson Warren and Phebe Gleason.

Died: Dec. 12, 1829, in Manlius [Onondaga Co.], Mariah Baker, formerly of Palmyra.

JANUARY 1, 1830

"Manchester" writes on subject of a canal between Canandaigua and the Erie Canal and also a macadam road to Palmyra.[!]

Married: Dec. 31st, in Palmyra, Allyn Williams and Delia Payne by Rev. A. E. C.

Married: Dec. 31, 1829, in Palmyra, William Hyde and Caroline Rose by Rev. Mr. Guion.

Married: Dec. 29th, in town, Capt. Harvey Cobb and Ann Durfee by Rev. Eustace.

Married: Dec. 29, 1829, Edmond Champion of Macedon to Delia Durfee of Palmyra.

Married: Dec. 24, 1829, in Hopewell, Albert G. Fuller and Eunice Lee, both of Palmyra.

Married: Dec. 31, 1829, in Pultneyville, James Holling and Rachel Throop.
Died: Dec. 25, 1829, John Vanwickle, ae 81 years.

JANUARY 8, 1830
Married: Dec. 31, 1829, in Pultneyville, Nathan N. Sheffield to Maria Stalp.
Married: Dec. 31, 1829, in Lyons, Bartlet R. Rogers and Belinda Leach.
Married: Dec. 31, 1829, in Lyons, Stephen Roe and Betsy Smith.
Married: Dec. 31, 1829, in Lyons, Richard Hough and Matilda Plumley.
Married: Dec. 31, 1829, in Phelps, Daniel Homan and Sally Avery.
Married: Dec. 31, 1829, in Arcadia, Thomas Parsly and Jane Adams.
Married: Jan. 1, 1830, in Arcadia, Jeremiah Van Ostrand and Jane Beckwith.
ADV: Stimpson & Pendergast, painters have moved to the 2nd story of the new Market House on the corner of Canal & Market St.

JANUARY 15, 1830
Treat & Curtis dissolve partnership.

JANUARY 22, 1830
Married: Sun. evening, Jan. 17, 1830, by Rev. Henry Davis, Mr. H. H. Treat of Palmyra to Miss Addela Bosworth, of PA.
Married: Jan. 14, 1830, by Rev. Mr. Bagley, David H. Sherman, of this town [Palmyra] to Mrs. Valina Marsh of Phelps.

JANUARY 29, 1830
The Palmyra Freeman discontinued and the first copy of the Countryman just received.
Donation party to be given Rev. A. E. Campbell at his home Feb. 5th at 4 p.m.
Thayer & Co. assigned to Thomas Rogers, 2nd.

FEBRUARY 5, 1830
Married: Jan. 21, 1830, in Phelps, Hiram B. Carothers of Manchester to Miss Lany Robinson.
Died: Jan. 30, 1830 in Phelps, James Westfall, ae 78 years.

FEBRUARY 12, 1830
The following were chosen directors of the Wayne Co. Bank at a meeting held at the hotel of Horace Church:

Cyrus Strong	Joseph Fenton	Pliny Sexton
George N. Williams	George Beckwith	N. H. Beckwith
Joseph S. Colt	Henry Jessup	Ovid Lovell
P. Grandin	Thomas Rogers, 2nd	Abraham Spear

Cyrus Strong - President & Joseph S. Fenton - Cashier

John C. Winters, "alias Jack" leaves town, people are warned.
Anthony Jorry of Palmyra reported insolvent. Feb. 2, 1830
Married: Feb. 5, 1830 at Palmyra, John Logan and Cordelia Howard, both of Canandaigua.
ADV.: P. West harness shop 2 doors east of Eagle Hotel; A. R. Tiffany become a law firm; E. R. Spear - painter, opposite Asa Lilly's Tavern; Thomas Rogers, 2nd, Claims Agent for Thayer & Co.

FEBRUARY 19, 1830
J. Allen, Principal of Palmyra High school invites public to visit school.
Postoffice has been moved to the building of A. Hendee at the corner of Main and Cuyler St. on Feb. 18, 1830.
Married: Feb. 11, 1830, in Manchester, Lyman W. Baker and Asenath Warner.

FEBRUARY 26, 1830
George W. Moore was advertised as an insolvent.
Married: Feb. 25, 1830, in Macedon, by Rev. Mr. Powell, Orlando Bates of Ridgeway, NY and Miss Irene Spear, dau. of Abraham Spear.

MARCH 5, 1830
J. & L. Thayer assigns boats to Allen Brown; Allen Brown assigns boats to Edward & Silas Browen [sic] and Peter Bain.
Married: Feb. 25, 1830, in Lyons, Erastus Wilder and Katherine Mead.
Married: Feb. 28, 1830, in Arcadia, Eber Thorn and Emily Tharp.
ADV: Perry & Mason - lumber - succeeds Meech & Woodward; Allen Brown assignees - 5 boats, horses, etc.

MARCH 12, 1830
Report of meeting on northern route and improved road to Canandaigua.
Married: Feb. 18, 1830, in Prattsburg, Jeremiah Hakes, late of Palmyra and Maria Smith of that place.
Married: Mar. 4, 1830, in Williamson, John J. Myers and Orella Stalp.
Died: March 7, in Palmyra, Mrs. Sophia Foster, wife of Jeter Foster, age 32 years.

MARCH 19, 1830
We are requested to announce that the "Book of Mormons" will be ready for sale in the course of the next week.
Birdsall & Stimpson dissolve; Edwin B. Stimpson continues.
Died: March 13, 1830, Sidney S. Seymour, ae 24 years.
Died: Feb. 27, 1830, in Arcadia, Sally Mighells, ae 34, wife of Elezear Mighells.
Died: March 7, 1830, in Canandaigua, Thaddeus Chapin, an early settler.
Died: Feb. 27, 1830, at Jerico, Long Island, Elias Hicks, of Quaker fame.

MARCH 26, 1830
Book of Mormon advertised by Howard & Grandin.
Died: March 18, 1830, in this town, William Colbrath.
Adv.: Samuel Rogers will not be responsible for debts; William Adams lost a saddle.

APRIL 2, 1830
Howard & Grandin dissolve - Grandin continues.
Adv.: Ira White has a house to let.
Meeting of Marion Republicans held at <u>Marion Springs House</u>, March 26, 1830; Marvin Rich, Chairman and Morton Eddy, Sec.. Object to the anti-masonic policy so prevalent at this time. Those in attendance:

Thomas Laky	Darius Pratt	Jesse Mason
George P. Eddy	Samuel Ball	J. L. Thayer
J. V. C. Teller	John Galloway	Wm. H. Dennison
John Wilber	Manchester Boice	Levi Clark
Hiram E. Eddy	John Atwood	William Boise
A. Galloway	Asa Skinner	Julius C. Hutchins
Henry Eddy	Silas S. Lyon	J. Sutton
Friend Webster	B. Bennett	Richard Bourne
Sidney Pratt	Truman Perry	Stephen Vaughn
Orlo Haskins	Levi Johnson	

APRIL 9, 1830
In Spring elections anti-masonry was defeated heavily.
Married: April 5, 1830, in this town, William Robinson and Mary Horton.
Died: April 8, 1830, in Palmyra, Mrs. Nancy Havens wife of E. Havens, ae 46 years.

APRIL 16, 1830
Wayne County Bank will begin operations within a few days; 10 of the 15 towns of this county are Republican; Wendell & Hyde dissolve partnership.
Adv.: William Hyde - bakery; P. Grandin - threshing machines.

APRIL 23, 1830
Died: April 21, 1830 in Palmyra, Mrs. Sarah Skellenger, wife of Stephen Skellenger, ae 55 years.
Died: April 18, 1830 in the town of Palmyra, Warren Sherman, ae 25 years.
Adv.: April 22, Stephen Skellenger - household furniture.

APRIL 30, 1830 - no news items copied.
MAY 7, 1830
Teachers Examination at H. Church's Tavern May 15, 1830.

Married: May 4, 1830, in Pittsford [Monroe] Co., by Rev. Mr. Mahan, Mr. Richard S. Williams, of this village to Miss Olive Ann Porter, daughter of Chauncey Porter, Esq. of the former place.

Died: in Lyons, the 2nd inst., Maria, daughter of Rev. L. Hubbell, aged about 5 years.

ADV: H. S. White - boarding house three door east of the Bunker Hill Hotel.

MAY 14, 1830

We understand that the mail stage from Albany by the way of Cherry Valley, arrived in this village Tues. last in 36 hrs. from time of starting.[!]

Married: May 4, 1830, in this town, Samuel H. Post and Elizabeth C. Hathaway.

Married: May 4, 1830, in Arcadia, Brian Johnson of Sodus and Phebe Perry, of Arcadia.

Married: May 8, 1830, in Gorham, John Saunders and Nancy Gage.

ADV: St. Lawrence - bath house; George W. Cuyler has a house for sale on Cuyler Street.

MAY 21, 1830

ADV: William Hyde & Co. - groceries under the Palmyra Market.

MAY 28, 1830

A concert by Hastings and Masons Musical Society at the Presbyterian Meeting House June 9, 1830 - adm. 25c

JUNE 4, 1830

ADV: J. Hermans - dry goods - one door west of Eagle Hotel - rents new store from Mr. Anderson.

JUNE 7, 1830

N.B.: **The next 10 entries appear in Mrs. Wiles' abstracts but do not appear in Mr. Van Alstine's abstracts of the same newspaper. Indeed, Mr. Van Alstine showed no evidence of a June 7th edition of the newspaper. However, the names of the individuals who appear in these entries do appear in separate indexes of male marriages, female marriages and deaths which Mr. Van Alstine compiled. This editor can conceive of no explanation for this happenstance.**

Married: in Groton, CT, on the 12th ult., Albert E. Smith of the firm of H. F. Smith & Co., of Rochester, to Julia A. Burrows of the former place.

Died: in Lyons on the 16th ult. Mr. Emery Hewlet.

Died: in Canandaigua on the 17th ult., Margaret, wife of Capt. William O'Hara ae 47 years.

Died: on the 21st ult., Rebecca, wife of Baily Hall, ae 30 years.

Died: in Geneva on the 27th ult., Mrs. Susannah Loncast, ae 37 years.

Died: in Rochester on the 27th ult., Harriet, wife of Levi A. Ward.

Died: in Fishkill, Mr. Jacob Vanbenschoten, ae 77 years.

Died: in Poughkeepsie, Mrs. Catharine G. Livingston, widow of the late Gilbert Livingston, ae 85 years.

Died: in Wheeler, [Steuben Co.], William Homes, ae 52 years.

Died: in Elmira, William Vial, son of Norris North, aged 16 months.

End of Mrs. Wiles Entries

....

JUNE 11, 1830

At a meeting at Miller's Franklin House a committee was named to arrange for the 4th of July celebration:

Charles Hotchkiss	Hiram Niles	Jehiel Todd
George Jessup	E. B. Grandin	G. C. Leach
George W. Cuyler	W. M. Bayard	P. Tucker
T. R. Strong	M. W. Willcox	J. M. Woodward

The first number of a new newspaper just received: The Western Spectator and Wayne Advertiser, Luther Howard, Prop. and Pub.; Erastus Sheppard, Editor and Printer; Democratic in politics.

Married: in Manchester, by David Howland, Esq., Mr. Howard Bement to Miss Lydia Bird.

Died: in this village, on Thursday, the 5th inst., Ann Sophia, daughter of Mr. Jeter Foster, aged 3 years.

Died: June 5, 1830, at West Macedon, Electa, wife of Samuel Rand, aged 23 years.

ADV: Hurlburt & Bennet - blacksmith - Francis Hurlburt takes in Franklin Bennet - near the Collectors Office.

JUNE 18, 1830

Rev. A. E. Campbell will give an address to the Palmyra society for the Promotion of Temperance.

The following were elected Directors of the Wayne County Bank by order of the Board of Managers: J. M. Woodward, Sec.:

Cyrus Strong	Loring Fenton	John Clapp
Joseph O. Fenton	Squire Smith	George Beckwith
Thomas Rogers, 2nd	Pliny Sexton	Abraham Spear
Nath. H. Beckwith	John Colvin	George M. Williams
	Philip Grandin	

Married: June 6, 1830, Ransom Blakmarr and Adeline Miller of Newark, by Rev. Peter Kanouse.

JUNE 25, 1830

Fourth of July Dinner will be given by H. Church of the Eagle Hotel.

Married: June 17, 1830, at Williamson, John Smith, Jr. of Marion and Mary Ann Johnson of Williamson.

JULY 2, 1830

Fourth of July Procession - Lt. Col. Ambrose Salisbury, Marshall; Maj. Durfee Chase and Capt. M. W. Willcox as assistants in parade.

Married: July, 1830, William R. Harrison and Ann Giberson, all of Williamson.

Died: June 22, 1830, Hannah Hill, dau. of David Hill, ae 22 years.

Died: June 30, 1830, in Newark, Mrs. Adeline Blackmarr, wife of Ransom Blackmarr.

Died: June 26, 1830, in Lyons, Mrs. Susan Kingsbury, ae 32 years.

Died: June 16, 1830, in Canandaigua, Jasper Reid, ae 41 years.

ADV: W. F. Jarvis - meat market; H. Nelson - meat market.

JULY 9, 1830

Peter VanAlstine has an uncalled for letter in the post office.

Married: July 8, 1830, in Palmyra, Clark Robinson of Albany, late of Palmyra, and Miss Delia Strong of Palmyra.

JULY 16, 1830

Married: July 5, 1830 in Lyons, Jeremiah Burch and Lucinda Smock.

Married: July 1, 1830, John Hawks, M. D. and Laura Louise Lathrop, 2nd dau. of Leonard E. Lathrop, all of Newark.

Married: July 1, 1830, in Arcadia, David Dunham and Mary Hillman.

Married: July 1, 1830, in Lockville, Jacob Keller and Mary Stansell.

Married: July 9, 1830, in Canandaigua, William Service and Miss Ann Bulrees.

Married: July 13, 1830, in Galen, Azariah Prentiss and Almira C. Brown.

Married: July 11, 1830, in Lyons, Louis Baltze and Mathalane Shuler.

Died: July 4, 1830, Mary A. Kipp, dau. of John L. Kipp, of Newark, ae 11 years.

ADV: Frederick Coppock - jeweller, 3 doors east of the Eagle Hotel.

JULY 23, 1830

On July 21st several bed pieces of aqueduct from the center pier to the west gave way but the Superintendent, Mr. Reeves had repairs made in ten hours time.

John Harris of Newark had his leg badly broken - it was taken off.

George W. Cuyler admitted to the bar at Utica recently.

Died: July 16, 1830, Mrs. Sarah Barker, wife of Samuel S. Barker, and dau. of Ezra Crandall, ae 23 years. (Wiles entered above as Barber)

ADV.: Wells Anderson & Samuel Beckwith - leather, etc.; Draper Allen wants to buy skins; Palmyra High School is open under the care of James F. Cogswell who has served at Cherry Valley for the past 6 or 7 years.

JULY 30, 1830

Married: July 8, 1830, at Seneca, Clark Wright and Polly Hammond, both of Palmyra.

Married: July 8, 1830, Jefferson Gates and Mary Ann Laver.

ADV: W (?) H. Bortles operates the Lottery office.

AUGUST 6, 1830

L. Tillottson of Canandaigua operates a line of post coaches with M. Kingman and has for some months - see early papers.

AUGUST 13, 1830

Henry Nelson and Barnabas VanTassell dissolve.
Meeting called for 8/18 at the Eagle Hotel, to discuss the propriety of erecting a steam flouring mill.
The death of King George reported in this issue [on] June 26, 1830.
Died: Aug. 3, 1830, in Palmyra, Mrs. Sally Lewis, a visitor here, ae 34 years.
Died: July 31, 1830, in Macedon, Angelica Hicks, wife of Joshua Hicks, ae 38 years.
ADV: Ezra Coon adv. stray colts; Henry Nelson.

AUGUST 20, 1830

Committee appointed to receive subscriptions to aid person who contemplates erecting a steam flouring mill.
Died: Aug. 19, 1830, in Palmyra, Juliet Ann Coppock, dau. of F. Coppock, ae 22 months.
Aug. 16, 1830. Flanders Dyke, a swindler, of Palmyra, adv. as an absconder; he had lived in Palmyra 5 or 6 yrs.; had m. the dau. of a wealthy farmer; left with Asa Hill and about $1000.00, for Michigan. The 5th trick played by members of this family: Samuel Dyke, Sr., Samuel Dyke, Jr., James Dyke, John Biggs, a son-in-law, and now Flanders Dyke.

AUGUST 27, 1830

Married: in Williamson, Eli W. Bartholomew and Hannah Brockway of Williamson.
Died: Aug. 20, 1830, in Palmyra, Miss Scott, dau. of John Scott, ae 16 months.
Died: Aug. 21, 1830, in Palmyra, Frederick A. Norton, son of Augustus Norton.
Died: Aug. 20, 1830, in Lyons, Candice Leach, ae 41 years.
Died: Aug. 22, 1830, in Manchester, Nathaniel Reed, ae 70 years.

SEPTEMBER 3, 1830

September 4, 1830 - 50 village lots sold at auction at the Eagle Hotel by James White & Co. on the south side of Main st., intersected by Jackson St., President and Governor Sts., equi-distant between two prominent roads from Canandaigua to Palmyra. In the center is a plot of 3 1/2 acres.
Married: Sept. 30, 1830, in Schenectady, Nelson Serviss and Martha Chandler.
Married: Sept. 1, 1830, in Sodus, William W. Nash and Lucy E. Green, dau. of Byram Green.
Married: Aug. 17, 1830, in Plainfield, NY, Phineas L. Sherman of Palmyra, and Miss Eveline Robinson.
Died: Aug. 28, 1830, in Lyons, Mrs. Abigail Price, wife of Benjamin Price, ae 38 years.
Died: Aug. 26, 1830, in Lyons, Harris Barrett, ae 30 years.
Died: Sept. 1, 1830, in Canandaigua, Eliphalet Taylor.

SEPTEMBER 10, 1830
Married: Sept. 4, 1830, in Marion, by Eld. Allen, Stephen Brown and Ann Bennett.
Married: Sept. 2, 1830, in Macedon, by Rev. Powell, William Crandall and Rebecca Rawson.
Married: Aug. 29, in Arcadia, Philip Sager and Sally Riggs.
Married: Aug. 22, 1830, in Clyde, James McDole and Mrs. Betsy George.

SEPTEMBER 17, 1830
Married: Sept 5, 1830, in Arcadia, George B. Burnet and Abigail Craw, both of Galen.
Married: Sept. 2, 1830, in Sodus, at Camp-meeting, James H. Kellogg and Mary Taylor.
Died: Sept. 12, 1830, the Rt. Rev. John Henry Hobart, at Auburn at 5:00 a.m.

SEPTEMBER 24, 1830 - No items copied or unavailable.
OCTOBER 1, 1830 - No items copied or unavailable
OCTOBER 2, 1840 - EXTRA
Married: Sept. 30, 1930, in Palmyra, Mr. Stevens and Elizabeth Trembly.
Married: Sept. 30, 1830, at the Friends Meeting house in Farmington, Loren Hathaway and Lydia Ramsdell.
Died: Sept. 25, 1830, in Palmyra, Mrs. Moore, wife of Dr. Samuel Moore, of Marion.
Died: Sept 24, 1830, in Palmyra, Mrs. Harriet Picket, age 30 years.

OCTOBER 8, 1830
The first number of the Western Argus [pub. in] Lyons [by] J. Baker, Jr. and D. Chapman, [appears].
Married: Sept. 30, 1830, in Albany, Joseph S. Colt and Henrietta L. Peckham.
Married: Oct. 7, 1830, in Palmyra, William Gordon and Delia M. Williams.
Married: Sept. 23, 1830, in Macedon, James Edmunds, Jr. and Cordelia Spear.
Died: Sept. 10, in Macedon, David Smith, ae 57 yrs., father of Benjamin F. Smith.
ADV.: Uriah S. McClave - stray colts; W[illiam] R. & F[rederick] Coppock, jewellers.

OCTOBER 16, 1830 - No items copied.
OCTOBER 22, 1830
Inspector announced poll will be held as follows: 1st day: at Ambrose Salisbury's dwelling house; 2nd day: forenoon at school house near Paul Goldsmiths; 2nd day: p.m. at Kingsley Miller's Inn; 3rd day: at Joel Stearns Eagle Hotel.
Married: Oct. 30, 1830, in Palmyra, by A. R. Tiffany, Esq., Thomas VanAlstine and Mary Costere, all of Arcadia.
Married: Oct. 11, 1830, at Waterville, NY, Dr. Horatio N. Loomis, of Palmyra and Cornelia Williams, dau. of Col. John Williams.
Died: Oct. 7, 1830, at Seneca Falls, Mrs. Mary Ann Beebe, wife of Joseph L. Beebe, late of Palmyra.

OCTOBER 29, 1830

Married: Oct. 27, 1830, by Rev. A. E. Campbell, Dr. Albert Curtis of Arcadia to Miss Mary A. C Lilly of Palmyra.

Died: Oct. 24, 1830, in Pultneyville, James Blithe, ae 69 years.

Died: Oct. 19, 1830, in Palmyra, Mrs. Polly Prentice, ae 35 years.

ADV: Dr. D. Chase on Clinton St.; Isaac Corey of Marion declared as insolvent, Oct. 29, 1830.

NOVEMBER 5, 1830

William J VanDoren lives at the corner of Fayette & Jackson Sts.

ADV: L. Morley - merchant tailor.

NOVEMBER 12, 1830

Married: Oct. 27, 1830, in Newark, Stephen Thorn and Mary Kean.

Married: Oct. 28, 1830, in Lyons, George Failing and Sally Lemoreau.

Married: Oct. 21, 1830, in Brockport, Jonas Woodward of Palmyra and Eliza S. Davis.

Died: Nov. 6, 1830, in Palmyra, Charles Payne Eggleston, oldest son of D. J. S. Eggleston, ae 3y 11m 24 days.

Died: Oct. 22, in Newark, Caleb Finch, ae 40 years.

Died: Oct. 25, 1830, Zebell, dau. of William Austin, ae 30 years.

Died: Oct. 16, 1830, at Farmington, Jonathan Smith, one of the lst settlers, ae 64 years.

Died: Nov. 7, 1830, in Macedon, Mrs. Fanny Hill, wife of Ira Hill, ae 30 years.

Died: Nov. 7, 1830, in Macdeon, a dau. of Ira Hill, ae 13 months.

NOVEMBER 19, 1830

The census of Wayne Co. of 1830 shows the town of Palmyra has a population of 3426 or 813 more than in 1825.

Married: Nov. 14, 1830, in Marion, by Rev. Mr. Boyle, William Steele and Almira Rice.

Married: Nov. 4, 1830, in Lyons, Erastus Marshall and Lucy Pitts.

NOVEMBER 26, 1830 - no items copied

DECEMBER 3, 1830

Wayne Sentinel offers $100 reward for detection and conviction of the person or persons who got up and first published the forged certificate of A. T. Bush in relation to the Witherill affair.

Married: Nov. 28, 1830, in Galen, William F. Holmes and Jane Pierce, eldest dau. of Jeremiah N. Pierce.

Married: Nov. 30, 1830, in Batavia, George W. Harris and Mrs. Lucinda Morgan, widow of the late Capt. William Morgan.

Married: Nov. 24, 1830, in Rose, Abel Grinnell and Polly Dawley.

Married: Dec. 1, 1830, in Macedon, Mr. Nelson and Maria Ostrom.

Died: Dec. 2, 1830, in Palmyra, at 11:30 a.m., Mrs. Clarissa Thayer, ae 43 yrs., wife of Levi Thayer, a dau. of Edward and Sibyl Seldon, b. in Haddam, CT, June 1787. Her parents moved to Windsor where she lived until her marriage.

ADV: J. C. Heath - umbrella factory opp. the Franklin House and 2 doors west of the Spectator office.

DECEMBER 10, 1830

The Newark Republican suspends publication.

L. F. Hutchinson of Newark commences a daily line of stages to start from Palmyra on Dec. 14 at 5 a.m. between Palmyra and Geneva via Port Gibson, Newark, Lockville, and Vienna. [This item copied from the Newark Republican of Nov. 25, 1830.]

Married: Nov. 25, 1830, in Macedon, George Dailey and Sarah Pound, both of Farmington.

Married: Dec. 7, 1830, in Galen, Jacob Stillwell of Lyons and Delilah Harmon, of Galen.

DECEMBER 17, 1830

Died: Dec. 17, 1830, in Palmyra, Lydia Clackner, ae 13 years.

[Henry E.] Perry & [James] Mason dissolve partnership.

DECEMBER 24, 1830

Marion Springs House owned by Enoch Turner burned.

Letter from Archer Galloway who had trouble in Philadelphia in 1828.

Married: Dec. 22, 1830, in Palmyra, Epanetus Howell and Miss Soper.

Married: Dec. 22, 1830, Marion Bailey Durfee and Abigail Rees by Rev. Mr. Burbank.

Married: Dec. 17, 1830, in Lyons, George G. Ellison and Hannah Drake.

DECEMBER 31, 1830

Married: Dec. 30, 1930, at the Friends Meeting House in Farmington or Macedon, Stephen Durfee of Palmyra and Mary Bristol of Macedon.

Married: Dec. 30, 1830, in Palmyra, Harvey Clark and Rhoda Tice, by Rev. A.E.C.

ADV: W. R. Coppock advertise as an auctioneer.

JANUARY 7, 1831

The following were elected officers of the Mechanics Institute: J. M. Woodward, Pres.; P. Tucker, V. P.; A. F. Woodward, Sec.; G. G. Jessup, Treas.; Hiram Niles, Lib.; John G. Pendergast, Auditor.

To exonerate from imprisonment: Thaddeus St. John of Walworth.

JANUARY 14, 1831

Biography of Roger Sherman in this and next two issues; Geneva Courier first published Jan. 6, 1831;

Meech & Woodward dissolve Dec. 30, 1830 - J. M. Woodward continues.

JANUARY 21, 1831

J. O. Balch first published the Vienna Republican at Vienna-Phelps;

Joseph A. Norton succeeds in warehouse near Collectors Office Mr. James Field, Jan. 20, 1831.

JANUARY 28, 1831

Wayne Co. with a population of 33,000 has five newspapers at this time.

Petition for the division of the County of Wayne.

The Geneva Courier says "We witnessed on Fri. last, a novel sight for this country. Two sleighs, each loaded with a coil of rope - the largest about 3" in diameter and 2700 feet in length, weighing about 4500 lbs., destined for the D. & H. RR Co. They were made at the ropewalk of Messers Townsend & Co. of Palmyra...they have a contract for a large quantity for the same company.

Married: Dec. 30, 1830, in Sodus, Alanson King and Charlotte Bell.

Married: Jan. 13, 1831, Jeremiah White and Sally Wright.

Married: Jan. 20, 1831, in Walworth, Vaniah Yeomans and Alzorah Boynton, dau. of Jonathan Boynton.

Died: Jan. 23, 1830 in Buffalo, Mrs. Amanda Rochester, wife of Hon. William B. Rochester, ae 32 years.

Died: Jan. 24, 1831, in Manchester, Abraham Stafford, ae about 50 years.

Died: Jan. 24, 1831, in Palmyra, the infant son of Elihu Durfee, ae 7 months.

FEBRUARY 4, 1831

Calvin Parker jumped into a well and was drowned Jan 31st.

Married: Dec. 30, 1830, Harvey Clark and Miss Rhoda Tice.

Married: in Clyde, Jan. 24, 1831, Lyman B. Dickerson, to Miss Sarah Ford.

Married: Jan. 24, 1831, in Clyde, J. S. Gildersleeve and Belinda McCarthy.

Married; Jan. 29, 1831, in Lyons, Liberty N. Straw and Lucy Phillips, both of Arcadia.

Married: Jan. 29, 1831, in Galen, Abraham Closs and Rhoda Holcomb.

Died: Feb. 1, 1831, in Palmyra, Margaret Newland, infant dau. of George and Mary Newland.

Died: Jan. 24, 1831, in Lyons, Louisa M., dau. of J. W. Goodrich, ae 1 yr. 9 months.

B. Taber adv. for stray animals.

FEBRUARY 11, 1831

The name of the Ontario Postoffice has been changed to Walworth.

Ira White and Pomeroy Tucker have been appointed as auctioneers.

A meeting has been called at Col. Joel Stearns tavern to vote a tax to defray the expense of building a culvert between H. Jessup's tannery and the canal for an engine house.

Married: Feb. 3, 1831, Joshua Hicks of Macedon and Mrs. Adaline Stearns.

Died: Feb. 4, 1831, in Palmyra, Joseph S. Colt, ae 64 yrs.; death followed a fall he received just before Christmas; he was an Episcopalian. Joseph S. Colt partnership ceased by death of Mr. Colt.

FEBRUARY 18, 1831

Married: Dec. 25, 1830, at Macedon, Luke Morley and Sarah Cooper, both of Palmyra.

Married: Feb. 1, 1831, in Marion, Sanford R. Hall of Geneva and Almira R. Huggins, a dau. of Zadock Huggins of Marion.

Married Feb. 10, 1831, in Sodus, Levi Ellsworth and Isabella McIntyre.
Married: Jan. 29, 1831, in Pittsford [Monroe Co.], Jeheil Dunning and Katherine Servis.
Married: Jan. 17, 1831, in Macedon, George Bradley and Sarah Williams.
Died: Feb. 11, 1831, in Palmyra, Sophia Jackson, ae 10 years.
Died: Feb. 3, 1831, in Sodus, Y. S. Alling, ae 55 years.

FEBRUARY 26, 1831
Married: Feb. 9, 1831 at Carbondale, PA, John M. Poor and Harriet Townsend.
Married: Feb. 24, 1831, in Macedon, S. Z. Ostrom and Relief Brown.
Married: Feb. 24, 1831, in Palmyra, Abraham Bromfield and Alvira Parker.
Married: Feb. 21, 1831, in Palmyra, Harvey Chase of Waterloo and Caroline Page.
Married: Feb. 10, 1831, in Manchester, James C. Sears of Arcadia and Lydia Elmira, dau. of David Howland.
Married: Feb. 14, 1831, in Lockville, James McDowell and Lucretia Hawser.
Married: Feb. 12, 1831, in Lockville, Isaac Losee and Roxy Torry of Manchester.
Died: Feb. 15, 1831, Mrs. Cynthia Howell, ae 53 yrs., wife of Col. Gilbert Howell.
Died: in Palmyra, Charles Lovell, infant son of Ovid Lovell, ae 3 mos.
ADV: Miss Morgan - teaches writing and painting at Mrs Sheppardson's.

MARCH 4, 1831
Married: March 2, 1831, Hiram Niles and Chloe Robinson, dau. of Dr. Gain Robinson.
Married: Feb. 22, 1831, in Lyons, Joseph Shaver and Paulina West, all of Arcadia.
Married: March 3, 1831, in Lyons, Chauncey L. Wright of Albany and Louisa Griswold.
Married: Feb. 17, 1831, in Sodus, Josiah Rice of Marion and Betsy Bennett of Sodus.
ADV: C. A. Batterson - stone cutting.

MARCH 11, 1831
Married: March 2, 1831, in Williamson, Thomas Atwater of Sodus and Harriet Conner of Williamson.
Married: Feb. 17, 1831, in Rushville, Joseph L. Hullett and Sarah Fairbanks, dau. of Rev. Ira Fairbanks.
Died: March 6, 1831, in Manchester, James Hill, son of Ephriam Hill, ae 26 years.
Died: March 5, 1731 in Palmyra, Edward Luck, son of William Luck, ae 10 years.
Died: Feb. 12, 1831, in Ontario, Dr. William Greenwood, ae 38 years.

MARCH 18, 1831
Letter of Rev. B. H. Hickox (3/14/31) addressed to Mr.Townsend, refuting a criticism in his sermon preached at the funeral of Mr. J. Colt.
E.[penetus] and J.[onah H.] Howell dissolve partnership.
Married: March 8, 1831, in Palmyra, James Aiken and Miss Adeline Cook.
Married: March 2, 1831, in Marion, George Belden and Mary Putnam.
Married: March 9, 1831, in Arcadia, Ira Stanbrough and Elizabeth K. Van Waggenen.

Married: March 9, 1831, in Ontario, Mr. Bean and Cordelia Carey.
Died: March 16, 1831, in Palmyra, Mrs. Jarvis, wife of William Jarvis.

MARCH 25, 1831
Details of the trial of the abductors of William Morgan [who was murdered for supposedly planning to give away secrets of the Masonic ritual.]
Married: March 13, 1831, in Pultneyville, Joseph Hopkins of Manchester and Pamelia Nichols.
Married: March 19, 1831, Joseph Morley of Walworth and Margaret Calhoun of Williamson.

APRIL 1, 1831 - no items copied
APRIL 8, 1831
A meeting scheduled to take measures for procuring a site for a public burying ground 4/8/31.
Died: April 2, 1831, in Canandaigua, Mrs. Hannah Sibley, mother of James Sibley.

APRIL 15, 1831
Married: in Palmyra, by Rev. Abner Chase, Dr. Samuel Moore of Marion to Mrs. Ruth Sherman, widow of Stephen Sherman.
Married: April 12, 1831, Gaylord Taber of Manchester, and Louisa Willcox.
Joel Stearns adv. his stallion "Hazard".

APRIL 22, 1831
A 4% dividend on Wayne Co. Bank stock announced.
Died: April 14, 1831, in Walworth, Mrs. Frances Ann Tucker, wife of Luther Tucker and dau. of Denison Smith, of Groton, CT. Buried in the public burying ground near the Presbyterian Meeting House.
ADV: William M. Bayard & George W. Cuyler - law firm.

APRIL 29, 1831
Mr. H. Hubbard of Canandaigua joined M. Kingman in running stages between Canandaigua and Palmyra, succeeded L. Tillotson.
Married: April 26, 1831, in Williamson, John W. Sherman and Jerusha L. Pratt, both of Williamson.

MAY 6, 1831
On May 3, 1831, Miss Sarah R. Galloway of Marion, ae 24 yrs., while riding with another lady was thrown out [of carriage/buggy] and instantly killed.
Married: May 6, 1831, in Farmington, Jonathan Sprague and Mary Smith.
Married: 21, 1831, in Macedon, Benjamin Billings and Mary Glover.
Married: April 14, 1831, in West Bloomfield, William White of Macedon and Jane A. Alexander.
Died: April 14, 1831, Lucy Mariah Billings, dau. of William Billings, ae 13 years.
ADV: Daniel G. Finch - dry goods, 1st door west of Zuill & White in Thayer's & Grandin's Row.

MAY 13, 1831

A letter from W. W. Phelps written in Lyons jail printed in this issue, q.v. To exonerate from imprisonment, Isaac Morse, of Marion (5/6).

Married: May 3, in Minaville, [Montgomery Co., NY], William R. Coppock and Mary Barlow.

Married: May 11, in East Palmyra, George Hopkinson and Mariah Howell.

MAY 27, 1831

Painesville, O. - May 17 [1831] - Mormon emigration:

"About 200 men, women and children of the deluded followers of Bro. Jo Smith's Bible speculation, have arrived on our coast during the last week from the State of New York and are about seating themselves down upon the "promised land" in this county. It is surely a melancholy comment upon human nature to see so many people at this enlightened age of the world, trucking along at the car[?] of a miserable imposter, submitting themselves, both soul and body, to his spiritual and temporal mandates, without a murmur, or presuming to question that it is all a command direct from Heaven. Such an abject slavery of the mind may endure for a season; but in due time, like the chains of Popery, the links which bind them will be rent asunder, and reason resume her empire. [Taken from the] Telegraph".

Several families, numbering about 50 souls, took up their line of march from this town last week for the "promised land", among whom was Martin Harris, one of the original believers in the "Book of Mormon". Mr. Harris was among the early settlers of this town, and has ever borne the character of an honorable and upright man, and an obliging and benevolent neighbor. He had secured to himself by honest industry a respectable fortune - and he has left a large circle of acquaintances and friends to pity his delusion.

Donation Party: For the benefit of Rev. A. E. Campbell to be held June 2nd at his house. [Sponsors]:

R. W. Smith	H. Linnell	L. Foster
C. Durfee	J. Horton	P. G. Ely
L. Spear	E. Shepard	P. West

If the weather is unpleasant, carriages will call for the ladies.

Died: May 25, 1831, in Marion, William Bixbe, ae 49 yrs. On the previous Sun., he was thrown from a wagon while riding to church.

Died: May 17, 1831, Nathaniel Rochester, founder of the village [of the same name], ae 80 years.

Died: May 10, 1831, in Detroit, Hon. John Trumbull, age 81 yrs., father of M'Fingal [Trumbull?].

Died: May 27, 1831, in Palmyra, Margaret Sexton, ae 33 yrs., wife of Pliny Sexton.

ADV: Archer Galloway has 25,000 acres of land in Illinois for sale. M. W. Willcox & J. M. Woodward.

JUNE 3, 1831

Bayard & Cuyler Law office on south side of Main St., opposite Wayne Co. Bank.

Adv.: Clark Robinson - dry goods, one door east of the Eagle Hotel; William White - fancy goods; P. Tucker settles accounts of Tucker & Lothrop.

JUNE 10, 1831

Married: June 2, 1831, by F. Smith, Eldredge Havens and Prudence Morgan.

Married: June 5, 1831 in Farmington, Jonathan Sprague and Mary Smith.

Married: In Lyons, May 26, 1831, by William Voorhees, Esq., Philip Hill, Jr. of Junius, and Barbara Snyder.

Married: At Newark, George W. Provost and Rebecca Lambright.

Died: In Sodus, Lois Turner, dau. of Capt. Enoch Turner, ae 29 years.

Adv.: Jessup, Smith & Co. - hides and skins bought.

JUNE 17, 1831

The following were appointed Directors of the Wayne Co. Bank for the ensuing year: Thomas Rogers, 2nd. Ebenezer Hale, J. S. Fenton, Joseph Moss, Nathaniel H. Beckwith, George Beckwith, Pliny Sexton, John Colvin, John Clapp, Abraham Spear, P. K. Leach, Hiram K. Jerome, and George Crane.

Married: In the Zion Church, Palmyra, by Rev. B. H. Hickox, Charles Smyth, Jr. of Rochester and Miss Catherine Colt, a dau. of the late Maj. Joseph Colt of Palmyra.

Died: June 12, 1831, in Albany, Mrs. Gertrude Lovell, wife of Ovid Lovell, of Palmyra, ae 28 years.

Adv.: L. Beatty advertises the Marion Springs as medicinal. Mr. Hemingway's stage leaves Palmyra on Tues. and Sat. mornings and arrives at the Springs at 9 a.m., returning at 3 p.m.

JUNE 24, 1831

Committee on arrangements for July 4th celebration: C. Foster, T. R. Strong, P. Tucker, S. Birdsall, Ira White, E. C. Foster, T. R. Strong, P. Tucker, S. Birdsall, Ira White, E. Shepard, R. S. Williams, H. Niles, M. W. Willcox, H. P. Thayer, E. B. Grandin, Burr Butler and T. Hemingway.

Died: June 21, 1831, in Palmyra, Dr. Gain Robinson, ae 62 years.

Died: June 3, 1831, in Macedon, Jacob Spear, ae 46 yrs.

Died: June 17, 1831, in Lyons, Cyrus Hecox, ae 49 yrs.

Adv.: Gardner Tiffany of Walworth, adv. a runaway apprentice, William Scantlin. Anthony Soules, of Macedon, adv. a stolen horse.

JULY 1, 1831

Died: June 29, 1831 in Palmyra, Mrs. Ann Norton, ae 24 yrs., wife of Joseph A. Norton.

Died: June 29, 1831, in Palmyra, Charles, son of Linus North, ae 2 yrs. 3 months.

Died: June 28, 1831, in Palmyra, Luman Harrison, ae 56 years.

Adv.: Joshua Drake wants ashes.

JULY 8, 1831

July 4th celebration finest ever held. About 1000 marched to the Episcopal Church under direction of of Lt. D. Chase and H. P. Thayer; W. R. Coppock was organist at church; Rev. John Parker, Meth. Church; Rev. B. H. Hickox, Episcopal Church, and Rev. Barber gave benediction; returned to Col. J. Stearns Eagle Hotel for dinner, toasts, etc.

Married: June 30, 1831, at Sulphur Springs House, by Rev. B. H. Hickox, John B. Knolls, and Eliza W. Barnhart, both of Palmyra.

Married: June 30, 1831, Elihu Hinman and Calista Inman, both of Palmyra.

Married: June 30, 1831 in East Palmyra, by Rev. Alverson, William C. Lovejoy and Emily H. Abbott, both of Newark.

JULY 15, 1831

Died: July 7, 1831 in Palmyra, Mrs. Lydia Rogers, ae 26 yrs., wife of Stephen Rogers.

Died: July 10, 1831 in Marion, Joseph Horton, ae 67 yrs.

JULY 22, 1831

Died: In Palmyra, Peleg Holmes, ae 76 yrs., an early settler, and a native of Warren, CT.

Died: July 14, 1831, Mrs. Betsey Chapman, ae 73 yrs.

News: A letter of James Culver re: Luman Harrison.

JULY 29, 1831

Forty-four persons appointed to serve on the Vigilance Committee Society for purpose of suppressing felony in Macedon; some are appointed riders to pursue criminals and they have power to hire horses to pursue felons.

AUGUST 5, 1831

News: Alfred E. Campbell, Corr. Sec. of the Wayne Co. Union Sabbath Schools.

J. Francis, Sec. announce meeting of the Palmyra Soc. for Promotion of Temperance.

Died: Aug. 1, 1831, Mrs. Hannah Clackner, wife of John S. Clackner, ae 42 yrs., [mother of] seven children.

Died: July 25, 1831, in Canandaigua, Maria Wells, wife of Dr. Richard Wells, ae 50 years.

Died: July 28, 1831, in New York, Dr. Pliny Hayes, Jr. of Canandaigua, ae 42 years.

Died: Aug. 2, 1831, in Bristol, Pliny Hayes, father of P. Hayes Jr., ae 65 years.

Died: Aug. 2, 1831, at Black Rock, Mrs. Latitia Porter, wife of Gen. Peter B. Porter, ae 43 years.

AUGUST 12, 1831

The Wayne Sentinel will hereafter be issued on Tuesdays instead of Fridays as heretofore.

The Western Spectator and Anti-Masonic Star which has been struggling in this village for several months with a certain disease, peculiar to Anti-Masonic newspapers, ceased publication on Tues. last. Our friend, Mr. Shepard, the printer (there has been no visible editor, since the original "proprietor" retired) who is altogether a very clever fellow, but an odd genius, intimates in his announcement of the catastrophe, an intention to locate himself elsewhere.

Town of Palmyra - School Districts Committees

R. S. Williams	Frederick Smith
N. Throop, Jr.	James P. Horton
Caleb Horton	Ambrose Salisbury
Lyman H. Tiffany	George Culver
S. S. Durfee	Nathan Parshall
Benjamin Cole	Lott Stone
M. W. Willcox	D. Chase
Joseph Willcox	J. Bingham
J. Patrick	J. Parshall
Lyman Reeves	Stephen Hopkins
William Corwin	Luther Reeves
Charles Davis	J. F. Sickles
E. D. Robinson	George W. Cuyler
Hiram Niles	E. Bortles
E. Hammond	Hiram Lester
D. H. Sherman	Caleb Beals
James Hubbell	J. L. Knowles
Barzillai Durfee	Thomas Eggleston
Gad C. Higby	

Married: Aug. 7, 1831, at Pultneyville, David C. Higgins and Eliza Smith, adopted dau. of Russell Whipple, Esq.

Married: Aug. 9, 1831, in Aurora, John L. Cuyler of Lockville and Elizabeth C. Marsh, dau. of E. C. Marsh of Aurora.

Died: July 30, 1831 in Jersey City, [NJ], Col. Richard Varick, ae 79 years.

Died: Aug. 5, 1831 in Canandaigua, Benjamin F. Day, ae 25 yrs., editor of the Ontario Messenger.

Died: Aug. 11, 1831, David Williams, last of the captors of Major Andre.

Died: Aug. 11, 1831, in Palmyra, Eugene, youngest son of Daniel D. Finch, ae 7 mos., resident of Fayette St.

Adv.: George Beckwith & Co. dissolve; Richard L. Clark continues; Henry Lupkins, barber on Fayette St., near the Eagle Hotel. Julius C. Hutchinson of Marion found a sum of money.

AUGUST 16, 1831

Rev. John A. Clark will preach in Zion Church, this village, Sunday next.

Married: Aug. 14, 1831 at the National House in Palmyra, by A. R. Tiffany, Esq., John Cole to Priscilla Lemunion, both of Manchester.

Married: Aug. 14, 1831, Anson Burger of Hopewell to Calista LaMunion of Manchester.

Married: Aug. 9, 1831 in Buffalo, William F. Jarvis and Harriet Maxon, of Buffalo.

Died: August 14, 1831 in Manchester, Luke Sawyer, ae 50 years.

Died: August 9, 1831, Frances Ann Steele, dau. of Joseph A. Norton, ae 8 weeks. [sic]

Died: August 13, 1831, infant son of Levi Thayer, ae 1 year.

AUGUST 23, 1831
Daniel Porter of Macedon, exonerated from imprisonment.
Adv.: A. Salisbury wants rye and corn at Harrison's Mill.

AUGUST 30, 1831 - No items copied.

SEPTEMBER 6, 1831
Died: At Lyons, Aug. 30, 1831, Isaac Rogers, ae 59 years.

SEPTEMBER 13, 1831.
Subscribers to apply to Legislature for and act of incorporation to construct a railway from the village of Palmyra to the village of Canandaigua.

Thomas Rogers, 2nd	J. Boynton
Elijah Kent	Cullen Foster
David Eddy	P. Tucker
H. K. Jerome	E. S. Townsend
Henry Jessup	A. R. Tiffany
W. M. Bayard	George Crane
George W. Cuyler	T. Heminway
J. S. Colt	William Parker
James White	F. S. Fenton
Truman Hart	A. Salisbury
P. Grandin	E. B. Grandin
John Colvin	P. Sexton
Ovid Lovell	D. G. Finch
R. W. Smith	L. Tucker

Married: Aug. 25, 1831, in Seneca, Charles K. Tooker and Cornelia Clark.
Died: Sept. 12, 1831, William T. Hussey of Palmyra.
Died: Aug. 16, 1831, at Randolph, NJ, Sylvanus Lawrence, ae 86 years.
Died: Aug. 22, 1831, at Randolph, NJ, Kemina [sic] D. Lawrence, ae 22 years.
Adv.: C. J. & L. Sutherland, hardware in the place where Elijah Linnell had a shoe store -two doors east of B. Butler's shop; S. S. Durfee - nursery stock; "Hunting Match-men" to meet at Nottingham's Hotel.

SEPTEMBER 20, 1831
A meeting to be held at the Episcopal Church to raise money to aid people of Poland against the Russians.
Abraham Shaduck assigns to William Parke and Wells Anderson; Clark Wright and Wilbert Hills, dissolve partnership.
Married: Aug. 13, 1831, at Pittsford, [Monroe Co.], by Rev. B. H. Hickox, Maj. George W. Cuyler and Caroline Porter, dau. of Chauncey Porter of Pittsford.

Married: Aug. 8, 1831, in Palmyra, John S. Clackner and Mrs. Elizabeth Walker.
Died: Aug. 15, 1831, Delia Strong, ae 14 yrs., youngest dau. of Cyrus Strong.
Adv.: John Amsden, Jr., Dry Goods, buys out Coleman; E. Linnell and E. P. Godard [form co.] E. L. Linnell & Co.; Mr. Bradish, painter.

SEPTEMBER 27, 1831
Married: Sept. 18, 1851, in Palmyra, Dr. Parley Hill and Mary Ann Stillman.
Married: Sept. 22, 1831, in Palmyra, Luke Wells and Samantha Coon.
Died: Sept. 6, 1831, in Shelby, MI, Mrs. Eliza Dart, wife of Jonathan Dart, formerly of Palmyra, ae 37 yrs.
Died: Sept. 16, 1831, in Sodus, Mrs. Catherine Pierce, ae 37 years.
Died: Sept. 18, in Canandaigua, Peter A. Mower, ae 27 years.

OCTOBER 4, 1831
See editorial on "Square Beny Durfee" and also one on Palmyra Umbrella Factory.
Belden [George, Jr.] & Winslow [Philander], dissolve business; E. B. Grandin now advertises the Lottery instead of J. H. Bortles.
Solomon Field, advertises a stray mare.

OCTOBER 11, 1831 ["This number of the newspaper seems to be missing."]
OCTOBER 18, 1832
Meeting to be held at the Eagle Hotel to hear new communications on the subject of steam power and take some measures toward erecting a steam mill in this place.
Married: Oct. 12, 1831 in Palmyra, by Rev. Whelpley, Dr. J. V. C. Teller of Massilon, OH, to Miss Lydia Ann Shepherdson of Palmyra.
Died: Oct. 11, 1831, in Manchester, Mrs. Hannah Bigelow, wife of John Bigelow.
Died: Oct. 14, 1831, Mrs. Cornelia Loomis, wife of Dr. H. N. Loomis.

OCTOBER 25, 1831 - No items copied
NOVEMBER 1, 1831
Young Men's Democratic Committee of Vigilance held a meeting at the Eagle Hotel, Oct. 8, 1831. M. W. Wilcox, Chm. and T. R. Strong, Sec.

Washington Beal	John F. Sherman	Sidney S. Durfee
G. A. Hathaway	Geo. W. Anderson	Epenetus Howell
Augustus Daggett	M. Kingman	Zebulon Williams
F. Woodward	Edwin Godard	Hiram Niles
William White	Henry Gardner	Robert Carr
Philo Durfee	Hiram Willcox	Dennis Clark
Burton Foster	R. S. Williams	James G. Howell
John Gillett	James Robinson	Moses Parke
Avery Havens	Addison K. Warner	J. A. Tiffany
William S. Seeley	Geo. W. Cuyler	Francis Bortle

L. H. Tiffany	H. W. Rogers	Hiram Wing
Wm. Billings, Jr.	John A. Ryerson	William Hyde
Zebulon Williams	Albert Jessup	Bortles, J. H.
G. C. Higby	H. R. Willcox	David Rogers
Joel Foster	Hiram Thayer	James Jenner
Clark Robinson	William F. Jarvis	Henry E. Perry
Levi Houghtaling	Henry Nelson	Parley Hill

Married: Oct. 16, 1831, in Williamson, Abram Gurney and Eliza Paddock, both of Sodus.

Married: Oct. 12, 1831 in Canandaigua, Louis Gabriel and Eliza Dexter.

Married: Nov. 1, 1831, in Canandaigua, Henry Morris of Buffalo, and Mary Natalie Spencer, dau. of John C. Spencer.

Died: Oct. 19, 1831, in Auburn, Hon., John W. Hurlburt.

Adv.: Solomon Carter - boots and shoes; George W. Cuyler, hardware at the arcade front, next to the bank, corner of Main and Williams St. in Palmyra.

NOVEMBER 8, 1831

Sketch of Morgan's abduction, q.v. [This abduction led to the great anti-masonic movement of the period. ed.]; notice of meeting to be held at J. Baker's Tavern (Eagle Hotel).

Died: Oct. 26, 1831, in Macedon, Henry Spear, son of Isaac Spear, ae 21 years.

Adv.: James Culver adv. for claims against Luman Harrison.

NOVEMBER 22, 1831

Notice of application to incorporate the Mutual Fire Insurance Co. - applicants: J. S. Fenton, Thomas Rogers, 2nd, Burr Butler, William Parke, Wells Anderson, P. Grandin, George Beckwith, J. S. Colt, Abner F. Lakey, Henry Jessup, Ovid Lovell, Pliny Sexton, Cephas Smith, and H. K. Jerome.

Married: Nov. 20, 1831, in Palmyra, Peter VanDine of Phelps and Mary Redfield.

Died: Nov. 10, 1831, at Vienna, Claudius V. Houghton, ae 47 years.

Died: Nov. 13, 1831, in Pultneyville, John Mason, ae 40 yrs.; drowned in the harbor.

NOVEMBER 29, 1831

Lyons Countryman discontinued - 3rd Anti-Masonic paper to quit.

Ira Lakey - exonerated from imprisonment for debt.

George E. Pomeroy buys out Robinson & Loomis.

Married: Nov. 24, 1831 in Palmyra, John Beam of Sodus to Mrs. Clara Miles.

Married: Oct. 30, 1831 in Lockville, Nelson Day and Jane Ammerman, both of Canandaigua.

Adv: George E. Pomeroy - drugs, etc. 3 doors west of Eagle Hotel; Lott Stone - house & lot [for sale?]; A. F. Woodward - claims of Meech & Woodward.

DECEMBER 6, 1831

News: Cuyler St., recently opened by G. W. Cuyler and J. B. Fenton, running south from Main St., just completed at their own expense..it is planned to continue this street north to the canal as soon as the gravel can be removed from the hill through which it will run.

The Life and Adventures of David C. Bunnell published at Palmyra by J. H. Bortles.

Adv.: Hoyt & May - doctors over Finch's store in Exchange Row; John Amaden, tailor; C.C. Coleman;s stock; Robert Powell adv. for a stolen horse and cutter.

Died: Nov. 29, 1831, Col. Daniel Hendee, formerly of Palmyra was drowned in the canal while locking a boat. [Left children.]

Married: Dec. 1, 1831 in Palmyra, Seth Knapp and Ann Marshall, both of Farmington.

Married: Nov. 30, 1831, in Macedon, Horace Chase of Medina and Amanda Turner, dau. of Capt. Noah Turner.

DECEMBER 13, 1831

Married: in Palmyra, by Rev. E. Blakesley, Samuel S. Barker and Mary Ann Eggleston.

Married: Dec. 1, 1831 in Lyons, George G. Kingman and Elizabeth D. Holley.

DECEMBER 20, 1831

James Jacklin a colored resident of Palmyra, got drunk and froze to death near his home, just outside the village.

Married: Dec. 20, 1831, at Sodus, Samuel C. Gordon of Lyons and Mrs. Elizabeth Denny.

DECEMBER 27, 1831

Married: Dec. 25, 1831, at Zion Church, Hiram P. Thayer and Sarah E. Williams of Macedon.

Married: Dec. 20, 1831, in Palmyra, William F. Applegate and Elizabeth Gardner, both of Macedon.

Married: Dec. 4, 1831, at Macedon, W. W. Abbey and Clarissa Houghton.

Married: Dec. 18, 1831 at Macedon, Joseph Slocum and Hannah David.

Married: at Macedon, James Sloan and Diane A. Hill.

Died: at Pultneyville, Rachel, dau. of Daniel Grandin, ae 12 years.

JANUARY 3, 1832

Married: Dec. 26, 1831 in Canandaigua, Amasa Jackson of New York and Jane E. Howell, dau. of Hon, N. W. Howell.

Married: Dec. 27, 1831, in Canandaigua, Philo S. Rawson and Charlotte Dobbin.

Married: Dec. 27, 1831, in Sodus, Col. Henry Sweet to Miss Juicy Baker.

Died: Dec. 31, 1831, in Palmyra, Emily Mariah Throop, dau. of Benjamin T. Throop, Jr., ae 6 mos. 13 days.

ADVERTISERS:

E. B. Grandin - Wayne sentinel

David White , Macedon, farm for sale.

Sylvannus Culver - Farm for sale in Farmington.

Lott Stone - Farm, house and lot for sale
James Culver - claims against Luman Harrison
Daniel D. Finch - Dry goods at No. 3 Exchange Row.
J. & L. Thayer - wheat wanted
Rogers and Grandin - Dry goods at Thayer's old stand.
John Amsden - Dry goods.
E. Linnell & Co. - Managed by E. P. Godard: Boots.
Richard L. Clark: Shawls etc.
Zuill & White
A. Salisbury - Corn and rye wanted.
George W. Cuyler
Joshua Drake - tallow wanted.
L. North - Jeweller.
Ovid Lovell - broad cloths
Giles S. Ely - Dry goods.
Dr. D. Chase - Clinton St.
George E. Pomeroy - Drugs
A. F. Woodward - Settles Meech & Woodward's accts.
Clark & Robinson Dry goods.
Hoyt & May - Physicians and Surgeons.
William White - Groceries.
M. Ritter - Meat market.
William Hyde & Co. - Dry goods.
Jessup, Smith & Co. - Hides and skins.
Solomon Carter - Boots and shoes.
P. West - Harness and saddle maker.
N. Niles - Honey wanted.

JANUARY 10, 1832

There have been several cases of horse stealing in Palmyra; on Jan. 5th a horse and cutter were stolen from in front of George Brown's; seen going east; overtaken by Philo Durfee; criminal sent to jail.

Married: January 8, 1832, George Styles of Albion to Harriet Rose of Palmyra.

Married: Jan. 9, 1832 at Palmyra, Henry P. Allen and Ann Maria Havens, all of Palmyra.

JANUARY 17, 1832

Married: Jan. 15, 1832, at Zion Church, Maj. Lovell Hurd and Sally Ann Taber, dau. of Capt. B. Taber.

Married: Jan. 10, 1832, at Brighton, E. P. Godard and Maria Fillmore of Walworth.

Married - Jan. 8, 1832 in Macedon, Valentine Champlin to Miss Phebe Wilbur.

Died: Jan. 16, 1832 in Lyons, Mrs. Mary Eddy, wife of John Eddy, and dau. of Hezekiah Miller, ae 27 years.

Adv.: School teacher wanted at once to take charge of Dist. No. 1 school in village of Palmyra. s/Levi Thayer, G. W. Cuyler, P. Tucker, Trustees.

James Field [has] 12 boxes of scythe rifles [for sale?].

JANUARY 24, 1832

William P. Bayard of Palmyra was admitted to the bar.

Married: Jan. 15, 1832 in Sodus, Thomas Judson and Almira Turner.

Adv.: Field & Robinson - canal lines - succeeds P. Grandin; C. Foster has farm for sale.

JANUARY 31, 1832

The proprietor of the Wayne Sentinel announces that he has formed a connection with Theron R. Strong, Esq., of this village, by whom, co-jointly with himself, the paper will hereafter be conducted, the new arrangement to commence with the next number.

Married: Jan. 19, 1832, James G. Horton of Palmyra to Maria Horton of New York.

TUESDAY, FEBRUARY 7, 1832

Rev. Samuel Whelpley of Macedon, thanks friends for their assistance.; E. Linnell & Co. dissolve.

Lorenzo Hudson, apprentice boy, runaway from R. W. Smith. Feb. 6. 1832.

Married: Jan. 30, 1832, in Arcadia, Archer Galloway of Marion to Mrs. Rosanna Hyde, widow of the late Dr. Henry Hyde of Arcadia.

FEBRUARY 14, 1832 - This issue missing from files.
FEBRUARY 21, 1832

Washington's Birthday to be celebrated with a Public Dinner at the <u>Bunker Hill Hotel</u> by Mr. Nottingham. M. W. Wilcox and P. Tucker, H. Niles, C. Robinson, and H. P. Thayer. [Comm?]

Married: Feb. 19, 1832 at Sodus, James Mason of Palmyra and Henrietta Harmsley of Sodus.

Married: Feb. 19, 1832 at Sodus, Alexander B. Williams and Sara M. McCarty.

Married: Feb. 12, 1832, Rufus Soules of Boston to Ursula Turner.

Married: Feb. 19, 1832, at Williamson, Sylvanus Bartlett and Isabel Van Duzer.

FEBRUARY 28, 1832

February 19, 1832: Died Nathaniel Beckwith, son of N. H. Beckwith, age 5 yrs.

TUESDAY, MARCH 6, 1832

Married: Feb. 14, 1832, in New York, Festus A. Goldsmith of Palmyra to Abigail Munsell, in New York.

Married: Feb. 16, 1832, in Macedon, Nathan Ramsdell and Mary Ann Hoag.

Married: Feb. 23, 1832, in Macedon, Thomas Bussey to Harriet Kelly.

Died: March 4, 1832 in Palmyra, Augustus Sherman, infant son of Alanson Sherman, ae 1 year.

MARCH 14, 1832 - no entries copied.

MARCH 21, 1832
Adv.: Frederick Smith, insurance; [Otis C.] Clapp and [Philo D.] Durfee. Clark Robinson's goods.

MARCH 28, 1832
Died: March 20, 1832, in Albany, Leonard Westcott, age 49 yrs., formerly a merchant of Palmyra.

APRIL 4, 1832
Married: March 30, 1832, in Williamson, John Sheffield, of Buffalo, to Mary Pratt, of Williamson.
Married: March 30, 1832, in Williamson, Maj. __ Sanford of Marion and Emeline Pratt, of Williamson.

APRIL 11, 1832
Wells Anderson and Samuel Beckwith dissolve.
Married: April 5, 1832, in Lyons, Charles T. Payne and Rebecca Pudney.
Married: March 29, 1832 in Palmyra, Marcus Coles and Rosannah Beals.
Died: April 9, 1832, in Palmyra, William Richards, formerly of New London, CT, ae 30 years.
Died: April 2, 1832, Frances Ann Brown, infant dau. of Nelson Brown.

APRIL 18, 1832
Died: April 4, 1832, in Rochester, of a lingering consumption, Ira West, ae 46 yrs. Mr. West was one of the earliest settlers and oldest merchants of that village. He opened a store in 1812, the first establishment of the kind made in that place.

APRIL 25, 1832
Deac. Henry Jessup's machine shops got afire [but] were saved Apr. 19, 1832. He thanks the citizens in a formal notice.

MAY 2, 1832
Married: April 26, 1832 in Walworth, Luther Tucker and Elmira Kent, dau. of Elijah Kent.
Adv.: [E. R.] Spear & [Samuel] Palmer, painting, opp. the Episcopal Church.

MAY 9 and MAY 16, 1832 - Nothing copied
MAY 23, 1832
Married: May 15, 1832, in Canandaigua, George W. Clinton of Albany and Laura Catherine Spencer, dau. of Hon. John C. Spencer.
Died: May 3, 1832, in Ontario, Mrs. Margaret Peckham, wife of Dr. William Peckham, ae 47 years.
Died: May 18, 1832, in Palmyra, Mrs. Hannah Baker, wife of James Baker, ae 24 years.

MAY 30, 1832
Married: May 9, 1832, in New London, CT, A. W. Tucker of Walworth and Frances E. Allen.
Married: May 9, 1832, in New London, CT, E. V. Stoddard and Mary S. Allen.

JUNE 6, 1832 - Nothing copied.

JUNE 13, 1832

Palmyra Baths & Gardens are opened by Mr. Niles; pleasure grounds connected with them; in the rear of the Post Office entrance from Cuyler and Main St. Ladies days too.

A course of Sacred, Roman, American and Promiscuous [sic] Oratory will be given in this village Sat. evening next by Mr. J. G. S. Empson...from London.

Died: June 11, 1832, in Palmyra, Joseph Henry Colt, son of Joseph S. Colt, ae 6 weeks.

Adv.: Lovell & Haven want to buy wool.

JUNE 20, 1832

Fourth of July Committee: Hiram Niles, Cephas Smith, William P. Nottingham, E. P. Godard, Isaac Beecher, Henry, Gardner, Philo Durfee, Draper Allen, Sydney S. Durfee, Arthur F. Woodward, Hiram P. Thayer, I. J. Richardson, William May, H. G. Williams, Kingsley Miller, Benjamin Homan, Mahlon Kingman, E. Clark, E. Bortles, J. W. M. Zuill, G. W. Cuyler, H. N. Loomis, C. E. Thayer, A. E. Evans, M. W. Wilcox, a Rochester Band secured to furnish music for the day.

Wayne County Bank Directors: Joseph S. Fenton, Abraham Spear, John Colvin, George Crane, Pliny Sexton, George Beckwith, Wm. M. Bayard, Nathaniel H. Beckwith, Jonathan Boynton, Ovid Lovell, Payne K. Leech, Hiram K. Jerome, Thomas Rogers, 2nd (Pres.).

The laying of the cornerstone of the new Presbyterian House will not be laid today as was expected, but is deferred.

Gaius Robinson & Horatio N. Loomis dissolve.

JUNE 27, 1832

Fourth of July arrangement similar to former years...Fireworks in the evening at the Palmyra Gardens.

Married: June 20, 1832 in Palmyra, Ovid Lovell and Cynthia D. Willcox, by Rev. S. W. W.

Married: June 25, 1832 in Hopewell, Ira White of the firm of Zuill & White of Palmyra, to Esther Bates, dau. of Stephen Bates of Hopewell.

JULY 4, 1832

Adv.: Pratt & Hill, drugs; Niles & Allen, groceries; F. A. Goldsmith lost a rifle;

Peter Ingersol adv. a stray colt; an Orange Outang is being shown at the <u>Eagle Hotel</u>.

JULY 11, 1832

Report of July 4th celebration: school children marched under Mr. Pierce, a tutor; Rev. Joseph Tompkinson offered prayer, Alexander McIntyre led a mixed choir; Theron R. Strong delivered an oration; Stephen Culver, a high school student, delivered an oration; and John Kedzia, a high school student read the Declaration of Independence.

Married; July 4, 1832, J. D. Dunning of Sodus to Endoxura Smith of Palmyra.

Adv.: Clark Robinson wants to leave Palmyra on account of cholera and wants his accounts settled.

JULY 18, 1832

Toast of Rev. B. H. Hickox, sent in to July 4th celebration as he left the room and table when toasts were begun.

Married: July 11, 1832, in Palmyra, Franklin Payne to Octavia J. Lewis.

Married - July 13, 1832, Royal Gurley, M. D. and Mrs. Silas Draper.

JULY 25, 1832

Cholera is quite prevalent at this time - two deaths in Rochester.

Notice of a meeting of Republicans of the town of Palmyra. signed:

A. E. Havens	Henry E. Perry
A. K. Daggett	Henry Gardner
A. Hendee	Hiram Wing
Abraham Martin	Hiram K. Jerome
Almond Pratt,	Hiram Niles
Asa Lilly	Isaac E. Beecher
Asabel Millard	J. D. Hayward
Benj. Homas	J. S. Fenton
Benj. Throop, Jr.	J. R. Avrill
C. Barnhart	J. S. Eggleston
C. E. Thayer	James Culver
C. S. Stanton	James Hubbell
Caleb Beal	James Mason
Clark Robinson	Jared Stillman
Daniel Crandall	Jas. Fenner
David H. Sherman	Joel Thayer
Draper Allen	John Amsden, Jr
E. Clark	John H. Gilbert.
E. Havens	John W. M. Zuill
E. B. Grandin	John W. Sherman
E. D. Robinson	Joseph C. Payne
E. P. Godard	K. Miller
E. Cooper	L. Hurd
Frederick Smith	L. O. Godard
G. G. Finch	L. H. Tiffany
George W. Cuyler	L. Reeves
George A. Hathaway	Levi Thayer
H. Cooley	Levi Houghtaling
H. Cobb	Levi Daggett
H. B. Williams	Lott Stone
H. P. Thayer	M. W. Willcox
Henry P. Allen	M. J. Godard

M. Kingman
Michael Ritter
N. H. Beckwith
P. Durfee
P. Bortle
P. Hill
P. Tucker
P. Grandin
R. S. Foote
S. Carter
Salisbury, A.
Hathaway, Salmon
Sydney S. Durfee
T. R. Strong

T. Hemingway
William Gardner
William L. Dowling
Wm. M. Bayard
Wm. May
Wm. P. Nottingham
Wm. Parke
Thomas P. Baldwin
Thomas Rogers, 2nd
Wells Anderson
Z. Williams
Wm. Wilcox
William White

Married, July 22, 1832, at Palmyra, James Milliman of Macedon and Amanda McMichael, of Palmyra.

Adv.: Dr. Stilwell, surgeon, 1st house west of Capt. Lilly's tavern, on Main St., opp. W. Ackleys.

AUGUST 1, 1832

Board of Health of the village of Palmyra, announce the death from cholera, July 22, 1832, of Andrew McCord, a boat man; many deaths in New York State.

Married: In Zion Church, July 29, 1832, John H. Merrill, of New York and Eliza Gardner of Boston.

Married: in Zion Church, John N. Correll, of New York and Angeline Gardner.

Died: July 30, 1832, Harriet Mariah Allen, dau. of Draper Allen, ae one year.

Adv.: E. R. Spear wants an apprentice printer.; Gurney & Post, groceries, corner of Main & Market St.

AUGUST 8, 1832

Salman Frisbee, a stranger, d. in Palmyra of cholera.

L. J. Littlejohn adv. for cow that strayed.

AUGUST 15, 1832:

Married: Aug. 1, 1832, in Palmyra, James Sullivan and Freelove Johnson.

Died: in Palmyra, Aug. 1, 1832, Noahdiah Hibbard, ae 32 [sic], a Revolutionary soldier. [The age given must be in error. The veteran was more than likely 82 ed.]

Died: in Walworth, Mrs. Maranda Hurley, ae 37 yrs., wife of Samuel Hurley.

Died: in Palmyra, Katherine Heath, dau. of J. C. Hurley, ae 14 weeks.

AUGUST 22, 1832

Died: in Palmyra, Frances Catherine Jerome, dau. of H. K. Jerome, ae 2 years.

Died: August 18, 1832, George Whitford (Whitfield?) Beckwith, son, of George B. Beckwith age 10 yrs. [A second source copied age as 10 mos.]

Died: Aug. 8, 1832, in Macedon, Mrs. Martha Delano, wife of Israel Delano, and dau. of Judge William Rogers, ae 55 years.

AUGUST 29, 1832

The cornerstone for the new Western Presbyterian Church will be laid Thursday [Aug. 30th], this week.

Married: in Palmyra, Aug. 21, 1832, William Prime and Eliza Ann Newbury.

Died: Aug. 27, 1832, in Palmyra, Lott Stone.

SEPTEMBER 5, 1832

Cornerstone of church laid; a leaden box containing a bible presented by E. B. Grandin, last number of the Wayne Sentinel, an account of the church and the Society, etc. Prayer by Rev Jesse Townsend, and Rev. B. H. Hickox, and procession escorted by Col. Horton's Cavalry.

Died: In Palmyra, Sept. 3, 1832, James Stewart, a native of Ireland.

Adv.: F. Pierce - select boarding school, opposite the Eagle Hotel.

SEPTEMBER 12, 1832:

Young men of the town invited to join a meeting of the Democratic Republicans at the Eagle Hotel Sept. 22, 1832, s/ by the following: Hiram P. Thayer, Noah Shaw, Henry Gardner, Chris E. Thayer, Clark Robinson, William L. Downing, P. R. Howell, J. K. Cummings, Almond Pratt, William H. Cuyler, Jarvis L. Thayer, Homer B. Williams, Theron R. Strong, M. Ritter, J. W. M. Zuill, James Terbuss, John M. Harlow, James McMichael.

JANUARY 2, 1833

Adv.: Palmyra High School, James F. Cogswell in charge; George M. Williams, Sec.; David H. Sherman and Stephen Alling, Assignees of Caleb Horton. Ira White & Co. put bills in hands of T. R. Strong for collection, Dec. 22, 1831. Clark & Ely -shawls, etc.; Daniel G. Finch, No. 2, Exchange Row; Clapp & Durfee - Dry goods; George E. Pomeroy Drugs; Pratt & White - drugs; Palmyra Brewery will pay cash for barley. John Amsden, Jr, - Tailor and draper at C. C. Coleman's old stand;

M. Ritter, market; L. North - jeweller, 3 doors east of old brick block; G. S. Ely "Stone Front Store"; Woodward & Co. - settling accounts; [M. W.] Willcox & [J. H.] Bortles, bookstore and bindery. Eagle Hotel, N. Homan; William T. Briggs, carriage builder, Fayette St.; William White - unsettled accounts; [C. C.] Robinson and [H. N.] Loomis - accounts to be settled; K. S. Eggleston - pectoral drops; Mr. Lupkins - perfumer and hair dresser; P. Grandin will pay cash for corn.

Death by smallpox of a lad in Palmyra, Sullivan by name, a Canal employee.

JANUARY 9, 1833
Philip Grandin, assigned [?] to Hiram Niles and J. S. Fenton.

JANUARY 16, 1833
F. A. Goldsmith's Library and Reading Room is established Jan. 15, 1833.
Celebration of the victory of Jan. 8th is given in detail; F. Smith, T. Heminway, and T. R. Strong in charge; a ball held in the evening.
Married: Jan. 10, 1833, in Walworth, Dr. Almond Pratt of Palmyra and Mary Boynton, dau. of Hon. Jonathan Boynton, of Walworth.
Adv: Mr. Gilbert's dancing school.

JANUARY 23, 1838
Married: Jan. 20, 1833, in Manchester, Corrin G. Johnson and Mary Ann White, both of Manchester.
Adv.: S. Jackson's rifle factory

JANUARY 30, 1833
Married: in Palmyra, Jan. 23, 1833, John Amsden, Jr. and Miss Ann Parker.
Married: Jan. 24, 1833, in Palmyra, Erastus R. Spear and Elizabeth Van Allen.
Married: Jan. 24, 1833, in Newark, Nelson Sherman and Temperance Goldsmith, both of Palmyra.
Adv. John Amsden, Jr. & Co.; Sutton Birdsall is the Co. tailor.

FEBRUARY 6, 1833
Medical School (Delamater & Loomis) begins in Palmyra, March 1, 1833.

FEBRUARY 16, 1833
Adv.: E. B. Grandin, having retired from business, wants accounts paid.

FEBRUARY 20, 1833
Joseph F. Fenton is appointed notary and Hiram Niles as auctioneer.
Married, Feb. 14, 1833, at Macedon, Stephen Spear, of Michigan and Lucinda Powell, dau. of Rev. R. Powell.
Married: Feb. 12, 1833, in Palmyra, Philip Durfee, of the firm of Clapp & Durfee, to Mary White, dau. of Dr. James White.

FEBRUARY 27, 1833
Eldredge Havens, appointed inspector of beef and pork.
Died: February 23, 1833, in Macedon, Dr. William P. Richardson, age 44, of apoplexy.

MARCH 6, 1833
Married: Feb. 21, 1833, in Marion, Aaron McGraw of Lyons, and Laura Huggins of Marion.
MARCH 13, 1833 - no events copied.

MARCH 20, 1833

Married: Feb. 28, 1833, in the Friends Meeting House, Otis Clapp, and Mary D. Ramsdell, dau. of Gideon Ramsdell.

Married: March 13, 1833, in Palmyra, George A. Hathaway, and Adaline Chase.

Married: March 13, 1833, in Palmyra, Cullen Loud [?] and Lucinda M. Bliss.

Married: March 10, 1833, in Macedon, Ephriam Davenport and Lodema Eggleston.

Died: March 7, 1833, in Macedon, Mrs. Eunice Capron, widow of the late Samuel Capron and mother of William P. Capron, ae 90 year.

MARCH 27, 1833

Married: March 20, 1833, in Palmyra, Israel T. Hatch, of Buffalo, and Lydia A. Powers, dau. of Gershom Powers, of Auburn [Cayuga Co].

Died: March 14, 1833, in Canandaigua, Spencer Chapin, ae 43 years.

Adv.: D. Hotchkiss, jeweller, formerly of Hotchkiss & Durfee; Jonathan Dart & Co., plow factory, 1 1/2 mi. east [of Palmyra?].

APRIL 3, 1833

Died: March 24, 1833 in Walworth, Catharine Calista Benham, dau. of David and Sally Benham, age 1 yr. 7 mos.

APRIL 10, 1833 - No items copied.

APRIL 17, 1833

Died: April 10, 1833, in Palmyra, Andrew Jackson, infant son of Philip Grandin.

Adv: Eddy & Elihu L. Clark, bought out William White.

APRIL 24, 1833

Stage line-east, goes to Vienna, Freebridge, etc. to Albany.

Died: April 21, 1833, in the town of Palmyra, Mrs. Hannah Rogers, wife of Maj. William Rogers, age 51 years.

Adv.: Jonah Howell, having sold out, wants to "settle up."

May 1, 1833

The great eastern mail is now received at this place via the Freebridge and Vienna from 8 to 10 hours earlier than before and before rider mail by horseback, leaving Elbridge [Onondaga Co.], at the same time as the other.

Palmyra Baths and Garden are open again; Niles and Allyn; Pratt & White dissolve partnership.

The new and splendid canal boat, <u>Saranac</u>, built by Samuel Randall for H. H. Treat & Co., was launched April 27, 1833.

Zuill & White assign to R. C. Jackson and J. S. Fenton, April 24, 1833.

Married: April 28, 1833, Samuel Palmer and Julia Decker.

MAY 8, 1833

Married: April 28, 1833, Morgan L. Schermerhorn of Hammondsport and Elizabeth Colt, dau. of Joseph Colt, of Palmyra.

Died: May 4, 1833, Mrs. Sally Thayer, ae 47 yrs., widow of Amasa Thayer.

Adv: George W. Cuyler will sue those who do not settle.

MAY 15, 1833

Charles J. Sutherland and Lemuel Sutherland, dissolve, 4 Apr. 1933.

Adv. Lemuel Sutherland buys old metal.

MAY 22, 1833.

Rev. B. H. Hickox, who has officiated at St. Paul's Church for six months, has accepted a call to said church to become its rector.

Married: May 9, 1833, Nathan T. Williams and Margaret Williams, dau. of John Williams.

Married: May 16, 1833, at Palmyra, George P. Eddy, of Marion, son of David Eddy and Catherine H. Rowe, dau. of Rev. Epicratus Rowe, deceased.

Died, May 21, 1833, at Palmyra, Mrs. Mary Winship, wife of Joseph Winship, age 32 yrs., also a daughter.

Adv. Augustus Hard, marble factory; Newton & Davis, wool carding, bought out Jonah Howe.

MAY 29, 1833:

Married: May 21, 1833, at Owasco, [Cayuga Co.], William H. Cuyler and Eliza Aikin, by Rev. B. H. Hickox, of Rochester.

Married: May 19, 1833, in Westminster, CT, Dr. David D. Hoyt, of Palmyra and Julia May, dau. of E. May of that place.

Adv.: Kingman & Coleman - livery.

JUNE 5, 1833

Married: June 4, 1833, in Zion Church, by Rev. Jesse Pound, Theron R. Strong and Abby L. Hart, dau. of the Hon. Truman Hart, of Palmyra.

JUNE 12, 1833

Adv.: A. Pratt - drugs - two doors east of the bank.

JUNE 19, 1833

Married: June 6, 1833, Horatio N. Loomis, M. D., of Palmyra, to Mrs. Mary Ann Mott, dau. of John Williams.

Married: May 30, 1833, at Massilon, OH, Arvine Wales and Mrs. Nancy Shepherdson, of Palmyra.

JUNE 26, 1833

The Indian captives, Black Hawk, the Prophet and Black Hawk's son, are expected to arrive in Palmyra via canal tomorrow evening.

Died: May 26, 1833, in Williamson, Alexander Stewart, a Revolutionary soldier, ae 85 yrs.; born in the Parish of Whitehorn, Scotland, came to America in 1774.

THEATRE: at the Eagle Hotel, June 26, 1833; Inn Keeper's Bride or Married Yesterday; four in the company. Admission only 25c.

JULY 3, 1833

Adv: Fireworks for July 4th at the Palmyra Gardens; Meeting for purpose of taking action toward inviting the President of the U. S. to visit Palmyra, on his tour; June 21, 1833 - J. Francis loses his apprentice, Isaac Letts, ae 18 yrs.

Died: July 1, 1833, John Hayward, ae 32 yrs.

JULY 10, 1833

CELEBRATION OF JULY 4th: Col. L. Hurd and Maj. H. N. Loomis in command: Prayer by Dr. James Hubbell; Jeremiah Russ read the Declaration of Independence; oration by Elisha Foot; choir of young men and women under Capt. John H. Gilbert. 300 people at the garden [for fireworks]; one citizen rubbering over the fence was discovered and shot at with a roman candle, fell into the cask.

JULY 17, 1833

M. Kingman owned a farm near Yellow Mills.

Toasts drank by following students at 4th July celebration: R. S. Hendee, F. M. Smith, F. C. Lovell, William Rogers, 3rd, F. D. Rogers, Phineas Homan.

Adv.: C. Aldrich - hats, etc.- bought out George Seymour.

The day of publication for this paper in the future, will be Friday, instead of Wednesday.

JULY 22, 1833 (Friday)

Clark & Ely dissolve - Clark sells to Col. George Beckwith.

Married: July 26, 1833, Lorenzo Saunders and Calista Taber, dau. of Capt. B. Taber.

Died: July 22, 1833, in Palmyra, William G. Newland, infant son of George Newland.

Isaac Jerome, adv. a stray horse.

AUGUST 2, 1833

Camp meeting will be held by the Methodists on the premises of Caleb Beal, in East Palmyra, beginning Aug. 6th, 1833.

AUGUST 9, 1833

A post office has been established in the east part of the town, called East Palmyra; Lyman Tiffany is postmaster.

Alexander Purdy is appointed Post Master in Macedon, Dr. Reed has removed.

Married: Aug. 5, 1833, in Palmyra, George E. Pomeroy and Helen E. Robinson, dau. of Dr. Gain Robinson.

Died: In Maumee, OH, Nathaniel McCollum, ae 23 yrs.

AUGUST 16, 1833

Married: In Palmyra, Moses Parke, of Sodus, formerly of Palmyra and Harriet Eliza Badger.

Married: Aug. 11, 1833, in Palmyra, John P. Dennis and Susan Hunt, of Palmyra.

Died: Aug. 10, 1833, Elsey Elizabeth Finch, dau. of Daniel D. Finch.

AUGUST 23, 1833

T. H. Strong announces to the public that George W. Cuyler has become a joint proprietor with him in this [news] paper.

AUGUST 30, 1833

Wheeler R. Crane was pastor of the Baptist Church at Marion at this time.

Died: Aug. 28, 1833, in Pittsford, James D. Williams, infant son of Richard S. Williams, formerly of Palmyra.

Adv.: Aaron McGraw - deaf and dumb school at Marion.

SEPTEMBER 6, 1833

Married: Aug. 29, 1833, at Farmington, Moses Power, Jr., and Chloe Terrill, all of Farmington.

Died: at Pittsford, Aug. 31, 1833, Helen P. Williams, dau. of Richard S. Williams, ae 2 yrs. 4 months.

SEPTEMBER 13, 1833

Application has been made to the Legislature to incorporate a company to construct a rail-road from Rochester, via Palmyra to Syracuse and also from the Erie Canal in Palmyra to Canandaigua.

Married: Sept. 12, 1833, in Macedon, Hiram Gallup of Williamson and Abigail Spear, dau. of Lemuel Spear.

Died: Aug. 31, 1833, in Hopewell, Israel Chapin, ae 70 years.

Joseph Lippincott offers a reward for a stolen pocket book; Abner F. Lake advertises a stray horse.

Adv.: William Fitch, jeweller, buys out L. North, east of Eagle House.

SEPTEMBER 20, 1833

Married: Sept. 25, 1833, in Palmyra, John S. Decker to Betsy Hammond.

Died: Sept. 14, 1833, Philena F. Lewis, infant dau. of Uriah Lewis.

SEPTEMBER 27, 1833

Adv.: Mr. E. N. Manning, dentist at the Eagle Hotel.

Married: September 26, 1833, in Palmyra, by Rev. Gideon Osband, Rev. Josiah D. Paris of Pike [Wyoming Co.] and Miss Elizabeth Winn, of Palmyra.

Married: Sept. 19, 1833, in Manchester, John Lathberry and Betsey S. Jones.

OCTOBER 4, 1833

An unclaimed letter in Post Office for Jacob Van Alstine.

Married: Sept. 27, 1833, in Canandaigua, Henry Gilbert and Charlotte Case, of Canandaigua.
Adv.: Beckwith & Ely - dry goods; B. Maynard, Wilcox and Bortles - old stand, books.

OCTOBER 11, 1833
Married: Oct. 9, 1833, in Palmyra, David G. Ely of "Beckwith & Ely" and Ruth E. Marvin.
Adv.: C. M. Hanner, dentist at The Bunker Hill Hotel.

OCTOBER 18, 1833
Died: Oct. 2, 1833, at her mother's home in Middlehaddam, CT, Mrs. Eliza Thayer, wife of Levi Thayer of Palmyra, ae 41 yrs. She was the dau. of Rev. David Selden.
Died: Oct. 13, 1833, Elijah Clark, Deacon of the Congregational Church in Marion, formerly of Amherst, MA, ae 50 years.

OCTOBER 25, 1833
Married: Oct. 17, 1833, in Marion, Rufus Sweezey and Philena Wait, of Marion.
Married: Oct. 14, 1833, in Rochester, Luther Tucker and Mary Sparhawk, dau. of E. Sparhawk.
Married: Oct. 17, 1833, Daniel Aylesworth and Betsey Perkins, both of Galen.
Adv.: Stephen Hyde, dry goods, #2 Exchange Row.

NOVEMBER 1, 1833
Four polling places: Methodist Church in East Palmyra, opposite Maltby Clark's; the schoolhouse near Goldsmith's; Bunker Hill Hotel and the Eagle Hotel.
Married: Oct. 24, 1833, in Walworth, William Morse and Mahala P. Freeman.
Died: Oct. 31, 1833, Laban S. Eddy, of the firm, Eddy & Clark, ae 22 years.

NOVEMBER 8, 1833
Died: Nov. 18, 1833, in Macedon, Isaac Spear, ae 51 yrs., formerly of Boston.

NOVEMBER 15, 1833
Article criticizing the Village Trustees for granting liquor licenses.
Married: Oct. 24, 1833, in Palmyra, David Vanderhoof and Sarah Jane Shirts, both of Arcadia.

NOVEMBER 22, 1833
A second article on Trustees granting licenses to sell liquor.
Marine and Canal Intelligence: Arrived at his port yesterday, the superior new canal boat, Buffalo, owned and commanded by Capt. Clark Robinson, ten days from New York with a full cargo of merchandise for Palmyra merchants, embracing many articles direct from England.

NOVEMBER 29, 1833
Married: Nov. 20, 1833, in Palmyra, William T. Briggs of Palmyra and Clarinda Farr, of Sodus.
Married: Nov. 14, in Walworth, Charles Chase and Orpha Bancroft.
Nov. 25, 1833: William Freeman, adv. his runaway son, Henry Washington Sidney Freeman.

DECEMBER 6, 1833
Article on Mormons at Kirtland, Ohio.
Married: Nov. 26, 1833, at Vienna, Col. Joel Stearns, Jr. and Mrs. Chloe Hotchkiss.

DECEMBER 13, 1833
Matter of the establishment of a new county again considered. Meeting called.

DECEMBER 20, 1833 - No items copied
DECEMBER 27, 1833
Report of the Committee on the "New County' in detail.
Married: Dec. 22, 1833, in Palmyra, Daniel Allen and Matilda Hoag of Farmington.

JANUARY 3, 1834
See article on new county of Wayne formed by act of April 11, 1823.
A new post office established in town of Macedon at Hoxie's corner, called Macedon Centre; Miles Andrus appointed postmaster; he d. Dec. 27th before the post office was organized. A new post office established at East Ridge, Sodus, to be called "Sodus".
Married: Dec. 29, 1833, in Macedon, Runa H. Talbot and Cynthia Ann Stimpson, of Macedon.
Married: Dec. 29, 1833, at Pultneyville, J. S. Phelps and Satah Ann Selby.
Married: Dec. 31, 1833, at Palmyra, James Stanbrough and Uretta Smith, both of Arcadia.
Advertisers: T. R. Strong, atty; G. W. Cuyler, atty.; Burr Butler, tailor; Beckwith & Ely, dry-goods; D. G. Finch, cutter, etc.; Assignees of William White; W. Winship, flour; Dr. J. Eggleston, drugs; George E. Pomeroy, drugs; Alanson Sherman, apprentice; Kingman & Coleman, livery; M. Kingman - pigs for sale; George Brown, stray cattle; Thomas Rogers, 2nd- cattle; George Beckwith- dry goods; C. Smith -house & lot; Philip Grandin - estate accounts; E. Maynard - boy wanted; Robinson & Loomis - wants settlement of accounts.

JANUARY 10, 1834
Notice of meetings at Walworth, Macedon and Marion re: erection of new county.
John Moore, of Macedon says his wife, Catherine, daughters, Margaret and Maria, and son, Martin, have left him without cause...
Married: Jan. 14, 1834, at Palmyra, by Rev. Doolittle, William H. Morey and Mary Gibbs.

JANUARY 17, 1834
Died: at Palmyra, Ruth Gilbert, dau. of J. H. Gilbert, ae 11 months.
Adv.: A Sherman & A. P. Crandall - blacksmiths, etc.

JANUARY 24, 1834
Married: Jan. 15, 1834, at East Bloomfield, P. W. Handy, of Palmyra and Sophronia Gaines.

JANUARY 31, 1834

Married: Jan. 28, 1834, at Potter, Henry Husted and Susan P. Williams, dau. of Richard M. Williams.

FEBRUARY 7, 1834

J. Amsden, Jr. & Sutton Birdsall (J. Amsden & Co.) to dissolve.

Married: Jan, 28, 1834, at Genoa, Alfred Avery and Mary Jane Underhill.

Married: Jan. 30, 1834, at Venice, Abraham Reynolds and Amanda Purdy.

FEBRUARY 14, 1834

The eccentric preacher, Lorenzo Dow, died at Washington City, Feb. 2, 1834.

Married: Feb. 12, 1834, in Aurora, William S. Post (of the firm. Gurney & Post), and Helen H. Wells.

Married: Jan. 29, 1834, in Walworth, Charles Hurlburt and Margaret Gregory.

Died: Feb. 8, 1834, at Palmyra, Capt. Benjamin Throop, ae 50 years.

FEBRUARY 21, 1834

William Parks assigns to Dennison and William Rogers, Jr., Feb. 13, 1834.

Benjamin T. Hoxie, appointed postmaster at Macedon Center in place of Miles H. Andrus, who d. before he had qualified. Allen Sisson has been appointed postmaster at Manchester, vice R. T. Field (reformed).

Married: Feb. 11, 1834, in Batavia, Orasmus Turner of Lockport and Julia Bush.

FEBRUARY 28, 1834

Palmyra High School: J. F. Cogwell, A. M., Principal and instructor in ancient languages; N. E. Spencer, A.P., instructor in French, Spanish, Math and Science; William Welsh, asst. in ancient languages; J. L. Elwood, asst. in English dept. FEMALE DEPT.: Miss Maria Sloane, Principal and instructor in French and Belles-letters; Miss Mary W. Dodd, instrumental music and vocal music; Miss Jane Brush, asst. in female dept.; 161 pupils - 63 ladies and 98 gentlemen; summer term begins 1st week in May and the winter term four week after the first Wed. in Oct.; each term to be for 22 weeks. A boarding house is connected with the school; $150.00 per year.

Friends of Rev. Whelpley requested to meet at the Presbyterian Church that a free and full expression of views and feelings may be had in regard to him. s/ Thomas Rogers, 2nd, F. U. Sheffield, Richard Sweet, Burr Butler.

John J. Myers, a swindler, is given free notice. (2/28/1834).

Married: Feb. 23, 1824, at Butler, Riley Merrill, age 17 yrs. and Charlotte Hubbard, age 15 years.

MARCH 7, 1834

Sketch of Lorenzo Dow and his wife, Peggy Dow.

Married: March 5, 1834, Jacob H. Bortles and Mary Colt, dau. of Joseph Colt. Mr. Bortles is of the firm, Wilcox & Bortles.

Died: Feb. 15, 1834, in Vienna, Mary Ann Hooker, age 15 years.

MARCH 14, 1834
Married: March 10, 1834, in Palmyra, Nelson Rich and Matilda Palmeter.
Married: March 12, 1834, in Palmyra, Nelson Lapham and Lucinda Parker.
Died: Feb. 21, 1834, Mrs. Dorcas Putnam, wife of Stephen Putnam, ae 26 years.

MARCH 21, 1834
George W. Cuyler has been appointed collector of canal tolls.
Married: March 20, 1834, in Palmyra, by Rev. Samuel Moore, Eliphalet Murdoch and Sally Hall of Palmyra.
Died: Feb. 21, 1834, in Macedon, Mrs. Marietta Osband, wife of Durfee Osband, ae 26 years.

MARCH 28, 1834
Married: March 19, 1834, at Pultneyville, William Rogers, Jr. and Mrs. Ruth Throop.
Died: March 26, 1834, Thomas E. Hall, formerly of Palmyra.
Adv.: Nathan Parshall, has a store to rent at Marion Corners.

APRIL 4, 1834
Died: at Port Glasgow, Mrs. Amy Horton, wife of Nathan Horton.
George Wilcox, assignee of William T. Briggs.

APRIL 18, 1834
F. Pierce opens a private school at the corner of Main and Washington St.; Wilcox & Bortles dissolve partnership - 4/16/1834.
Adv: J. K. Cummings - ground plaister for sale; James Williams, Johnson St., has a stallion [for breeding purposes].

APRIL 25, 1834
The new Presbyterian Church is to be dedicated Wed., May 7th; Rev. Josiah Hopkins, of Auburn will preach.

MAY 2, 1834
Married: April 27, 1834, in Palmyra, by Rev. William Staunton, Oliver Niles and Hannah A. Gardner.
Died: April 22, 1834, in Palmyra, Mary Thayer, dau. of Joel Thayer, ae 7 years.

MAY 9, 1834
Died: May 7, 1834, in Sodus, Thomas Judson, ae 32 years.
Niles & Allyn, dissolve partnership 4/29/1834; Dorcas Gear advertises stray cattle.

MAY 16, 1834

Adv. James Hodges, dentist, one door east of Lilly's Inn.; June, Titus & Angevine Circus will be here May 28th and go to Canandaigua the next day - 14 piece band, etc.

MAY 23, 1834

Married: May 17, 1834 in Canandaigua, John Wallis and Annie C. Howland, both of Palmyra.

MAY 30, 1834

Many could not get into the circus and were turned back.

JUNE 6, 1834

Adv: J. Atwood, portrait painter at Bunker Hill Hotel; E. M. Clifford, portrait painter, at the Eagle Hotel.

JUNE 13, 1834 - No items copied.

JUNE 20, 1834

The first number of a new paper, Wayne County Gazette, edited by John M. Holley was issued June 18, 1834.

An Anti-slavery meeting will be held at the old Preb. Meeting house at early candle lighting, June 20.

JUNE 27, 1834

Married: June 20, 1834, at Palmyra, John Colvin, Jr., of Macedon and Rachel Smith of Marion.

Married, June 20, 1834, at Palmyra, John Devine and Sarah Barnes.

Married, June 23, 1834: in Palmyra, Alexander Finley and Lydia Ann Chilson.

Died: Mrs. Permilla Durfee, wife of William Durfee, ae 28 years.

Adv.: Orin Collins, harness shop, at S. Carter's old stand.

JULY 4, 1834 - No items copied.

JULY 11, 1834

Married: July 7, 1834, at Pultneyville, Horatio N. Throop, and Mary F. Ledyard, dau. of Samuel Ledyard.

Married: In Palmyra, July 6, 1834, Alanson Todd and Mary R. Bingham, of Palmyra.

Married: July 9, 1834, Job Barnhart and Fidelia Lapham, dau. of Aretus Lapham.

JULY 18, 1834

Adv: Letter at postoffice for Peter Van Alstine.

JULY 25, 1834

E. R. Spear and Samuel Palmer dissolve partnership.

AUGUST 1, 1834

Levi Hanks adv. a stolen mare;

Francis Bortle, constable, "lost" a jail bird, Amos Walker.

AUGUST 8, 1834
Alexander McIntyre and D. D. Hoyt, dissolve partnership, 8/7; Asa Piper's barn, one mi. south of Palmyra, burned by lightning, 8/7; Property of N. H. Beckwith, sold at auction by executors, George Beckwith and Norton B. Burchard.

Married: Aug. 6, 1834, Levi Thayer and Susan Westcott.

Married: Aug. 5, 1834, in Manchester, Eugene L. Morgan and Dorothea Armington.

Married: Aug. 7, 1834, in Seneca Falls, John G. Woren and Lois P. Howland.

AUGUST 15, 1834
Report of a riot and outrage at Palmyra over a slave girl in the employ of some visitors here at Palmyra; Rochester Negroes involved.

Adv.: Jacob H. Quimby, attorney; Epenetus Howell, adv. a stray mare.

AUGUST 22, 1834
Theron R. Strong has transferred his undivided half of the Wayne Sentinel and the printing establishment connected with it to Pomeroy Tucker - 8/20.

Adv.: R. C. Hodgkin - barber.

AUGUST 29, 1834
This issue contains names of 168 voters - but not copied here.

Married: Aug. 23, 1834, Joseph Winship of Palmyra to Nancy Belden.

Died: Aug. 22, 1834, Lorenzo Spear, formerly of Macedon, enroute from Buffalo to Detroit.

Died: At Lewiston, [Niagara Co.], Aug. 24, 1834, Salmon Hathaway.

SEPTEMBER 5, 1834
Married: at Palmyra, Sept. 1, 1834, Francis Bortles and Emily Lilly.

SEPTEMBER 12, 1834
Three fatal cases of cholera reported in the past week - emigrants.

T. R. Strong and J. H. Quimby, form partnership on 8/11.

Died: Sept. 6, 1834, Frances Ann Gilbert, dau. of G. H. Gilbert, 3 1/2 years of age.

Adv.: Mons[sieur?] Glowacke - [teaching?] French and Italian at the Eagle Hotel; Mons. Wilezewski -[teaching?] writing and painting at the Eagle Hotel; Strong & Quimby - lawyers.

SEPTEMBER 19, 1834
Another death from cholera reported - foreigners to Palmyra.

Married: Sept. 17, 1834, in Walworth, Joseph Sheets, of Erie and Eveline Rawson.

Died: Sept. 15, 1834, Seth Williams, ae 20 yrs, of cholera.

Adv.: Tucker & Cuyler - have type for sale; Eugene L. Morgan - draper; Charles A. Thompson tailor.

SEPTEMBER 26, 1834
Married: Sept. 18, 1834, in Palmyra by Rev. Shumway, James Williams and Sarah Osborn.
Married: In Walworth, Sept. 11, 1834, Elihu L. Clark and Isabella Bean.
Died: Sept. 8, 1834, at Clyde, James Dickson.
Died: Sept. 9, 1834, in Buffalo, John Dorrin, ae 70 yrs.
Died: Sept. 3, 1834, at Phelps, James Humphrey, a Revolutionary soldier, ae 80 years.
Died: Sept. 4, 1834, at Canandaigua, William A. Williams, ae 70 yrs.

OCTOBER 3, 1834 - Nothing copied.

OCTOBER 10, 1834
Married: Sept. 29, 1834, at Palmyra, Alonzo Smedley and Sylvia King.

OCTOBER 17, 1834
Regimental Parade: The different companies of the 39th Regt., commanded by Col. D. Chase, rendezvoused in this village for military discipline, inspection and review, Friday last.
Died: Oct. 28, 1834 [sic] [prob. should be Sept. 28. ed.] O. Russell Ensworth, formerly of Rochester.
Adv: Z. Williams - groceries; A. Martin & Co., carters - buys out M. Kingman.

OCTOBER 24, 1834
Married: Oct. 23, 1834, in Palmyra, Charles B. Bingham and Abigail Tice.
Married: Oct. 23, 1834, in Canandaigua, Stephen Scantling and Louisa Cooper, both of Palmyra.
Adv.: J. Johnson - barber.

OCTOBER 31, 1834
Thanksgiving day proclaimed by the Governor to be Dec. 11, 1834.
Adv.: The Misses [Louisa & Amanda) Gardner, - private school for ladies; Israel Vail, adv. a stray cow.

NOVEMBER 7, 1834
Married: Nov. 5, 1834, Joseph Lippincott and Mary Williams.

NOVEMBER 14, 1834
Married: Nov. 13, 1834, Elisha Clark and Elizabeth A. Bristol, both of Palmyra.

NOVEMBER 21, 1834
Adv.: W. G. Gardner - dry goods at Market & Canal Street.

NOVEMBER 28, 1834
Elijah Smith of Walworth leaves for parts unknown.

DECEMBER 5, 1834
Married: Dec. 4, 1834, in Farmington, Elias H. Lapham and Dirce [sic[Ann Brown.
Married: Dec. 4, 1834, Gideon R. Payne and Mary B. Smith.
Died: Dec. 1, 1834, in Palmyra, Eugene L. Morgan, ae 24 years.
Died: Dec. 3, 1834, in Macedon, Silas Stoddard Sheffield, son of F. U. Sheffield, ae one week.

DECEMBER 10, 1834
Alanson Sherman adv. Randall B. Saunders as a runaway.

DECEMBER 19, 1834
The British schooner, General Brock, goes ashore at Pultneyville, Dec. 14th with 17 person aboard; all were saved.
L. W. Hard, of Pittsford and Augustus Hard, seek a brother, Burton Hard, who left his home on June 23, 1833.
Died: Dec. 15, 1834, Mrs. Mehitable Reeves, wife of James Reeves, age 67 yrs.; she came to this town from Southampton, L. I. in 1792.
Died: Dec. 8, 1834 in Schenectady, Joseph Gavitt, of Palmyra, ae 40 yrs.
Adv.: Daniel H. Conner, tailor, takes shop of E. L. Morgan, deceased; John Balcom - adv. a boar [for breeding purposes].

DECEMBER 26, 1834
The installation and ordination of Rev. George R. H. Shumway to take place at the Brick Church in this village, Jan. 1, 1835; sermon to be preached by Dr. Richards, of Auburn.
Killed: Dec. 23, 1834, Goodale Foskett of Walworth was killed by being struck by a threshing machine cylinder, when it burst.
Meeting called for Jan. 7, 1835, to discuss building a railroad along the canal from Rochester to Syracuse.

JANUARY 2, 1835
Railroad meeting at Homan's Hotel Jan. 8th to nominate delegates to attend meeting at Vienna Jan. 7th to discuss a contemplated railroad from Auburn to Rochester.
Inhabitants of Ontario, Walworth, and Macedon, are to meet at Aldrich's Inn at Walworth Corners Jan. 5, to discuss the question of the location of the county buildings.

Adv: P. Bortle, tax collector; R. C. Hodgkin - barber; J. H. Bortle - Palmyra Book Store; C. T. Payne - improved Fire Frames; Collector's Office - coat left for Rev. Ward Stafford, not taken; Daniel Tuttle - military caps; Daniel H. Conner - tailoring; M. W. Willcox -Dr.

C. C. Robinson's house for sale; J. Williams & Co. - Groceries; Z. Williams - groceries; J. Williams & Co. - saddles; Sherman & Crandall- carriage painting; David H. Sherman and John H. Cummings -assignees of Hollister & Hildreth; E. P. Godard & Co. - oysters etc.

JANUARY 9, 1835
Married: Jan. 8, 1835, in Palmyra, by Eld. Richards, Capt. Wareham Wilson of Whitehall and Miss Cordelia Gardner, dau. of Isaac Gardner, of Palmyra.
Married: Jan. 1, 1835, in Palmyra, Seymour Monroe and Miss Mary Brockway.
Married: Jan. 1, 1835 in Sodus, James Ackley and Betsy Lumbard, of Lyons.
Died: Jan. 2, 1835, Thomas Eggleston, ae 57(?) years.
Died: Jan. 2, 1835, in Palmyra, Mrs. Cynthia Johnson, wife of David J. Johnson, ae 37 years.
Died: Dec. 27, 1834, in Macedon, Isaac Eddy, ae 55 years.
Died: Jan. 5, 1835, in Palmyra, Dr. James B. Eddy, ae 55 years.
Gurney & Post dissolve - Thomas W. Gurney continues [dry goods].

JANUARY 16, 1835
Young Men's Society giving a series of lectures this winter - those who will lecture: Rev. William Staunton, H. Jerome, Dr. H. N. Loomis, Rev. G. R. H. Shumway, Joseph Hyde, T. R. Strong, Truman Hart, G. W. Cuyler, Dr. D. D. Hoyt, Abner F. Lakey, and James F. Brown.
Elijah Drake, an imposter leaves town in debt to many citizens.
Died: Jan. 13, 1835, in Palmyra, Christian Barnhart, ae 57 years.
Died: Jan. 15, 1835, in Palmyra, Stephen Durfee, son of Elihu Durfee, ae 7 years.
Adv.: Beers and Richmond - Macedon Furnace.

JANUARY 23, 1835
Married: Jan. 21, 1825, in Palmyra, by Rev. G. R. H. Shumway, Alfred Spear and Catherine Shirts, both of Lockville.

JANUARY 30, 1835
A committee appointed to superintend and survey of the railroad route between Vienna and Palmyra.
Married: Jan. 28, 1835, in Palmyra, by Rev. Shumway, Richard L. Clark of New York and Julia J. Fenton, dau. of Joseph S. Fenton of Palmyra.
Died: Jan. 20, 1835, in Lyons, Thomas Payne, ae 57 years.
Died: Jan. 20, 1835, Isaac Rogers, ae 44 years.
Died: Jan. 24, 1835, William H. Birch, ae 38 years.
Died: Jan. 25, 1835, Mrs. Richard Jones, ae 83 years.

FEBRUARY 6, 1835
Theron R. Strong appointed District Attorney of Wayne Co.; report of Benjamin H. Brown, Engineer in charge of survey re: railroad route between Vienna and Palmyra.
Married: Jan. 29, 1835, by Rev. Mr. Filmore, Harry Fish and Polly Russell.

Died: Jan. 30, 1835, in Palmyra, Cynthia Ann Beckwith, dau. of N. H. Beckwith, ae 15 years.

FEBRUARY 13, 1835
Palmyra Anti-Slavery meeting will be held in Preb. Meeting house Feb. 25th.
Married: Feb. 5, 1835, in Palmyra, Stephen Clark and Ann Hathorn.
Died: Feb. 8, 1835, William S. Post, ae 28 yrs. of Gurney & Post.
Died Jan. 30, 1835, Henry P. White, son of Dr. James White, ae 3 years.
Died: Feb. 1, 1835, William E. Allen, infant son of Draper Allen.
Died: Jan. 24, 1835, Solomon St. John, formerly of Palmyra.

FEBRUARY 20, 1835
Married: Feb. 15, 1835, by Rev. William Staunton, Henry Gardner and Barbara Marie Todd.
Married: Feb. 17, 1835, in Lawrenceville, PA, Rev. G. R. H. Shumway and Emily C. Ford, a dau. of James Ford of that place.
Married: Feb. 11, 1835, in Walworth, Charles D. Hinckley, and Margaret VanWagoner.
Died: Feb. 15, 1835, in Palmyra, Jonah Howell, ae 32 years.
Died: Feb. 11, 1835, in Sodus, Robert McCollum, ae 71 years.
Adv: Joseph S. Hyde, Attorney at law; E. S. Townsend adv. a stray colt.

FEBRUARY 27, 1835 - No items copied
MARCH 6, 1835
H. K. Jerome has been appointed Master and Examiner in Chancery by the Governor and confirmed by the Senate.
Capt. Clark of the ship, Washington, reports Feb. 26, 1835, that Edward B. Saultenstall, fell from its royal top-mast head, off Cape Horn and was lost. Saultenstall came to Hudson and shipped with Morgan L. Bingham of Palmyra; he was b. in New York, lived at Geneva and by trade was a book-binder.
Adv.: T. N. and J. S. Eggleston, admns. of Thomas Eggleston, announce an auction; D. Tingley offers a tavern stand for sale; John G. Crowl loses a pocketbook and $123.00.

MARCH 13, 1835
The traders of Palmyra hold a meeting and agree to close their stores during the funeral of Ovid Lovell, in respect to his memory.
Married: March 13, 1835, in Palmyra, M. T. Rollin Robinson late of Palmyra and Celestia Corbett.
Died: March 11, 1835, Ovid Lovell, ae 45 yrs.
Died: March 6, 1835, at Ransomville, Henry Clapp, ae 26 years.
Adv.: Foster [Samuel], Clapp [Otis], & [Philo] Durfee - dry goods.

MARCH 20, 1835
Adv.: A. E. Havens - dry goods

MARCH 27, 1835

Married: March 13, 1835, at Palmyra, Augustus Heacox and Mrs. Ann Hibbard.

Died: March 5, 1835, in Hollidaysburgh, PA, Capt. Simon Disbrow, ae 43 yrs., his wife and child.
[Unclear whether wife and child died or if they survived him. ed.]

APRIL 3, 1835 - no items copied.

APRIL 10, 1835

John Colvin, of Macedon hung himself April 9th; he bought a 400 acre farm in Marion and finally sold it and bought old place at a loss.

Married: April 8, 1835, Levi Warner and Ann Jagger, all of Palmyra.

J. Williams & Co. (James Williams & Pelitiah West) dissolve, April 9, 1835; Pomeroy Tucker and George W. Cuyler, as P. Tucker & Co. have transferred their entire interest in the establishment of the Wayne Sentinel to Festus A. Goldsmith, by whom, as sole proprietor, it will hereafter be conducted.

APRIL 17, 1835 - No items copied.

APRIL 24, 1835

Mr. B. Harding speaks on stenography before Young Men's Society.

The Rhinoceros exhibited at Palmyra in 1834, d. recently; it was the only one in the United States.

Died: April 2, 1835, at Macedon, Capt. Thomas Stimpson, ae 64 yrs.

MAY 1, 1835

Married: April 27, 1835, in Walworth, Rufus Sweeting, of Paris, [Oneida Co.], NY and Lucy Tucker of Walworth.

Died: April 24, 1835, in Canandaigua, Chauncey H. Coe, ae 40 years.

Died: April 19, 1835, in Batavia, Gen. Ethan B. Allen, ae 48 years.

Harvey Cobb adv. a stray horse.

MAY 8, 1835

A society was formed for the improvement of sacred music, "The Palmyra Musical Society"; Daniel Tuttle, Pres.; John H Gilbert, V. P.; Joseph Hyde, Sec.; Josiah Francis, Treas.; Robert W. Smith, Librarian.

Died: April 30, 1835, in Macedon, Emma Lancaster, ae 15 years.

Adv.: S. Cole - select school at the Stone School House; R. C. Jackson - dry goods; buys out Eddy Clark & Co.

MAY 15, 1835

Died: May 9, 1835, Frederick M. Niles, son of Hiram Niles, ae 3 years.

Died: May 13, 1835, Levi Daggett, ae 67 years.

Died: May 1, 1835, at Sandy Hill, John Blaney, ae 103 years.

Adv: A. J. Grover - boots - 3 doors east of the Eagle Hotel; Grandin & Gardner - want to buy wool; William Bacon adv. a stray mare.

MAY 22, 1835
Died: May 21, 1835, in Palmyra, Hezekiah Miller, ae 83 years.
J. Williams & Co., saddlery, now Williams & Cook.

MAY 29, 1835
J. Orville Taylor, sent out by the State, will lecture on Popular Education.
Married: May 7, 1835, at Spring Hill, OH, Samuel Pease and Ann Louisa Shepherdson, late of Palmyra.
Married: May 28, 1835, at Palmyra, Cyrus Fuller and Mrs. Lucina A. Haight.

JUNE 5, 1835
Notice of Damon's hanging at Mayville, copied from the Fredonia Censor.
Adv.: Epenetus Howell and Albert A. Allen, admns. of Jonah Howell.

JUNE 12, 1835
Fourth of July Committee: Joseph Hyde, T. Hemingway, Durfee Chase. Isaac A. Beecher, Ambrose Salisbury, P. Tucker, Hiram Niles, Jehial Todd, Chris. E. Thayer, Richard S. Hendee, Henry Gardner, John L. Mason, Festus A. Goldsmith, William Gardner, Hiram P. Thayer, L. O. Godard, John H. Gilbert, Gardner Straight, Daniel Tuttle. Jeremiah Russell, George W. Cuyler, Philo Durfee, Avery E. Havens, Sutton Birdsall.
Married: May 30, 1835, at Valatie [Columbia Co., NY] Daniel H. Philip and Charlotte Baker.
Married: June 8, 1835, at Palmyra, George Redfield, of St. Joseph, M. T. [Missouri Territory?] and Julia Ann Mason.
Adv.: Buckley Weeks & Co. - Amphitheatre near the Eagle Hotel; 80 men; boxes 50c; pit 25c; boxes for 1000 ladies; circus will show at Palmyra, June 24, 1835.

JUNE 19, 1835 - no items copied.

JUNE 26, 1835
A gun the size and denomination of a six-pound carronade to be used July 4th, has been made at the steam furnace by E. Williams.
William Wilcox is appointed Marshall to take the Town census.
Dr. Villery Beer refuses $15,000 for a 189 acre farm, 1 1/2 miles west of Palmyra village; he gave $8,000 for it two years ago.
Notice: Priscilla Cadawallader, of the denomination of Friends has appointed a meeting at the Baptist Meeting House in Palmyra, for Sun. afternoon next.
Died: June 12, 1835, in Sodus, Joseph Green, age 81 yrs., a Revolutionary soldier, father of Byram Green.
Died: June 19, 1835, in Geneva, Capt. John Sheather, a Revolutionary officer.
Adv.: E. P. Lane, dentist, now with Dr. Chase on Clinton Street.

JULY 3, 1835

The carronade built by E. Williams exploded when being tested - no damage and another procured for the 4th celebration.

Williams & Cook dissolve - Williams continues the business.

Albert Chandler, formerly of Palmyra, buys an interest in The Michigan Statesman and with Henry Gilbert continues it.

Adv: N. Duggan advertises farm for sale; Exchange House for sale by B. Newton -at the foot of Canal St.; [Gardener] Straight and [David] Glossender - groceries one door east of the Franklin House.

JULY 10, 1835

July 4th address by Charles McEwen, of New York.

Married: July 10, 1835, in Marion, Stacey White and Hannah Sutton.

Died: July 7, 1835, in Macedon, Capt. James Robinson.

Died: July 4, 1835, in Walworth, Mrs. Dr. John Hinman, ae 35 years.

Died: May 22, 1835, in Branford, Upper Canada, Burdette Crothers, late of Palmyra, ae 22 yrs.

Adv.: George W. Norman - New York Paper; Associations Menagerie & Aviary Circus.

JULY 17, 1835

An act passed authorizing enlargement of the Erie Canal; 6 ft. of water - 60 ft. wide; locks 105 ft. long and 15 ft. wide.

Married: July 15, 1835, Benjamin Rockwell and Lavina B. Fenton, dau. of J. S. Fenton.

Married: July 15, 1835, Elias Richards and Matilda Barnhart.

Married: July 14, 1835, in Seneca Falls, William M. Bayard late of Palmyra and Romana Dashnell.

Married: July 11, 1835, at West Avon, Stephen Cook, late of Palmyra and Charlotte Hale.

Died: July 15, 1835, in Rochester, Abner Cole, late of Palmyra.

Died: July 11, 1835, in Palmyra, Charles B. Ford.

JULY 24, 1835

Died: July 19, 1835, in Canandaigua, Ashahel Harvey, ae 36 years.

Died: July 11, 1835, in Auburn, Harriet Augusta Barnum, ae 27 yrs., wife of Philo B. Barnum.

Adv.: C. Southwick, adv. metallic shingles - patentee.

JULY 31, 1835

Meeting called for 7/31 at the Eagle Hotel, to devise a way of getting rid of so many vagabond Negroes from the village.

A. Robb adv. for stolen horseshoes marked "A. Robb".

P. W. West & L. G. Buckley - saddlery.

AUGUST 7, 1835

Died: July 29, 1835, in Geneva, Samuel Mott, ae 38 years.

Adv.: H. R. Willcox - land for sale.

AUGUST 14, 1835
Foster, Clapp & Durfee, dissolve; Clapp & Hathaway - merchants where G. S. Ely was opposite the Eagle Hotel.

AUGUST 21, 1835
Died: Aug. 18, 1835, in Palmyra, Mrs. Susan Sexton, ae 37 yrs., wife of Pliny Sexton.
Died: Aug. 12, 1835, in Palmyra, Miss Sarah Tingley, dau. of Daniel Tingley, ae 18 years.
Died: July 14, 1835, in Natchez (MI), George Aiken, ae 22 yrs., late of Auburn [Cayuga Co.].
Died: in Cleveland [OH or Oswego Co., NY?], Harriet D. Sloane, dau. of Douglas W. Sloane, ae 18 years.

AUGUST 28, 1835
Census of Palmyra village taken by Mr. Willcox, as marshall; males - 690; females -667; colored - 47; total -1404 people.
George Hickely, of Marion, hung himself Aug. 21, 1835.

SEPTEMBER 4, 1835
Married: Sept. 2, 1835, in Macedon, Jacob Robins and Barbara Crater, of Arcadia.
Died: Sept. 2, 1835, Helen Augusta Pomeroy, ae 26 mos., dau. of George E. Pomeroy.
Adv.: Dr. S. C. Parsons - dentist at Mr. Nicholas' High School Boarding House; S. & T. T. Birdsall (Bros.)-hats.

SEPTEMBER 11, 1835
Sept. 8, 1835: William Spear of Macedon hung himself.
Died: Sept. 4. 1835, at Palmyra, Mrs. Margaret Fitzsimmons, wife of John Fitzsimmons.

SEPTEMBER 18, 1835
Van Buren Point at Dunkirk, is laid out into lots for sale.
Married: Aug. 30, 1835, Henry Lewis and Harriet Nickerson, both of Penfield [Monroe Co.].
Married: Aug. 12, 1835: at Palmyra, Calvin Powers, and Maria Emeline Corey, both of Farmington.
Married: Aug. 13, 1835, at Macedon, John Wicks and Sarah Hoag.
Married: Aug. 13, 1835, at Riga, Robert Pomeroy and Elizabeth Rogers.
Married: Aug. 9, 1835, in Auburn, John Williams, Jr. and Harriet B. Martin.
Married: Aug. 9, 1835, Chipman P. Turner and Louisa Bush.
Married: Aug. 3, 1835, William Maltby and Delia W. Chapman.
Died: July 22, 1835, in Coldwater, MI, Job Barnhart, late of Macedon.
Adv.: Cuyler & Godard - fish; Henry Snyder adv. a stray cow.

SEPTEMBER 25, 1835
Married: Sept. 23, 1835, in Palmyra, Abram Martin and Esther Chadwick.

Married: Sept. 19, 1835, Joseph Van Duzer and Mrs. Sarah McMellen.

Married: Sept. 17, 1835, in Geneva, M. W. Williams and Caroline Tippets.

Married: Sept. 20, 1835, in Rochester, Burdette Cruthers, late of Palmyra and Irena Springer of Marion. (His death was reported last July) [?].

Adv.: J. D. Everingham - executors sale.

OCTOBER 2, 1835

Sheriff sells out William G. Gardner's store at the corner of Canal and Market St.

John Kellogg of Plymouth, MI, late of Palmyra, advertises 60 to 100 lots for sale; settling Michigan fast.

CENSUS OF PALMYRA: Statistics of this town for the year ending 1 July 1835: Males - 1676; females - 1649; militia - 338; voters - 680; aliens - 89; colored - 49; married females under 45 yrs. - 343; unmarried females from 16-45, 356; unmarried females over 16 -699; marriages - 21; male births - 58; female births -41; male deaths - 39; female deaths - 28; total 3325, 101 less than the census of 1830. From 1825- 1830 population increased by 813, so think something is wrong in the census

Married: Sept. 29, 1835, in Palmyra, Charles Lee, son of Joshua Lee, of Penn Yan and Mary M. Hall, eldest dau. of Ambrose Hall.

Married: Sept. 24, 1835, by Rev. Merritt, James Reeves and Caroline Sanford, dau. of Luther Sanford, all of this town.

Died: Sept. 18, 1834, in Ithaca, [Tompkins Co.], David Woodcock, ae 50 years.

Died: Aug. 9, 1835 in Auburn [Cayuga Co.], Joshua Driscoll, formerly of Palmyra, ae 34 years.

OCTOBER 9, 1835

An old man, Mr. North, was stabbed in the groin at Palmyra, Oct. 3rd - not too serious.

Married: Oct. 5, 1835, at Palmyra, Martin Butterfield, of Sexton & Butterfield, and Nancy May, of Westminster, VT.

Died: Oct. 5, 1835, Clarissa Thayer, 4th dau. of Joel Thayer.

Died: Oct. 8, 1835, in Palmyra, Mrs. Elizabeth Duggan, ae 81 years.

Adv.: Mr. Benedict, writing teacher - in upper room of Hendee's bldg. opposite the Bank; Leonard & Linnell succeed L. O. Godard.

OCTOBER 16, 1835

Draper Allen and Henry Gardner, dissolve partnership Oct. 14, 1835.

Died: Oct. 3, 1835, in Perrysburg, OH, Thomas Rogers, late of this town, ae 75 years.

OCTOBER 23, 1835

Married: Oct. 20, 1835, Morgan Robinson and Lucy R. Booth, both of Macedon.

Married: Oct. 20, 1835, at the Eagle Hotel, by Elder Henry V. Jones, Joseph Harris, of Rochester and Lucinda Harris, of Marion.

Married: Oct. 14, 1835, in Rochester, George Smith and Miss Sophia Hoffman.

OCTOBER 30, 1835

Married - Oct. 26, 1835, in Palmyra, Samuel W. Osborne and Ann Goldsmith.

Married: Oct, 18, 1835, in Walworth, Abner Tucker and Ann Asa.

Married: October 6, 1835, in Canandaigua, Stephen P. Seymour, merchant of Erie, PA, to Almira Norton, of Canandaigua.

NOVEMBER 6, 1835

Married: Oct. 29, 1835, in Palmyra, Enoch Cosart and Caroline Osborne.

Died: Sept. 19, 1835, in St. Catherine's [Ont.], Mrs. Maria Buel, wife of Rev. A. K. Buell.

NOVEMBER 13, 1835

Cooper Culver, East Palmyra - 15 onions = (one) peck.

Married: Nov. 19, 1835, in Canandaigua, Thomas Neele and Laura A. Wolcott, of Canandaigua.

Adv.: Sydney S. Durfee & Co. and E. S. Townsend & Co., dissolve. Edward S. Townsend becomes a merchant.

NOVEMBER 20, 1835

Thanksgiving Proclamation calls for celebration on Dec. 10, 1835.

Adv.: Drs. Hoyt and May succeed George E. Pomeroy.

NOVEMBER 17, 1835

The Eagle Hotel caught fire on the morning of Nov. 24th and gutted the interior of the garret.

DECEMBER 4, 1835 No news reported.

No news reported December 11, or 18, 1835.

DECEMBER 25, 1835

Dr. White's farm, partly in the village, sold for $118.00 per acre.

Married: Dec. 7, 1835, David McNiel, Judge of Ontario Co. to Sarah Young.

JANUARY 1, 1836

Contains lists of advertisers from 1835.

JANUARY 8, 1836

An elegant hotel to be erected on the site of the present Eagle Hotel.

Married: Jan. 2, 1836, in Farmington, Mr. Lilly Stafford and Susan Patch.

Died: Jan. 7, 1836. Mrs. Margaret Southworth.

Died: Jan. 1, 1836, at Macedon, Stephen Putnam, ae 47 years.

JANUARY 15, 1836

Snow storm began Jan. 8th and raged for four days; snow 4 to 5 ft. deep.

Married: Jan. 4, 1836, at Manchester, Alvenzo Tanner of Palmyra and Mary Wentworth of Walworth.

Died: Jan. 9, 1836, Margaret Todd, ae 19 years.

Died: Jan. 12, 1836, Nathan Parshall, ae 70 years, an early settler.
Died: Jan. 14, 1836, William Rogers, Sr., ae 82 yrs.; a pioneer from Rhode Island.
Died: Jan. 10, 1836, Charles McEwen, in New York. He visited a dau. in Palmyra in June and July.

JANUARY 22, 1836
Died: Jan. 19, 1836, Deborah Southworth, of Palmyra.

JANUARY 29, 1836 - no items copied.
FEBRUARY 5, 1836
The blacksmith shop of Alanson Sherman on Fayette St., burned Jan. 29th with its contents.
Married: Feb. 2, 1836, Philo Robinson and Eunice Straight.
Married: Jan. 27, 1836, Gilbert Sherman of Arcadia and Hannah Rowley.
Married: Jan. 27, 1836, at Northville, MI, Norman C. Baker and Harriet Robinson of Manchester.

FEBRUARY 12, 1836
Adv.: August Hard - marble factory on upper Main St.
Married: Feb. 11, 1836, in Palmyra, Caleb Van Huzen and Catherine Jackson, dau. of R. C. Jackson.
Died: Suddenly, 36, Peletiah West, ae 43 yrs., elder of the Presbyterian Church.

FEBRUARY 19, 1836
Proposals to be submitted for building the Palmyra Hotel... s/: C. Jackson, T. Rogers; B.Butler, and H. K. Jerome.
A mob at the Holland Land Co. office, at Mayville [Chautauqua Co.], destroyed the building, Feb. 6, 1836.
Married: Feb. 14, 1836, in Macedon, Daniel F. Rush, of Farmington and Mary Ann Lancaster.
Adv.: James Jenner buys out Mr. Lakey - cabinet ware rooms; A. P. Crandall and Daniel Palmer wants accounts settled.

MARCH 4, 1836
The interest of F. A. Goldsmith in this paper has been transferred to Jacob H. Bortles. Mar. 1, 1836.
The house of Samuel Sherman, in Marion burned Feb. 19, 1836 - a loss of $600-$800; his mother was badly burned in the fire and died soon after.
Married: Feb. 18, 1836, in Palmyra, by the Rev. Mr. Lucky, Rev. (?) Carleton and Jane Sherman.
Married: Feb. 25, 1836, in Palmyra, by Rev. Moore, Abraham Woodbeck and Mary Ann Duer.
Married: Feb. 25, 1836, in Palmyra, Asher B. Webster and Susan Duer, all of Palmyra.
Married; Feb. 19, 1936, in Lyons, William F. Ashley and Eliza Jane Denton.
Married: Feb. 28, 1836, in Ontario, Alvah J. Atwood and Mary Northrup, dau. of R. K. Northrup.
Married: Mar. 2, 1836, in Palmyra, Marcellus J. Godard and Eliza M. Woodward, dau. of William Woodward.
Married: Feb. 25, 1836, in Branchport, Robert B. Wheeler, and Hannah Doolittle, of Penn Yan.
Died: March 1, 1836, in Palmyra, Catherine Fenton, ae 18 yrs., third dau. of Joseph S. Fenton.

Died: Feb. 22, 1836, in Palmyra, Mrs. Zenas Foster.
Died: March 3, 1836, in Palmyra, Elizabeth Thayer, wife of Smith Thayer and dau. of Stephen Durfee, ae 37 years.
Adv.: Tripp & Thompson - tailors; A. P. Crandall and Daniel Polhamus adv. for claims; Susannah Durfee has farm for sale; Oliver Grow lost a pocket-book.

MARCH 11, 1836
Published Fridays by Jacob H. Bortle.
Married: March 10, 1836, Christopher D. Thayer and Prudence Rogers.
Married: March 8, 1836, in Sodus, Nelson D. Young and Achsah M. Kingsley.
Married: March 11, 1836, in Ontario, William A. Peckham and Lydiaette Chapin.
Married: March 21, 1836, in Marion, Joseph Corey and Caroline Jackson of Walworth.
Adv. P. A. Parnell will give lectures on phrenology at the Eagle Hotel.

MARCH 18, 1836
Married: March 9, 1836, in Lyons, William E. Whitney and Harriet B. Moore.
Married: March 17, 1836, in Waterloo, Henry C. Swift and Mary Swift.

MARCH 25, 1836
The Palmyra Band will give a concert Tues. evening, Mar. 31 at the old Presbyterian Meeting house. 25c adm.
Married: March 23, 1836, by Rev. Mr. Barrel, Nathaniel Johnson of Manchester and Ann Sax, of Greenfield.
Adv.: Dr. J. D. Delamater and H. N. Loomis dissolve partnership.

APRIL 1, 1836
George W. Cuyler, collector of tolls and Zebulon Reeves, Supt. of Canal.
Lemuel Spear, of Macedon, hung himself March 14, 1836.
Adv.: D. Hotchkiss and I. Laker, jewelers.

APRIL 8, 1836
March 25, 1836, the blacksmith shop of Charles Chase was burned - $1000 loss.
Adv.: Jarvis Barrows - tailor, 2nd bldg. west of bank.

APRIL 15, 1836
Adv.: F. A. Goldsmith wants settlement; Fobes Southworth adv. for claims against Margaret Southworth, deceased.
Married: April 14, 1836, in Macedon, Timothy D. Jackson of Palmyra and Elizabeth C. Carpenter, dau. of M. Carpenter.

APRIL 22, 1836
Adv.: T. Chase [teaches] penmanship, corner of Market and Canal st.

Married: April 11, 1836, at Addison [Steuben Co.], William M. Fenton and Adelaide S. Birdsall, oldest dau. of Hon. James Birdsall.
Married: April 17, 1836, in Penfield, George Boynton, of Walworth, and Sarah Hibner.
Married: April 16, 1836, in Palmyra, by Isaac E. Beecher, Esq., Chester Purdy and Mariah Bradley.
Married: April 21, 1836, at Macedon, Ira Horton and Ruth Spear of Macedon.

APRIL 29, 1836
Adv.: Miss E. Bradbury - milliner
Married: April 21, 1836, Davis Johnson and Mrs. Case, of Manchester.
Married: April 28, 1836, Wilson Beckwith, and Mary J. Post, both of Palmyra.
Married; April 28, 1936, in Williamson, Shadrach Hildreth and Laura Culver.

MAY 5, 1836
George W. Cuyler and E. P. Godard dissolve.
Peter Doney's five year old boy was burned in the fire place on Sat. and d. Mon., May 2, 1836.
Married: May 5, 1836, in Palmyra, Morey Goodell and Charlotte Hall.
Married: May 1, 1836, in Marion, Abiah Angell and Lucy Parker.
Adv.: Mrs. Reed - millinery; Miss Shaw - dress making.

MAY 13, 1836
Married: May 5, 1836, in Canandaigua, F. C. Buckley of Walworth and Louisa Delano of Canandaigua.
Married: May 12, 1836, in Macedon, Stephen C. Carpenter and Ambaline Aldrich.

MAY 20, 1836
Died: in Pittsford, Chauncey Porter, ae 58 years.
Adv.: James Johnson's coat left at E. P. Lane's tavern.

MAY 27, 1836
Married: May 24, 1836, in Zion Church, by Rev. Orange Clark, George H. Mumford of Rochester and Ann Elizabeth Hart, dau. of Truman Hart.

JUNE 3, 1836
Married: May 25, 1836, in Detroit, George C. Bates and Susan DeWitt, dau. of Simon DeWitt.

JUNE 10, 1836
Died: in Vienna [Oneida Co.], Mrs. Hetty Davis, wife of Dr. James Davis, and eldest dau. of Dr. John Delamater, of Palmyra, ae 34 years.
Adv.: Buell & Robbins - marble shop at Main & Fayette St.; D. G. Ely has a farm for sale.

JUNE 17, 1836

Three priests belonging to the Mormon sect, passed through Palmyra two days since. Who do you guess they were? They belong to old neighbor Smith, the money digger, father of Joe, the Mormon prophet. The boys were on their way to Boston to preach to the unenlightened.

Died: June 9, 1836, in Williamson, Mrs. Sarah Fairbanks, relict of the late, Rev. Eleazer Fairbanks, ae 77 yrs. She had been insane for 30 yrs. until the last 11 mos. when she seemed alright again.

Adv.: A. Tanner: baths formerly H. Niles Place; William A. Delavan, Eagle Circus on Canandaigua St.

JUNE 24, 1836

Joseph S. Fenton gives Wayne Sentinel Editor some strawberries.

JULY 1, 1836

Died: John C. Chapman, son of William Chapman, ae 7 years.

JULY 8, 1836

Married: July 7, 1836, George Lard and Eveline Hubbard.
Died: July 7, 1836 in Manchester, William Raynear, ae 83 years.

JULY 15, 1836

Died: Dr. Levi Ward, late of Walworth, ae 67 yrs.; [left?] wife and four daughters.

JULY 22, 1836

Charles Caldwell, of Jamestown [Chautauqua Co.] was shot and robbed of $900, at Albion.
Married: July 21, 1836, William Howard and Ann Phelps, all of this town.

JULY 29, 1836

Palmyra Manufacturing Co. - $30,000 of stock to be sold at $50.00 a share. Truman Hart, Truman Heminway and George W. Cuyler will distribute the stock.

P. Durfee & Co. have erected a rope manufactory at Black Rock, more extensive than any perhaps in the U. S., 100 ft. long - 60' x 30 'at one end and 28' x 28" at the other. [Employs?] 50 men.

Died: July 27, 1836, Harriet Elizabeth Bortles, infant dau. of J. H. Bortles.
Died: July 27, 1836, Louisa Billings, dau. of William Billings, ae 35 years.

AUGUST 5, 1836

Married: July 31, 1836, in Palmyra, Moses Cook, of Phelps and Roxina Carlow, of Hopewell.
Died: July 28, 1836, at Ashtabula [OH], Miss Sarah Booth, late of Palmyra.
Married: Aug. 2, 1836, in Macedon, Harmon Griswold, of Palmyra to Emily Spear.

AUGUST 12, 1836

On Aug. 1, 1836, the Railroad from Schenectady to Albany was opened - a train with 18 coaches and two baggage cars and two engines.

Died: In this village yesterday afternoon, Mr. Jacob H. Bortles, after a short but severe illness, ae 28 yrs.; leaves a wife, mother and brother; funeral Sat. a.m. at 10 o'clock.

AUGUST 19, 1836

The afflictive event announced last week having deprived this paper of it its editor and publisher, it remains undetermined upon the future management of the same will devolve. It is expected that the necessary arrangements in regard to this contingency will be effected in a few days. In the meantime, the paper will continue to be regularly issued as heretofore.

Married: Aug. 17, 1836, Hiram Baker, of Ohio, and Catherine Hagaman of Macedon.

Married: Aug. 18, 1836, in Benton [Yates Co.], Freeman Soule and Mariah Slaughter.

Died: Aug. 14, 1836, Mary Ann Millard, age 8 yrs., dau. of Asahel Millard.

Died: Aug. 18, 1836, John Groves, ae 39 years.

AUGUST 26, 1836

The printing establishment connected with the Wayne Sentinel newspaper together with the Palmyra Bookstore, belonging to the estate of Jacob H. Bortles, deceased, are offered for sale by Theron R. Strong and Francis Bortles, admns. Aug. 26, 1836.

A. Tanner is reported as an innkeeper at Palmyra.

Married: Aug. 18, 1836, in Perry [Wyoming Co.], Mortimer N. Birchard and Louisa J. Gregg, late of Palmyra.

Married: Aug. 21, 1836, in Palmyra, Paul Phelps and Polly Drake.

Adv. Samuel Clark - dyeing.

SEPTEMBER 2, 1836

The Wayne Sentinel is now published every week for the benefit of the estate of Jacob H. Bortles, deceased by the Administrators.

Married: Sept. 1, 1836, in Palmyra, Joseph Kellogg and Adeline Goodwin.

Married: Sept. 1, 1836, in Palmyra, Myron Sickles and Harriet M. Salley.

Adv.: House of J. H. Bortles for rent by F. Bortles.

SEPTEMBER 9, 1836

Died: Sept. 6, 1836, in Palmyra, Cornelia Jackson, ae 3 yrs., infant of S. Jackson.

SEPTEMBER 16, 1836

Balloon ascension in Rochester; humbug; later took place.

SEPTEMBER 23, 1836

Married: Sept. 15, 1836, in Macedon, Charles M. L. Andrews and Leah Mallory of Macedon.

Married: Sept. 15, 1836, in Farmington, Jesse Balcom of Palmyra and Martha Ann Reed of Farmington.
Married: Sept. 15, 1836, in Farmington, William Balcom of Palmyra and Rhoda Reed.
Adv.: L. W. Post & Co.

SEPTEMBER 30, 1836
Married: Sept. 28, 1836, William Siverson, and Catherine Grove, both of Walworth.
Married: Sept. 21, 1836, Rensselear Cobb and Mary Gibson.
Died: Sept. 29, 1836, Mrs. Eliza Godard, wife of M. J. Godard and dau. of William Woodward, ae 25 years.

OCTOBER 7, 1836
Married: Oct. 5, 1836, John W. Cromwell, a merchant of Fishkill Landing , Dutchess Co.], and Miss Louisa Brumfield, dau. of A. D. Brumfield, of Palmyra.

OCT0BER 14, 1836
Railroad Convention held at Lyons Oct. 3, 1836; Young Men's County Convention held at Lyons, Oct. 1, 1836.
Archer Galloway sent to prison for three years for fraud.
Married: Oct. 13, 1836, at Palmyra, Caleb C. Church of Lockport and Chastina A. Fisher, of Newark.
Married: Oct. 5, 1836, at Geneva, Josiah J. Fenton, of Buffalo, and Frances R. Conklin, of Geneva.
Died: Oct. 5, 1836, in Palmyra, Mrs. Lucy Durfee, widow of the late Abel Durfee, ae 35 years.
John Groves adv. stray sheep.

OCTOBER 21, 1836
October 17, 1836, the Bank of Lyons began operations.
Married: Oct. 25, 1836, at Manchester, Capt. Peter B. Salpaugh and Sabrina Bird, dau. of John Bird.
Married: Oct. 12, 1836, at Macedon, Lewis Robinson and Mary Hall, dau. of James Hall.
Married: Oct. 13, 1836, Lester O. Godard and Mabel Robinson, dau. of Bartlett Robinson.
Married: Oct. 19, 1836, in Palmyra, Alfred B. Kinney and Harriet Bennett.
Married: Oct. 19, 1836, at East Palmyra, Henry Miles and Hannah Clark.

OCTOBER 28, 1836 - No items copied.
NOVEMBER 4, 1836
Polling places: Stone school house near East Palmyra; school house near Paul Goldsmith's; Asa Lilly's tavern, and Higby's Hotel all day the 3rd day.
Palmyra's Young Men's Society begins again, R. S. Hendee, Secretary.
Married: Nov. 11, 1836, at Palmyra, Joel Foster and Mary Jessup, dau. of Henry Jessup.
Married: Oct. 23, 1836, at Brooklyn, NY, O. Henry Spencer and Diana Williams.
Married: Oct. 30, at Butler, Eron N. Thomas and Lucy Ann Davis, dau. of Paul H. Davis.

Died: Nov. 1, 1836, in Albany, Charles Knower, son of Benjamin Knower, ae 21 yrs., brother-in-law and Private Secretary to Governor Marcy.

Died: Oct. 22, 1836, in Newark, Louisa Miller, wife of Joseph A. Miller, ae 32 years.

NOVEMBER 11, 1836

Nelson Lapham, one mile north of Palmyra, loses house.

Died: Nov. 11, 1836, in Marion, Amasa Hall, aged 62 years.

NOVEMBER 18, 1836

Died: Nov. 11, 1836, at Palmyra, Amasa Miner, age 81 years; served 7 years in the Revolutionary War, a native of New London [CT].

Died: Nov. 15, 1826, at Palmyra, Daniel Crandall, ae 50 years.

ADV.: Clapp, Hathaway & (Gilbert H.) Moore; George Monroe adv, a stray mare; James Hickey - a house and lot.

NOVEMBER 25, 1836

Married: Nov. 24, 1836, Simeon Dennis and Julia Ann Capron, both of Manchester.

Married: Nov. 20, 1836, at Palmyra, Marvin Allen and Mary Gardner, both of Farmington.

Died: Nov. 23, 1836, Ralph N. Hotchkiss ae 10 yrs. 5 months, a child of David Hotchkiss.

DECEMBER 2, 1836

Married: Nov. 27, 1836, in Palmyra, Moses Day and Matilda Fisher.

Died: Nov. 19, 1836, in Macedon, Calvin W. Stoddard, ae 35 years.

DECEMBER 9, 1836

E. P. Godard & Co. buy Yellow Mills of Edward Birdsall; Leonard & Linnell dissolve partnership.

DECEMBER 16, 1836

Richard T. Mead, of Macedon, fell on the ice with a sharp axe in his hand and was horribly cut; he d. Dec. 12th, aged 50 yrs.; he came from Dutchess Co.

Stillman Jackson, as a rifle maker becomes noted for his rifles - one in particular in gold and silver; he has a shop near the foot of Market St.

Married: Dec. 15, 1836, in Williamson, Philip Palmer of Macedon and Lucinda Potter, of Williamson.

Married: Dec. 15, 1836, Noah Palmer, Jr. and Louisa Davenport, both of Macedon.

Died: Dec. 15, 1836, at Palmyra, Israel Mabee, of Glen [Montgomery Co.], NY. ae 35 yrs., was on his way to Rochester by stage when taken sick; burial at Palmyra.

DECEMBER 23, 1836 - no items copied.
DECEMBER 30, 1836

Married Dec. 29, 1836, Capt. Alden Barker, of Rochester, and Mrs. Fidelia Barnhart, a dau. of Aretus Lapham.

Married: Dec. 29, 1836, at the Friends Meeting House in Farmington, Hiram Willits and Lydia R. Lapham, both of Macedon.

Died: Dec. 29, 1836 at Palmyra, Robert Foster, son of Cyrus Foster, ae 25 years.

JANUARY 6, 1837

Theron R. Strong and F. Bortles, as administrators of Jacob H. Bortles, deceased, sell Wayne Sentinel and printing establishment, to Henry Spencer and William M. M. Myers, Dec. 31, 1836.

Married: Jan. 4, 1837, in Palmyra, Abraham Walker and Mrs. Betsey Newton, both of Farmington.

JANUARY 13, 1837 - no items copied.

JANUARY 20, 1837

Married: Jan. 12, 1837, in Palmyra, Abram Norris and Cynthia Horton, dau. of Samuel T. Horton.

Married: Jan. 12, 1837, in Macedon, John Ketchum and Alma Tedman.

Adv.: 25 village lots for sale in Michigan by T. Heminway, auctioneer.

JANUARY 27, 1837

Married: Jan. 24, 1837, Daniel Greenvault, of Lockport and Mary Price, of Farmington.

FEBRUARY 3, 1837

Pliny Sexton criticizes Dr. Munro's preparation for teeth.

FEBRUARY 10, 1837

Dr. Munro answers Pliny Sexton and furnishes recommendations.

Adv.: Christopher C. Hyde - dentist.

FEBRUARY 17, 1837

Hotckkiss & Lake, dissolve partnership.

Married: Feb. 14, 1837, William R. Spear of MI and Maria A. Foster, dau. of Cyrus Foster.

Married: Feb. 9, 1837, in Pultneyville, William Palmer and Pamelia Heath, of Penfield [Monroe Co.].

Died: Phebe Gurney, ae 14 yrs., only dau. of Thomas W. Gurney.

FEBRUARY 24, 1837

Married: Feb. 22, 1837, Caleb Thompson and Lydia S. Godard.

Married: Feb. 22, 1837, in Vienna, [Oneida Co., NY], William D. Wylie of Walworth and Mrs. Eliza Ann Lewis.

Adv.: L. W. Post & Co. - stone ware.

MARCH 3, 1837

Died: Feb. 1, 1837, in Ann Arbor [MI], Delia Hart Thayer, ae 10 yrs. 11 mos., only child of Charles and Mary Ann Thayer, late of Palmyra.

MARCH 10, 1837

Died: March 2, 1837, in East Palmyra, Jane Allen, only child of Joseph and Sophia K. Allen, ae 1 yr. 9 months.

Died: March 4, 1837, at Palmyra, Julia Maria Strong, ae 8 mos., dau. of T. R. Strong.

Adv.: J. K. Merrill - chair factory.

MARCH 17, 1837

The Flouring Mills at Manchester burned, Mar. 12th, 10 or 15,000 bu. of wheat, 300 bbls. of flour destroyed; a distillery nearby suffered a loss of $50 - $80,000 - no insurance.

Married: March 15, 1837, John Beal and Melissa Sanford, both of this town. [Palmyra]

Died: Feb. 23, 1837, at Gambier, OH, by Rev. Nelson E. Spencer, Principal of the Senior Dept. of Grammar School. of Kenyon College, formerly asst. teacher in Palmyra Academy, ae 25 years.

MARCH 24, 1837

Col. Durfee Chase was elected Brig. Gen. of the 24th Brigade Infantry of NY State Militia at a meeting in Canandaigua March 18, 1837.

Married: March 16, 1837, Almond Galloway and Celestia A. Knowles, of East Palmyra.

Adv. E. M. Klapp has farms for sale.

MARCH 31, 1837

James M. Mott is appointed Postmaster at Macedon Centre [replacing] B. T. Hoxie who resigned.

Married: March 27, 1837, Chauncey Osborn and Deborah P. Haver, all of this town.

Married: March 16, 1837, Capt. Ammi C. Smith, of Walworth and Lydia Eddy of Macedon.

Died: March 24, 1837, at Macedon, Paul Sheffield, ae 75 yrs, a Revolutionary soldier; he came here in 1818.

Died: March 27, 1837, in Palmyra, Mrs. Margaret Hallhimer, ae 81 years.

Died: March 1, 1837, in Ohio, Jeremiah Bingham, late of Palmyra, ae 45 yrs.

Adv.: James Macown, adv. his wife, Sally Macown.

APRIL 7, 1837

Letter for Jacob Van Alstine is at postoffice;

Eldridge Havens appointed inspector of beef and pork.

Died: April 4, 1834, Mrs. Abigail Goldsmith, ae 23 yrs., wife of Festus Goldsmith.

APRIL 14, 1837

Frederick Smith appointed as a loan commissioner;

J. D. Hayward appointed inspector of beef and pork.

APRIL 21, 1837

A. E. Havens sells out his business.

Married: April 18, 1837, by Rev. H. K. Ware, Alfred Hubbard and Lydia P. Shove, all of Palmyra.

Adv.: Miss Lemmon [conducts] a private school in the place lately occupied by Miss Wallingford; D. S. Aldrich continues A. E. Havens business; Henry Gardner - leather (for sale?); George Newland, loses an apprentice, Simeon Orvil Hibbard; Grandin & Gardner dissolve partnership.

APRIL 28, 1837 - issue missing

MAY 5, 1837

Benjamin Billings, Jr. has been appointed postmaster at Walworth.

MAY 12 AND MAY 13, 1837 - no items copied.

MAY 26, 1837

Married: May 20, 1837, Edward Dubois and Silvena Wolcott, both of Madison.

Married: May 17, 1837, Barnabas Adams of Williamson, and Eliza Hicks, of Palmyra.

JUNE 2, 1837

Died: May 21, 1837, Caroline Bogart, dau. of Peter J. and Susan Bogart, ae 2 yrs. 10 mos. 18 days.

JUNE 9, 1837

Committee appointees to make arrangements for July 4th celebration: Truman Heminway, George W. Cuyler, William M. Myers, William P. Nottingham, Zebulon Williams. William May Lewis Beers, Henry Spencer, Burr Butler, William F. Aldrich, J. B. Fenton, Durfee Chase, Samuel Cole, Theron R. Strong, Ambrose Salisbury, M. Smith Waters, M. W. Willcox, Edmund M. Klapp, Asahel Millard, John H. Gilbert, Stillman Jackson, S. O. Goddard, F. S. Lovell, Bailey Durfee, Joseph C. Lovett, Clemens Hathaway.

JUNE 16, 1837

A hotel being erected on the corner of Main and Fayette St., now all but completed; a steam mill is also being erected. The Zoological Institute of New York will give a circus in a lot on Fayette St., June 28th.

Married: June 4, 1837, in Palmyra, J. C. Lovett, of Hyde & Lovett, and Electa Thayer, dau. of Joel E. Thayer.

Died: June 4, , at Palmyra, Mary Elvira Sherman, ae 3 yrs. 10 mos. 6 days, dau. of Alanson Sherman.

Died: June 10, 1837, in Palmyra, Mrs. Eunice Robertson, wife of Philo Robertson, and dau. of Gardner Straight.

Died: June 9, 1837, in Palmyra, Minerva Nye Beckwith, ae 16 years.

JUNE 23, 1837

Theron Strong will deliver an oration as part of July 4th celebration.

Adv. - William H. Wheeler offers $15.00 reward for stolen harness.

JUNE 30, 1837

Directors of the Wayne Co. Bank elected: Pliny Sexton; Jareb [sic] D. Rogers; George W. Beckwith; Abraham Spear; William Willcox; Jonathan Boynton; Oliver Clark; D. Rossiter; P. H. Leach; D.G. Ely; S. Beckwith; P. W. Handy; and J. S. Fenton. Pres., George Beckwith; Cashier, J. S. Fenton; R. C. Jackson, Abner F. Lakey and Wells Anderson, inspectors.

JULY 7, 1837

Married: July 4, at Williamson, Joseph Carpenter, of Lancaster [Erie Co, NY] and Cynthia Rogers, of Williamson.

Adv.: Warren & Robbins - marble factory, succeeds Buell & Robbins.

JULY 14, 1837 - no items copied.

JULY 21, 1837

Married: July 19, 1837, at Palmyra, Charles Dozen and Rachel Cogswell, both of Michigan.

Died: July 15, 1837, in Palmyra, Mary Newland, wife of George Newland.

JULY 28, 1837

McIntyre & Dunn - three doors west of the hotel; New York Circus to be in Palmyra, Aug. 28th; adm. 50c; pit, 25c.

AUGUST 4, 1837

Died: July 28, 1837, Avery E. Havens, ae 27 yrs. of consumption.

AUGUST 11, 1837

Jack Frost visited Palmyra on August 5, 1837!

Died: Aug. 7, 1837, Jane Terry, ae 19 years.

AUGUST 18, 1837

Married: July 27, 1837, at North Ontario,, Rufus Dolbeat and Miss C. M. P. Lawrence, only dau. of Rev. A. B. Lawrence.

AUGUST 25, 1837 - no items copied.

SEPTEMBER 1, 1837

Beckwith & Ely dissolve.

Married: Aug. 24, 1837, in Williamson, Peter V. More and Maria H. Selby.

Married: Aug. 24, in Williamson, Daniel Ward and Phebe Ann Selby.

Married: Aug. 29, in Hanover, M. J. Godard and Adeline Fillmore.

SEPTEMBER 8, 1837

Sept. 6, 1837, Peter V. More hung himself in Grandin & Gardner's barn on Canal St.; the testament lay by his body turned to St. John 4:32. [But he said unto them, I have meat to eat that ye know not of.] [Note his marriage above.]

SEPTEMBER 15, 1837 - No items copied.

SEPTEMBER 22, 1837

The Wayne Sentinel will be issued on Wed. instead of Sat. hereafter; The steam Flouring mill will be in operation this fall.

The Palmyra Hotel is now completed and ready for occupancy.

Married: Sept. 10, 1837, in Ontario, Dewitt C. Norrin of Walworth and Mrs. Lucy Rood.

Philip Palmer adv. a stray cow.

SEPTEMBER 27, 1837

Married: Sept. 24, 1837, Mason D. Foster and Romina Bird, dau. of John Bird, of Manchester.

Married: Sept. 21, 19376, in Marion, Rufus Clark and Jemima Moody, of Amherst, MA.

OCTOBER 4, 1837

Married: Sept. 28, 1837, Theron G. Yoemans, merchant of Walworth, and Lydia A. Stearns, of Gorham.

OCTOBER 11, 1837 - No items copied.

OCTOBER 18, 1837

Married: Oct. 12, 1837, in Palmyra, by Rev. S. W. Wooster, P. R. Howell and Alinda Drake.

A lecture to be delivered every Sabbath evening by Rev. Wheeler I. Crane; Clapp & Hathaway sell out to Higby & Coleman.

OCTOBER 25, 1837

Adv.: [W. W.] Gordon & [Z.] Williams - groceries.

NOVEMBER 1, 1837

Married; Oct. 29, 1837, Ebenezer Davenport and Mrs. Mariam Munroe, of Macedon.

NOVEMBER 8, 1837

Married: Nov. 1, 1837, at the Friends Meeting House, Thomas W. Mead and Sarah Hoag.

Married: Nov. 2, 1837, at the Friends Meeting House, James S. Hoag and Judith Mead, all of Macedon.

NOVEMBER 15, 1837

The tavern and store owned by James Lovett and the store occupied by Benjamin Homan, of this village, 3 miles east of Penfield [Monroe Co.], burned 11/9 with a loss of $6000 with only $1275 in insurance.

Died: Oct. 26, 1837 in New York: Caius Robinson, a native of Palmyra, 2nd son of son of Dr. Gain Robinson; he went to Palmyra, MI in 1832; bur. at Palmyra Nov. 3rd. [Burial prob. in NY as funeral was 8 days after his death - time to ship the body home.]

Died: Nov. 13, 1837, Mrs. Elizabeth Woodward, wife of William Woodward, ae 51 years.

Died: Nov. 14, 1837, in Palmyra, Carlton Rogers Grandin, son of E. B. Grandin, ae 8 years.

Libeus Hammond adv. his wife, Cyntha P. Hammond.

Married: Nov. 16, 1837, at Port Glasgow, George R. Parburt and Frances Ann Cole, dau. of Abner Cole.

Thanksgiving to occur this year on Nov. 30th.

NOVEMBER 22, 1837

Married: Nov. 16, 1837, in East Palmyra, Seth F. Betts and Jane Hopkinson, by Rev. S. W. Wooster.

Adv.: A. Elemendorf (first) - Fish.

NOVEMBER 29, 1837

The Steam Mill is ready for operation; three stories high with 3 run of stone.

Adv.: David Bill - pork barrels.

DECEMBER 6, 1837

Married: Nov. 29, 1837 at the Friends Meeting House, Elihu Durfee and Maria Howland.

DECEMBER 13, 1837

(Russell) Galloway & (Nelson W.) More - dissolve.

Died: Dec. 9, 1837, in Palmyra, Frances Woodward, dau. of William Woodward, ae 19 years.

DECEMBER 20, 1837

Married: Dec. 6, 1837, Durant Rushmore and Eliza Ann Culver, of Macedon.

Adv.: C. W. White - dry goods at #4 Exchange Row.

DECEMBER 27, 1837

Died: Monday, Dec. 25, 1837, Mary Eliza, daughter of Robert and Mary Ann Withers, of this village, aged 6 years and 4 months.

JANUARY 6, 1838

The Committee on Canada Affairs will meet at Smith's Franklin House on Jan. 8, 1838, Levi Thayer, Chairman.

Married: Jan. 6, 1838 in Macedon, Powers Aldridge and Eliza Andrus.

Married: Jan. 1, 1838, in Palmyra, J. J. Delamater and Ann S. Beckwith.

JANUARY 10, 1838

L. C. Smith is credited with running the Franklin House.

Married: Jan. 2, 1838, in Sodus, Z. Williams of Palmyra to Amanda M. Collins.

Married: Jan. 1, 1838, in Pultneyville, Valentine Hahn, Jr. and Harriet G. Selby.

Married: Jan. 4, 1838, at Williamson, William W. Rogers, and Sarah C. Throop.

Married: Jan. 3, 1838, in Ballston [Saratoga Co.], Solomon D. Hollister and Phebe Smith, dau. of D. K. Smith.

Adv.: Allyn Williams joins Burr Butler forming Butler & Williams; George Newland - music teacher.

JANUARY 17, 1838

Report of an editorial trip to Macedonville, Walworth, Ontario, Williamson, Sodus, Arcadia, and back to Palmyra.

Married: Jan. 11, 1838, Joseph Wilcox and Eliza Barrows, of the town of Palmyra.

Married: Jan. 10, 1838, Charles Allyn and Sarah C. Ally, of the town of Palmyra.

JANUARY 24, 1838

A lad found a box under the ice in the canal, containing a double barrelled gun and 107 Sovereigns ($500).

Adv.: Abram Norris, Capt. of the boat, Robert Hunter, lost a trunk.

JANUARY 31, 1838

Comment on the Palmyra Freeman paper, now in its 5th stage of existence.

Adv.: Henry Gardner wants an apprentice tanner; John Rawling offers 24 family burial plots for sale, contiguous to the burying ground in this village - inquiries to Mr. Gibson, the sexton.

FEBRUARY 7, 1838 - No items copied.

FEBRUARY 14, 1838

The Palmyra Whig & Wayne County Advertiser is the title of a paper just established in his village by the Federal party, conducted by W. N. & S. J. Cole...

The Investigator is the title of a semi-monthly periodical of 8 quarto pages which has made its appearance in our village during the past week, purporting to be published by an association of young men and edited by Anthony Bramble, Esq. To applaud virtue and condemn vice are its chief objects.

Married: Feb.8, 1838,, in Palmyra, Edward D. Wentworth and Mary McNutt, both of Manchester.

Margaret Woods advertises for her brother, John Woods.

FEBRUARY 21, 1838

Married: Feb. 20, 1838, in Palmyra, Wesley Newcomb, of Albany and Helen Post of Palmyra.

Died: Feb. 6, 1838, in Baltimore, MD, Jacob Quimby, late professor of Latin and Greek in the Academical Dept. of the University of Maryland, late of this village.

FEBRUARY 28, 1838
Pomeroy Tucker has been appointed as Postmaster for this village, in place of Mr. Willcox, who resigned.
A barn roof crushed in in the village by heavy fall of snow.
Died: Feb. 25, 1838, in Palmyra, Adoniram Wilson, ae 38 years.

MARCH 7, 1838
An anti-slavery meeting was held in Walworth.
Died: Suddenly, Feb. 22, 1838, in Williamson, Erastus Chappel.
Died: Feb. 22, 1838, Nell Alexander, an early settler.
Married: Feb. 17, 1838, in Detroit, [MI], Albert Chandler, late of Palmyra, and Eliza Frances Abbott.
Married: Feb. 17, 1838, in Batavia, B. W. C. Massett and Harriet Hart.

MARCH 14, 1838
Married: Feb. 28, 1838, in Macedon, John Lawrence and Catherine Kipp.
Married: March 11, 1838, Jacob Smith and Deborah Weeks.

MARCH 21, 1838
First Business Directory:
A. Elmemdorf - east of Wayne Co. Bank
C. W. White - 4 Exchange Row
Gordon & Williams - old stand of Z. Williams
L. W. Post - corner of Main & Market St.
S. & T. T. Birdsall - 1st door east of P. O.
Constant Terry - 2 doors w. of Collector's office
E. P. Godard - 1 door w. of Collectors Office
Hoyt & May - Main St. - sign of the Golden Mortar
Seaman & Thompson - 2 doors east of the bank
Butler & Williams - 5 doors east of P. O.
M. W. Willcox - Main St. - Sign of the Bible.
Isaac E. Beecher - on Canal, fronting foot of Market St.
J. K. Cumings - 3 doors w. of Collectors office
J. & L. Thayer - east of Collectors office
M. Ritter - Market St.
Stillman Jackson - Canal St., foot of Market St.
Henry Gardner - n. side of Canal, opp. I. E. Beecher's storehouse.
Frederick Smith - attorney, few doors w. of bank.
P. Tucker - corner of Main & Market St.
Adv.: Stephen Sanford and Daniel Russell, assignees sale - boat, etc.
William Woodward has land for sale.

The undersigned will sell at auction, the Palmyra Hotel, April 7, 1838: H K. Jerome, B. Butler, Thomas Rogers, R. C. Jackson.

MARCH 28, 1838

The partnership of Henry Spencer and William M. Myers dissolved; all books and accounts are placed in the hands of Truman Heminway for settlement. The Sentinel will hereafter be conducted by Henry Spencer.

Died: March 21, 1838, at Palmyra, Henry Fenton, 3rd son of Joseph S. Fenton, ae 18 years.

Married: March 22, 1838, at Palmyra, Azor Leflen and Emeline N. Tracy, both of Palmyra.

Adv.: Primus Leblan - barber; Benjamin T. Gregory - Plasterer; Beecher & Glossender succeeds Hiram Niles; Beecher & Drake succeeds Hiram Niles.

APRIL 4, 1838

Died: March 31, 1838, at Palmyra, Mary Ware, ae 5 mos., child of Rev. Joseph K. Ware.

Adv.: Asahel Millard - architect and builder.

APRIL 11, 1838

The election last week resulted in a triumph of Democracy.

The Palmyra Hotel was sold, Sat., last to William P. Nottingham and will soon be opened for the accomodation of the public. Adv: Henry Spencer - printer. Schedule of mails leaving Palmyra Post Office for: Newark and Lyons; Macedon & Rochester; Manchester & Canandaigua; Port Glasgow & Phelps; Marion & Williamson to Pultneyville and Walworth. The Post Office was open daily, 6 a.m. to 9 p.m. and on Sun. 8 - 9 a.m., 12 to 1 p.m. and 6 - 8 p.m. [!!!!]

APRIL 18, 1838

Miss Knowles, of Farmington, who recently married, hung herself.

Married: April 11, 1838, Isaac Howland, of Manchester and Prudence Church, of Palmyra.

APRIL 25, 1838

W. W. Gordon and Zebulon Williams - dissolve;

Description of the F. C. Brown lots (for sale).

Married: April 19, 1838, Lemuel H. Spear and Matilda Hart, dau of George Hart.

Adv.: "Lady of the Lake" is playing at the Franklin House theatre; Lyman W. Post - dry goods; Cyrus Leonard - boots and shoes.

MAY 2, 1838

Two steam packets, the SS Sirus from Cork, and the Great Western from Bristol, cross the Atlantic in 18 and 15 days, respectively; The Great Western is 234 x 58".

MAY 9, 1838

A serious accident on Mon., last, while several individuals were moving an old building from the premises of Samuel T. Horton, in the rear of the corner of Main & Fayette St., the blocking gave way and Mr. Horton, Mr. Buchanan, and Mr. Lamberton were injured. Lamberton lost the whole end of his hand.

Married: May 7, 1838, in Palmyra, Avery W. Stowell, of Syracuse, [Onondaga Co.] and Louisa Gardner, of Palmyra.

Died: May 7, 1838, in Palmyra, Mary A. Hurlburt, ae 17 years.

Died: May 1, 1838, in New York, John P. Haff, Sr., ae 69 years.

MAY 16, 1838

Adv.: Williams & Fillmore - livery.

MAY 23, 1838

Married: May 16, 1838, in Canandaigua, Amasa Hall, 2nd, of Marion to Laura A. Delance.

MAY 30, 1838

Luther Reeves advertises a stray colt.

JUNE 6, 1838

The Wayne Standard printed at Newark - being The Lyons American, David M. Keeler conducts its printing.

JUNE 13, 1838

Circus [coming] - Rockwell, Hopkins & Co. June 20, 1838.

JUNE 20, 1838

The George Washington, a 500 ton boat, burned off Silver Creek, June 16th.

Anti-slavery meeting at the Preb. Church June 27th. J. J. Thomas, Sec.

Fourth of July Committee:

George W. Cuyler	Samuel Cole	Durfee Chase
Joseph C. Lovett	Levi Thayer	V. Beers
S. Scantlin	P. Tucker	William May
Burr Butler	Constant Terry	T. Heminway
J. B. Fenton	William B. Tilden	J. J. Delamater
William Chapman	Homer B. Williams	Henry Gardner
James Jenner	E. P. Godard	Wm. F. Aldrich
Ambrose Salisbury	James Hubbell	Isaac Gardner
A. Elmendorf	Samuel B. Randall	

Wayne County Bank Directors elected June 12, 1838:

George Beckwith	Jonathan Boynton	William Willcox

J. S. Fenton	Abraham Spear	Jareb D. Rogers
Payne K. Leach	Pliny Sexton	Samuel Beckwith
Oliver Clark	David Rossiter	D. G. Ely
W. P. Handy	George Beckwith (Pres.)	

JUNE 27, 1838
S. W. Cole adv. a stray horse.

JULY 4, 1838
Adv.: Perry B. Lee - barber.

JULY 11, 1838
Died: July 5, 1838, Elizabeth Cole, widow of Samuel Cole, of Baltimore [Cortland Co., NY..or MD]

JULY 18, 1838
Died: July 14, 1838, in Farmington, Mrs. Maria Minor, consort of James Minor and only dau. of George and Betsey Spencer, of the same town. She leaves a husband and two children.
Died: July 14, 1838: Died in this village (Palmyra), Rev. Jesse Townsend, aged 73 years.

JULY 25, 1838
A four year old son of Capt. Allen, was run over on Main St., and lived but a few hours.

AUGUST 1, 1838
This paper will hereafter be issued on Friday instead of Wednesday.
Palmyra Democracy met at the Palmyra Hotel, July 23rd.: T. Heminway, Pres.; Stephen P. Jordan, V. P.; W. F. Aldrich and Caleb Van Husen, Secretaries. About 100 names appear in this issue.

AUGUST 8, 1838 - No items copied.

AUGUST 15, 1838
W. H. Cuyler, takes over the Palmyra Steam Mill of Palmyra Mfg. Co.

AUGUST 24, 1838
Died: August 6, 1838, in Indiana, Austin Capron, late of Palmyra, son of William P. Capron, of Macedon.

AUGUST 31, 1838
Palmyra High School opens Aug. 30th, under charge of Chauncey Giles, assisted in the female Dept. by Miss F. White.
Married: Aug. 15, 1838, in Michigan, George W. Pattison and Mary Ann Wright, dau. of Benjamin Wright.

Died: Aug. 29, 1838, in Palmyra, Louis M. Butterfield, son of Martin Butterfield, ae 10 months.
Died: Aug. 15, 1838, in Rochester, Mrs. Hannah Culver, wife of Cornelius B. Culver, of Macedon, ae 42 years.

SEPTEMBER 7, 1838
Married: Aug. 29, 1838, in Palmyra, by Prof. G. W. Watson, Philetus B. Spear, and Esther Jackson, dau. of R. C. Jackson.

SEPTEMBER 14, 1838
Base slander refuted: comment on George N. Williams and P. Tucker.

SEPTEMBER 21, 1838
Two boats conveying the delegates from Niagara and Monroe counties passed through Palmyra, Sept. 17th on the way to the Convention [in Albany, ed.] - 80 delegates and a band on each. Wayne Co. delegates left Monday with the Palmyra band.
Married: Sept. 13, 1838, in Lewiston [Niagara Co.], P. C. H. Brotherson and Cyntha R. Scovell, dau. of Seymour Scovell.

SEPTEMBER 28, 1838 - No items copied.
OCTOBER 5, 1838
Educational meeting held Sept. 27; committee of six to investigate schools in this village: J. S. Fenton, Robert W. Smith, Samuel Cole, George C. Jessup, T. Heminway, and Chauncey Giles.
Married: Sept. 30, 1838, William May and Elizabeth Thayer, dau. of Levi Thayer.
Died: Sept. 25, 1838, in Palmyra, Alanson Impson, ae 17 yrs., of lockjaw.

OCTOBER 12, 1838
Died: Samuel J. Cole, youngest son of the late Samuel Cole, ae 21 years.
Died: Sept. 27, 1836 [sic], in Detroit, William Myers printer, late of Palmyra, ae 28 years.
Died: Oct. 5, 1838, in Palmyra, Mary Elizabeth Norris, dau. of Abram Norris, ae 9 months.

OCTOBER 19, 1838
Married: Oct. 14, 1838, in Macedon, Philo Robinson and Jane Thomas, both of Macedon.
Married: Oct. 11, 1838, in Palmyra, George Albritt and Mary McCumber.

OCTOBER 26, 1838
Adv: Miss H. L. Putnam - ladies school in Horton's brick block.

NOVEMBER 2, 1838
Lt. William Grandin, late of Palmyra, has received the appointment of Aid-de-Camp, on the staff of Gen. Taylor of Florida.

Died: Luther Tucker, of Walworth, d. at Bloomingdale Lunatic Asylum, ae 40 years. [Date not given]

NOVEMBER 9, 1838
Married: Nov. 4, 1838, Alonzo Buckley and Catherine DeMunn, both of Walworth.

NOVEMBER 17, 1838
Joseph B. Fenton has been admitted to the bar.
A fire occurred in this village, Wed. morning last, abt. 6 a.m. which entirely destroyed the old Presbyterian Meeting House, lately used by the Baptist Soc. of this place. It was thought to have originated in the deposit of ashes in a wooden vessel; one hour saw the building leveled.
Married: Nov. 8, 1838, in Palmyra, John Smolten and Louisa Walton.
Married: Nov. 14, 1838, William Duel and Maria Garlock, both of Marion.
Died: Nov 10, 1838, Mrs. Delia Skidmore, dau. of Timothy Howland, of Dutchess Co., NY.
Died: Oct. 2, 1838, in Canandaigua, William Billings, Sr., late of the town of Palmyra, ae 55 years.
Adv: Seaman & Thompson dissolve; L. L. Seaman, barber; Miss Charlock & Co. - milliner.

NOVEMBER 24, 1838
A new line of stages has been extablished, running from Rochester to Auburn via Palmyra, Vienna, etc. instead of the old Canandaigua route, this thought being preferable on account of distance and roads. The stages began for the season on Tues. (Nov. 6) and will run daily, both ways in connection with the railroad cars at each end of the route.
Died: Nov. 29, 1838, in Palmyra, Eliza Malvina Merrill, 4th dau. of John M. Merrill, from the croup.

DECEMBER 6, 1838
Married: Dec. 1, 1838, Abram Vandine and Loretta Tinney.
Adv.: Joseph B. Fenton - attorney; Miss Benson - milliner.

DECEMBER 14, 1838
Married: Dec. 10, 1838, George Sampson and Eliza Walker, both of Palmyra.
Died: Dec. 12, 1838, in Palmyra, Arnold E. Rice, proprietor of the Bunker Hill Hotel.

DECEMBER 21, 1838 - No items copied.
DECEMBER 28, 1838 -No items copied.
JANUARY 4, 1939 - No items copied
JANUARY 11, 1839
Died: Jan. 7, 1839, in Palmyra, Mrs. Caroline Cosart, of consumption.

JANUARY 18, 1839
Married: Jan. 16, 1839, in Williamson, C. B. Wade and Esther Allen.

JANUARY 25, 1839 - No items copied.
FEBRUARY 1, 1838
A sleigh ride party from Rochester stopped at the Palmyra Hotel, Jan. 30th, consisting of two sleighs, each drawn by six horses.

FEBRUARY 8, 1839
Married: Feb. 3, 1839, in Palmyra, George Hicks and Mary Eliza Carpenter, both of Farmington.
Married; Feb. 4, 1839, in Palmyra, Samuel Adams and Lucinda McLouth, both of Farmington.
Married: Jan. 31, 1839, in Marion, Asa Briggs and Maria Dunlop.
Died: Jan. 29, 1839, Mary Ann Smith, wife of John Smith, Jr., ae 29 yrs.
Adv.: J. Friedheim & Co. - spectacles, etc.

FEBRUARY 13, 1839
CONGO - 5 ft. 2 inch high- saw and buck on shoulder usually; large family worked hard to support them - see copy of conversation printed.
History of Fredonia's supply of natural gas in this issue.
Married: Feb. 13, 1839, in Palmyra, Thomas Dickerson and Charlotte Leonard, dau. of Cyrus Leonard, of Palmyra.
Married: Feb. 5, 1839, in Athens, PA, Samuel White and Elizabeth McDuffee, of Palmyra.
Died: Feb. 6, 1839, in Williamson, Myron J. Tuttle, ae 22 years.

FEBRUARY 22, 1839
Died: Feb. 9, 1839, in town, Hannah Adams, wife of William Adams, ae 45 years.
Died: Feb. 20, 1839, in Palmyra, Mrs. A. E. Rice.

MARCH 1, 1839
At Macedon, a sheep buried alive in deep snow for two weeks, still lived.
Married: Feb. 21, 1839, at Macedon, J. W. Post and Jane A. Mott.
Died: Feb. 23, 1838, in Marion, Laura Ann Hall, wife of Amasa Hall, ae 2 days and 20 years.

MARCH 8, 1839
Married: Feb. 27, 1839, in Marion, Peter Hayner and Mrs. Kerzander Hayner.

MARCH 15, 1839 - No items copied.
MARCH 22, 1839
Died: March 21, 1839, in Palmyra, Daniel Webster Hinman, son of Elihu and Calista Hinman, ae 1 1/2 years.
Adv.: Hiram Payne has 25,000 mulberry trees for sale.[!]

MARCH 29, 1839 - No items copied.
APRIL 5, 1839
John Rossman d. of consumption, ae 72 years.

Adv.: The Palmyra Steam Mill revived - passes into hands of L. W. Post, Levi Thayer, and Constant Terry.

APRIL 12, 1839
Died: in Michigan, Mrs. Elizabeth Finch, wife of Daniel G. Finch, ae 40 years.

APRIL 19, 1839
Married: April 11, 1839, Augustus Babcock, of Rochester and Nancy S. Ford, of Palmyra.

APRIL 26, 1839
Married: April 18, 1839, in Walworth, Lorenzo Boynton and Philura Main, of Ontario.
Married: April 22, 1839, in Geneva, Martin Dunn, M. D. and Lucinda Fairbanks, dau. of Rev. Ira Fairbanks.

MAY 3, 1839
The origin of Mormonism appears on the 4th page of this edition.
Married: April 17, 1839, Jeter Jagger and Ruth Tripp.
Died: April 16, 1839, in Palmyra, Abdilla Cutter.

MAY 10, 1839
Ira Odell has been appointed Postmaster at Macedon Centre, in place of J. M. Mott, who resigned.
Married: May 1, 1839, Morgan C. Ketchum and Laura Jenks, of Farmington.
Died: March 20, 1839, Mrs. Helden [sic], wife of Thomas Brown, ae 46 years.
Adv.: Dr. A. Evans, M. D.

MAY 17, 1839
Adv.: New York Arena and Circus Co. to be in Palmyra, May 31st; Perry & Crandall - tailoring.

MAY 24, 1839
D. Hotchkiss & Co., Jewelers, take in B. R. Norton.
Died: May 16, 1839, in Marion, Caroline Rice, eldest [child?] of William and Anna Rice, ae 24 yrs. and 8 months.
Building Committee for proposed new church to be built in village of Palmyra: Stephen Spear, Samuel T. Horton, S. B. Jordan, Dennis Rogers, Samuel Palmer, and A. Sherman.

MAY 31, 1839
The office of the Wayne Sentinel, is offered for sale, the proprietor having other engagements in contemplation. This paper is the oldest in the County.

JUNE 7, 1839
An editorial appears concerning a new game, "Essex Money".
The H. H. Rockwell circus to be in Palmyra, June 28, 1839.

Died: May 30, 1839: Died James Benson, age 57 yrs.

JUNE 14, 1839

The editorial on "Essex Money" maddens some and the following stop the paper: Joseph S. Fenton, D. D. Hoyt, William May, Burr Butler and A. Williams.

Fourth of July Committee:

A. Elemendorf	O. H. Palmer	George W. Cuyler
S. B. Jordan	Samuel Cole	T. Heminway
L. G. Buckley	E. Hinman	A. D. Bromfield
Wm. H. Cuyler	Lyman Reeves	Wm. Woodward
O. B. Bingham	J. Peddie	T. R. Strong
F. Smith	Dr. Hubbell	J. C. Lovett
E. Parshall	F. Lakey	Otis Clapp
C. Leonard	H. Linnell	J. J. Delamater
Isaac Gardner	E. P. Godard	B. Randall
William F. Goodrich	William H. Southwick	

Died: June 1, 1839, in Rochester, James F. Brown, Atty., late asst. teacher in Palmyra High School.
Died: June 1, 1839, in Canandaigua, Reuben Sutherland, early settler of Ontario Co., ae 71 years.
Adv.: Assignees of Solomon Crowell; Nancy Throop adv. a stray cow.

JUNE 21, 1839

Jacob Sherman has been assigned Postmaster at East Palmyra in place of L. H. Tiffany, who resigned.
Ezra Jewell, editor of the Lyons Argus, suicided by shooting, June 17, 1839.
Mr. and Mrs. Austin and 12 year old son, upset (wagon or buggy) on way home from Palmyra, and the boy was instantly killed.

JUNE 28, 1839

Died: June 25, 1839, in Palmyra, Christopher E. Thayer, ae 32 yrs., of consumption.
C. W. Sanders New Spelling Book is recommended by: Rev. G. R. H. Shumway, pastor of the Preb. Church; C. M. Butler, rector of Zion Church; W. I. Crane, pastor of the Baptist Church; Samuel W. Wilson, Principal of Palmyra H. S.; Horace Cummings, Preceptor, of Palmyra H. S., Stephen Hyde and Isaac E. Beecher and Samuel Cole, Commmrs. of Common Schools.

JULY 5, 1839

A letter, uncalled for, is at the Macedon P. O. for Jacob Van Alstine.
William L. Hall, of Walworth, eldest son of Joel Hall, ae 30 yrs. was crushed July 4th, while attempting to bury a large rock.
Adv.: J. H. Wade - portrait painter.

JULY 12, 1839

Adv. Stephen Sanford - 3 doors east of Butler & Williams in the Rogers Block, has chairs from Auburn prison [made by the convicts?], for sale.

JULY 19, 1839

The People vs Joseph S. Fenton, cashier of the Wayne Co. Bank.

Some people oppose the 4th of July celebration and have for several years. A Committee from the four churches is named to arrange a different kind for another year: William N. Cole and James E. Walker, of the Episcopal Church; Philip Crandall and Stephen Spear from the Baptist Church; James Seeley and J. K. Cummings of the Methodist Church and J. S. Eggleston and P. W. Handy from the Presbyterian Church.

JULY 26, 1839

Miss H. L. Putnam ladies school will open again August 14th.

AUGUST 2, 1839

The following committee appointed to find a proper location and erect a suitable building for the High School in this village: T. Heminway, Stephen Hyde, Draper Allen, Edwin F. Townsend, Robert W. Smith, Stephen Spear, James Hubbell, Samuel Moore, and Otis Clapp.

Died: June 13, 1839, in Detroit, Freeman Smith, late of Ontario., ae 31 yrs.

AUGUST 9, 1839

Died: July 30, 1839, in Macedon, Ephriam Davenport, ae 28 years.

AUGUST 16, 1839

The new distillery just erected and owned by Durfee A. Sherman, at East Palmyra was destroyed by fire, Aug. 5, 1839. A $1200.00 loss.

C. Terry and George W. Cuyler dissolve.

Married: Aug. 14, 1839, in Palmyra, William E. Pickett, of Sodus and Mary Kellogg, of Palmyra.

AUGUST 23, 1839

June Titus An.?.vine & Co. Circus to be in Palmyra, August 31st.

Married: Aug. 21. 1839, John W. Drum and Miss Elizabeth Hazen, both of Manchester.

Died: Aug. 17, 1839, Mrs. Mary Goldsmith, relict of the late Festus A. Goldsmith, an early settler, ae 69 years.

AUGUST 30, 1839

The Palmyra Whig has gone to Lyons bag and baggage; The Wayne Standard, the other Whig paper ceases to exist also.

A select school for young ladies is organized with the Rev. C. M. Butler, as principal and Mrs. May S. Root (from Mrs. Willard's Female Seminary in Troy). teacher, will open Sept. 2nd, in the new building in Canandaigua St., opposite Zion Church rectory. Rev. C. M. Butler, Martin Butterfield, Levi Thayer, T. Strong, Esq., D. D. Hoyt, T. Heminway, Allyn Williams, William N. Cole, William B. Tilden, and George W. Cuyler, Trustees.

SEPTEMBER 6, 1839
The Palmyra Whig is now being published at Lyons, NY.
Adv.: E. Edmunds, has imported bucks [male sheep] for sale; Robert McKechnie wants to purchase barley at the Palmyra Brewery.

SEPTEMBER 13, 1839
H. Linnell, chair dealer criticizes S. Sanford's chairs. [Sanford got the chairs from Auburn Prison, viz.]
Married: Sept. 10. 1839, in Zion Church, by Rev. Clement M. Butler, Frederick T. Hurxthal, of Ohio, and Emily Maria Smith, dau. of Frederick Smith, Esq.
Married: Sept. 4, 1939, in Sodus, William C. Hoyt, of Buffalo, and Harriet M. Green, dau. of Hon. Byram Green.
Married: Sept. 12, 1839, in Palmyra, Philip G. Cramer and Sarah Morehouse, of Vermont.
Died: Sept. 10, 1839, in Farmington, Mrs. Polly Moore, wife of Phineas Moore, and dau. of David DeCamp, of Rahway, NJ.
Died: September 4, 1939, in Palmyra, Albert H. Sherman, son of Durfee A. and Susannah H. Sherman, ae 1 yr. 9 months.

SEPTEMBER 20, 1839
Stephen Sanford tells H. Linnell to "keep cool" and continues to advertise.
Married: Sept 18, 1839, at Zion Church, Samuel P. Breck, of Branchport [Yates Co.], and Mary H. Baldwin, of Palmyra.
Married: Sept. 8, 1839, Ambrose Camp, and Phebe Jane Mills, both of Macedon.
Adv.: Dr. Lemon, Botanic Physician -"tomato pills".

SEPTEMBER 27, 1839
Adv.: S. W. Wilson - music teacher; Joseph F. Lippincott buys out Elbridge Williams foundry.

OCTOBER 4, 1839
Elder Isaac Goff from Rochester, a minister of the Christian Connection will preach on Sunday next, (Oct. 7)
Died: Sept. 23, 1839, in Michigan, Nancy Bradish, wife of Calvin Bradish, formerly of Macedon.

OCTOBER 11, 1839
Adv.: Bostwick's Hotel in Macedon; Farnham's Walworth House; Beers & Payne -mulberry trees for sale;
W. E. & B. Everson, open a dry Goods store at the corner of Main & William St., formerly occupied by George W. Culver as a hardware store.

OCTOBER 18, 1839
Married: Oct. 9, 1839, in Saratoga, Schuyler R. Parshall, of Palmyra, and Mary Perkins.
Married: Oct. 17, 1839, in Walworth, Harvey Miller and Sally Bancroft.

OCTOBER 25, 1839
Died: Oct. 19, 1839, Mary Joannah Spencer, dau. of Henry and Diana Spencer, ae 2 years.
Died: Oct. 18, 1839, in Manchester, Myndert Groesbeck, ae 72 yrs., late of Rensselaer Co.
Adv: Miss Hine - millinery; Mrs. Chase - millinery.

NOVEMBER 1, 1839
Adv.: Orson Whiting - dentist.
Died: Oct. 26, 1939, Clement Amos Spencer, son of Henry and Diana Spencer, ae 3 mos. 26 days, of Scarlet Fever; his sister died of the same disease one week ago.

NOVEMBER 8, 1839
Married: Nov. 3, 1839, Emulous Sweet and Phebe Warren.
Married: Nov. 3, 1839, Samuel Brigham and Emily Ann Street, all of Penfield.
Died: Nov. 1, 1839, Joseph Henry Lovett, son of J. C. Lovett, ae 1 yr 10 months.

NOVEMBER 15, 1839
W. E. and Bruce Everson dissolve - Bruce continues.
Samuel Beckwith was killed on Sat. night by his horse taking fright and throwing him from his wagon.
Adv. Uriah McClave; Bruce Everson - groceries.
Married: Nov. 5, 1839, in Manchester, Mr. Piper and Mrs. Hibban.
Married: Nov. 5, 1939. in Palmyra, Andrew Fergy of Brighton and Isabella Adams.
Married: Nov. 13, 1839, in Palmyra, Samuel Brigham and Emily Ann Sweet, all of Penfield [Monroe Co.]
Married: Nov. 13, 1839, in Marion, Phineas Leach and Julia Ann Rice of Walworth.

NOVEMBER 22, 1839
Mr. Babcock, a boatman, was crushed to death between his boat and the lock while locking through between Palmyra and Syracuse.
Dr. A. Evans absconds from the village and leaves some debts.
Gen. Winfield Scott passed through Palmyra Nov. 20, 1839.
The Palmyra Thespian Society will present "The Golden Farmer" Nov. 26th. - 25c.

NOVEMBER 29, 1839
Palmyra Select School for Young Ladies began Nov. 21st; Rev. C. M. Butler and Mrs. Mary M. Root; Mrs Butler - Music. One more boarder can be accommodated in the Principal's home.
Married: Nov. 14, 1839, William Johnson and Arsena Phelps.

DECEMBER 6, 1839

Married: Nov. 26, 1839, in Marion, Darius F. Kinney and Harriet Rice, dau. of William Rice.

DECEMBER 13, 1839

A dinner was hosted by Messrs Nottingham & Martin to thank those who contributed to the erection of same.

Married: Nov. 26, 1839, Moses Barret and Fanny A. White, late principal of the Female Dept. of Palmyra H. S.

Married: Dec. 8, 1839, Charles N. Lewis and Hannah Daily, both of Seneca Falls [Seneca Co.].

Married: December 12, 1839, by Mr. Osburn, Mr. Squire B. Johnson to Miss Rachel Beal, daughter of Caleb Beal, all of this town.

Married: Dec. 2, 1839, Abner F. Lakey and Chloe Harris.

Married: Dec. 5, 1839, in Walworth, William B. Smith and Lucy Yoemans.

Adv.: A. G. Wheeler - late of Rochester, tailor.

DECEMBER 20, 1839

Article on Mormons in this issue.

Married: Dec. 17, 1839, in Macedon, Tues. evening, by Rev. A. W. Stowell, of this village, Mr. Namon S. Bachus, of Groton, Tompkins Co., to Miss Hannah A., daughter of Deacon Stephen Spear, of the former place.

Married: Dec. 18, 1839: Married on the 10th inst., by Rev. Mr. Walling, Mr. John H. Galloway to Miss Delia Ann Brown.

Married: Dec. 19, 1839: Mr. Mathew Hickey, to Miss Emily Galloway, all of Macedon.

Stephen Mosher adv. stray cattle.

DECEMBER 27, 1839

"X" criticizes the play of the Thespian Society, in a garret of a produce store - terrible conditions and an awful attempt.

With this edition closes three years of our connexion with this paper. The next number will not be issued until Jan. 8, 1840, and will hereafter be published on Wednesdays instead of Fridays.

Married: Dec. 25, 1839, in Walworth, Amos Morse and Lucina Finley.

Married: Dec. 23, 1839, Robert Nelson and Catherine Bedell, both of Greene Co.

Died: Dec. 18, 1839, at Shelby [Orleans Co.], NY, Samuel R. Thompson, ae 90 yrs., a Revolutionary Soldier.

Died: Dec. 21, 1839, in Palmyra, Marvin Woodward, ae 19 years.

JANUARY 8, 1840

With this number, ends our editorial connexion [sic] with the Wayne Sentinel, this department will hereafter be conducted by O. H. Palmer.

Married: Dec. 26, 1839, in Pultneyville, John Pollitt, of Farmington and Catherine Hohn, dau. of Valentine Hohn.

Married: Dec. 25, 1839, in Marion, Shubael Smith of Palmyra to Margaret Ann Turck.

Married: Jan. 1, 1840, in Palmyra, Thomas Cornwell and Lena Marie Brizzee, of Victor.

Married: Jan. 1, 1840, in Palmyra, Moses L. Whitney and Delight Curtis, both of Rushville [Yates Co.].

Married: Jan. 4, 1840, Asa H. Doty and Laura Clark, both of Macedon.

Married, Jan. 5, 1840, in Palmyra, James Shaw and Marietta Risley.

Died: Dec. 29, 1839, Delia Marie Thayer, dau. of Levi and Susan Thayer, ae 4 yrs. 2 months.

Adv: J. K. Cummings & Co.-Commission - consists of J. K. Cummings, Chauncey Cummings, Luther Reeves, and Abram Martin; Abram Norris has a house for sale.

JANUARY 15, 1840

O. H. Palmer, as editor of the <u>Wayne Sentinel</u>, states principles, etc. Paper is published each Wednesday.

Married: Jan. 11, 1840, John W. Foreman and Julietta S. Day.

JANUARY 22, 1840

Tragedians known as the Palmyra Thespian Society, decamp.

Butler & Williams dissolve - B. Butler continues.

Married: Jan. 21, 1840, in Palmyra, James Bowdish and Laura Hine.

Married: Jan. 15, 1840, A. P. Sawyer, of Macedon and Fanny Rice, dau. of Charles Rice of Pineville. [There are two villages of the name, Pineville, one in the town of Conquest, Cayuga Co., the other in Oswego Co.]

Married - Jan. 15, 1840, in Macedon, I. O. Edwards and Philena Spear, dau. of Deacon A. Spear

Married: Jan. 8, 1840, in Orleans [Ontario Co.], William Moore and Sarah Ann Bolkcom, late of Palmyra.

Married: Jan. 17, 1840, Horace Bigelow and Mary Moore, both of Macedon.

JANUARY 29, 1840

Married: Jan. 22, 1840, Albert G. Wheeler of Rochester and Mary S. Thompson, of Palmyra.

Married: Jan. 22, 1840, Alvah N. Buell and Hannah M. Bowdish.

Died: Jan. 21, 18140, in Marion, Jane Eddy, ae 68 yrs.; suicided with a skein of yarn.

FEBRUARY 5, 1840

Abram K. Jerome has been appointed First Judge of Wayne County.

Married: Jan. 31, 1840, in Pultneyville, Ansel A. Cornwall and Martha Brewer.

Died: Jan. 31, 1840, Eleazer Huntington May, son of Dr. William May, from scarlet fever, ae 7 months.

Died: Feb. 4, 1840, William May Hoyt, son of Dr. D. D. Hoyt, ae 4 yrs. 6 months.

FEBRUARY 12, 1840

Nelson Beers becomes Postmaster at Macedon, in place of A. Purdy; W.(?) Tucker becomes Postmaster at Walworth, in place of B. Billings who resigned.

Died: Feb. 6, 1840, Mary Eliza Cuyler, ae 4 yrs., 2nd dau. of William H. and Eliza Cuyler.

Died: Feb. 5, 1840, George Henry Newland, only child of George Newland.

Olney Briggs adv. his lost pocketbook; Mrs. Mary A. Root's private school; Rev. C. M. Butler to be Principal.

FEBRUARY 19, 1840

Jessup, Smith & Co. (Henry, Albert J. and Robert Smith dissolve. [an adv.in the same issue lists partners as Henry, Albert and George Jessup and Robert W. Smith.]

Married: Feb. 13, 1840, Lucius Strong and Hannah E. Fillmore, all of Walworth.

Married: Feb. 12, 1840, in Marion, Mr. Wilcox and Betsey Cogswell, both of Marion.

Died: Feb. 16, 1840, in Sodus, Gertrude Proseus, age 14 yrs. 9 months.

Died: Feb. 16, 1840, in Palmyra, Sutton Sylvester Birdsall, son of Sutton and Eliza Birdsall.

FEBRUARY 26, 1840

William D. Wylie appointed Postmaster at West Walworth.

Died: Feb. 20, 1840, in Palmyra, Samuel P. Cummings, son of Chauncey Cummings, ae 2 yrs. 4 months.

Died: Feb. 25, 1840, George A. Tucker, son of Albigence W. Tucker, ae 3 yrs. 8 months.

MARCH 4, 1840

Married: Feb. 26, in Arcadia, George Hutchins, of Marion and Amanda Philips.

Married: Feb. 27, 1840, Albert Aldrich and Marietta Osband, dau. of Rev. William Osband.

Married: Feb.20, 1840, in New York, B. Throckmorton and Sarah Marie Grandin, dau.of P. Grandin.

Died: March 3, 1840, Uriah Westfall, ae 29 years.

MARCH 11, 1840

P[omeroy] Tucker, Esq., formerly editor of this paper and its original founder in 1823, will be hereafter associated with the subscriber in its publication. s/O. H. Palmer.

S. Eggleston replies to a challenge; Stephen Sanford still importing chairs from Auburn for sale. [These chairs were purchased from the Auburn Prison and were probably made there by the prisoners. ed.];

NOTICE: My interest in the publication of the Wayne Sentinel, having ceased with the last number (March 11), it becomes necessary for me to call upon the patrons of the establishment for a prompt settlement. s/Henry Spencer

Married: March 14, 1840, Adin B. Smith and Eliza Ann Hitchcock, both of Macedon.

Married: March 10, 1840, at Farmington, George H. Smith and Adeline E. Smith.

Married: March 13, 1840, Horace N. Barnes and Harriet A. Powers.

Married: March 12, 1840, William P. Power and Alice Sheffield, all of Farmington.

MARCH 25, 1840

Adv: N. K. Lamson - hats - next east of Burr Butler's.

APRIL 1, 1840

Philo [or Milo] S. Rawson, late of Palmyra, the swindling cashier of the Mich. [?] Bank, and skipped to Texas, has been arrested.

Adv.: Moses B. Russell - first dealer in milk.

APRIL 8, 1840 - No items copied.

APRIL 15, 1840

Female Dept. Palmyra High School under Miss Caroline Jacobs, Alex C. Huestis, A. B., Principal.

Married: April 6, 1840, James Munsey and Welthy Huntington, both of Palmyra.

Married: April 13, 1840, R. S. Foote, of Buffalo, and Mrs. Eliza Moses, all of Palmyra.

Married: April 9, 1840, in Palmyra, Henry Nottingham and Mary Jane Hathaway.

Died: March 31, 1840, Laura Ann Warren, wife of Nathaniel Warren, ae 26 years.

Died: March 24, 1840, in Geneva, Sarah Whiting, dau. of E. H. Gordon, ae 25 years.

Died: April 5, 1840, in Palmyra, Susan Mary Gordon, only child of William W. and Delia M. Gordon ae 5 years.

APRIL 22, 1840

Adv.: Terry & Post - wants to buy wheat; D. Andrews has land for sale.

APRIL 29, 1840

Married: Apr. 22, 1840, William F. Parke and Mary Jane Foster, dau. of Cyrus Foster.

Married: Apr. 22, in Lyons, J. Nelson Sherman of Palmyra and Harriet Myers, of Lyons.

Married: April 28, 1840, at Port Glasgow, Albert Barnard, of Buffalo, and Elizabeth A. Jenkins.

MAY 6, 1840

Due to the continued ill-health of J. S. Fenton, P. W. Handy is now Asst. Cashier [of the bank].

Married: April 12, 1840, at Walworth, Lucius B. Titus, of Ontario, and Sophia M. Smith of Walworth.

Died: April 24, 1840, at Auburn, Isaac Sherwood, stage proprietor and mail carrier, ae 70 years.

Adv.: The Equestrian Co. will show at Palmyra May 25, 1840; William S. Gramesley will buy hides and leathers.

MAY 13, 1840

E. P. Godard & Co. dissolve partnership May 11, 1840; [E. P.] Godard & [Selden] Williams, dissolve the same day.

Married: May 11, 1840, at the Palmyra Hotel, George W. Taylor and Charlotte Rose, both of Farmington.

Married: May 13, 1840, at Geneva, Peter Moore of Phelps, and Ann Staunton.

Adv.: William Theodore Downs - Attorney; M. J. Godard & Co.

MAY 20, 1840

S. Fenton resigns as cashier of the Wayne County Bank.

Married: May 17, 1840, Isaac Stockton and Fanny Goodrich.
Married: May 13, 1840, Abram R. Bullis and Lydia P. Lapham, all of Macedon.
Died: May 1840, at Palmyra, Joseph Warren, son of Nathaniel Warren, ae 8 years.
Died: May 18, 1840, at Palmyra, Celia L. Rogers, dau. of David Rogers, ae 10 years.
Died: May 12, 1840, in Palmyra, Sarah Springer, wife of Richard Springer, ae 23 years.
Adv.: John Robinson has a stallion, "Samson". George Harrison adv. a stray horse.

MAY 27, 1840
Married: May 21, 1840, Capt. John Stacy, of Port Glagow, master of canal boat, Delaware, and Dorothy Duffie, of Palmyra.
Died: May 23, 1840, in Macedon, David Warner, ae 75 years.
Adv.: Prof. M. Holst will give a concert at the Palmyra Hotel; Heman Martine-groceries; Bowman & Seymour, hardware at old stand of J. S. Colt, recently occupied by Aldrich & Havens; William Palmer adv. a stray colt.

JUNE 3, 1840
Died: May 27, 1840, in Palmyra, Margaret Ann Howell, ae 23 years.

JUNE 10, 1840
Married: May 31, 1840 in "Town", George Scotten of Geneva and Caroline Smith, of Palmyra. ["Town" may refer to town of Palmyra.]
Married June 2, 1840, in Manchester, Alonzo Teachout and Anna Dewey.
Adv.: E. S. Thayer - silk worms and eggs; [Philip] Palmer & [James H.] Bowdish dissolve.

JUNE 17, 1840
Ladies of the Dorcas Society will hold a fair.
Married: June 3, 1840, in Sodus, Solomon M. Burbank, of Newark, and Laura Ann Irwin.
Married: June 11, 1840, in "Town", John Bresee and Louise Stantial, both of Arcadia.

JUNE 24, 1840
Sodus Centre Post Office established with Myron Homes as Postmaster.
Adv.: Dr. A. H. Howland - room #5 at the Palmyra Hotel.

JULY 1, 1840
The trunk of J. W. Phillips, of Akron, OH, was stolen from the boot of the Swiftsure stage between this place and Vienna, on Saturday.
Sabbath School Celebration - Preb. Church - Comm.: William Cole, James E. Walker, P. M. Crandall, James Seeley, W. Chase, P. W. Handy, and J. S. Eggleston.
Election of officers of Wayne county Bank: Abram Spear, Pres.; Peter W. Handy, Cashier; and...

Oliver Clark	Pliny Sexton	Abram Spear
Payne Leach	Jonathan Boynton	David G. Ely
Williams Willcox	Abner F. Lakey	William Ely

Charles Curtis   George G. Jessup   Burr Butler
David Hotchkiss

Married: June 29, 1840, in Palmyra, A. J. Brown and Mercy Foskett, both of Walworth.

Died: June 20, 1840, in "Town", Mrs. Mary Jane Huntington, wife of Samuel D. Huntington, ae 38 years.

Died: June 16, 1840, in Albany at home of his brother, J. S. Colt, Judah Colt, son of the late Joseph Colt, formerly of Palmyra and late of Cleveland, OH, ae 30 years.

JULY 8, 1840

New Counterfeit on Wayne County Bank at Palmyra: on 3-dollar bills, letter A, Vignette of Perry's victory; on the right end, head of Washington and on the left Franklin; signed E. Fenton, Cashier: G. Burkurth, [sic], President; purporting to be engraved by Rawdon, Wright, Hatch & Co., N. Y.

John Miller was hooked by a bull yesterday and killed instantly.

Married: July 2, 1840, in "Town", Jeremiah Flint of Marion and Sarah Gibbs.

Married: July 4, 1840, in Palmyra, Paul Hines and Koziah Crandall.

Married: July 4, 1840, in Palmyra, Rhodes H. Sherman and Elizabeth Craig, both of Palmyra.

Married: July 3, 1840, James Goff, Jr. and Serepta J. Nott, both of Canandaigua.

Married: June 29, 1840, in Sodus, Samuel C. Wilkinson and Rachel Butler.

James M. Jennings adv. a lost shawl.

JULY 15, 1840

William's tailor shop is in 2nd story over shoe store of Wells Anderson, adj. to the <u>Palmyra Hotel</u>.

Summer term of school begins July 27th with Alex McG. C. Huestis as Principal and Caroline Jacobs in the Female Dept.

Married: July 12, 1840, H. H. Sawtell, of Palmyra and Eleanor Mason, of Pultneyville.

Died: June 24, 1840, in Adrian [MI?], John Barker, Sr., ae 83 yrs., a Revolutionary Soldier.

JULY 22, 1840

Died: July 12, 1840, in Walworth, Nathaniel Palmer, ae 76 years.

JULY 29, 1840

THE SILK BUSINESS: The cocoonery of Hiram Payne, Jr., of this village, over the store of J. & L. Thayer, is well worth a visit by our citizens, the entire process from the invisible egg of the worm to the silk itself. Mr. P. is feeding 250,000 and will 450,000. Mr. Payne will accept cocoons for reeling silk.

Died: July 21, 1840, in "Town", James Galloway, ae 75 yrs.; came to Palmyra in 1792.

AUGUST 5, 1840

Married: July 22, 1840, at W. P. N. [?], Cornelius Glimpse and Caroline Davis, both of Phelps.

Palmyra Library Assoc., will meet at George Cuyler's office Aug 10th.

AUGUST 12, 1840

Jacob J. Delamater has been admitted to the bar.

Adv.: S. P. W. Douglas - penmanship and stenography; J. Johnson, barber.

Died: August 9, 1840, in "Town", Mrs. Abigail Harris, wife of Peter Harris, ae 76 years.

AUGUST 19, 1840

Rev C. M. Butler about to move from Palmyra, will sell his household goods at auction at the rectory Aug, 24th.

AUGUST 26, 1840

John Driscoll was killed at Albany when a bridge fell in with a crowd on it.

Married: Aug. 19, 1840, at Romulus [Cayuga Co.], Gilbert Howell, of Palmyra and Mary Ann Stout.

Married: Aug. 20, 1840, Elbert A. Jackways and Nancy A. Bingham, all of Palmyra.

Died: Aug. 21, 1840, at Leroy [Genesee Co.], Mrs. Eliza Gates, wife of Hon. S. E. Gates.

Died: Aug. 23, 1840, in Palmyra, Emily Armington, infant dau. of Henry and Aurelia Armington.

SEPTEMBER 2, 1840

David M. Keeler has revived his Wayne Standard, at Newark, as a neutral paper.

Benjamin Nichols is made postmaster at Williamson.

A watermelon exhibited grown by Capt. George Culver 2' 2" long and 2'11" in circumference; weighed 34 1/4 pounds.

Dr. Perrine, late of Palmyra, was killed by Indians in Florida.

Married: Aug. 27, 1840, Maj. E. C. Cosart of Palmyra and Ann M. Hill.

SEPTEMBER 9, 1840

Massacre at Indian Key, FL. Mrs. Perrine, two daughters and a son, ae 13, escaped while the husband was killed.

SEPTEMBER 16, 1840

Married: Sept. 4, 1840, James McCarthy and Christina Thompson.

Married: Sept. 8, 1840, in Marion, William H. Clark and Sybil A. Swan.

Married: Aug. 26, 1840, in Farmington, Capt. John Bosworth and Mrs. Anna Markham.

Married: Sept. 10, 1840, in Macedon, John T. Tripp and Eliza Mott, of Macedon.

Adv: James S. Williams Saddlery.

SEPTEMBER 23, 1840 - No items copied.

SEPTEMBER 30, 1840

Married: Sept. 24, 1840, Roland Booth and Susannah Keith, both of Farmington.

Married: Sept. 27, 1840, Ira Hulse and Nancy Doolittle, both of Canandaigua.

OCTOBER 7, 1840

Married: Oct. 1, 1840, Lott C. Carpenter and Caroline S. Underhill.

Married: Oct. 3, 1840, Elbridge F. Clark and Georgiana Short, both of Victor [Ontario Co.].

Died: Sept. 30, 1840, at Williamson, Eliza A. Richard, dau. of Charles G. Richard, ae 3 yrs. 5 mos. 12 days.

CENSUS OF PALMYRA TOWN AND VILLAGE: Males - 1869; Females - 1741; Total -3610; 3326 in 1835, a gain of 284.

OCTOBER 14, 1840

Married: Oct. 11, 1840, in Walworth, Hezekiah Hill and Pamela Strickland, both of Walworth.

Married: Oct. 5, 1840, David W. Cross, of Cleveland (OH or Oswego, Co. NY?) and Loraine P. Lee, dau. of Capt. Seth Lee.

Married: Oct. 8, 1840, in Manchester, William H. Cooke, of Palmyra and Mary Benett, of Manchester.

Adv.: H. Park - portrait painter; J. C. Pettit wants a stray steer.

OCTOBER 21, 1840

Married: Oct. 15, 1840, in Palmyra, Horatio N. Johnson and Elizabeth Tice, of Palmyra.

Married: Oct. 19, 1840, in Marion, Daniel Sawyer and Mary Lyon.

Adv.: Miss Jacobs adv. a new term Oct. 19th in lower room of the Academy; George Pratt, Jr. - groceries in store of Higby & Gates, opposite the <u>Palmyra Hotel</u> of W. P. Nottingham.

OCTOBER 28, 1840

Married: Oct. 22, 1840, in Macedon, Hiram Hoag and Sally Ann Wyman.

Adv.: John O. Vorse - jeweller, next to S. Scantlin's shoe store.

OCTOBER 30, 1840

XTRA XTRA - Our next paper will be issued Fri. a.m. Nov. 6th, and after that on Wednesdays as usual on account of the election number.

NOVEMBER 6, 1840

Republicans won out in election - <u>Wayne Sentinel</u> admits it.

Married: Oct. 28, 1840, Perry Parker and Narcissa Lapham, all of Palmyra.

Married: Oct. 29, 1840, in Williamson, Leonard P. Rising and Harriet J. Lathrop.

NOVEMBER 11, 1840

Notice: This paper will hereafter be published for the proprietor, by Festus A. Goldsmith, the temporary engagement of the undersigned...having expired. s/ P. Tucker and O. H. Palmer.

Died: Nov. 5, 1840, in Buffalo, Mrs. Jane E. Starr, wife of Albert J. Starr, and dau. of Joel Thayer, late of Palmyra, ae 23 years.

Adv.: (James) Bowdish & (Alvin N.) Buell; David Johnson adv. a lost steer.

NOVEMBER 18, 1840

Married: Nov. 8, 1840, in Marion, by B. B. Durfee, Esq., Asahel Chapman and Ann Everitt, both of Palmyra.

Died: Nov. 11, 1840, Mrs. Jane Goldsmith, wife of Thomas Goldsmith, ae 30 years.

NOVEMBER 25, 1840

Married, Nov. 10, 1840, Peter Reed and Anna Maria Thurston, dau. of Isaac Thurston.

Married: Nov. 11, 1840, in Elizabeth, NJ, Daniel O. Scott, of Arcadia and Susan E. Meeker.

Died: Nov. 18, 1840, in Walworth, Nehemiah Straight, ae 70 years.

DECEMBER 2, 1840

Winter term of Palmyra High School to commence Dec. 14 - C. Robinson, a graduate of Williams College is to be Principal and Caroline Jacobs will have charge of the Female Department.

Palmyra Select School opened Nov. 2nd in the upper room of the High School Bldg. by J. L. Sanford.

DECEMBER 9, 1840

Having purchased the Wayne Sentinel, this paper will be published by me in the future. My interest in said paper dates from the 11th of March last. s/P. Tucker.

Married: Dec. 2, 1840, in Clyde, Barnet B. Johnson and Ann Maria Hilman [sic], oldest dau. of Dr. John Hinman. [n.b.: Mr. Van Alstine lists the groom in his index as Johnston and the bride always as Hilman but her father as Hinman.]

Adv.: James Peddie, attorney.

DECEMBER 16, 1840

Married: Dec. 16, 1840, in Victor, Henry P. Wilson of Macedon and Emily Bickford, of Victor [Ontario Co].

Adv.: I. E. Beecher - will pay cash for wheat and oats; Charles B. Bingham - axe factory.

DECEMBER 23, 1840

Allen W. Horton, constable, offers reward of $25.00 for capture of Flanders Dike, who escaped 12/5/1840.

Married: Dec, 15, 1840, in Palmyra, Isaac L. Smith of Walworth and Charlotte Nichols, of McConnellsville [Oneida Co.].

Married: Dec. 21, 1840, in Arcadia, Samuel D. Huntington of Palmyra and Philura Reeves of Arcadia.

DECEMBER 30, 1840

Mr. Gilbert will commence Dancing School, at W. P. N., Dec. 30th. [The meaning of W. P. N. is unknown.]

Married: Dec. 25, 1840 at Richmond [NY or VA?], Nathaniel Warren, of Palmyra and Mrs. Eliza Ann Hinman, dau. of Gilbert Wilson.

JANUARY 6, 1841

Article on Mormonism, by Rev. J. A. Clark. q.v..

Bowdish & Buell dissolve partnership.

Married: Dec. 24, 1840, at Manchester, Henry Post and Ann Jennett Saulpugh, dau. of Philip Saulpugh.

Married Dec. 10, 1840, in Lynn, CT, Enoch Noyes and Catherine Lord.

JANUARY 13, 1841

Celebration of the Victory of Jan. 8th; Col. A. Salisbury, Pres. of the day, Drs. A. McIntyre and Truman Heminway, V. P.; Rev. T. S. Brittan, Chaplin;, Maj. J. H. Gilbert's band; O. H. Palmer, orator.

Abraham Huntoon is made postmaster at Port Gibson, J. Nottingham resigned.

Felix Grundy is no more - he died Dec. 19, 1840.

Died: Jan. 7, 1841, Margaretta R. Gardner, dau. of Henry Gardner, ae 3 yrs. 9 months.

Died: Jan. 8, 1841, Henry Fenton Eggleston, son of J. S. Eggleston, ae ---yrs. and 4 months.

JANUARY 20, 1841

Hon. Samuel Miller, of Rochester has been appointed Receiver of the Wayne Co. Bank. See pedigree of each of the Bank Directors, P. S. [Pliny Sexton?] and others.

The new Baptist Church has been completed and will be dedicated on Jan. 28.

Died: Jan. 18, 1841, Sally Moore, dau. of Phineas and Polly Moore, ae 38 yrs.

Adv.: Chauncey Cummings will run a grocery.

Anti-slavery Convention to be held in Palmyra, Feb. 2nd. J. C Hathaway, clerk.

J. K. Cummings & Co. dissolve; Stephen Sanford will sell stock of chairs at auction, Jan. 30, 1841.

JANUARY 27, 1841

Married: Jan. 21, 1841, in Lenox, [Madison Co.], NY, John Marble, M. D., of Marion and Sarah Whitman, a dau of John Whitman.

Married: Jan. 24,, by Rev. Samuel Wilson, Chester Pardy [Purdy?], and Rhoda Mitchell, all of Palmyra.

Died: Jan. 23, 1841, in Albany, Hon. Charles E. Dudley.

FEBRUARY 3, 1841

The Free Religious Society of Palmyra, under the care of Elder Isaac C. Goff, will commence religious worship next Sabbath, the 7th inst., in the room in the Horton Block, lately occupied by the Baptist Society.

Married: Jan. 28, 1841, by Rev. T. S. Brittan, Bruce Everson and Lucy Crowell.

Died: Jan. 27, 1841, in Walworth, Edward Augustus Tucker, son of A. W. Tucker, ae 7 months.

FEBRUARY 10. 1841

Pierce & Osborn of Rochester close up their branch store [in Palmyra?]

Married: Jan. 31, 1841, in Arcadia, Alva Briggs and Ischa Leonard by I. C. Goff.

Married: Feb. 4, 1841 in Pulaski, [Oswego Co., NY], Erasmus D. Stearns and Sarah M. Cole.

FEBRUARY 17, 1841

Peter W. Handy now Notary Public in place of Joseph B. Fenton.

A gang of thieves located on Canandaigua Outlet...14 of them arrested.

Statement of condition of Wayne Co. Bank: $150,407 deficit; reporting committee lay blame to Cashier Fenton as he had been speculating in a number of ways.

Married: Feb. 11, 1841, George Newland and Mrs. Lodema P. Davenport, both of Palmyra.

FEBRUARY 24, 1841 - No items copied.

MARCH 3, 1841

Many applicants reported for the Newark Post Office.

Married: Feb. 25, 1841, William Walton and Susan Carpenter, dau. of George S. Carpenter.

Died: Feb. 23, 1841, in Marion, Orville Dwight Kinney, son of D. F. Kinney, ae 3 mos., 6 days.

Died: March 1, 1841, in town of Palmyra, Edward Durfee, ae 21 yrs.

MARCH 10, 1841

Died: March 4, 1841, Myron Holley d. at Rochester.

Married: March 4, 1841, at Palmyra, by Rev. G. R. H. Shumway, Leonard Van Alstyne, of Victory, Cayuga Co. and Miss Tabitha H. Preston, of Palmyra.

Married: March 4, 1841, Jesse Vine and Lucy Ann Chappel, all of Palmyra.

Adv. B. Frost - jewellery auction.

MARCH 17, 1841

Married: March 4, 1841, in Palmyra, Welcome Reed and Sarah Booth, both of Manchester.

Married: Feb. 25, 1841, in Macedon, Isaac Durfee and Mrs. Ann Hoag, of Macedon.

Married: March 10, 1841, in Walworth, D. T. Hannah, of Macedon and Laura H. Nims.

Died: March 12, 1841, in Palmyra, Moses Norris, ae 73 years.

Adv.: P. Palmer - groceries.

MARCH 24, 1841

The Sheriff offers a reward of $100 for Deacon (?) George N. Williams who escaped from arrest for crime in connection with the Wayne Co. Bank.

General Scott passed through Palmyra, March 22, 1841.

Married: March 18, 1841, Richard Brumfield and Electa Eggleston.

Married: March 21, 1841, in Palmyra, William Ingersoll and Elizabeth M. Lee.

Married: March 14, 1841, in Macedon, Valentine Perry and Mrs. Abigail Gannett.

Adv.: W. & N. Drake have seeds for sale.

MARCH 31, 1841

Dr. D. D. Hoyt has been appointed postmaster at this place, vice Pomeroy Tucker "Frank'd" out. [This is a joke, i.e. Mr. Tucker was tired of stamping letters.]

Lewis P. Beers leases the Godard Mills, one mi. west of Palmyra.

Married: March 24, 1841, by G. R. H. S., Nelson Drake and Delia C. Duggan, eldest dau. of Nathaniel Duggan.

Married: March 10, 1841, in Palmyra, Daniel Vine and Emily Howland, of Manchester.

APRIL 7, 1841

A letter for Leonard Van Alstine is uncalled for.

Adv.: Lewis P. Beers - miller; Thomas Austin & Co. - meat market.

APRIL 14, 1841

Death of President, William H. Harrison.

April 14, 1841: Thomas Turner desiring to return to England, offers his lease of Barnhart's mill - unexpired [lease] of 8 yrs. with privilege of seven years more if desired.

Married: April 12, 1841, in "Town", Lucius A. Hunt of CT and Susan Harris of Palmyra.

Married: April 14, 1841, James H. Willson and Rachel Booth, both of Manchester.

Adv.: J. K. Cummings & Co. - "& Co. is Remus Ferrin."

Married: April 21, 1841, in Arcadia, Luther Sanford, Jr. of East Palmyra, and Ruth Culver, dau. of Cooper Culver.

Adv.: E. Parker - auction of farm utensils; Gramesly & Robinson - leather.

APRIL 28, 1841

Cyrus Leonard is appointed as inspector of sole leather; D. Tingley wants to buy oats.

MAY 5, 1841

J. L. Sanford announces his select school summer term begins 5/24, in the 3rd story of Brown's Block over Beckwith's store; Louisa Cobb will have charge of the Ladies Department.

Married: April 28, 1841, in Palmyra, William S, Gramesly and Phebe J. Hildreth, of Sag Harbor (Long Island.)

Married: April 29,1841, in Palmyra, Henry King and Mrs. Minerva Kingsley, both of Farmington.

Died: May 4, 1841, in Macedon, Mrs. Chloe Lily, wife of Enoch Lilly, ae 60 years.

Adv.: Mrs. A. M. Cosart; Joseph C. Lovett - continues Hyde & Lovett; G. Collins and L. C. Smith adv. their stallion, Black Hawk.

MAY 12, 1841

Memorial service for President Harrison, May 14, 1841.

Ann Eliza Newton, dau. of Butler Newton, ae 9 yrs., burned to death, May 8, 1841; she had put her young sister to bed and waiting for her to go to sleep, fell asleep and her sleeve caught fire.

Married: May 9, 1841, in Macedon, Edward Knox and Lutha A. Barrager, of Macedon.

Died: May 9, 1841, in Walworth, Enoch Lilly, ae 60 years.

Adv.: Southwick & Johnson - dry goods; Mrs. Chase and Miss Crandall - Millinery; Albert A. Allen wants to buy wool.

MAY 19, 1841

Married: May 6, 1841, in Scriba, Charles Poucher, editor of the Western Argus of Lyons, and Mary E. Wales, dau. of George Wales.

Married: May 13, 1841, Elisha Willis and Alantha Jackways, dau. of David S. Jackways.

Adv.: Bunker Hill Hotel - Newton & Parshall; Alanson Todd - Palmyra Bakery; D. Whiting - ploughs.

MAY 26, 1841

William F. Aldrich and Charles W. Torry, admitted to the bar.

Married: May 22, 1841, Henry Mathewson, of Walworth and Ruth Tiffany, of Canandaigua.

Died: May 22, 1841, in West Bloomfield, Ariel Hendee, ae 61 years.

Died: in "Town", John Graves, ae 78 years.

Died: May 18, 1841, in Utica [Oneida Co.], Gurdon C. Leech, late of Palmyra, ae 29 years.

Adv.: J. S. Williamson, tailor.

JUNE 2, 1841

Married May 27, 1841, in Palmyra, by Rev. Samuel Wilson, James McKnight Severs, of Canandaigua, and Maria Angelica Bradt.

Died: May 29, 1841, in Palmyra, Mrs. Rebecca Hathaway, wife of Ebenezer Hathaway, ae 67 years.

Died: May 17, 1841, in Walworth, Elon Galusha Levi Church, son of Alonzo Church.

Died: June 4, 1841, in Palmyra, Mrs. Lydia Selina Thompson, wife of Caleb Thompson, ae 28 years.

Adv.: George Priest - saddlery.

JUNE 9, 1841

The Steam Grist and Saw Mills of William Coggshall, burned June 3, 1841.

Jerry Johnson, the barber, has a lamp which burns lard at his shop.

William Ninde Cole, sold the Lyons Whig to Morley & Tobey.

Married: June 9, 1841, Fay H. Purdy of Penn Yan and Caroline Hall, of Palmyra.

Married: June 17, 1841, at Oak Ridge, by Rev. B. B. Durfee, of Marion, Jeremiah Shupheldt and Mrs. Ann Edgintin, both of East Palmyra. [There is an Oak Ridge in Montgomery Co. but I doubt this marriage took place there but rather at a local Wayne Co. site.]

Died: April 27, 1841, in Connecticut, Mrs. Mary H. E. Reed, wife of Rev. Royal Reed, late of Palmyra, ae 28 years.

Adv.: James H. Bowdish - groceries; John W. Hodson succeeds John O. Vorse - dry goods; Albany Amphitheatre - circus coming June 22nd; Stephen Spear adv. a stray horse.

JUNE 16, 1841

Adv.: George Knight - candy and toys; Josiah Drake - adv. a stray sheep.

JUNE 23, 1841

Another article on Mormons: Jo. Smith arrested; Martin Harris reported killed - shot through the head - a false report however.

Butler Newton is arranging a 4th of July celebration.

Benjamin Clark, of Marion, cut his throat, June 21, 1841, ae 45 years.

JUNE 30, 1841

Married: June 23, 1841, at Zion Church, William H. Southwick, and Henrietta Chapman, dau. of William Chapman.

Died: June 28, 1841, at Palmyra, Mrs. Sarah Randall, wife of Samuel B. Randall, ae 31 years.

Died: June 26, 1841, Calvin Crowell, son of Solomon Crowell, Sr., ae 18 years.

JULY 7, 1841

Celebration of July 4th, with bands from Palmyra and Clyde. A large arbor was built to seat 500 at dinner.

Married: July 4, 1841, at Macedon Centre, Eli Hill, of Palmyra and Phebe L. Baker of Farmington.

Married: July 3, 1841, at Palmyra, Charles LaForge and Sally Shaver, both of Savannah.

Died: June 25, 1841, at Pittsford [Monroe Co.], Mrs. Julia Ann Calhoun Burlingame, wife of Rev. A. H. Burlingame, pastor of the Baptist Church in this village and dau. of Nathan and Hannah Calhoun.

Bailey Durfee adv. a stray mare.

JULY 14, 1841

Married: July 7, 1841, in Palmyra, Marvin Macomber, of Williamson, and Eliza Octavia Sears, oldest dau. of John Sears.

Married: July 4, 1841, in Walworth, Thomas Downing and Delphena S. Parks, both of Palmyra.

Married: July 11, 1841, at the Methodist Chapel, Franklin Horton and Mrs. Betsy Ann Lane, both of Palmyra.

Died: July 4, 1841, in Williamson, Hon., Daniel Poppino, county judge, ae 64 years.

G. S. Carpenter adv. a horse stolen; Adv. M. B. Russell & L. B. Corey bought out P. Palmer - groceries.

JULY 21, 1841

The Poor House barn in Lyons was struck by lightning and burned, July 14th.

Bunker Hill livery stables bought by Nelson Lapham and Ebenezer Terry.

JULY 28, 1841

Information wanted of ___ Leonard, a Swiss, working on a farm near Palmyra; his father and friends want to know where he is.

Married: July 19, 1841, in Palmyra, David Agin of Onondaga [co. or village?] and Euphemy Bayles, of Lyons.

Married: July 21, 1841, A. S. Tyler of Buffalo, and Frances C. Robson.

AUGUST 4, 1841

Why so many private schools and no ACADEMY?

Married: July 28, 1841, in Manchester, Rodman Hart, of Junius [Seneca Co.] and Nancy Lemunyon.

AUGUST 11, 1841

Died: August 5, 1841, in Williamson, Robert Alsop Richards, son of Charles G. Richards, ae 7 months.

Died: Aug. 5, 1841, in Palmyra, Cornelius C. Coleman, ae 36 years.

Adv.: John McCarty - sheep - living on Townsend farm.

AUGUST 18, 1841

Leonard W. Jerome appointed Notary Public in place of P. W. Handy, who resigned.

F. Aldrich and B. Newton hold an assignees sale of George Priest's goods.

Married: Aug. 15, 1841, John Beam and Desdemona Wallace, both of Sodus.

Died: Aug. 18, 1841, in Walworth, Mrs. Mary Jessup, wife of Henry Jessup, Jr.

Died: Aug. 14, 1841, in "Town", Mrs. Betsey Day, wife of Nathaniel Day, ae 47 years.

AUGUST 25, 1841

Died: in East Palmyra, Lucinda Hathaway, dau. of Josiah Hathaway, ae 9 years.

Died: Aug. 15, 1841, in Palmyra, William Robert Gordon, son of Robert Gordon, ae 1 year.

Died: Aug. 21, 1841, in Geneva [Ontario Co.], Gideon Lee, late of New York.

Adv.: Jacob Mattison, administrator of C. C. Coleman.

SEPTEMBER 1, 1841

Seth Antisdale, of Walworth, while drunk, fell into a well and was killed, Aug. 23, 1841, ae 45 years.

Married: Aug. 25, 1841, in "Town", Thomas Goldsmith and Sophia Rich.

SEPTEMBER 8, 1841

Married: Aug. 29, 1841, in Pultneyville, Martin Terwilliger and Sylvia Prentiss, both of Ontario.

Married: Aug. 29, 1841, in Pultneyville, Horton Faulkner and Susan Prentiss, of Ontario.

Married; Sept. 5, 1841, in Pultneyvillle, David Tubbs, of Macedon, and Mary Everts, of Marion.

SEPTEMBER 15, 1841

Married: Sept. 8, 1841, Chauncey C. Giles, of Ohio, and Eunice Lakey, dau. of Abner F. Lakey.

Married: Sept. 9, 1841, James M. Palmer, of Minden and Hannah Louisa R. Tice, of Palmyra.

Died: Sept. 12, 1841, Aurelia F. Jackson, ae 18 years.

SEPTEMBER 22, 1841

Married: Sept. 19, 1841, Erastus R. Calhoun, and Harriet Drake.

Married: Sept. 12, 1841, in Manchester, Philo Clark, of Port Glasgow and Elizabeth Fitzgerald, of Manchester.

Died: Sept. 15, 1841, Joseph McMichael, age 86 yrs., served with George Washington and Arnold [in Revolutionary War].

Adv.: R. G. Pardee & Co. - dry foods; Cuyler & Aldrich, attorneys.

SEPTEMBER 29, 1841

Mechanics meeting - opposed to State Prison labor, Sept 27th at the Boston Hotel.

Married: Sept. 10, 1841, in Salamanca [Chautauqua Co.], Zalmon Rice of Lyons and Eliza Ann Bleeker.

Married: Sept. 7, 1841, at Franklinville, [Cattaraugus Co.], Claudius Victorius Broughton Barse and Mary Helen Wade.

Married: Sept. 27, 1841, in Palmyra, Jacob R. Crandall and Julia Ann Cook, both of Palmyra.

Died: Sept. 15, 1841, in Rhode Island, William Lapham, father of Aretus Lapham, ae 74 years.

OCTOBER 6, 1841

___ Birdsall and T. T. Birdsall dissolve; T. T. Birdsall and A. C. Sanford, form partnership.

Married: Oct. 5, 1841, at [home of] Gen. Lyman Reeves, in East Palmyra, by Rev. A. E. Platt, Edwin S. Foster and Nancy E. White, all of East Palmyra.

OCTOBER 13, 1841

Aldrich & Havens dissolve partnershp.

Macedon Academy winter term. Eaton B. Northrup, principal; Stephen Wood, Math.; Stephen Ramsdell, Austin Mandeville, assts.; and Gideon Freeman, penmanship.

Married: Oct. 6, 1841, in Macedon, Joshua Drake of Palmyra and Agnes Green, dau. of John N. Green, of Macedon.

Married: Oct. 12, 1841, in Walworth, Marcellus McKeen and Clarissa Robinson, of Walworth.

Died: Sept. 13, 1841, in Lewiston, IL, Stephen Phelps, ae 73 yrs. Judge Phelps was among the earliest settlers of this village. He opened the first public house here on the spot now occupied by the Palmyra Hotel; moved to Canandaigua and then in 1821, moved to Illinois.

Died: Oct. 6, 1841, in Palmyra, Elizabeth Clinton, dau. of Asahel and Aurelia Millard, ae 8 months.

OCTOBER 20, 1841

Winter term of J. L. Sanford's select school begins Oct. 26th - R. C. Wells teaches the ancient languages.

Married: Oct. 7, 1841, in Albion, [Oswego Co.], James McKnight, of Palmyra, and Nancy Thatcher.

Married: Oct. 14, 1841, in Palmyra, William Smelt and Margaret Hartman, both of Alloway.

Married: Oct. 9, 1841, in Walworth, Theron M. Robinson and Sarah Maria Brown, all of Walworth.

OCTOBER 27, 1841

Married: Oct. 21, 1841, in Walworth, Allen W. Horton and Catherine Knapp, dau. of Elias Knapp, of Walworth.

Married: Oct. 6, 1841, in Geneva [Ontario Co.], Hiram M. Higby and Polly Harris, both of Palmyra.

Married: Oct. 19, 1841, in Manchester, Stoughton Hayward, of East Bloomfield, [Ontario Co.], and Eliza C. Throop.

NOVEMBER 3, 1841

William Grandin admitted as counsellor at Rochester term [of court].

Married; Oct. 20, 1841, in CT, George Capron of Macedon and Tabitha Frances Stoddard.

Married: Oct. 28, 1841, in Palmyra, Charles Maynard and Maria Carey, both of Hopewell [Ontario Co.].

Married: Oct. 27, 1841, in "Town", Erastus Brumfield and Amy Brockway.

Adv.: Bowman & Seymour - hardware.

NOVEMBER 10, 1841

A Democratic victory reported at the election in Wayne Co.

Married: Oct. 28, 1841, in "Town", S. Joseph Bailey of MI, and Celina Reeves, dau. of Luther Reeves.

Adv.: (D. H.) Hotchkiss & (B. R.) Horton Co.

NOVEMBER 17, 1841

Married: Nov. 11, 1841, William Rushmore, of Farmington and Jane Hall, dau. of James Hall, of Macedon.

NOVEMBER 24, 1841 - No items copied.

DECEMBER 1, 1841

Married: Nov. 18, 1841, in Brighton, D. W. Metcalf, of Palmyra, and Cornelia L. Marcy, of Brighton. [There are various villages of the name Brighton, in NY but this one is in all likelihood the one in Monroe Co.].

Married: Nov. 12, 1841, in Sag Harbor [Long Is.], H. N. Taft, of Lyons, and Mary M. Cook, dau. of Halsey Cook.

Married: Nov. 24, 1841, in Palmyra, Henry Phelps, of Pultneyville, to Martha Moses of Palmyra.

Married: Nov. 25, in Palmyra, Sylvester Rowley, of Manchester and Mary Ann Drake, of Palmyra.

DECEMBER 8, 1841

Died: at Macedon, Mrs. Bathsheba Stoddard, wife of Silas Stoddard, ae 84 years.

Adv.: Misses Nearing - milliners; Isaac Barnhart wants to sell the Walworth mill.

DECEMBER 15, 1841

J. K. Cumings & Remus Ferrin dissolve.

DECEMBER 22, 1841

Married: Dec. 25,[?], 1841 in Oswego, Hon. Theron R. Strong and Cornelia Barnes, dau.of Wheeler Barnes of Oswego.

DECEMBER 29, 1841

Married: Dec. 22, 1841, in Macedon, William L. Tucker, and Marietta Barnhart, dau. of Isaac Barnhart.

Died: Dec. 24, 1841, in Palmyra, Mrs. Lucy Terry, wife of Constant Terry, ae 31 years.

Public oyster supper Dec. 30th at 7 p.m. -- sleighs for the ladies.

JANUARY 5, 1842

Married: Jan. 1, 1842, in Ontario, William H. Gardner of Palmyra and Clarissa Decker.

Married: Jan. 3, 1842, in Palmyra, Julius McLean and Jane D. Eggleston.

Married: Dec. 30, 1841, Abram Hagerman of Port Glasgow and Maria Cobb, dau. of Elisha W. Cobb.

Married: Dec. 30, 1841, in Manchester, Asa T. Chase and Betsey Ann Phelps.

Died: Dec. 30, 1841, in Newark, Ransom Blackmar, ae 39 years.

JANUARY 12, 1842

The Steam Saw Mill, of Millard & Allen has a fine engine in it made at the foundry of E. Williams of Palmyra.

Married: Dec. 10, 1841, at Palmyra, Morgan L. Bingham and Lydia Ann Tice.

Adv.: A. Robinson - milk.

JANUARY 19, 1842

Married: Jan. 13, 1842, in Manchester, Chauncey Miner and Sally McKnutt, dau. of Archibald McKnutt.

Adv.: Eldred Parker runs the Bunker Hill Hotel livery and Nelson Lapham acts as his agent; Remus Ferrin succeeds J. K. Cummings & Co.

JANUARY 26, 1842

Hereafter this paper will be published by William Turner, Jr. to whom the establishment has been leased for a term with the intention on his part of his becoming some day the permanent proprietor.

J. H. Fenton has been admitted as a counsellor.

Having relinquished the chief charge of the Wayne Sentinel, the subscriber intends here-after, to devote a larger share of his attention to the book selling business. s/P. Tucker.

Died: Jan. 17, 1842, in Manchester, Benjamin Throop, ae 88 yrs. He was b. in Lebanon, CT, where he married in May preceding the Declaration of Independence, to Rachel Brown. He was a Revolutionary soldier.

Died: Jan. 19, 1842, in Manchester, David Short, ae 34 years.

Died: Jan. 1, 1841, in Castor, Upper Canada, Mrs. Sophronia Tisdale, wife of James Tisdale, and dau. of Mrs. Susannah Durfee, of Palmyra, ae 44 years.

FEBRUARY 2, 1842
The Democratic Republicans of the village will meet at L. U(?) Smith's tavern..
Adv.: M. Cooke - tailor
Deacon Pliny Foster, two miles west of Newark, lost his house, wagon shop, and blacksmith shop, Jan. 26, 1842 [fire?].
Died: Jan. 30, 1842, in Macedon, James Hall, formerly of Stamford, NY.

FEBRUARY 9, 1842
Hiram K. Jerome, for 20 years a resident of Palmyra resigns as County Judge, and will move to Rochester soon.
J. H. Cumings & Co. dissolve partnership.
Married: Jan. 26, 1842, in Farmington, Walter Robinson, of Macedon and Eliza O. Johnson, dau. of Robert Johnson, of Macedon.
Married: Jan. 22, 1842, in Sodus, Francis Boyle and Sally M. Phelps, of Sodus.
Married: Jan. 23, 1824, at Lyons, John W. Daily and Charlotte Hill, all of Arcadia.

FEBRUARY 16, 1842
Adv.: Hiram K. Jerome - attorney; A. Jessup - leather business and tannery; Robert W. Smith - shoe business.
Henry Jessup, Albert Jessup, George G. Jessup, and Robert W. Smith, dissolve Feb. 16 -George G. Jessup settles accounts - R. W. Smith continues.
Died: Feb. 8, 1842, in "Town", Sheaver Houghton, a Revolutionary soldier, ae 88 years.
Died: Feb. 8, 1842, in Arcadia, Pliny Hudson, ae 53 years.
Died: Feb. 4, 1842, in Lyons, William Paine, ae 24 years.
Died: Feb. 15, 1842, Mrs. Mary Hendee, wife of Alva Hendee, and dau. of the late David Willcox. She was the first person born in the town of Palmyra of civilized parents.

FEBRUARY 23, 1842
Married: Feb. 15, 1842, in Lyons, Morton Browson and Harriet J. Taft.
Married: Feb. 10, 1842, John W. Bullock and Jane Olmstead, both of Lyons.
Married; Feb. 10, 1842, in Wolcott, Charles M. Green and Elizabeth Cuyler.
Married: Feb. 20, 1842, at the Baptist Church in Palmyra, Sun. afternoon, Ezra P. Day and Mary C. Baxter.
Died: Feb. 9, 1842, in Canandaigua, Fanny Howell, wife of Hon. Nathaniel W. Howell, ae 61 years.
Adv.: William B. Tilden - hardware dealer.

MARCH 2, 1842
Wayne County Mills, between the Yellow Mills and Macedon Locks run by Ira Baylis, although owned by Hiram K. Jerome.

Married: Feb. 3, 1842, in Palmyra, James Tannehill and Altha Norton, both of Ovid.
Died: Feb. 25, 1842, in Palmyra, Luther Reeves, ae 46 years.
Died: Feb. 20, 1842, in Newark, John McCarn, a Revolutionary soldier.
Died: Jan. 16, 1842, in the West Indies, Edwin A. Hendee, ae 27 years.
Died: Feb. 4, 1842 in Henrietta, John Russell, ae 76 yrs.; one of Palmyra's earliest inhabitants and a Quaker - kicked by a horse.
Adv.: Levi Thayer - wheat at the red warehouse at Jessup's basin.

MARCH 9, 1842
Married: Feb. 27, 1842, in Lyons, George I. Warden, of Arcadia and Hannah Eliza Moore, of Lyons.
Died: Feb. 27, 1842, in Sodus, Josiah Dunning, a Revolutionary soldier, late of Vermont.

MARCH 16, 1842
Died: March 13, 1842, at N. K. Lamson's, in Palmyra, Mrs. Hannah Isaacs, formerly of South Salem [Westchester Co.], ae 67 years.
Adv.: O. H. Palmer - attorney.

MARCH 23, 1842
The temporary lease of Mr. Turner, having expired, an arrangement, has been made whereby the publication of this paper will be continued by him for P. Tucker.
Married: March 15, 1842, in Aurora, Samuel C. Jennings, of Palmyra, and Charlotte E. Wood, a dau. of Isaac Wood, of Aurora.
Married: March 19, 1842, in Manchester, Festus A. Goldsmith, of Palmyra and Martha Thompson.
Died: March 16, 1842, Chade Southwick, ae 67 yrs. 5 mos. 11 days.
Died: March 9, 1842, in Newark, Mrs. Polly Hutchinson, wife of Luther F. Hutchinson.
Died: March 14, 1842, in Newark, Col. Lathrop S. Bristol, ae 38 years.
Died: March 14, 1842, in Newark, Lois Mosely.
Died: March 19, 1842, in Newark, Mrs. Adelaide Morrin, ae 39 years.
Died: Feb. 26, 1842, in Michigan, Daniel G. Finch, ae 44 yrs., a founder of Tecumseh, MI, and formerly of Palmyra.
Died: March 15, 1842, in Macedon, Mrs. Tabitha Frances Capron, wife of George Capron and dau. of Wait Stoddard, of Connecticut.

MARCH 30, 1842
Married: March 29, 1842, in Zion Church, James McIlwain, of Lyons and Susan Durfee, dau. of Mrs. Susannah Durfee.
Married: March 23, 1842, in Macedon, Charles B. Rogers, and Mary Jane Scovill.
Married: March 24, 1842, in Palmyra, Hugh Reed and Sarah Mills, both of Farmington.
Married: March 13, 1842, Stephen Post and Sarah Ann Gifford.

Married: March 19, 1842, in Canandaigua, Gilbert Oliver, of Palmyra and Elizabeth Judson, of Canandaigua.
Died: March 27, 1842, in Palmyra, Maria Rosman, dau. of Samuel I. Rosman, ae 5 yrs. 4 mos. 29 days.
Died: March 23, in Arcadia, Mrs. Frances Marsh, wife of Dr. Marsh, ae 40 years.
Died: March 9, 1842, in Sodus, Ira R. Paddock, ae 55 years.
Adv.: Grandin & Thurber - forwarding at the yellow warehouse lately occupied by H. K. Jerome.

APRIL 6, 1842
J. D. Phelps is the mail carrier to Pultneyville from Palmyra.
Democratic Town Officers elected - see list in the paper.
Ambrose Salisbury is appointed a Commissioner of Deeds for Pennsylvania.
Married: March 30, 1842, in Marion, Orrin Hicks, of Palmyra and Maria Pooley, of Marion.
Married: March 2, 1842, in Lima [Livingston Co.], W. H. H. Barton and Lydia Jane Lane, second dau. of Col. Lane.
Married: March 23, 1842, in Sodus, Mungo Patterson and Agnes Clow, dau. of Robert Clow.
Died: April 2, 1842, in Manchester, Mrs. Mary Bement, ae 95 years.
Died: April 1, 1842, in Walworth, Vanaih Yoemans, ae 37 years.
Died: March 26, 1842, in Lyons, Mrs. Roxana Barnes, ae 60 yrs., wife of Sherman Barnes.
Died: March 28, 1842, in Newark, Mrs. Mary S. Rogers, wife of Hamilton Rogers.

APRIL 13, 1842
Fall term of Palmyra Academy to commence the summer term...under supervision of J. L. Sanford and Lady; Mr. R. G. Wells will teach Belles Lettres, etc.

MARCH 24, 1842 - EXTRA.
Bound in the file of newspapers at this date] ANOTHER RUNAWAY SUBSCRIBER -Leonard Van Alstine "sloped to Wisconsin". Such is the notice that appears upon the margin of a number of Wayne Sentinels returned from the Postoffice in Macedon. "The scamp has taken the paper for 18 months without paying for it!"
Married: April 6, 1842, in Newark, Warren Powers and Jane C. Schermerhorn, both of Lyons.
Married: April 6, 1842, in Newark, John Vine, of Palmyra, and Harriet N. Robinson, of Newark.
Died: April 4, 1842, in Williamson, Mrs. Mary Calhoun, wife of James Calhoun, ae 62 years.
Died: March 31, 1842, in Lockport [Niagara Co.], Dr. Isaac W. Smith, ae 58 years.

APRIL 20, 1842
Fire broke out in this village on Sat. afternoon last in the dwelling house occupied by B. Homan, owned by B. F. Lakey - furniture was saved but house practically destroyed - no insurance.
Edwin F. Townsend and Otis Clapp are bankrupt, (New Law).
Miss Jacob's School - this well conducted seminary removed to Mr. Dewey's Bldg. at the corner of Main and Canandaigua St.

Married: April 10, 1842, at Walworth, Elihu Davis and Sarah Strickland.

Married: April 14, 1842, in Newark, Thomas B. Higby, of Chapinville, [Ontario Co.] and Mary A. Rogers, a dau. of Shubal G. Rogers, of Newark.

Adv.: Palmyra Academy - Mr. R. G. Wells, J. L. Sanford & Lady, instructors; Nancy Galloway, Exec. - James Galloway's things to be auctioned off.

APRIL 27, 1842

Married April 14, 1842 at Canandaigua, Jonas Miller and Sarah J. Walker.

MAY 4, 1842

Died: April 26, 1842, in Canandaigua Mrs. Delia Willson, wife of Jared Willson, ae 46 years.

Died: April 19, 1842, in Sodus, John M. Sentell, ae 26 years.

MAY 11, 1842 - No items copied.

MAY 18, 1842

Died: May 18, 1842, in Southport, [Chemung Co.], NY, Elisha M. White, printer, late of Palmyra, ae 30 years.

Died: March 12, 1842, in Ohio, Col. Hooker Sawyer, late of Manchester, ae 71 years.

Adv.: W. M. Howell will sell Russell & Corey's stock of groceries.

MAY 25, 1842

Married: May 18, 1842, at Pittsford, [Monroe Co.], P. Milford Crandall, of Canandaigua, and Celestia M. Calhoun, dau. of Nathan Calhoun.

Married: May 17, 1842, in Canandaigua, Thomas Fish and Adelia Hart, both of Manchester.

Died: May 13, 1842, in Penn Yan, [Yates Co.], Abraham H. Bennett, ae 46 years.

Died: May 17, 1842, in Arcadia, Henry Drum, ae 29 years.

Married: May 17, 1842, in Canandaigua, Thomas Fish and Adelia Hart, both of Manchester.

Died: May 13, 1842, in Penn Yan, Abraham H. Bennett, ae 46 years.

Died: May 17, 1842, in Arcadia, Henry Drum, ae 29 years.

Died: May 16, 1842, in Rochester, Thomas M. Watson, ae 31 years.

Adv.: W. L. Tucker at corner of Main & Market St., opposite C. Aldrich's hat store; Sherman & Crandall, Maple Ave. near Nottingham & Martin's Hotel; Mr. Conant invents a new kind of lock with a burglar alarm.

JUNE 1, 1842

William Ninde Cole buys the interest of A. B. Tobey, in the <u>Wayne County Whig</u> and the paper will be published under the firm of Morley & Cole.

Caroline M. Russell and Hamlin G. Russell, children of Daniel R. Russell, leave their home and are advertised by their father.

Died: May 25, 1842, in "Town", Harriet Johnson, dau. of David Johnson, ae 22 years.

Adv.: J. L. Clark & Co. - groceries.

JUNE 8, 1842

Villeroy Beers of Macedon and Cyrus Leonard, of Palmyra are bankrupts.

W. H. Kieth, a celebrated accordion player, will give a concert June 17th at the Nottingham Hotel - 25c; sings and plays both.

Died: May 28, 1842, in Hudson, MI, Harvey Cobb, ae 45 years, late of the town of Palmyra.

JUNE 15, 1842

Two daily lines of packet boats, Syracuse to Rochester - $2.00 with board; $1.00 without. Run in the following order, passing Palmyra twice ech day:

    Liberty..Capt. Burrows   Lyons...Capt. Wiggins
    Minerva..Capt. Wheeler   Palmyra a..Capt. Petrie
    Seneca..... Capt. Vedder

Married: June 9, 1842, at East Palmyra, Stephen Culver of Newark and Helen Mary, dau. of dau. of Hon. Ambrose Salisbury.

Married: June 3, 1842, in Port Glasgow, Charles B. Hill, of Newark and Hester Ann Stiles, of Port Glasgow.

Adv.: Great Western Amphitheatre Circus on June 24, 1842.

JUNE 22, 1842

The Rochester Theatrical Co. [will present "London Assurance", Feb. 22 - adm. 25c.

JUNE 29, 1842 - No items copied.

JULY 6, 1842

Married: July 4, 1842, in Palmyra, Benjamin Fitts and Aurilla Bristol, of Palmyra.

Married: June 29, 1842, in Williamson, Adam Nash and Mary Johnson, both of Williamson.

Died: July 3, 1842, in Marion, Dr. Seth Tucker, formerly of Woodstock, CT.

No large celebration on July 4th.

JULY 13, 1842

Attention is called to the cabinet shop of Col. James Jenner.

Married: July 3, 1842, Hollis Johnson of Evans, [Erie Co.], and Mary Feester, of Marion.

Married: July 4, 1842, in Arcadia, Hilliard Creig, of Lyons, and Melissa Turner.

Adv.: [Thomas] Smith & [George] Pooley Rope factory, succeeding Townsend & Durfee; Jacob C. Pettit - storage in B. Frost's old stand; E. Hinman adv. stray cattle.

JULY 20, 1842

Married: July 4, 1841, at Fishkill [Dutchess Co.], Maj. Samuel B. Randall, of Palmyra and Maria M. Dates.

Married: July 3, 1842, at Pultneyville, James Johnson, Jr. and Eliza Ann Geralamon [Jeralamon?].

Died: July 4, 1842, in Macedon, Mrs. Malinda Johnson, wife of William C. Johnson.

JULY 27, 1842
Married: July 15, 1842, in Lyons, Cornelius Putnam of Marion and Matilda Bradley, of Palmyra.
Died: July 3, 1842, in Dubuque, [IA], Edwin Reeves, oldest son of Zebulon Reeves, ae 27 years.
Died: July 18, 1842, in Newark, Leonard P. Hutchinson, age 40 years.

AUGUST 3, 1842
Died: July 31, 1842, in Manchester, William Johnson, ae 58 years.
Adv.: J. B. Fenton & T. C. Miller, attorneys; J. K. Wing - wants to buy wheat; McKnight & Walton - settlements wanted; Frederick M. Smith - drugs.

AUGUST 10, 1842
David Smith of Farmington, cut on the leg by a scythe in the hands of another workman, bled to death in one hour.
Married: July 28, 1842, in Palmyra, Horace Burnett and Delinda Smith, both of Macedon.
Married: Aug. 7, 1842, in Arcadia, John Hewson and Jane Rogers.
Adv.: K. Jerome - Wayne Co. Mills.

AUGUST 17, 1842
--- Flouring Mills pass into the hands of J. K. Wing, late of Albany; 100 bbls. of flour a day are turned out at this mill.
William Jackson and Jonathan T. Flint of Palmyra - bankrupts.
Married: July 26, 1842, at Morrisville [Madison Co.], William S. Packer and Harriet L. Putnam, of Morrisville, [Madison Co.], but late of Palmyra.

AUGUST 24, 1842
Married: Aug. 21, 1842, Garrett Henry Hiney and Sophia Ann O'Neil.

AUGUST 31, 1842
Pupils from N. Y. institutions for the blind, gave an exhibition Aug. 26th.
Married: Aug. 30, 1842, in Palmyra, Enoch Straight of Macedon, and Elizabeth M. Whitfield, of Farmington.
Died: Aug. 31, 1842, Mrs. Cynthia Lakey, wife of Thomas Lakey, ae 45 years.

SEPTEMBER 7, 1842
Married: Aug. 6, 1842, William Whitmore, of Columbia Co. and Fanny Ripper, of Washington Co.
Married: Aug. 4, 1842, in Newark, Philo Phelps and Emeline Dewey, both of Manchester.
Died: in Palmyra, Josiah G. Lord, ae 25 years. [No date given]

SEPTEMBER 14, 1842
John Chase, conductor of the steam mill, south of Newark, was killed in the machinery. He was caught in the wheel while oiling Aug. 31, 1842.
Married: Aug. 29, 1842, in Macedon Locks, Luther E. Hathaway, and Clarissa L. Ripley.

Married: Aug. 31, 1842, Adoniram J. Rice, of Newport [Herkimer Co.], and Ann S. Ripley.
Adv.: Rockwell & Stone's Circus will be here Oct. 5th.

SEPTEMBER 21, 1842
Bank of Lyons fails, Sept. 14, 1842.
Married: Sept. 14, 1842, in Lyons, Edward Fitch, of Buffalo, and Betsey Jane Grawbadger.
Died: Sept. 17, 1842, Sarah W. Hall, youngest dau. of Ambrose Hall, ae 15 years.
Died: Sept. 12, 1842, in Lyons, Daniel Dunn, ae 73 years.
Died: Sept. 7, 1842, in Manchester, William McKnutt, Jr., ae 18 yrs. 3 mos. and 7 days.

SEPTEMBER 28, 1842
June, Titus, Angevine & Co. Circus to be in Palmyra Sept. 30, 1842.
Married: Sept. 16, 1842, in Pultneyville, Adam Rutherford, of Palmyra and Sarah Reed, of Williamson.
Adv.: Frank Johnson & Co. - concert - 25c

OCTOBER 5, 1842
Married: Sept. 17, 1842, in Saratoga Co., Cyrus Smith and Jane Thompson Sherman.
Died: Sept. 23, 1842, in Sodus, John Williams, ae 65 years.

OCTOBER 12, 1842
Palmyra Academy begins fall term with E. Fobes, A. M., Principal; H. G. Wells, Math. teacher; Amerila D. Colton, Preceptress.
Orson Whiting, dentist, takes in L. C. Whiting [as partner.]
Died: Sept. 17, 1842, at Walworth, Richard P. Robinson.

OCTOBER 19, 1842
FIRE! The old one story building owned by William Woodward, of Walworth, and occupied by C. B. Rumsey, burned Oct. 13th (No loss).
Married: Oct. 23, 1842, at Palmyra, John L. Clark and Martha A. Flower, all of Palmyra.

OCTOBER 26, 1842
Married: Oct. 24, 1842, in Palmyra, J. P. H. Deming, M. D. and Mrs. Mary Bortles, both of Palmyra.
Married: Oct. 20, 1842, at Port Glasgow, Samuel D. Carpenter and Laura Wakeman.
Died: Oct. 26, 1842, at Lyons, Ira Panker, late of Port Glasgow, ae 52 years.

NOVEMBER 2, 1842
L. Bickford & Co., consisting of Lyman Bickford, Silas Richmond, and Henry Hoffman, organize at Macedon to succeed the co-partnership of Silas Richmond, Henry Hoffman, and Hiram Wilkinson.

Married: Oct. 26, 1842, in Williamson, Theodore V. R. Miller, and Harriet G. J. Fish.

Adv.: J. P. H. Deming, M. D., for two yrs. with A. McIntyre, lives one door west of the Franklin House.

NOVEMBER 9, 1842

Married: Nov. 1, 1842, at Watertown [Jefferson Co.], Frederick M. Smith, of Palmyra, and Delia F. McKnight, youngest dau. of Judge McKnight.

Died: Oct. 31, 1842, in Phelps, Elijah Cole, ae 34 years.

Died: Nov. 1, 1842, in Macedon, Phebe Jane Birdsall, only child of Daniel Birdsall, ae 18 yrs. 11 months.

NOVEMBER 16, 1842

Died: Nov. 6, 1842, at West Sand Lake [Rensselaer Co.], Caleb Thompson, ae 22 yrs., late of Palmyra.

NOVEMBER 23, 1842

[The by-line] "William Turner, Jr. for P. Tucker, Prop." disappears in this issue of the paper and just "P. Tucker" takes its place. [Owners of the newspaper.]

NOVEMBER 30, 1842

Walworth people within a year have built the Academy Building, and the same will be opened Dec. 5, 1842.

Married: Nov. 24, 1842, in Palmyra, Phineas Moore, of Farmington, and Mrs. Mary Johnson, of Palmyra.

Married: Nov. 20, 1842, in Palmyra, A. H. Wentworth, of Manchester and Mary Hine, of Palmyra.

Married; Nov. 22, 1842, Samuel Wilber and Sarah Allen, both of "Town".

Adv.: Miss M. Fowler - milliner.

DECEMBER 7, 1842 - No items copied.

DECEMBER 14, 1842

Married: Nov. 24, 1842, in Marion, Rev. Isaac Braman, of Chautauqua Co. and Sally Hoyt, of Marion.

Died: Dec. 12, 1842, in Marion, Ann Eliza Brown, dau. of Ezra W. Brown, ae 23 months.

DECEMBER 21, 1842 - No items copied.

DECEMBER 28, 1842

Mr. Adams preaching to crowded audiences on the "Millennium" - to come in 1845.

Married: Dec. 22, 1842, in "Town", Aaron H. Hedden, of Arcadia, and Ruth Aramantha Harrison, of Palmyra, both deaf mutes.

Married: Dec. 22, 1842, in Arcadia, Joseph H. Burrows and Rowena L. Osband, dau. of Rev. Wilson Osband.

Married: Dec. 21, 1842, in Marion, Cyrenus C. Eddy, of Williamson, and Cornelia S. Miller, of Marion.
Died: Dec. 24, 1842, in Macedon, Mrs. Charlotte Rogers, wife of Denison Rogers, ae 54 years.
Died: Dec. 31, 1842, in Macedon, Jeremiah Monroe, ae 21 yrs., of smallpox.

JANUARY 4, 1843

The Wayne Sentinel will be published hereafter by William L. Tucker & Co. This change will not effect the present relations of our patrons further than require the immediate settlement of all long standing subscriptions and printing accounts. W. L. Tucker, at his book store will wait upon those interested and is authorized to make all collections for this office. 1/1/1843
Coon (or Cohn's) Mill on Canandaigua outlet burned Jan. 1, 1843.
Married: Dec. 29, 1842, at Pultneyville, Charles Farewell and Mary Holling.

JANUARY 11, 1843

Theron R. Strong appointed receiver of the Bank of Lyons.
Bruce Everson sells out to William E. Everson.
Married: Jan. 1, 1843, at Seneca Falls, [Seneca Co.], John J. Cross and Harriet E. Brooks, of Lysander [Onondaga Co.].

JANUARY 18, 1843

Married: Jan. 11, 1843 in Macedon, Calvin Tucker, of Walworth and Uretta Knapp, of Macedon.
Married Jan. 11, 1843, in Williamson, Andrew Cornwall and Mary Calhoon.
Married: Dec. 28, 1842, in Manchester, Leander P. Mosely of Marion, and Elizabeth Dewey, dau. of Jedidiah Dewey.
Married, Jan. 10, 1843, in Lyons, George E. Mooney and Climena Landon, dau. of Jarvis Landon.
Died: Jan. 10, 1843, in Macedon, Mary Jane Rogers, wife of Charles Rogers, ae 19 years.
Adv.: Mr. Lund - Singing school.

JANUARY 25, 1843

L. L. Seaman buys the Godard Mills, one mile west of Palmyra.
Married: Jan. 19, 1843, at Farmington, Lorenzo Whitney, of Fairport [Monroe Co.] and Mary A. Johnson.
Married: Jan. 12, 1843, at Lyons, Frederick Morley, of the Wayne Whig and Eleanor Ninde, dau. of the late Rev. William Ninde, of Baltimore [Cortland Co.].

FEBRUARY 1, 1843

Ladies of the "Hive" will hold a fair at W. P. Nottingham's.
Married: Jan. 26, 1843, Franklin Lakey and Terrissa Page, both of Macedon.
Died: Jan. 29, 1843, in "Town", Oliver Clark, ae 76 years.

FEBRUARY 8, 1843 - No items copied.

FEBRUARY 15, 1843

The Baptist Meeting House in Williamson burned.

Several cases of small pox in the village are reported.

B. Grandin and Remus Ferrin in the storage business.

FEBRUARY 22, 1843

Grandin & Thurber dissolve partnership.

MARCH 1, 1843

Died: Feb. 22, 1843, Mrs. Lettis Reynier, ae 80 years.

Died: Feb. 5, 1843, in Cazenovia, [Madison Co.], Miss Louisa H. Cobb, member of the Baptist Church.

MARCH 8, 1843

Died Mar. 3, 1843, in Palmyra, Christopher E. Thayer, son of C. E. Thayer, ae 4 years.

Died: Feb. 26, 1843, in Penfield, [Monroe Co.], Miss Mary L. Bryan, dau. of J. B. Bryan.

MARCH 15, 1843

Married: March 19, 1843, in Palmyra, William Clark Johnston, of Macedon and Phebe Hine.

Died: March 18, 1843, in Newark, Abel Blackmar, ae 72 years.

Adv.: H. Williams - auction of horses.

MARCH 29, 1843

Married: March 26, 1843, at Jesse Eddy's, Isaac Shove and Phebe Fairbanks, all of this town.

Married: March 15, 1843, at the Bunker Hill Hotel [in Palmyra], John Millet, of Ontario and Mary Smith of West Williamson.

Died: March 24, 1843, William Smith, ae 24 years.

APRIL 5, 1843

Thomas Austin & Richard Ford dissolve. List of Town Officers recently elected is published. q.v.; R. G. Pardee & John S. Gay dissolve.

Married: April 2, 1843, in Palmyra, Edward Knox and Lucinda Pelham, both of Palmyra.

Married: March 29, 1843, in Phelps, Capt. Richard Ford and Emily Tingley.

Died: April 1, 1843, Joseph Daniel, son of A. P. and Ann P. Crandall, ae 21 months.

Died: April 1, 1843: in Palmyra, Eli Seymour, ae 81 years.

Died: March 23, 1843, in Buffalo, Maria Louisa Durfee, oldest dau. of Philo Durfee, ae 9 years.

APRIL 12, 1843

David G. Ely & Richard Ely dissolve.

Married: April 4, 1843, in Phelps [Ontario Co.], Joseph F. Fillmore of Palmyra and Harriet J. Adams.

Adv.: Elisha Flower, wants boarders at the bank building.

Married: April 19, 1843, Samuel J. Bragaw, of Rhode Island and Elizabeth E. Hawker, of Palmyra.
Married: April 12, 1843, in Newark, David S. Fox and Elizabeth Culver, both of Palmyra.
Adv.: Williams Drake - Commission business; William Drake and Nelson Drake dissolve; Red Mills - or Jerome Mills, 2 mi. west [of Palmyra] again put in operation by Albert Wells.

APRIL 26, 1843
Married: Apr. 17, 1843, in Lyons, Jonas W. Goodrich, and Sarah Beaumont, all of Lyons.
Married: April 17, 1843, in Watertown, [Jefferson Co.], Simon V. W. Stout, County Sheriff and Caroline Cole.
Married: April 13, in Manchester, Rev. George Switzer and Lucy Armington, dau. of Benjamin Armington.
Married: April 20, 1843, in Geneva [Ontario Co.] Joseph Stow and Mary Robinson, dau. of Peter Bours.
Married: April 6, 1843, in Seneca Falls [Seneca Co.], Sylvester Pew and Electa Cox, dau. of William Cox.
Married: April 18, 1843, in Lewiston, [Niagara Co.], Henry F. Hotchkiss and Maria Scovell, dau. of Seymour Scovell.

MAY 3, 1843
Died: April 26,1843, Marianna Cornelia Woodward, age 20 years.
Died: April 29, 1843, Mrs, Anna Sophia Hiney, wife of Garrett H. Hiney, ae 21 years.
Died: May 1, 1843, Lysander C. Smith, ae 30 years.
Adv: David G. 0. Ely & Oscar F. 0. Avery - dry goods.

MAY 10, 1843
Married: May 3, 1843, in Williamson, Levi Clark and Paulina Truax.
Died: May 1, 1843, in Newport [Herkimer Co.] NY, Henrietta, wife of Cephas Smith, late of Palmyra.
Adv.: A. F. Dodge - dentist.

MAY 17, 1843
Horace Cumings, a commissioner of Common Schools has been granting certificates without the presence of the other inspectors, O. H. Palmer and James Hubbell.
Sexton & Butterfield, sell out to M. Butterfield, William P. Lamson and James E. Walker.
Adv.: Lyman Willcox - cow strayed; James N. Sanford - wants to buy eggs and has pumps for sale; Robert Withers - shoes for sale.

MAY 24, 1843
Rev. Mr. Lee of Newark, will preach in the Universalist room in this village next Sabbath.
Married: May 16, 1843, William Ninde Cole and Emily W. Goldsmith, dau. of Ovid Goldsmith.

MAY 31, 1843

Married: May 29, 1843, Henry Jessup, Jr., of Walworth, and Rebecca F. Seaman, of Palmyra.

Married: May 14, 1841, Artemas Garlock and Mary Lewis, both of Palmyra.

Married: May 29, 1843, Spencer G. House and Elizabeth Brown.

Married: May 29, 1843, in Marion, Hezro Nimo and Sylvia Rice.

Died: May 28, 1843, Maria Horton, dau. of Samuel T. Horton.

Adv.: F. U. Sheffield - lands for sale; Pliny Sexton - land for sale; D. Chase and Charles A. Stevens - doctors.

JUNE 7, 1843

Married: June 1, 1843, in "Town", Edwin Stacy and Caroline Luce, both of Palmyra.

Married: June 6, 1843, in Palmyra, William Henry Smith and Sarah Ann Salard.

JUNE 14, 1843

J. L. Clark & Co. lease Yellow Mills for a term of years.

Died: in Town, Elias Reeves ae 80 yrs., the first one to emigrate from Long Island to this country in 1792.

Adv.: George R. Herrick - teaches penmanship; R. Tallent - upholstery; George Beckwith & Co. on north side between D. S. Aldrich and J. C. Lovett in Brown's new block.

JUNE 21, 1843

Fourth of July arrangements - Thomas Miller, orator; R. S. Hendee, reader and S. B. Randall, marshall of the day. Adv: S. G. Hill - painting.

Married: June 8, 1843, in Sodus, J. Clark Rogers and Louisa Green, dau. of Hon. Byram Green.

JUNE 28, 1843

Maj. J. H. Gilbert's band will play at Fourth of July celebration and dinner at the Bunker Hill Hotel.

Married: June 21, 1843, by Rev. Mr. Piersoll, Abisha Goodell, of Fairhaven [Cayuga Co.] and Mary Lemon, dau. of Dr. Richard Lemon.

Adv.: Ely & Avery - dry goods; Albert Wells - flour;

Ebenezer Davenport advertises his wife, Marium Davenport, April 14th.

JULY 4, 1843

Married: June 29, 1843, in Williamson, William Cragg and Jane Wake.

Hendee Parshall adv. a stray cow.

JULY 12, 1843

The Wayne Standard passes into the hands of H. S. Wiants.

Died: June 29, 1843, in New York, Mrs. Angeline Carroll, sister of Mrs. Isaac Gardner, of Palmyra, ae 44 years.

Adv.: T. C. Miller - farm wanted; T. Rogers - grindstones.

JULY 19, 1843

Married: July 12, 1843, in Penfield, [Monroe Co.], Christopher C. Thompson, of Palmyra and Caroline G. Gibson.

Died: July 13, 1843, John L. Sanford, ae 72 years.

Died: July 9, 1843, in Williamson, William Cragg.

JULY 26, 1843

Married: July 23, 1843, in Palmyra, Andrew M. Rykard and Eunice Burnett, both of Arcadia.

Married: July 18, 1843, in Geneva [Ontario Co.], Isaac M. Schermerhorn of Canandaigua and Maria Barkley of Geneva.

Died: July 19, 1843, in Palmyra, Charlotte Eaton Thayer, ae 17 yrs., youngest dau. of Levi Thayer.

AUGUST 2, 1843

Died: July 5, 1843, in Marion, Mrs. Laura A. Burbank, wife of Solomon M. Burbank and dau. of William P. Irwin, of Sodus.

AUGUST 9., 1843

Died: Aug. 4, 1843, in "Town", Israel Parshall, a Revolutionary soldier, ae 84 years.

Died: Aug. 1, 1843, at Henry P. Wilson's in Macedon, Charity Wilson, dau. of David Wilson.

Adv.: D. Coe - lost a package.

AUGUST 16, 1843

Adv.: Throop & McCarty - harness - dissolving partnership; William H. Throop - takes over. Andrew Beard has a farm for exchange.

AUGUST 23, 1843

Died Aug. 17, 1843, in Macedon, Dr. Allen A. Jordan, ae 26 yrs.; his wife and two children survive him.

AUGUST 30, 1843

Mrs C. A. Stevens will teach piano during the fall term of the Palmyra Academy; Mr. Edson Fobes is principal of the school.

Water from the Palmyra Springs available at W. P. Nottingham's; J. K. Sexton has a general store at Port Gibson; B. P. Seymour leases Godard's mills - George Neward is in charge.

Married: Aug. 21, 1843, in Ontario, Isaac Barnhart of Macedon and Mrs. Anne Wooster.

ADV.: S. P. Seymour - Yellow Mills.

SEPTEMBER 6, 1843

Nottingham & Martin run carriages to and from Soda Spring - round trip 6 1/4c - a discount to families of three.

Died: Aug. 20, 1843, in Pultneyville, Joseph Stewart, a Revolutionary soldier, ae 86 years.

SEPTEMBER 13, 1843

J. E. and Miss Hughes gave a recital Sept. 11 & 12 on violin and Harp - last of their concerts at Horton's Block.

Grandin & Ferrin shipped on the boat, J. S. Holcomb, Capt. James McKeller, 2,226 bu. of wheat, 7 bbls. of agge (?) and 3 bales of wool - in all 78 tons.

Married: Sept. 6, 1843, in Marion, James Byron Cooper, son of Griffith Cooper of Williamson, and Sarah W. Rogers, dau. of John Rogers, of Marion.

Died: Sept. 3, 1843, in Mt. Morris, Graham H. Chapin of Rochester, ae 45 yrs., late of Lyons.

Died: Sept. 3, 1843, George L. Riker, son of John and Mary T. Riker, ae 1 yr. 11 mos. 24 days.

Died: Sept. 10, 1843, Abel Sanford, ae 78 yrs., late of Wallingford, CT.

SEPTEMBER 20, 1843

Married: Sept. 13, 1843, in Palmyra, Isaac Underhill Wilbur and Welthy Ann Thomas.

SEPTEMBER 27, 1843

Marion Democrats will meet at Van Camp's Temperance House.

Married: Sept. 21, 1843, in Palmyra, Carlton H. Rogers and Sarah Perrine, eldest dau. of the late Dr. Henry Perrine.

Married: Sept. 20, 1843, in Marion, William H. Whipple, of Wyoming Co., and Susan H. McCumber.

OCTOBER 4, 1843

Married: Sept. 26, 1843, in Williamson, Myron H. Bennett, and Mary E. Fish, dau. of Isaac Fish.

Married: Sept. 2, 1843, in Palmyra, Howard Fisher of Palmyra and Sarah Maria Hubbard, of Farmington.

Married: Sept. 26, 1843, in Macedon, William H. Manchester and Mrs. Martha Glover Billings, by Rev. D. Harrington, of Palmyra.

Died: Sept. 26, 1843, in Palmyra, George S. Newton, son of Butler Newton, ae 17 months.

Died: Sept. 28, 1843, in Rochester, George H. McKnight, ae 19 years.

OCTOBER 11, 1843

Died: Aug. 14, 1843, in Hoosick [Rensselaer Co.], Mrs. Sally Ann Hurd, wife of Col. Lovell Hurd, late of Palmyra, dau. of Capt. Benjamin Taber, of Manchester.

Adv.: Jenner & Seely - furniture.

OCTOBER 18, 1843

Married: Oct. 12, in "Town", Joseph Allen, Jr. and Julia L. Galloway, both of Palmyra.

Married: Sept. 28, 1843, in Canandaigua, Jeremiah Haskett and Caroline Smith, both of Canandaigua.

Married: 1843, in Black Rock, [Erie Co. NY]; George Pooley of Palmyra and Mary Ann Clinton.

Died: Oct. 12, 1843, in Palmyra, Mrs. Harriet E. Calhoon, wife of Erastus R. Calhoon, ae 22 years.

Died: Oct. 17, in "Town" Edward Westfall. ae 25 yrs., funeral at his father's J. Westfall. James Peddie, Town Superintendent puts in notice: Resolutions passed in School Districts Nos. 1, 2, & 3 of Palmyra to call a meeting to consider the consolidation of the said districts...

OCTOBER 25, 1843
Adv.: Thomas Stead - red oak timber; Andrus Dennis - farm for sale.
Married: Oct. 24, 1843, in Farmington, Norris Sawyer and Caroline Johnston, dau. of Robert Johnston.
Married: Oct. 20, 1843, in Palmyra, J. D. Hornsby and Sarah A. Beeching, of Palmyra.
Married: Oct. 22, 1843, in Ira Edwards and Mary Chapman, eldest dau. of Rev. Joseph Chapman.
Died: Oct. 17, 1843, in Macedon, Eaton B. Northrup, Principal of Macedon Academy, ae 28 years.
Died: Oct. 28, 1843, in Lockport [Niagara Co., NY], Wright Latten, late of Palmyra.

NOVEMBER 1, 1843
Died: Oct. 28, 1843, in Lyons, Harriet W. Poucher, ae 1 yr 6 mos. 10 days, dau. of Charles and Mary Poucher.

NOVEMBER 8, 1843
Oron Archer is principal of Marion Institute.
Married: Nov. 2, 1843, in Rochester, Oliver H. Palmer, of Palmyra and Susan Hart, dau. of Truman Hart.
Married: Nov. 1, 1843, in "Town", William H. Throop and Jane A. Granger.
Died: Oct. 25, 1843, in Manchester, Hiram Rich, son of Hon. M. Rich, of Marion, ae 22 years.
Died Nov. 2, 1843, in Port Glasgow, Lucy Maria Alling, youngest dau. of Stephen and Amanda Alling.
Adv.: Samuel Lyon - dyer.

NOVEMBER 15, 1843
Election resulted in a decided Democratic victory locally.
Adv.: Mrs. Enos - milliner.

NOVEMBER 22, 1843
Adv.: Seales & Mead - photographers.

NOVEMBER 29, 1843
Durfee Chase & Charles A. Stevens dissolve.
James E. Walker, Sec., Engine Co. #2, calls a meeting.
Married; Nov. 16, 1843, in Palmyra, by the Rev. D. K. Lee, Aaron Hosmer, Jr. and Catherine Sherman, both of Newark.
Died: Nov. 21, 1843, in Williamson, Duane Wing Kinney, son of D. F. and Harriet Kinney, ae 3 mos. 16 days.

Died: Nov. 15, 1843, in Philadelphia, Rev. Augustine Palmer Provost, Rector of Canandaigua, ae 36 yrs., at his father's house.

DECEMBER 6, 1843
Adv.: Williams & Williamson -- tailors.

DECEMBER 13, 1843
Twelve merchants agree to close up Thanksgiving Day; Mr. Gilbert opens his dancing school.
Married: Dec. 7, 1843, in Town, Horace Cumings and Lucy G. Thompson.

DECEMBER 20, 1843
Married: Dec. 10, 1843, in Williamson, Morris Boughton of Michigan, and Lucretia Culver.
Married: Dec. 13, 1843, in Manchester, William E. Bement and Laura Ann Newell.
Died: Dec. 14, 1843, in Palmyra, Thaddeus Merrill, son of John Merrill, ae 7 months.

DECEMBER 27, 1843 - No items copied.

JANUARY 3, 1844
Married: Dec. 20, 1843, in Macedon, D. C. Hicks and Rebecca Young.
Married: Dec. 31, 1843, in the M. E. Chapel, Cain R. Allen and Amelia Potter, both of Perinton [Monroe Co.].
Married: Jan. 1, 1844, in Palmyra, James Webb, and Charlotte Hersey.
Married: Jan. 1, 1844, Lyman Monroe Phelps and Harriet Angeline Hunt.
Married: Dec. 25, 1843, in Arcadia, Daniel A. Kenyon and Antoinette E. Bartle, both of Newark.
Married; Dec. 25, 1843, in Sodus, William Van Camp and Margaretta Williams
Married: Jan. 1, 1844, in Canandaigua, Solomon Crowell, Jr., of Palmyra, and Miss L. D. C. Manley.
Died: Dec. 28, 1843, in Westford, [Otsego Co.], NY, James Brumfield, father of James I. and Andrew D. Brumfield, a Revolutionary soldier, ae 94 years.
Letter for William Van Alstyne at the Post Office.

JANUARY 10, 1844
Married: Dec. 30. 1843, at Ontario, George W. Hill and Margaret Sutton.
Married: Dec. 30, 1843, at Walworth, Newton Lyon and Caroline Smith, both of Walworth.
Married: Jan. 2, 1844, at Chili [Monroe Co.] Samuel S. Lacy and Mary A. Akin.

JANUARY 17, 1844
Married: Jan. 11, 1844, Blaker [?] L. Shear of Floyd [Oneida Co., NY] and Phebe Ann Eastwood, of Macedon.

JANUARY 24, 1844
Married: Jan. 17, 1844, in Palmyra, William R. Johnson and Lucy Willson, all of this town.

Married: Jan. 18, 1844, in Palmyra, James Fosman and Lydia Young, both of Arcadia.

Died: Jan. 17, 1844, in Gorham [Ontario Co.], Aaron Younglove, ae 81 yrs., a Revolutionary soldier.

Died: Jan. 13, 1844, in Detroit, George R. Miller, ae 29 years.

Adv. Miss L. C. Rolph - Select school, in 2nd story of F. M. Smith's Drugs.

JANUARY 31, 1844

Bill passed authorizing Trustees to buy land for a cemetery.

Married: Jan. 16, 1844, in Williamson, Zebina Crane and Hannah P. Peer.

Died: Jan. 26, 1844, in Palmyra, Capt. Asa Lilly, ae 67 yrs.; came to Wayne Co. from Ashfield, MA in 1802 and always lived in or near Palmyra. Began as a mechanic and later kept a hotel.

Died: Jan. 26, in Williamson, George Pearsall, ae 67 years.

Adv.: Mr. and Mrs. Canderbeeck will give a concert.

FEBRUARY 7, 1844

Married: Jan. 30, 1844, in Sodus, James K. Sexton of Port Glasgow, and Miss Augusta Jewell, of Sodus.

Married: Jan. 30, 1844, in Ga.[Galen?], Samuel R. Wilson and Mary A. Spear, oldest dau. of Harry Spear.

Died: Jan. 17, 1844, in Canandaigua, Emily Frances Tousley, 3rd dau. of L. B. and A.M. Tousley, ae 3 years.

FEBRUARY 14, 1844

Cataract Fire Co., # 4, of Rochester, thanks the Eagle Hotel for entertainment while visiting Palmyra on the eve of Jan. 31st.

Married: Feb. 8, 1844, in Pittsford, Monroe Co., Dr. John Bristol and Mary Anne Birdsall.

Married: Feb. 11, 1844, in Palmyra, Edward F. Allen and Hannah Tinney.

FEBRUARY 21, 1844

Died: Feb. 15, 1844, in Palmyra, Mary Williams, ae 17 yrs., dau. of George N. Williams.

Died: Feb. 8, 1844, in Boston, MA, Mrs. Mary D. Clapp, wife of Otis Clapp, late of Palmyra, and dau. of Gideon Ramsdell, ae 34 years.

FEBRUARY 28, 1844

Died: Feb. 16, 1844, in Lyons, Thomas D. G. Sisson, son of William Sisson, ae 22 years.

MARCH 6, 1844

The Palmyra Bank of Wayne Co, is the title of a new bank organized in this village by Pliny Sexton...The bills are secured by a pledge of Stocks of the State of New York and real estate... The Bank office is for the present at the store of David S. Aldrich.

Joseph Gibbs, as sexton, has charge of Horton's Hall.

Methodist Chapel for sale: The Methodist Episcopal Society of this village is contemplating erecting a new edifice on a more central site and are offering their chapel for the use of the Town of Palmyra.

Married: Feb. 26, 1844, Joseph D. Lambert and Julia Prime.

MARCH 13, 1844

Married: March 7, 1844, M. T. Tinker, M. D., of Perrinton, [Monroe Co.] and Harriet Culver.

Married: Feb. 27, 1844, at Sag Harbor [Long Is.], Capt. Jeremiah Sayre and Maria C. Payne.

Died: March 8, 1844, in Albany, Mrs. Mary S. Tucker; she was buried in Mt. Hope Cemetery.

Adv.: Henry S. Flower and John L. Clark - dissolve; Flower continues with Boston City Cash Store.

MARCH 20, 1844

Married: March 6, 1844, in Walworth, Rev. E. Ferdinand Ring of Ohio, and E. Greenleaf Bates, of MA.

Died: March 14, 1844, Mrs. Sarah Tingley, mother of Daniel Tingley, ae 81 years.

MARCH 27, 1844

Married: March 25, in Palmyra, Dr. Richard Lemon and Mrs. Mary Parshall, all of Palmyra.

Married: March 26, 1844, in Macedon, High Colbrath, of Palmyra and Anna S. Colvin, of Macedon.

Married: March 19, 1844, in Palmyra, Jason Pearse and Mrs. Mary Keckel, all of Palmyra.

Died: March 17, 1844, in Arcadia, Ebenezer Smith, ae 86 yrs., a Revolutionary soldier.

Adv.: H. B. Williams - dentist.

APRIL 3, 1844

Pomeroy Tucker apologizes for article re: George N. Williams.

Thomas C. Miller will lecture April 3, before P. L. A. on "Woman as she has been, as she is and as she should be."

Married: April 2, 1844, in Palmyra, William Foster and Esther Young, both of Palmyra.

Married: March 26, 1844, in Williamson, Chauncey Fish, and Phebe Jane Cottrell.

Died: March 27, 1844, in Williamson, Robert Alsop, ae 62 years.

APRIL 10, 1844

David G. Ely in the store 1st door west of Bank Bldg., now G. W. C. office.

Three new canal warehouses; 3 new dry goods stores; 2 new produce stores, a new book store and several shops and dwellings in Palmyra!

Died: April 3, 1844, in Walworth, George Mathewson, ae 69 yrs., a native of Rhode Island and a first settler in the Town of Walworth; a land surveyor for 40 years.

Adv.: Schuyler Parshall - canal store, W. F. Jarvis in charge of market; James Jennings adv. a lost pocket book.

APRIL 17, 1844
Adv.: Rogers & Scotten - dry goods.

APRIL 24, 1844
School District No. 1 classes to commence April 29, Mr. J. R. Vosburgh, teacher.
Married: April 17, in Zion Church, Edward H. Groot, of Auburn, [Cayuga Co.], and Sarah A. Smith, dau. of F. Smith, of Palmyra.
Married: April 16, 1844, in Macedon, Abraham Vosburgh and Louisa Foot.
Married: April 18, 1844, in Walworth, Rev. Harley Strickland and Charlotte Andrew, of Ontario.
Married: April 21, 1844, in Walworth, George Tiffany of Ohio, and Angeline Cady, of Ontario.
Adv: O. H. Palmer has a 200 acre farm for sale; S. O. Seelye - photographer; S. P. Seymour & J. K. Sexton, - dry goods.

MAY 1, 1844
Mr. J. M. Francis will assist in the editorial dept. of the Wayne Sentinel.
Editorial on packet lines: Two boats per day pass Palmyra in each direction regularly, stopping here to land and receive passengers. Name of boats:

South American	Capt. Vedder
North American	Capt. Green
Boston	Capt. Wheeler
Albany	Capt. Cole
Toronto	Capt. Smith

Married: April 11, 1844, Uriah L. Leonard, of Augusta, [Oneida Co.], and Cassandra M., a dau. of Col. Stephen Drane.
Married: April 16, 1844, in Williamson, Amasa O. Miller and Amanda Lewis, both of Williamson.
Married: April 16, 1844, by Rev. D. H. May, Alexander R. Terwiliger and Rebeckah C. Lemon, all of Palmyra.
Adv.: North American Circus - 50c; Aldrich & Gallup - dry goods.

MAY 8, 1844
Married: May 2, 1844, Freeman Clark and Lydia Robinson.
Died: April 23, 1844, in Lyons, Capt. Elisha Sisson, father of Hon. William Sisson, age 81 years.
Adv: I. E. Beecher & Co. - shoe store; Richard Ford - market, rents M. J. Godards's; James H. Sanford - patent pumps.

MAY 15, 1844
Married: May 8, in "Town", Alexander G. Melvin of Webster [Monroe Co.] and Emeline M. Foster, a dau. of Cyrus Foster.
Married: May 25 [sic], at Nashua, NH, Alfred Lund of Palmyra and Mary Antoinette Whitney, a dau. of Jesse Whitney.
Adv.: A. M. Bayles takes over H. Linnell's chair store;

J. L. Clark wants to buy wheat, etc.

F. Williams, late of Auburn is jeweller with D. Hotchkiss.

MAY 22, 1844

Editorial on the libel suit in re: George N. Williams.

Adv.: N. Allen - teaches penmanship.

Married: May 16, 1844, in "Town", William Eggerton (Adgeton?) and Calista Avery.

MAY 29, 1844

Married: May 16, 1844, in Canandaigua, Thomas B. Hahn and Flora Shepard.

JUNE 5, 1844

Married: May 26, 1844, in Macedon, Paul H. Davis, of Ridgeway [Orleans Co.], and Charlotte Spear, youngest dau. of Deacon Stephen Spear.

Adv.: William Anderson & Son - boot and shoe store.

JUNE 12, 1844

Article on the Morse Telegraph system, q.v.

Married: June 5, 1844, in Palmyra, by Rev. N. W. Fisher, S. Smith Pettit, of LaGrange, [Wyoming Co], NY, and Gertrude Everitt, of Poughkeepsie.

Died: May 22, 1844, in Canandaigua, Mrs. Elizabeth E. Oliver, consort of Gilbert Oliver and dau. of Hannah Judson, of Canandaigua.

JUNE 19, 1844

Married: June 12, 1844, Eliab W. Capron and Rebecca M. Cooper, dau. of Griffith M. Cooper, of Williamson.

JUNE 26, 1844

Democrats erect liberty pole in front of Horton's Block.

Died: June 22, 1844, in Macedon, Joseph Carpenter, a Quaker.

JULY 3, 1844

The Fourth will be ushered in by the usual salute and the flag will float from the Democrat's Liberty Pole; the Victor Band will give a concert in Horton's Hall July 4th.; Raymond & Co. Circus to be here July 8th - adm. 25c.

Married: June 25, 1844, Chester Acher and Elizabeth Coon, all of this town.

Married: June 18, 1844, in Auburn [Cayuga Co.], Charles J. Folger and Susan R. Worth, dau. of Capt. C. B. Worth.

Died: June 21, 1844, in East Palmyra, Sally, wife of Dr. James Hubbell, ae 53 yrs. 3 days.

Died: June 18, 1844, in New Brunswick, NJ, Zalmon Rice of Lyons, ae 56 years.

JULY 10, 1844

The Hose & Bucket Co. #1 of Palmyra thank Mr. B. Nowton [sic], of the Bunker Hill Hotel for the sumptuous repast he served the evening of the 4th of July. s/ J. H .Chase, Foreman and H. Williams, Sec.

Married: July 4, 1844, John F. Jackson and Lucy Ann Pierce.

Married: July 4, 1844, Jonathan Turner of Macedon and Betsey M. Dumond, of Walworth.

Died: July 6, 1844, in Newark, Capt. Nathan Hull, ae 37 years.

JULY 17, 1844

June 27, 1844, Joe and Hyrum Smith reported killed at Carthage [IL].

Married: July 11, 1844, in Palmyra, at the Bunker Hill Hotel, Erastus R. Calhoun of Vienna [Oneida Co.], and Lucinda Newton.

JULY 24, 1844

Theron G. Yoemans is appointed Post Master at Walworth.

Died: July 17, 1844, in Palmyra, Mrs. Ruth S. Ely, ae 35 yrs., 20 yrs. a member of the Presbyterian Church.

Died: July 16, 1844, at Williamson, Harriet Kinney, wife of Darius F. Kinney, ae 28 years.

JULY 31, 1844

Mr. Hammond will commence his select school Aug. 7th over Mr. Jackson's rifle factory.

Died: July 5, 1844, Avery W. Stowel, ae 30 yrs. 3 months.

Died: July 30, 1844, Sylvester Willcox, ae 69 yrs - [lived?] for 20 yrs. in Albany.

Adv.: Lamson, Butterfield & Walker dissolve, (Martin) Butterfield & (James S.) Walker [continue].

AUGUST 7, 1844

(Nathaniel) Warren & (Loring G.) Robbins dissolve.

Died: July 28, 1844, in Windham, [Greene Co], NY, Lucretia Vorse, wife of Charles Vorse, ae 72 years.

AUGUST 14, 1844

Died: Aug. 8, 1844, in Marion, at his father's, Robert Hogoboom, George C. Hogoboom, ae 24 years.

Died: Aug. 11, 1844, at Palmyra, Mary Ellen Fobes, dau. of Edson and Jane A. Fobes, ae 1 yr. 3 months.

AUGUST 21, 1844 - No items copied.

AUGUST 28, 1844 - Issue missing from the collection used.

SEPTEMBER 4, 1844

Married: Aug. 28, 1844, in Palmyra, Samuel Lunn and Sarah Allen, both of Sodus.

SEPTEMBER 11, 1844

Samuel G. Martin, chief engineer in J. K. Wing's steam flouring mill, was scalded Sept. 4th so bad that he died in 10 hours, ae 35 yrs.; left wife and 2 children.

Dr. Lund has a singing school in the Brown Block.

Died: Sept 5, 1844, in Palmyra, Irving W. Church, a son of Warren Church, ae 9 years. (This internment is the first one made in the new cemetery.)

SEPTEMBER 18, 1844

Wayne Co. Fair to be held in Lyons this year, Oct. 8th & 9th.

Miss Lusk teaches the piano.

Married: Sept. 11, 1844, in Prattsburgh [Steuben Co.], David Tuthill and Annis H. Francis.

SEPTEMBER 25, 1844

Married: Sept. 9, 1844, in Princeton, NJ, Daniel Scotten and Elizabeth H. Perine, dau. of Maj. John A. Perine.

Married: Sept. 24, 1844, in Macedon, James Gallup and Hannah Capron, dau. of William P. Capron.

Married: Sept. 25, 1844, in Canandaigua, James Jennings and Melvina Reynolds, dau. of Isaac Reynolds.

Died: Aug. 26, 1844, Mary Ann Addicott, dau. of Henry Addicott, ae 5 years.

Died: Sept. 14, 1844, in Ontario, Miss Rebecca L. McCreery, ae 19 years.

OCTOBER 2, 1844

The Wayne Sentinel to-day enters its 21st year of publication, having commenced Oct. 1, 1823.

Jacob C. Pettit discontinues business; there is a letter in the P. O. for William Van Alstyne.

Married: Sept. 23, 1844, Thomas Lakey and Mary Terry, both of the Town [Palmyra].

Married: Oct. 14, 1844, in Canandaigua, John Ganson and Mary Hopkins Sibley, dau. of Mark H. Sibley.

Married: Oct. 24, 1844, by Rev. John W. Clark, James Gallup of Palmyra and Hannah W. Capron, dau. of William P. Capron, of Macedon.

Died: Sept. 23, 1844, Elizabeth Westfall, dau. of Jacob Westfall, ae 25 years.

OCTOBER 9, 1844

Our Democratic Boys raised a noble hickory tree at the corner of Main and Canandaigua Thurs. last.

Died: Oct. 4, 1844, Mrs. Catherine Tingley, ae 52 yrs., wife of Daniel Tingley.

Married: Sept. 29, 1844, at Hopewell [Ontario Co.], John B. Haynes and Freelove Kingsley.

Married: Oct. 1, 1844, in Canandaigua, Charles H. Chesebro and Georgiana Martha Rosewarne, dau. of Dr. John Rosewarne.

OCTOBER 16, 1844

H. M. North - dentistry over D. Hotchkiss store, two doors west of W. P. Nottingham's Hotel.

OCTOBER 23, 1844

Fire broke out in the dwelling house of Daniel Tingley in this village, Sun. night last, originating in a box of ashes in the cellar - no damage. Another fire broke out Mon. night in the apartment of Mrs. Willcox in the Jarvis block.

Bruce Everson in poor health was in New York and being no better, sailed for the Island of Maderia Oct. 16th.

Decidedly the best Hickory performance of the season is the display of a "Polk & Dallas" banner from an elegant flag staff run up some 30 ft., above the top of the tall hickory tree by the residence of Col. Horton, on the eastern margin of the village... Two poles in Macedon were sawed or bored down.

Died: Oct. 18, 1844, in Palmyra, Maria Stoddard, ae 19 yrs., only dau. of Col. James S. Stoddard.

OCTOBER 30, 1844

Married: Oct. 16, 1844, in Williamson, William Palister and Elizabeth Church, both of Williamson.

Married: Oct. 16, 1844, in Williamson, John Lewis, of Iowa and Deborah Malcomb of Williamson.

NOVEMBER 6, 1844

John O. Vorse appointed postmaster vice Dr. D. D. Hoyt removed.

[James K. L.] Polk won with about 100 majority in the county.

Married: Oct. 3, 1844, in Marion, Samuel R. Sanford, of Geneva [Ontario Co.] and Susan Sophia Huggins, of Marion.

Married: Nov. 5, 1844, in Farmington, Benjamin Franklin Taber and Susan Ann Price, dau. of Isaac Price.

Died: in town, Mrs. Elizabeth Post, wife of Samuel H. Post, and dau. of Ebenezer Hathaway.

Adv.: Palmyra Recess - Charles Reeves - restaurant.

NOVEMBER 13, 1844

Married: Nov. 11, 1844, at Fishkill Landing [Dutchess Co.], Capt. David Glossender, of the firm Beecher & Glossender, and Mary E. Lamson, dau. of Nathaniel K. Lamson, both of this village.

Married: Nov. 8, 1844, in Newark, Paul J. Culver and Mary Tupper, of Palmyra.

Died: Nov. 7, 1844, in Palmyra, Mrs. Jane Elizabeth Ferrin, ae 35 yrs.

Died: Oct. 30, 1844, in Ann Arbor, MI, Col. Nathan Thayer, ae 74 years.

NOVEMBER 20, 1844

H. P. Sterling - marble shop, succeeds Warren & Robbins.

Died: Nov. 17, 1844, in "Town", Benjamin Cole, ae 54 years.

Died: Nov. 14, 1844, Ephriam Soper, ae 57 years.

Died: Nov. 13, 1844. in this village, [Palmyra], Catherine Gordon, ae 4 yrs., dau. of John Gordon.

Adv.: Solomon Carter is located opposite the Post Office on Market St.

NOVEMBER 27, 1844

E. T. Grant, Post Master at Newark vice R. P. Williams.

Albany State Normal School to be opened Dec.18, 1844.

Married: Nov. 7, 1844, in Ashtabula [OH], Stephen F. Selby, M. D., late of Palmyra, and Sarah A. Fisk, dau. of Hon. Amasa Fisk.

Married: Nov. 13, 1844 in Troy, Hon. John Wentworth, M. C. and R. Maria Loomis, dau. of Riley Loomis.

Married: Nov. 21, 1844, in Palmyra, John Pierce and Ann J. McOmber, both of town.

Died: Nov. 17, 1844, in Macedon, Mrs. Polly Cheesman, ae 60 years.

Died: Nov. 23, 1844, in Macedon, Mrs. Mary Billings, wife of Benjamin Billings.

Died: Nov. 24, 1844, in Palmyra, Betsey Bump, ae 48 years.

Died: Nov. 24, 2844, Mrs. Soper, widow of Ephriam Soper, who died last week.

Died: Nov. 19, 1844, Mary Ann Mix, dau. of Thomas Mix, ae 21 years.

DECEMBER 4, 1844

Married: Dec. 2nd, in Palmyra, Albert Wells and Catherine Beckwith, dau. of George Beckwith.

Married: Nov. 28, 1844, in Palmyra, Thomas Pierce and Jane Tassell, both of Williamson.

Married: Nov. 27, 1844, Loring O. Banks and Mary N. Hildreth, both of Palmyra.

DECEMBER 11, 1844

Married: Dec. 5, 1844, John E. North and Deborah H. Johnson, both of Palmyra.

DECEMBER 18, 1844

Married: Dec. 16, 1844, Charles W. Wooster, of Boston and Ann Maria Barnhart, dau. of Isaac Barnhart, of Walworth.

Married: Dec. 11, 1844, in East Bloomfield, Daniel S. Baker, and Rachel B. Pomeroy.

Died: Dec. 16, 1844, Edward S. Thayer, son of Levi Thayer, of Palmyra, ae 24 years.

DECEMBER 25, 1844

Married: Dec. 18, 1844, Edwin E. Rogers and Aurelia Sherman.

Died: Dec. 16, 1844, in Farmington, Amanda M. Payne, dau. of Allen Payne, ae 20 years.

JANUARY 8, 1845

Hiram Axtell kept the Manchester House in Manchester.

The Office of the Wayne Sentinel removed to the west end of the Horton Block; Mason & Tuttle are agents for the Wayne Sentinel in N. Y.

Charles Poucher, late editor of the Lyons Argus, is appointed Postmaster vice, Maj. E. Price, removed. Mr. Price was the first Post Master at Lyons in 1811 and held it most of the time since. His son-in-law, R. H. Foster held it a few years.

Died: Jan. 2, 1845, in Macedon, Mary M. Downing, ae 19 yrs., dau. of George Downing.

Died: Jan. 3, 1845, in Macedon, Ann Eliza Downing, ae 17 yrs., dau. of George Downing.

Died: Jan. 2, 1845, in Sodus, Mrs. Clarissa Brayton, wife of William L. Brayton, ae 55 years.

Adv.: William S. Wilcox, of Marion - dried fruit.

JANUARY 15, 1845

Married, Jan. 8, 1845, David Nettleton, of Penfield [Monroe Co.], and Anna M. Shaver, of Macedon.

Married: Jan. 17, 1845, in N.O. [New Oregon, Erie Co.; New Ohio, Broome Co. or New Orleans, LA ?], Daniel T. Lilly of N. O. and Eliza S. Lakey, dau. of Abner Lakey. [NB: This date copied as it appeared in the original transcription is an error.]

Died: Jan. 12, 1845, in Palmyra, Mrs. Maria Butler, wife of Burr Butler, ae 38 years.

Died: Jan. 14, 1745, Dr. Jonathan S. Eggleston, ae 46 years.

JANUARY 22, 1845

Abner Tucker is collecting agent for the Wayne Sentinel.

Married: Jan. 14, 1845, Benjamin Parker, of Manchester and Eliza Ann Edmonston, dau. of John A. Edmondston.

Married: Jan. 15, 1845, in Manchester, George A. Adams and Cynthia Parker, both of Manchester.

Married: Jan. 1, 1845, in Williamson, Rufus P. Fairbanks and Mary A. Cottrell.

Died: Jan. 20, 1845, in Macedon, George Downing, ae 55 years.

Died: Jan. 20, 1845, in Macedon, Mrs. Kozia Wilkinson, ae 67 years.

Died: Jan. 19, 1845, in Macedon, Mrs. Wooster, wife of Albert Wooster.

JANUARY 29, 1845

Married: Jan. 1, 1845, in Michigan, James B. Tucker and Susan Hall.

Married: Jan. 23, 1845, at the Bunker Hill Hotel, James Pollock and Ellen Stout, both of Arcadia.

Died: Jan. 23, 1845, in Palmyra, Mrs. Alcymany Flower, ae 52 yrs., wife of Elisha Flower, of Arcadia.

FEBRUARY 5, 1845

The Warehouse of William Hegeman in Port Glasgow, burned Jan. 31, containing 600-800 bushels of grain.

Died: Jan. 29, 1845, in Williamson, William B. Grandin, ae 27 years.

FEBRUARY 12, 1845

Committee named for Inauguration celebration and dinner at the Bunker Hill Hotel, March 4th.

Levi Clark named Post Master at Marion vice Dr. Wright removed.

Married: Feb. 11, 1845, Elijah Thompson and Sophronia Allen, both of Palmyra.

Died: Dec. 20, 1844, at Madeira, Bruce Everson [q.v.], of Palmyra, ae 50 years.

Died: Jan. 28, 1845, in Palmyra, Mrs. Mary Ann Wells, wife of Rufus G. Wells, ae 29 years.

FEBRUARY 19, 1845

Married: Feb. 12, 1845, in Macedon, Hiram Smith, of Manchester and Juliett Quance, dau. of King H. Quance.

Married: Feb. 9, 1845, in Williamson, Leonard Lord and Emma Jane Dusenbury.
Died: Feb. 13, 1845, in "Town", Hannah Eddy, ae 63 years, wife of Jesse Eddy, a Quaker.
Died: Feb. 16, 1845, in Walworth, Silas Downing, age 56 years.

FEBRUARY 26, 1845

Married: Feb. 25, 1845, Henry F. Sterling and Lois Nobles, all of Palmyra.
Married: Feb. 22, 1845, in Palmyra, Isaac Gifford and Jemima Ann Austin, both of Arcadia.
Died: Feb. 18, 1845, in Palmyra, Franklin A. Thayer, son of Levi Thayer, ae 14 months.
Died: Feb. 17, 1845, in Willett [Cortland Co.], Elijah Thompson of this town, ae 31 yrs.; he was running behind a rig to get warm and slipped and fell; he was a member of the M. E. Church of Palmyra.
Died: Feb. 14, 1845, in Manchester, Ebenezer Bird.
Died: Feb. 17, 1845, in East Bloomfield [Ontario Co.], Mrs. Lucy Haywood, wife of Asa Haywood, ae 85 years.
Died: Feb. 22, 1845, in Lyons, Maj. Ezekiel Price, ae 80 years.
Died: Feb. 21, 1845, in "Town", Jesse Brown, ae 50 years.

MARCH 5, 1845

Inauguration dinner; ball in the evening; cannonading from Mt. Holmes.
Several new buildings in progress in Palmyra; large dry goods store of J. L. Clark.
William H. Cuyler's house caught fire Feb. 28th.
Richard Lemon adv. a house and lot at the corner of Main & Clinton St.

MARCH 12, 1845

The Cleveland Medical College confers an honorary degree of M. D. on Dr. Alexander McIntyre, a pupil of the late Gain Robinson.
Jonathan Silsby Eggleston, a native of Orwell, VT, born Aug. 10(?), 1798, d. Jan. 14, 1845; came to Palmyra when a young man, studied with Dr. Gain Robinson; graduated at Fairfield, Feb. 15, 1825; was a Dr. in Palmyra for 21 years and a member of the Presbyterian Church.
Married: Mar. 5, 1845, in Town, Orrin McOmber and Frances Pierce, all of the town of Palmyra.
Died: Feb. 26, 1845, in Lyons, Capt. Peter Perrine, ae 68 years.
Died: Feb. 26, 1845, in Newark, Mrs. Sarah Middleton, wife of George H. Middleton, ae 31 years.
Died: March 5, 1845, in Pultneyville, Peter Powers, ae 58 years.

MARCH 19, 1845

Died: March 13, 1845, in Walworth, Nathan Palmer, ae 64 yrs., a native of Granville, [Washington Co.], NY.
Adv. H. B. Johnson - leathers; R. H. Sheldon, M. D. - in office of J. S. Eggleston.

MARCH 26, 1845

(John) Williamson & (Allyn) Williamson dissolves; J[ohn] Williamson continues.

Died: March 22, 1845. in Palmyra, Hiram Payne, ae 83 yrs., a native of CT, b. Jan. 13, 1785; a graduate at Darmouth, NH, a resident of Palmyra for 20 years.

Died: Jan. 12, 1845, Mrs. Maria Butler, wife of Burr Butler and a dau. of Hiram Payne, ae 39 years.

APRIL 2, 1845

Boats running on the Erie Canal through Palmyra:

South America	Capt. S. E. Vedder
Boston	Capt. T. Wheeler
St. Louis	Capt. J. B. Cole
Knickerbocker	Capt. W. H. A. Smith
North America	Capt. D. K. Green

Died: March 28, 1845, in Walworth, Hon. Jonathan Boynton, ae 65 yrs.; he settled on the farm where he died, in 1805; in 1827 and 1829 served as a legislator. In 1832, he joined the Free Will Baptist Church.

Died: March 20, 1845, in Williamson, Enoch Giberson, age 75 yrs. on Dec. 17, 1844 and Jerusha Giberson, d. March 21, 1845 - she was ae 74 yrs on June 17, 1844. A double funeral was held.

Died: March 31, 1845, in Palmyra, Robert Withers, Sr., ae 75 years.

APRIL 9, 1845

Fire in the old (Aldrich) Block, on Main St. - put out without much damage.

W. H Southwick and B. B. Johnston dissolve.

Died: April 3, 1845, in Walworth, Julia Boynton, dau. of the late Jonathan Boynton, ae 23 years.

APRIL 16, 1845

Editorial on J. W. Netterville's chair and furniture factory.

Died: April 13, 1845, Martha Flower Clark, dau. of John L. and Martha A. Clark, ae 18 months.

Died: April 8, 1845, Mrs. Sarah Huntington, wife of Jedidiah Huntington, ae 76 years.

Died: April 13, 1845, in Palmyra, Mrs. Salome Seymour, widow of the late Eli Seymour, ae 72 years.

Died: April 13, 1845, in "Town", Mrs. Ann Smith, wife of Barzillai, ae 58 years.

Died: April 15, 1845, in "Town", Samuel W. Jordan, ae 46 years.

Adv.: Boston Quartette Club at Horton's Hall.

APRIL 25, 1845

Married: April 18, 1845, at the Beacon Hill Hotel, John Van Kirk, and Mrs. Jane House, both of Orleans [Ontario Co.].

Married: April 22, 1845, in Pittsford [Monroe Co.], Rodney A. Rogers, of Albany and Augusta Parker, a dau. of Sylvester Parker.

APRIL 30, 1845

Married: April 29, 1845, in Walworth, Prof. A. G. J. DaLee, of Pittsford [Monroe Co.] and Clarinda E. Findly, dau. of Jones Findly.

Died: April 28, 1845, in Palmyra, Mary Jane Gilbert, dau. of John H. Gilbert, ae 5 years.

Died: April 28, 1845, Lydia Amanda, dau. of David P. Daggett, ae 18 years; funeral to be at the Presbyterian Church with sermon by Rev. Mr. Fisher.

Died: April 29, 1845, in Palmyra, Mrs. Aurelia Millard, wife of Asahel Millard, ae 42 years.

Adv.: C. E. Thurber - grain; Seymour & Sexton dissolve - Seymour continues.

Joseph Gibbs, Village Sexton, has removed to the home lately occupied by S. S. Durfee, near Col. Horton's.

MAY 7, 1845

Thomas C. Miller, attorney, went to Detroit.

Adv.: Wells Anderson & Son - dissolve; Pooley & Butterfield - Rope Walk; E. M. Anderson - shoe store.

MAY 21, 1845

Married: In Michigan, Samuel W. Sawyer, of Macedon, and Hannah Nelson.

Died: April 27, 1845, in Farmington, Mrs. Delia Aldrich, wife of Silas Aldrich, ae 21 years.

Died: May 9, 1845, in Pultneyville, Deacon Abraham Pepper, ae 88 yrs., a native of Holland.

MAY 28, 1845

The Palmyra Courier, by F. Morley, formerly associated in the publication of the Wayne County Whig, makes it first appearance in our village, this week.

Married: May 22, 1845, in "Town", by Rev. George R. H. Shumway, of Newark, Byram Green Sherman and Cynthia Ann Rogers, dau. of Jareb D. Rogers.

Married: May 18, 1845, in Groton [Tompkins Co.], Luther F. Spear of Macedon, and Lydia Dexter.

Died: May 24, 1845, Josephine Lovett, ae 4 yrs., dau. of J. C. Lovett.

Died: May 22, 1845, Deborah Ann Daggett, ae 22 yrs, dau. of David P. Daggett.

Died: May 19, 1845, George Post Jessup, son of George G. Jessup, ae one year.

Died: May 22, 1845, William H. Williamson, son of John Williamson, ae 3 years.

Died: May 26, 1845, Alfred Hubbard, ae 28 years.

Died: May 25, 1845, George S. Carpenter, ae 53 years.

Died: May 5, 1745, in Williamson, Orinda Adams, dau. of Merritt Adams, ae 25 years.

Died: Rufus G. Wells, ae 32 yrs., admitted to the bar in 1834, and formed a partnership with James Paddie - now dissolved.

JUNE 4, 1845

Married: June 1, 1845, in Walworth, Enoch Johnson of Williamson, and Martha Seymour, of Marion.

Died: May 31, 1845, in "Town", Maria Smith, dau. of Barzillai, ae 20 years.

Died: May 27, 1845, in Port Glasgow, Benjamin Drake, ae 58 years.
Died: May 25, 1845, in Walworth, Mrs. Eunice Tiffany, wife of Edwin Tiffany, ae 40 years.
Adv.: William H. Southwick, insurance; Welch, Mann & Delavan - circus.

JUNE 11, 1845
Died: June 8, 1845, Joel Thayer Gilbert, ae 11 mos., son of J. H. Gilbert.

JUNE 19, 1845
The new cemetery belonging to this village has been beautifully laid out into lots, with walks, avenues and carriage roads.
Died: June 11, 1845, in East Palmyra, the infant son of John and Mary Ann Ditton, ae 8 months.
Died: June 17, 1845, in Palmyra, Ebenezer Hathaway, ae 65 years.
Married: June 16, 1845, at the Temperance House, of S. Cole, Esq., Edward Sherman and Jane Pendle, both of Arcadia.

JUNE 25, 1845
Sale of cemetery lots brought in $600.00.
June 24, 1845, Marquis D. Coe and Isaac Sanford, adv., auction of Benjamin Cole's property.
Married: June 23, 1845, at Mt. Morris [Livingston Co.], Jesse R. Smith, of Manchester, and Jane M. Smith of Palmyra.
Married: June 11, 1845, at Palmyra, David Goldsmith and Eliza Ann Smith.
Died: June 15, 1845, Mary E. T. Ely, dau. of Joseph N. and Hannah M. R. Ely, ae 20 months.
Died: June 24, 1845, in Palmyra, Jane Williams, ae 3 yrs., dau. of Elbridge Williams.

JULY 2, 1845
D. Hotchkiss discontinued the jewellery business - sells out to Messrs. Williams and Douglas.
Fire Co. #2, held meeting at their engine house, June 30th; election of officers: Oliver Olson, foreman; Luther M. Chase, asst. foreman; Peter S. Lockwood, Sec.; DeWitt C. McIntyre, Treas.
Married: June 26, 1845 in Port Glasgow, Benjamin T. Babbitt, of New York and Rebecca McDufee.
Married: June 26, 1845, in "Town", William M. Horton, and Helen Shermerhorn, both of "Town".
Married: June 26, 1845, in Williamson, Allen Deo and Marietta Culver.
Died: June 28, 1845, in Walworth, Mrs. Burissa Hill, wife of Francis Hill, and dau. of the late Jonathan Boynton, ae 36 years.

JULY 9, 1845
Report of the Fourth of July celebration: Macedon and Palmyra Band and also a band under Mr. Doty; torch light procession in the evening, toasts, etc.
John M. Francis and James Culver are census enumerators.
Ornon Archer is principal of the Academy in Walworth.
Married: July 3, 1845, in Sodus, William Beswick and Eleanor M. Paddock, of Sodus.

JULY 16, 1845

A drunken man broke his leg at one of the stores in Palmyra, July 4th.

Married: July 3, 1845, in East Palmyra, John H. Parker and Anna Christina Feller, dau. of John D. Feller.

Married: July 9, 1845, in Syracuse, Benjamin R. Norton and Mrs. Louisa Stowell, both late of Palmyra.

Married: July 2, 1845, at [Utica [Oneida Co.], J. F. Jones, of Syracuse and Eveline R. Grannis of Utica.

Died: July 9, 1845, in Vermont, Eleazer May, father of Dr. William May, ae 79 years.

Adv.: L. D. Stone - Doctor.

JULY 23, 1845

Abram Fish ae 72 yrs, was killed at Manchester by Isaac Lockwood while drunk.

Dr. Wenzer - dentist at Room #5 at the Palmyra Hotel.

Married: Job Clark and Mrs. Prudence Smith, dau. of Joseph Lewis.

Died: July 20, 1845, in "Town", William Murray, ae 40 years.

Died: July 12, in Michigan, Stephen Winslow, late of Palmyra, ae 67 years.

JULY 30, 1845

Wayne County Bank Property sold by receiver at Rochester: $13,100; $235,000 of paper; 1127 acres of land in PA; 1776 a. in MI, 325 a. in Genesee Co. and also some in Palmyra village.

Died: July 28, 1845, in Walworth, Mark Newell, ae 51 yrs. fell dead while mowing. He was b. in CT.

AUGUST 6, 1845

Married: Aug. 4, 1845, in Palmyra, Orrin Barron and Ann E. Davis.

Married: Aug. 1, 1845, in Marion, Prof. S. Wood, Principal of Macedon Academy and Miss Emma M. Sanford, dau. of Isaac R. Sanford, of Marion.

AUGUST 13, 1845

Died: Aug. 10, 1845, Samuel Hudson, ae 29 yrs., at the home of his father, Col. Pliny E. Hudson.

Died: Aug. 7, 1845, in "Town", Mrs. Mary Lakey, ae 35 yrs., wife of Thomas Lakey.

Died: July 27, 1845, in Howell, MI, Mrs. Delia Ann Galloway, wife of John Galloway, late of Marion, ae 22 years.

Died: July 31, 1845, in Walworth, Mrs. Mary Strickland, ae 77 yrs.; came from Hartford, CT, converted in 1809.

Died: July 20, 1845, in Lawrenceville, PA, Mary Lindsley Shumway, oldest dau. of Rev. G. R. H. Shumway, of Newark, ae 8 yrs. 8 mos. 18 days.

Adv: H. R. Phelps - stage line to Pultneyville; 50 - 75c; runs three times a week; has a four year contract to carry the mail.

AUGUST 20, 1845

Dowingsville Mills - same as Hodard's Mills or Yellow Mills.

Married: Aug. 10, 1845, at the Methodist Chapel in Palmyra, Morrison Ford and Margaret McDonald.

Married: July 22, 1845, Hon, Stephen Clark, of Rochester, and Mrs. Sarah L. Phillips, of Waterford [Saratoga Co.?]

Married: Aug. 17, 1845, in Newark, George Wheeler and Catherine Brown, both of Palmyra.

Died: Aug. 13, 1845, in New Jersey, Frederick W. Cole, ae 30 yrs., clerk in the Albany Argus office.

Died: Aug. 15, 1845, in Albany, Obadiah R. Van Benthuysen, ae 59 years.

AUGUST 27, 1845

John C. Spencer, of Macedon, was found dead in Gen. Rogers barn - he was a drinker.

Stephen D. Wilson appointed Post Master in Macedon, vice Henry Reed, removed.

Henry F. Winchester, late with H. S. Flower, is now with J. C. L. [?]

Married: Aug. 20, 1845, in DeRuyter [Madison Co.], Purdy M. Willits, of Macedon and Sarah L. M. Arnold, oldest dau. of Ephriam Arnold.

Married: Aug. 19, 1845, in Buffalo, Dr. Ryland J. Rogers, of Holland, [Erie Co.] and Eliza Pomeroy, dau. of Robert Pomeroy.

Died: Aug. 3, 1845, in Palmyra. only son of Charles and Julia Bortles, ae 7 days.

SEPTEMBER 3, 1845

The population of this village acc. to the census just taken (embracing several families not actually within the corporate limits, but within what is regarded as Village territory) is 819, of which 903 are males and 916 females. In 1840, the population was 1709 showing a gain of 110 persons in five years. Statistics for the village:

295 dwelling houses	1 public hall
14 dry goods stores	1 hall/young Men's Assoc.
2 hardware stores	1 IOOF Hall
2 drug stores	1 Sons of Temperance
4 hat stores	8 tailor shops
8 boot/shoe shops	4 cooper shops
1 wholesale grocery	2 wagon shops
9 grocery/provision stores	3 cabinet & chair shops
2 book stores	5 joiners shops
2 newsp. printing offices	3 paint shops
2 jewellery stores	1 portrait painted
10 canal warehouses	1 rifle factory
1 steam flouring mill	1 marble factory
5 produce offices	3 tin & copper shops
2 wool depots/cloth stores	3 millinery shops
4 lawyers offices	3 Mantua-making/tailoress

3 magistrates offices	5 blacksmith shops
2 dentists offices	3 saddle/harness shops
7 Doctors offices	3 tanneries
1 academy (unincorpated.)	1 morocco factory
3 dist. schoolhouses	1 steam pump factory
1 select school	1 steam furnace/machine
5 hotels	1 soap/candle factory
1 bakery	1 weaving shop
3 turning lathes	2 saw mills
2 fire engine houses	1 canal collector/office
1 State boatyard/shop	1 canal drydock
1 bank	2 barber shops
1 brewery	2 livery stables
3 beef markets	3 confection/candy shops
1 candy mfgr.	3 soda fountains

[Editorial comment: In what village with a population of 1,819 in this year (1996) could you possibly find all such businesses as this? Are we progressing or sliding backwards?]

Died: Aug. 27, 1845, in Sodus, Matthew Clark, of Westhampton, MA, ae 45 years.

Adv.: J. Shimer, proprietor of the Railroad Stage, leaves Palmyra daily at 7 a.m. via Newark and ar. in Vienna at 10:30 a.m.; leaves Vienna at 11;00 p.m. and reaches Palmyra at 2 a.m. The line also runs to Auburn in 8 hrs. Pal. to Newark - 25c; Vienna - 50c; Auburn $1.25.

SEPTEMBER 10, 1845

Nathaniel Lamson, father of N. K. Lamson, committed suicide in New York, on Thurs. last, by shooting himself.

Counterfeiters found in some house near Palmyra - prominent men.

Married: Sept.4, 1845, in "Town", Peter P. Huyck and Frances C. Miller, dau. of Kingsley Miller.

Married: Sept. 3, 1845, James Tassell and Elizabeth Husker, dau. of William Husker.

Married: Sept. 3, 1845, in town, in a Quaker ceremony, Dr. Reuben Eves, of Macedon, and Amy E. Carpenter.

Married: Aug. 27, 1845, in Lyons, John P. McGregor and Maria Antoinette Goldsmith of Lyons.

Died: July 20, in Woodsock, CT, Theodore Lyon, youngest son of William Lyon, 2nd, ae 26 years.

SEPTEMBER 17, 1845

Selden Williams, Elbridge Williams, and James Ackley, held for being the counterfeiters found in a place in Palmyra.

Married; Sept. 5, 1845, in Chicago, IL, Constant Terry and Mrs. Maria H. Moore, of Palmyra.

Died: Sept. 2, 1845, in Jackson, MI, Lyman Post, ae 43 yrs., late of Palmyra (L.W.P.)

SEPTEMBER 24, 1845

John L. Clark's grain store house broke away from the second story on Sept. 18th, and let grain into the cellar and canal - 15,000 bushels in the building.

Married: Sept. 18, 1845, at the Beacon Hill Hotel, Charles A. Boutell and Harriet N. Paine, both of Michigan.

Married: Sept. 22, 1845, Joseph Johnson and Caroline Quaife, both of Palmyra.

Married Sept. 7, 1845, in Manchester, Loren Buck, of Palmyra and Louisa Smith.

OCTOBER 1, 1845 - No items copied.

OCTOBER 8, 1845

Married: Oct. 5, 1845, in Williamson, James Peckham, of Farmington and Marilla Gilbert, of Williamson.

Married: Oct. 5, 1845, in Walworth, Robert Clark and Ruth Stevens, both of Rochester.

Married: Oct. 1, 1845, Allen Hornby of Sweden, [Monroe Co.] and Harriet Beeching of Palmyra.

Died: Oct. 5, 1845, in Palmyra, Mrs. Hannah Albright, wife of J. F. Albright, ae 69 years.

Died: Sept. 3, 1845, in Wisconsin, Stephen Bates, late of Ontario Co., ae 72 years.

Died: Sept. 30, 1845, in Rochester, Mortimer F. Delano, Surrogate of Monroe Co.

Died: Sept. 25, 1845, in Chicago, Mrs. Jane E. Page, wife of Peter Page, ae 31 years.

Died: Oct. 5, 1845, in Palmyra, Marietta N. Chadwick, ae 19 years.

Cuyler & Aldrich dissolve - W. F. Aldrich continues.

OCTOBER 15, 1845

Married: Oct. 13, 1845, in Newark, John Van Duesen and Electa Bostwick.

Died: Oct. 9, 1845, in Rochester, Van Rensselaer Jackson, ae 29 yrs., brother of Stillman Jackson; he lived in Palmyra and learned the gunsmith trade.

Died: Oct. 13, 1845, in Palmyra, Lucinda, dau. of Thomas Huxley, ae 15 years.

OCTOBER 22, 1845

Married; Oct. 16, 1845, in Walworth, Sidney Lovell, of MA. and Sarah M. Stone of Walworth.

Died: Oct. 5, 1845, in Manchester, Evans Fitzgerald, ae 41 years.

OCTOBER 29, 1845

Married: Oct, 21, 1845, in "Town", Jacob Stupplebeen and Lucinda D. Smith, dau. of George W. Smith.

Married: Oct. 22, 1845, in the Village, James N. Sanford and Alma A. Allen, all of Palmyra and m. with a Quaker ceremony.

NOVEMBER 6, 1845

William L. Tucker's house caught fire Nov. 4, 1845; Rogers & Cuyler's slaughterhouse burned Oct. 31, 1845; Albert G. Heminway admitted to the bar.

Married: Oct. 28, 1845, in Walworth, Francis Heth, of Michigan and Permelia Palmer.

Married: Oct. 30, 1845, in Lyons, William H. Gray, of Geneva and Mary Jane Faling, dau. of Daniel Faling.

Married: Oct. 26, 1845, in Hillsdale, MI, Isaiah H. McCollum and Caroline E. Hammond.

NOVEMBER 12, 1845

The Baker family - 4 brothers and a sister give a concert at Horton's Hall, Nov. 14th.

Died: Nov. 11, 1845, Mrs. Lydia Lovett, ae 55 yrs., mother of J. C. Lovett.

Adv.: Heminway & Hart, attorneys in Brown Block; Southwick & Thurber - want to buy pork.

NOVEMBER 19, 1845

A series of cotillion parties to be held once in two weeks will commence Dec. 3rd at W. P. N, under management of Maj. Gilbert; terms per night, inc. carriages $1.50. Hall to be opened at 6 p.m.

Married: Nov. 12, 1845, at Zion Church, by Rev. John W. Clark, William F. Aldrich and Louisa H. Klapp, both of Palmyra.

Married: Nov. 11, 1845, in Rochester, Dr. James Hubbell, of East Palmyra and Maria Grace Davis, dau. of Thomas Davis.

Married: Nov. 11, 1845, in Marion, Ezekiel Clark and Harriet Mason.

Married: Nov. 15, 1845 in the Village, Gilson Malona of Macedon and Marcia C. Shoemaker.

Married: Nov. 7, 1845, in Vienna, William Dillon and S. Cornelius [sic] Drake, of Vienna [Oneida Co.].

Married: Nov. 7, 1845, David King, of Phelps, and Aurelia Graves.

NOVEMBER 26, 1845

Married: Nov. 24, 1845, in "Town", Edwin Leslie and Catherine Patison, of St. Lawrence Co., NY.

Died: Nov. 17, 1845, in Newark, Mrs. Laura Button, wife of Dr. Cyrus S. Button, ae 49 years.

Adv.: Charlotte B. Gage - painting and music.

DECEMBER 3, 1845

Married: Nov. 30, 1845, in Palmyra, Eli Nickerson and Lydia L. Cook, all of Palmyra.

Married: Nov. 26, 1845, in Webster [Monroe Co.], Ezekiel S. Barnhart of Walworth and Mary A. Dayton.

Married: Nov. 29, 1845, in Walworth, Russell Foster, of Walworth, and Eliza C. Hunt, of Penfield, [Monroe Co.].

Died: Dec. 1, 1845, in Williamson, Mrs. Polly Maria Fish, wife of Harry S. Fish, and dau. of Daniel and Lucy Russell, ae 30 years.

Died: Nov. 25, 1845, in Hammondsport, [Steuben Co.], Sarah Isabelle Gordon, dau. of Williams W. Gordon, ae 6 years.

DECEMBER 10, 1845

Died: Nov. 26, 1845, at New London, CT, Ansel D. Cady, ae 33 years.

DECEMBER 17, 1845

Henry S. Flower assigns to John L. Clark and A. McIntyre.

Married: Dec.11, 1845, in Newark, Stuteley [Studeley?] D. Palmer, of Palmyra and Mary M. Fish.

Married: Dec. 16, 1845, in Egypt [Ontario Co.], Albert H. Van Ness of Perrinton, [Monroe Co.] and Mary Prichard, dau. of James Prichard.

Died: Dec. 12, 1845, in Palmyra, Truman Johnston, 3 yr. old son of B. B. Johnston.

DECEMBER 24, 1845

Married: Dec. 18, 1845, in Walworth, Henry H. Howland and Eliza Lewis both of Walworth.

Married: Dec. 10, 1845, in Utica [Oneida Co.] Henry G. Balis and Sarah E. Jones.

Died: Dec. 12, 1845, Truman Sylvester Johnston, son of Barnet B. and Ann Maria Johnston.

DECEMBER 31, 1845

Died: Dec. 25, 1845, Mrs. C. A. McBane, formerly Maria Benson, of Palmyra, burned to death in Rochester. [Had] a fit and fell onto a fire.

Died: Dec. 20,1845, in Marion, Mrs. Julia Ann Smith, wife of John Smith, ae 31 yrs.; leaves a husband and three children.

Died: Dec. 18, 1845, Diantha, wife of Samuel Norris, ae 21 years.

Married: Dec. 25, 1845, in Zion Church, Samuel O. Scudder, of Waterloo and Harriet A. Chase, dau. of Dr. D. Chase.

Adv.: P. P. Nottingham - guyuscutus.

MARCH, 10, 1847

Married on the 3rd inst., by Rev. Mr. Beebe, David Poucher, Esq., of Sodus to Mrs. Delia Hinman, of the former place,

JUNE 2, 1847

Died: in Auburn, [Cayuga Co.], on the 8th ult., Hon. David Arne, formerly of this county, aged 62 years.

Died: in Walworth, on the 19th ult., of erysipelas, Mrs. Chloe Baker, daughter of Mr. Enoch Lilly (deceased), aged 28 years.

JUNE 16, 1847

Married: in Wethersfield, CT, on the 2nd inst., by Rev. O. E. Duggett, Jared Willson, Esq., of Canandaigua to Mary, dau. of the late William Warson, of Hartford.

Married: in Rochester on the 10th inst., by Rev. Mr. Dewey, George H. Middleton, Esq., of Newark, to Miss Mary Sophia Jerome, of the former place.

Married: in this village on the 12th inst., by I. E. Beecher, Esq., Mr. Benjamin Brown to Miss Catharine Porter,

Died: in this village on the 14th inst., of consumption, Miss Eliza Clarinda Crandall, in the 35th year of her age.

Died: in this village on the 10th inst., of pulmonary consumption, Alvin N. Buel, aged 36 years.

OCTOBER 27, 1847

Married in the Presbyterian CHurch, Palmyra, NY, on the 21st inst., by Rev. Mr. Platt, Mr. Hubbard Trowbridge, of Southfield, MI, to Miss Edna J. West, of the former place.

Died: in the village on the 25th inst., Richard Henry, son of Mr. William Shannon, aged 4 years.

APRIL 18, 1849

Died: in this village on the 6th inst., of consumption, Mrs. Hannah Myrick, wife of A. T. Myrick, aged 32 years.

Died: on the 10th inst., Mrs. Jane Graves, relict of the late John Graves, aged 80 years.

Died: On the 13th inst., Emma Dart, daughter of the late Jonathan Dart, aged 4 years.

Died: in this town on the 12th inst., Mrs. Prudence Durfee, relict of the late Samuel Durfee, aged 85 years.

MAY 2, 1849

Mr. Platt Williams is mysteriously lost in New York city. He was bound for California in company with his brother, Homer Williams, and both were waiting for the sailing of a vessel on which passage had been engaged.

APRIL 4, 1849

Died: in this village on the 28th ult., Mary Alida, daughter of P. Tucker, aged 2 years 8 months.

Died: in Pultneyville, on the 27th ult., Julia Augusta, daughter of Andrew Holling, aged 1 year 6 months.

Died: in East Palmyra, on the 17th of March last, of scarlet fever, Huron C., 2nd son of Luther and Ruth Sanford, aged 3 years, 11 months, 7 days also on the 28th of the same month of the same disease, Dexter C., eldest son of Luther and Ruth Sanford, aged 6 years, 2 months and 28 days.

Died: at Key West, FL, on the 21st of March, of typhus fever, Mrs. Sarah Hope Folker, in the 22nd year of her age. The deceased was for several years a resident of this village.

JUNE 13, 1849

Married: on the 20th inst. [ult?], by Rev. D. Harrington, Mr. Edwin E. Rogers of Palmyra to Miss Eveline Dexter of Macedon.

Two children were drowned in the canal in this village last week, one the son of Mr. Whipple, aged 6 years and the other the son of Mrs. DeClair, of the same age.

Died: in this village, on the 31st ult., Mrs. Mabel Goddard, wife of L. C. Goddard, 57[?] years of age.

Died: on the 9th inst., Joseph Henry, son of Joseph W. and Julia Corning, aged 2 years 10 months.

Died: on the 11th inst., George S., only son of George and Sophia Brown, of this town, aged 3 years.

MAY 21, 1850

Married: on the 19th inst., by Rev. D. Herrington, Mr. Stephen D. Willets of New York, to Miss Julia Willets, daughter of Henry Willets, Esq. of Macedon.

MAY 26, 1850

Died: in this village, on the 24th inst., Mrs. Harriet Brown, ae 23 years.

JUNE 5, 1850

Died: in this village, on the 30th inst., Paul Goldsmith, aged 80 years.

JUNE 12, 1850

Married: by Rev. Horace Eaton, June 9, 1850, Mr. John Thayer of Republic, OH, to Miss Serepta Stickney of this village.

JULY 24, 1850

Died: in Buffalo, on the 19th inst. of apoplexy, Mrs. Susan Thayer, wife of Levi Thayer, aged 47 years.

Died: in Marion, on the 18th inst., Miss Emily Crandall, daughter of Joseph Crandall, aged 14 years.

Died: in Lyons, on the 18th inst., Mrs. Rosetta Foster, wife of Rueben H. Foster, Esq.. ae 46 years.

Died: in Walworth, July 16th, Sarah Tabor, only daughter of Mr. Abraham Tabor, aged three years. (New Bedford Mercury, please copy)

Died in the same place [Walworth] on the 17th inst., Luther Tucker Freeman, son of Benjamin Freeman, aged 21 years.

SEPTEMBER, 18, 1850

Died: in Manchester, on the 14th inst., Mrs. Elizabeth Tabor, wife of Capt. B. Tabor, aged 69 years.

MAY 26, 1852 - No items copied.

JUNE 1, 1852

Married: in this village on the 20th inst., by the Rev. R. Herrington, at his residence, Mr. John Stone, of Columbus, OH to Miss Lucy Hall of Charlton, MA.

JUNE 23, 1853

Died: in Lyons, on the 11th inst., Mrs. Sally Smith, widow of Nathan Smith, and mother of Mrs. Amarilla Voorhees, in the 89th year of her age. She was a resident of this village for 35 years and a member of the Baptist Church for 45 years. She was the oldest person to die in Lyons within the last half century.

Died: at the residence of James Walker in East Palmyra, on the 6th inst., Margaret Jane Dunbar, aged 15 years, 7 months.

JUNE 25, 1853

Married: Thursday a.m. in Tioga Village, PA on Tuesday the 14th inst., by Rev. A. A. Marble of the Episcopal Church in this borough, Frederick Smith, Esq., Attorney-at-Law, to Miss Stella, youngest daughter of Hon. Levi Bigelow of the former place.

Married: in Palmyra by Rev. H. Eaton, June 20th, Mr. Edward C. Davenport of Macedon to Miss Catharine Cone of Palmyra.

JULY 14, 1853

Died: at Battle Creek, MI, June 30, 1853, Elias Rood, ae 21 yrs. one day.

Married: in Richmond, Ontario Co., NY, July 2nd, by Rev. George Gage, Mr. Cornell Morey, Teacher of Mathematics in Macedon Academy, to Miss Ann M. Hawes of Richmond, [Richmond Co., NY].

Married: in Mt. Morris on Tuesday A. M., June 14th, by Rev. O. L. Sprague, James T. Norton, Editor of the Livingston Republican, [at] Geneseo, to Miss Sarah A., 2nd daughter of Lester Phelps, Esq. of the former place.

Married: in Marion, July 7th, by Rev. A. Stanton, Mr. Thomas Brown to Miss Eleanor Gardiner, both of this place.

NOVEMBER 16, 1853

Married: Tuesday a.m., November 15th, by Rev. Horace Eaton, Mr. Alfred Hibberd, to Miss Mary Wilcox, all of Palmyra.

Married: on October 28th, by Rev. Horace Eaton, Mr. George Cunningham to Miss Isabella Harris, of Palmyra.

Married: in Farmington, November 15, 1853 by Rev. P. McKinstry, Richard A. Shedell of Georgetown, DC to Miss Lottie, A. youngest daughter of John A. Edmondston, Esq., of the former place.

NOVEMBER 23, 1854

Married on the 9th inst., in Walworth by Rev. H. Eaton, Mr. George Sanford of Fairport [Monroe Co], and Miss Mary E. Barnum, only daughter of E. Barnum. Esq. of the former place.

Married: in Palmyra on the 17th inst., by Rev. H. Eaton, Mr. Nicholas Daniels and Miss C. A. Crothers, both of Arcadia.

DECEMBER 22, 1859

Married: in Lyons, on Wednesday, December 7th by Rev. Van Benschoten at the residence of the bride's father, Mr. Levi Bashford of Oshkosh, WI to Miss Mary E., daughter of Cullen Foster, Esq. of Lyons.

Married: on Arcadia, the 7th inst., by Rev. Van Benschoten, Mr. Daniel Barton of Lyons, to Miss Sophie Miller, of Arcadia.

Married: on the 1st inst., at the residence of the bride's father, by Rev. A. Saxe, Mr. James W. Ford and Miss Libbie Rockefeller.

Died: on the 5th inst., in Huron, Miss Mary E. Dowd, aged 19 years.

Died: on the 3rd inst., in Port Byron, [Cayuga Co.] of putrid sore throat, Edward B. only son of John S. and Sophia Burt, aged 6 years.

NOVEMBER 8, 1860

Married: in this village on Wednesday morning, November 7th, by Rev. Horace Eaton, Albert L. Wheedon, M. D., of Wolcott and Miss Belle Gardner of Walworth.

Married by James Peddie, Esq., at the residence to the bride's father in Palmyra, Wayne Co., on the 1st day of November, Mr. Frank Chadsey of Brockport to Miss Helen Collins.

Married: at Grace Church, Lyons, on Wednesday, October 31st, by Rev. Sidney Wilbur, the Rev. George Seymour Lewis, Rector of St. Peter's Church, Lewes, Delaware Co. and Eliza Clarke, youngest daughter of John Adams of this village.

ADDENDA

NO DATE OF ISSUE

Gates & Thompson: stage line Pultneyville to Palmyra, bought out E. Steger: April 28, 1852.

Tripp, Mary Ann adv. claims against Timothy Tripp, Oct. 8, 1853.

Henderson & Hibberd, livery, bought out O'Neil & Finley,

C. Seeley - carriages, bought John Warrens' interest in Warren & Seeley; shop situated on Market St., north from Nottingham's hotel; Do not mistake the brick block with a tunnel through the center.

Mr. Zimmerman adv. as music teacher.

E. C. Wilder adv. a farm for sale , recently occupied by Rev. D. D. Francis, one mi. east of the village of Palmyra.

B. B. Johnston, miller, buys L. L. Seamans's (Yellow) Mills - store 2nd door east of Nottingham's Hotel,

A. Sherman, carriages, bought out A. P. Crandall's interest [now] Alanson Sherman and A. R. Sherman.

J. W. Williamson and Francis Hislop, tailors.

J. C. Benedict states that with the issue of Feb. 8, 1854 he ceases his connection with the paper having sold to B. C. Beebe who has issued a paper to be called The Wayne County

Banner: the first number to be issued Feb. 20, 1854 as announced; The Courier was discontinued for want of support; another reason was that if the Courier would not sell, another papaer would be started."

Married: in Zion Church, in this village, by Rev. Mr. Gillespie, William H. Farnham, merchant, and Miss Mary C. Chapman, all of this village. "We promised not to say anything about the "yellow boy" the accompanied the above, and of course we won't."

AUGUST 9, 1833

Died: Aug. 9, 1833, in Palmyra, Sarah Elizabeth Gordon, dau. of William W. Gordon, of Jacksonville.

William Adams advertised a stray horse.

INDEX

In using this index, the reader should bear in mind that many names were spelled in various ways. It is therefore necessary to explore all possible spellings of any given name.

Abbey, W. W., 68
Abbott, Eliza Frances, 111
Abbott, Emily H., 63
Acher, Chester, 160
Ackley, Aurelia, 31
Ackley, James, 89, 172
Ackley, W., 74
Adams, Barnabas, 106
Adams, Eliza Clarke, 179
Adams, George A., 165
Adams, Hannah, 117
Adams, Harriet J., 150
Adams, Isabella, 122
Adams, Jane, 48
Adams, John, 179
Adams, Merritt, 168
Adams, Mr., 148
Adams, Orinda, 168
Adams, Robert, 15
Adams, Samuel, 117
Adams, William, 50, 117, 180
Addicott, Henry, 162
Addicott, Mary Ann, 162
Adgeton. See Eggerton, 160
Agin, David, 136
Aiken, Eliza, 78
Aiken, George, 94
Aiken, James, 59
Aikin, Rev., 16
Aker, Thomas L., 39
Akin, Mary A., 156
Albright, Hannah, 173
Albright, J. F., 173
Albritt, George, 115
Albro, Abigail, 21
Albro, Job, 14
Aldrich & Havens, 127, 138

Aldrich & Gallup, 159
Aldrich, Albert, 125
Aldrich, Alsady, 20
Aldrich, Ambaline, 99
Aldrich, C., 79, 144
Aldrich, Cuyler &, 138
Aldrich, D. S., 106, 152
Aldrich, David S. 157
Aldrich, Delia, 168
Aldrich, F., 137
Aldrich, Julian, 17
Aldrich, Lusina, 43
Aldrich, Moses, 13
Aldrich, Mowry, 17
Aldrich, Rachel, 40
Aldrich, Silas, 168
Aldrich, Stephen, 13
Aldrich, W. F., 114, 173
Aldrich, William F., 106, 135, 174
Aldrich, Wm. F., 113
Aldridge, Powers, 109
Alexander, Jane A., 60
Alexander, Nell, 111
Allen, Albert A., 92, 134
Allen, Alma A., 173
Allen, Almira, 18
Allen, Betsey, 29
Allen, Cain R., 156
Allen, Capt., 114
Allen, Daniel, 82
Allen, Draper, 72, 73, 74, 90, 95, 120
Allen, Edward F., 157
Allen, Eld., 55
Allen, Esther, 116
Allen, Ethan B., 91

Allen, Frances E., 71
Allen, Harriet Mariah, 74
Allen, Henry P., 69, 73
Allen, J., 49
Allen, Jane,, 105
Allen, Jason, 45
Allen, Joseph, 105
Allen, Joseph Jr., 154
Allen, Lucina, 45
Allen, Margaret P., 11
Allen, Marvin, 103
Allen, Mary S., 71
Allen, Millard &, 140
Allen, N., 160
Allen, Nathaniel, 29
Allen, Niles &, 72, 77
Allen, S., 12
Allen, Samuel, 11
Allen, Sarah, 148, 161
Allen, Sophia K., 105
Allen, Sophronia, 165
Allen, William E., 90
Allert, Nathaniel, 18
Alling, Amanda, 155
Alling, Lucy Maria, 155
Alling, Stephen, 37, 75, 155
Alling, Y. S., 59
Ally, Sarah C., 110
Allyn, Charles, 110
Allyn, Niles &, 84
Alsop, Albert, 39
Alsop, Robert, 158
Alverson, Rev., 63
Amaden, John, 68
Ammerman, Jane, 67
Ampitheare, 92
Amsden, J., Jr., 83
Amsden, John, 69
Amsden, John, Jr., 66, 73, 75, 76
Amsden, John Jr. & Co., 76
Anderson, E. M., 168
Anderson, Geo. W., 66
Anderson, Mr., 51

Anderson, Wells & Son, 168
Anderson, Wells, 9, 38, 53, 65, 67, 71, 74, 107, 128
Anderson, William & Son, 160
Andre, Major, 64
Andrew, Charlotte, 159
Andrews, Charles M. L., 101
Andrews, D., 126
Andrus, Eliza, 109
Andrus, Miles, 82
Andrus, Miles H., 83
Angell, Abiah, 99
Anthony, Rev., 28
Anti-Slavery meeting, 85, 90, 111, 113, 132
Antis, Mary, 44
Antis, William, 44
Antisdale, Seth, 137
Applegate, William F., 68
Archer, Ornon, 169 ?????
Archer, Oron, 155
Archer, Stephen, 46
Armington, Aurelia, 129
Armington, Benjamin, 151
Armington, Dorothea, 86
Armington, Emily, 129
Armington, Henry, 129
Armington, Lucy, 151
Arne, David, 175
Arnett, S. W., 22
Arnold, Ephriam, 171
Arnold, Mariah, 20
Arnold, Sarah L. M., 171
Aru---, J. Steinmetz, 16
Asa, Ann, 96
Ashley, William F., 97
Atwater, Clarissa, 31
Atwater, Thomas, 59
Atwood, Alvah J., 97
Atwood, J., 85
Atwood, John, 50
Austin, family, 119
Austin, Jemima Ann, 166
Austin, Thomas, 150

Austin, Thomas & Co., 134
Austin, William, 56
Austin, Zebell, 56
Avery, Alfred, 83
Avery, Calista, 160
Avery, Ely &, 152
Avery, Oscar S. O., 151
Avery, Sally, 48
Avrill, J. R., 73
Axtell, Henry, 40
Axtell, Hiram, 164
Axtell, Rebecca, 40
Axtell, Rev., 34
Aylesworth, Daniel, 81
Ayres, John, 43
Babbitt, Benjamin T., 169
Babcock, Augustus, 118
Babcock, Lyman, 17
Babcock, Mary, 33
Babcock, Mr., 122
Bachus, Namon S., 123
Bacon, William, 91
Badger, Harriet Eliza, 80
Bagley, Rev., 48
Bailey, Rev., 32
Bailey, S. Joseph, 139
Bain, Peter, 49
Baker, Charlotte, 92
Baker, Chloe, 175
Baker, Daniel S., 164
Baker, Experience M., 40
Baker family, 174
Baker, Hannah, 71
Baker, Hiram,. 101
Baker, J., 67
Baker, J. Jr., 55
Baker, James, 71
Baker, Juicy, 68
Baker, Lyman W., 49
Baker, Mariah, 47
Baker, Moses C., 33
Baker, Norman C., 97
Baker, Phebe L., 136
Balch, J. O., 57

Balcom, John, 88
Balcom, Jesse, 102
Balcom, William, 102
Baldwin, Cole &, 10
Baldwin, Mary H., 121
Baldwin, Riley, 47
Baldwin, T. P., 9, 13, 15, 18, 22, 38
Baldwin, Thomas P., 10, 42, 74
Balis, Henry G., 175
Ball, Samuel, 50
Balloon ascension, 101
Baltze, Louis, 53
Bancker, Hiram S., 29
Bancroft, Orpha, 81
Bancroft, Sally, 122
Bancroft, Thomas, 18
Banks, Loring O., 164
Banks, Wayne Co., 170
Barber, Azuba, 23
Barber, John, 19, 23
Barber, Rev., 63
Barden, Betsey, 37
Barden, Jerusha, 32
Barker, Alden, 103
Barker, James F., 30, 34
Barker, John, Sr., 128
Barker, Samuel S., 53, 68
Barker, Sarah, 53
Barkley, Maria, 153
Barlow, Mary, 61
Barnard, Abner, 43
Barnard, Albert, 126
Barnes, Amanda, 24
Barnes, Cornelia, 140
Barnes, Horace N., 125
Barnes, Roxana, 143
Barnes, Sarah, 85
Barnes, Sherman, 143
Barnes, Wheeler, 140
Barney, Vincent G., 12, 15
Barnhart, Ann, 33
Barnhart, Ann Maria, 164
Barnhart, C., 73

Barnhart, Christian, 89
Barnhart, Eliza W., 63
Barnhart, Ezekiel S., 174
Barnhart, Fidelia, 103
Barnhart, Isaac, 139, 140, 153, 164
Barnhart, Job, 85, 94
Barnhart, Marietta, 140
Barnhart, Mary, 24
Barnhart, Matilda, 93
Barns, James, 25
Barnum, E., 178
Barnum, Harriet Augusta, 93
Barnum, L. B., 12, 14
Barnum, Mary E., 178
Barnum, Philo B., 93
Barnum, Thomas B., 31
Barnum, Thomas P., 43
Barrager, Lutha, 134
Barrel, Rev., 98
Barret, Moses, 123
Barrett, Alfred G., 15
Barron, Orrin, 170
Barrows, Eliza, 110
Barrows, Jarvis, 98
Barse, Claudius Victorius Broughton, 138
Bartholmew, Eli W., 54
Bartle, Antoinette, 156
Bartle, James, 42
Bartle, James P. 39
Bartlett, Mary, 34
Bartlett, Sylvanus, 70
Barton, Daniel, 178
Barton, W. H. H., 143
Bashford, Levi, 178
Bassy, Elias B., 44
Bates, Bennett, 14
Bates, David B., 24
Bates, E. Greenleaf, 158
Bates, Esther, 72
Bates, George C., 99
Bates, Orlando, 49
Bates, P. P., 27

Bates, Phineas, 24
Bates, Sarah, 27
Bates, Stephen, 72, 173
Batterson, C. A., 59
Baxter, Mary C., 141
Bayard & Cuyler, 62
Bayard, W. M., 39, 52, 65
Bayard, William M., 43, 60, 93
Bayard, William P., 70
Bayard, Wm. M., 72, 74
Bayles, A. M., 159
Bayles, Euphemy, 136
Baylis, Ira, 141
Beach, Fanny, 14
Beach, Sheldon, 19
Beal, Caleb, 73, 73, 79, 123
Beal, John, 105
Beal, Rachel, 123
Beal, Washington, 66
Beale, T. & Co., 14
Beals, B., 39
Beals, Caleb, 64
Beals, Deborah, 39
Beals, Rosannah, 71
Beam, Ann, 19
Beam, John, 67, 137
Bean, Isabella, 87
Bean, Mr., 60
Bean, William, 23
Beard, Andrew, 153
Beatty, L., 62
Beaumont, A. L., 45
Beaumont, Sarah, 151
Beckwith & Ely, 81, 82, 107
Beckwith, Ann S., 109
Beckwith, Catherine, 164
Beckwith, Cynthia Ann, 90
Beckwith, Emma E., 46
Beckwith, George, 38, 39, 46, 48, 52, 62, 67, 72, 82, 86, 107, 113, 164.
Beckwith, George & Co., 64, 152
Beckwith, George B., 75

Beckwith, George W., 107
Beckwith, George Whitfield, 75
Beckwith, H. H., 33
Beckwith, Jane, 48
Beckwith, Minerva Nye, 106
Beckwith, N. H., 24. 46, 48, 70, 74, 86, 90
Beckwith, Nath. H., 52
Beckwith, Nathaniel, 46, 70
Beckwith, Nathaniel H., 62, 72
Beckwith, S., 107
Beckwith, Samuel, 53, 71, 114, 122
Beckwith, Wilson, 99
Bedell, Catherine, 123
Beebe, B. C., 179
Beebe, Fanny, 10
Beebe, Joseph L., 55
Beebe, Joseph S., 40
Beebe, Mary Ann, 55
Beebe, Rev., 175
Beebe, Sarah, 40
Beecher & Glossender, 112, 163
Beecher, I. E. & Co., 159
Beecher, I. E., 111, 175
Beecher, Isaac, 72
Beecher, Isaac A., 92
Beecher, Isaac E., 73, 99, 111, 119,
Beeching, Harriet, 173
Beeching, Sarah A., 155
Beer, Villery, 92
Beers & Payne, 121
Beers & Richmond, 89
Beers, Laura, 35
Beers, Lewis, 106
Beers, Lewis P., 134
Beers, Nelson, 124
Beers, V., 113
Beers, Villeroy, 145
Belden, George, 59
Belden, George, Jr.. 66
Belden, Nancy, 11, 86
Bell, Charlotte, 58

Bell, John M., 37
Belote, John, 22
Bement, David, 38
Bement, Hiram, 47
Bement, Mary, 143
Bement, William E., 156
Bemis, J. D., 18
Benedict, J. C., 179
Benedict, Mr., 95
Benett, Mary, 130
Benham, Catharine Calista, 77
Benham, David, 12, 14, 77
Benham, Mary, 15
Benham, Rev., 20
Benham, Sally, 77
Benjamin, Sophronia, 15
Bennet, Franklin, 52
Bennett, Abraham H., 144
Bennett, Ance Ann Ande, 20
Bennett, Ann, 55
Bennett, B., 50
Bennett, Betsey, 59
Bennett, Harriet, 102
Bennett, Myron H., 154
Benson, J., 12
Benson, James, 119
Benson, Maria, 175
Benson, Miss, 116
Bentley, Elnathan, 29
Bently, Nathan, 31
Beswick, William, 169
Betts, Seth F., 109
Bickford, Emily, 131
Bickford, L. & Co., 147
Bickford, Lyman, 147
Bidwell, Daniel, 16
Bidwell, M., 33
Bigelow, Charlotte, 32
Bigelow, Hannah, 66
Bigelow, Horace, 124
Bigelow, John, 66
Bigelow, Levi, 178
Bigelow, Stella, 178
Biggs, John, 54

Bill, David, 109
Billings, B., 124
Billings, Benjamin, Jr., 106
Billings, Benjamin, 60, 164
Billings, Louisa, 100
Billings, Lucy Mariah, 60
Billings, Martha Glover, 154
Billings, Mary, 164
Billings, William, 60, 100
Billings, William, Sr., 116
Billings, Wm., Jr. 67
Bingham, Charles B., 87
Bingham, J., 64
Bingham, Jeremiah, 105
Bingham, Mary R., 85
Bingham, Morgan L., 90, 140
Bingham, Nancy A., 129
Bingham, O. B., 119
Biollet, Adelia E., 23
Birch, William H., 89
Birchard, Mortimer N. 101
Bird, Lydia, 52
Bird, Ebenezer, 166
Bird, Eliza, 38
Bird, Gardner, 33
Bird, John, 102, 108
Bird, Romina, 108
Bird, Sabrina, 102
Birdsall & Stimpson, 49
Birdsall, Adelaide, 99
Birdsall, Daniel, 148
Birdsall, Edward, 103
Birdsall, Eliza, 125
Birdsall, Horace, 45
Birdsall, James, 99
Birdsall, Mary Anne, 157
Birdsall, Phebe Jane, 148
Birdsall, S., 62, 111
Birdsall, S. & T. T., 94
Birdsall, Sutton, 42, 76, 83, 92, 125
Birdsall, Sutton Sylvester, 125
Birdsall, Sylvester, 42

Birdsall, T. T., 111, 138
Birdsey, Nancy, 17
Bixbe, William, 61
Black Hawk, 78
Black Rock, 100
Blackman, David, 39
Blackmar, Abel, 150
Blackmar, Ransom, 140
Blackmarr, Adeline, 53
Blackmarr, Ransom, 52, 53
Blakesley, E., 42, 68
Blakesley, Rev., 27, 28, 35, 40
Blanchard, Almina, 29
Blanchard, Elizabeth, 20
Blaney, John, 91
Bleeker, Eliza Ann, 138
Blind institutions, 146
Bliss, Lucinda, M., 77
Blithe, James, 56
Blossom, Isaac, 42
Bockhoven, Hannah, 36
Bogart, Caroline, 106
Bogart, Peter J., 106
Bogart, Susan, 106
Bogert, Cathalina, 34
Bogert, H. H., 34
Boice, Manchester, 50
Boise, William, 50
Bolkcom, Sarah Ann, 124
Booth, Lucy R., 95
Booth, Rachel, 134
Booth, Roland, 129
Booth, Sarah, 100, 133
Bortle, Francis, 66, 86
Bortle, J. H., 88
Bortle, Jacob H., 98
Bortle, P., 74
Bortles, Charles, 171
Bortles, E., 64, 72
Bortles, F., 101, 104
Bortles, Francis, 86, 101
Bortles, Harriet Elizabeth, 100

Bortles, J. H., 66, 67, 68, 75, 100
Bortles, Jacob H., 83, 97, 101, 104
Bortles, Julia, 171
Bortles, Mary, 147
Bortles, W. H., 53
Bortles, Wilcox &, 81, 83, 84
Boston Quartette Club, 167
Bostwick, Electa, 173
Bosworth, Addela, 48
Bosworth, John, 129
Bosworth, Mills H., 23
Bosworth, Seth W., 37
Boudinot, Elias, 28
Boughton, Delia, 12
Boughton, Morris, 156
Bourne, Richard, 50
Bours, Mary Robinson, 151
Bours, Peter, 151
Boutell, Charles A., 173
Bow, William, 23
Bowdish & Buell, 132
Bowdish, Hannah M., 124
Bowdish, James, 124, 130
Bowdish, James H., 127, 135
Bowen, Phebe, 32
Bowman & Seymour, 127, 139
Boyle, Francis, 141
Boyle, James, 18
Boyle, Patrick, 41
Boyle, Rev., 56
Boynton, Alzorah, 58
Boynton, Caroline, 21
Boynton, George, 99
Boynton, J., 29, 65
Boynton, Jonathan, 18, 20, 24, 40, 58, 72, 76, 107, 113, 127, 167, 169
Boynton, Julia, 167
Boynton, Lorenzo, 118
Boynton, Mary, 76
Boynton, Sophronia, 21
Brace, Lucinda, 15

Brace, Rev., 12
Bradbury, E. (Miss), 99
Bradish, Calvin, 121
Bradish, Curran, 41
Bradish, John, 22
Bradish, Mr., 66
Bradish, Nancy, 121
Bradish, Sarah, 37
Bradley, George, 59
Bradley, Matilda, 146
Bradley, Mariah, 99
Bradt, Maria Angelica, 135
Bragaw, Samuel J., 151
Braman, Isaac, 148
Bramble, Anthony, 110
Brayton, Clarissa, 164
Brayton, William L., 164
Breck, Samuel P., 121
Breese, Arthur, 23
Bresee, John, 127
Brewer, Martha, 124
Brewery, Palmyra, 45, 75, 121
Brewster, William R., 42
Bridgen, Thomas, 30
Briggs, Alva, 132
Briggs, Asa, 117
Briggs, Olney, 125
Briggs, William T., 81, 84
Brigham, Samuel, 122
Bristol, Aurilla, 145
Bristol, Elizabeth A., 87
Bristol. John, 157
Bristol, Lathrop S., 142
Bristol, Mary, 57
Brittan, T. S. 132
Brizzee, Lena Marie, 124
Brockway, Amy, 139
Brockway, Hannah, 54
Brockway, Mary, 89
Bromfield, A. D., 119
Bromfield, Abraham, 59
Bromfield, A. D., 119
Brotherson, P. C. H., 115
Browen, Edward, 49

Browen, Silas, 49
Brown, A. J., 128
Brown, Allen, 49
Brown, Ann Eliza, 148
Brown, Benjamin, 175
Brown, Benjamin H., 89
Brown, Catherine, 171
Brown, Delia Ann, 123
Brown, Dirce Ann, 88
Brown, Elizabeth, 152
Brown, Elvira, 40
Brown, Ezra, W., 148
Brown, F. C., 112
Brown, Frances Ann, 71
Brown, Francis, 34
Brown, George, 34, 69, 82, 176
Brown, Harriet, 39, 177
Brown, Helden, 118
Brown, James F., 89, 119
Brown, Jesse, 166
Brown, Lucy, 34
Brown, Maria, 27
Brown, Nelson, 71
Brown, Paul S., 33
Brown, Relief, 59
Brown, Rosamond, 14
Brown, Sarah Maria, 138
Brown, Sophia, 16, 176
Brown, Stephen, 55
Brown, Thomas, 118, 178
Brown, Wealthy, 20
Browson, Morton, 141
Brumfield, A. D. 102
Brumfield, Andrew D, 156
Brumfield, Erastus, 139
Brumfield, James, 156
Brumfield, James I., 156
Brumfield, Louisa, 102
Brumfield, Richard, 133
Brundage, Ruth, 17
Brush, Jane, 83
Bryan, J. B., 150

Bryan, Mary L., 150

Bryant, Lydia, 20
Buchanan, Mr., 113
Buck, Daniel, 30, 41
Buck, Gordon, 13
Buck, Hepsibath T., 30
Buck, Loren, 173
Buckley, Alonzo, 116
Buckley, F. C., 99
Buckley, L. G., 93, 119
Buckley, Weeks & Co., 92
Buel, Maria, 96
Buell, A. K., 96
Buell, Alvah N., 124, 130, 175
Buell & Robbins, 99, 107
Buell, Bowdish &, 132
Bull, Caroline, 17
Bullis, Abrahm, 127
Bullock, John W., 141
Bulrees, Ann, 53
Bump, Betsey, 164
Bunnell, David C., 68
Bunnell, Mary, 24
Burbank, Laura A., 153
Burbank, Rev., 57
Burbank, Solomon M., 127, 153
Burch, Jeremiah, 53
Burchard, Norton B., 86
Burden, Phebe, 38
Burger, Anson, 64
Burkurth, G., 128
Burlingame, A. H., 136
Burlingame, Julia Ann Calhoun, 136
Burnall, E. W., 35
Burnet, George B., 55
Burnett, Eunice, 153
Burnett, Horace, 146
Burnett, William, 22
Burrow, Capt., 145
Burrows, Joseph H., 148
Burrows, Julia A., 10, 51
Burt, Edward B., 179
Burt, John S., 179
Burt, Sophia, 179

Bush, A. T., 56
Bush, Julia, 83
Bush, Louisa, 94
Bushnell & Stevens, 12
Bussey, Thomas, 70
Bustell, Silas, 20
Butler & Williams, 110, 111, 120, 124
Butler, B., 65, 97, 112, 124
Butler, Burr, 15, 62, 67, 82, 83, 106, 110, 113, 119, 128, 165, 167
Butler, C. M., 120, 121, 122, 125, 129
Butler, Clement M., 121
Butler, Maria, 165, 167
Butler, Mrs., 122
Butler, Rachel, 128
Butterfield, Louis M., 115
Butterfield, M., 151
Butterfield, Martin, 95, 115, 121, 161
Butterfield, Pooley, &, 168
Button, Cyrus S., 174
Button, Laura, 174
Butts, Daniel, 10
Butts, Miss, 19
Butts, Ruth, 23, 30
Cadawallader, Priscilla, 92
Cady, Ansel D., 174
Cady, Angeline, 159
Caldwell, Margaret, 21
Caldwell, Charles, 100
Calhoon Erastus R., 154
Calhoon, Harriet E., 154
Calhoun, Celestia M., 144
Calhoun, Erastus R., 137, 161
Calhoun, Hannah, 136
Calhoun, James, 143
Calhoun, Margaret, 60
Calhoun, Mary, 143, 149
Calhoun, Nathan, 136, 144
Camp, Ambrose, 121

Campbell, A. E., 47, 48, 52, 56, 61
Campbell, Alfred E., 63
Campbell, Rev., 36, 39, 40, 41
Campbell, William, 40
Canal, 9, 88
Canal authorities, 98
Canal intelligence, 41, 81, 145
Cande, Lasher &, 10
Canderbeek, Mr. & Mrs., 157
Cantine, Christina, 13
Cantine, Moses, I., 13
Capron, Austin, 114
Capron, Eliab W., 160
Capron, Eunice, 77
Capron, George, 139, 142
Capron, Hannah, 162
Capron, Hannah W., 162
Capron, Julia Ann, 103
Capron, Samuel, 77
Capron, Tabitha Frances, 142
Capron, William P., 77, 114, 162
Carey, Cordelia, 60
Carey, Maria, 139
Carleton, Rev., 97
Carlow, Roxina, 100
Carothers, Hiram B, 48
Carpenter, Amy E., 172
Carpenter, Eliza, 11, 117
Carpenter, Elizabeth C., 98
Carpenter, Fuilealema, 43
Carpenter, G. S., 136
Carpenter, George S., 133, 168
Carpenter, Joseph, 107, 160
Carpenter, Lott C., 130
Carpenter, M., 98
Carpenter, Samuel D., 147
Carpenter, Stephen C., 99
Carpenter, Susan, 133
Carr, Robert, 66
Carroll, Angeline, 152
Carter, S., 74, 85

Carter, Solomon, 67, 69, 163
Cary, William Washington, 11
Case, Charlotte, 81
Case, Mrs., 99
Caulkins, Augustus, 27
Cemetery, 169
Census, 1840, 130
Census enumerators, 169
Census statistics, 1845, 171
Census statistics 1835, 95
Chadsey, Frank, 179
Chadwick, Esther, 94
Chadwick, Marietta N., 173
Chamberlain, Rev., 38
Champion & Howell, 40
Champion, Edmund, 47
Champion, Smith &, 12
Champlin, Valentine, 69
Chandler, Albert, 111
Chandler, Martha, 54
Chapin, Andrew, 27
Chapin, Graham H., 154
Chapin, Israel, 80
Chapin, Lydiaette, 98
Chapin, Spencer, 77
Chapin, Thaddeus, 49
Chapman, Ashael, 131
Chapman, Betsey, 63
Chapman, D., 55
Chapman, Delia W., 94
Chapman, Henrietta, 136
Chapman, John C., 100
Chapman, Joseph, 155
Chapman, Mary, 155
Chapman, Mary C., 180
Chapman, William, 100, 113, 136
Chappel, Erastus, 111
Chappel, Lucy Ann, 133
Chappell, Amaziah, 42
Chappell, Jerusha, 42
Charlock, & Co. (Miss), 116
Chase, Abner, 60
Chase, Adaline, 77

Chase, Ann, 11
Chase, Asa T., 140
Chase, Charles, 81, 98
Chase, D., 26, 56, 63, 64, 69, 87, 152, 175
Chase, Dr., 92
Chase, Durfee, 11, 16, 53, 92, 105, 106, 113, 155
Chase, Harriet A., 175
Chase, Harvey, 59
Chase, Horace, 68
Chase, J. H., 161
Chase, John, 146
Chase, Luther M., 169
Chase, Mrs, 122, 134
Chase, Orin, 21
Chase, Rev., 28
Chase, T., 98
Chase, W., 127
Cheesman, Polly, 164
Chesebro, Charles H., 162
Chilson, Lydia Ann, 85
Chittenden, William, 27
Cholera, 86
Church, Alonzo, 135
Church, Caleb C., 102
Church, Elizabeth, 163
Church, Elon Galusha Levi, 135
Church, H., 52
Church, Horace, 41, 42, 47, 48
Church, Irving, W., 162
Church, Margaret, 19
Church, Prudence, 112
Church, Warren, 162
Circus, Albany Ampitheatre 135
Circus, Angevine & Co., 147
Circus, Eagle, 100
Circus, Great Western, 145
Circus, H. H. Rockwell 118
Circus, June Titus Angevine, 85, 120
Circus, Menagerie & Aviary, 93
Circus, New York Arena, 118
Circus, New York, 107

Circus, North American, 159
Circus, Raymond & Co., 160
Circus, Rockwell & Stone, 147
Circus, Rockwell, Hopkins & Co., 113
Circus, Titus & Angevine, 85
Circus, Welch, Mann & Delevan, 169
Circus, Zoological Inst., 106
Clackner, Hannah, 63
Clackner, John S., 63, 66
Clackner, Lydia, 57
Clapp & Hathaway, 94, 108
Clapp & Durfee, 75, 76
Clapp, Hathaway & Moore, 103
Clapp, Henry, 90
Clapp, John, 52, 62
Clapp, Mary D., 157
Clapp, Otis, 77, 71, 90, 119, 120, 143, 157
Clapp, Otis C., 71
Clark & Ely, 75, 79
Clark & Robinson, 69
Clark, Benjamin, 136
Clark, Capt., 90
Clark, Cornelia, 65
Clark, Dennis, 66
Clark, E., 72, 73
Clark, Eddy &, 81, 91
Clark, Elbridge, F., 130
Clark, Elihu, 87
Clark, Elihu & Eddy, 77
Clark, Elijah, 81
Clark, Elisha, 87
Clark, Ezekiel, 174
Clark, Freeman, 159
Clark, Gideon, 26
Clark, Hannah, 102
Clark, Harvey, 57, 58
Clark, J. A., 132
Clark, J. L., 160, 166
Clark, J. L. & Co., 144, 152
Clark, Job., 170
Clark, John A., 36, 37, 44, 64

Clark, John W., 162, 174
Clark, John L., 147, 158, 173, 167, 175
Clark, Kazia, 43
Clark, Laura, 124
Clark, Levi, 50, 151, 165
Clark, Lorenzo, 9
Clark, Maltby, 39, 81
Clark, Martha A., 167
Clark, Martha Flower, 167
Clark, Matthew, 172
Clark, Oliver, 107, 114, 127, 149
Clark, Orange, 99
Clark, Philo, 138
Clark, Rev., 36, 37,
Clark, Richard L., 46, 64, 69, 89
Clark, Robert, 173
Clark, Rufus, 108
Clark, Samuel, 101
Clark, Stephen, 90. 171
Clark, William, 33
Clark, William H., 129
Clarke, George, 30
Clifford, E. M., 85
Clinton, George W., 71
Clinton, Mary Ann, 154
Closs, Abrahm, 58
Clow, Agnes, 143
Clow, Robert, 143
Clyde, 44
Cobb, Eli, 44
Cobb, Elisha W., 140
Cobb, H., 73
Cobb, Harvey, 47, 91, 134, 145
Cobb, Louisa, 134
Cobb, Louisa H., 150
Cobb, Maria, 140
Cobb, Rensselear, 102
Coe, Chauncey H., 91
Coe, D., 153
Coe, Joel, Jr., 10
Coe, Joseph, 14

Coe, Marquis D, 169
Coffin, Ebenezer, 34
Coffin, Robert S., 34
Coggshall, William, 135
Cogswell, Betsey, 125
Cogswell, Daniel, 37
Cogswell, J. F., 83
Cogswell, James F., 53, 75
Cogswell, Rachel, 107
Cogswell, William, 37
Colbrath, High, 158
Colbrath, William, 50
Cole, Abner, 10, 18, 13?, 23, 30, 93, 109
Cole, Adrian, 18
Cole, Benjamin, 9, 64, 163, 169
Cole, Capt., 159
Cole, Caroline, 151
Cole, Dorastus, 14
Cole, Elijah, 148
Cole, Elizabeth, 114
Cole, Fanny, 9
Cole, Frances Ann, 109
Cole, Frederick W., 171
Cole, George C., 45
Cole, J. B., 167
Cole, John, 64
Cole, Luther, 18
Cole, Morley &, 144
Cole, S., 169
Cole, S. J., 110
Cole, S. W., 114
Cole, Samuel, 106, 113, 114, 115, 119.
Cole, Samuel J., 115
Cole, Sarah M., 133
Cole, Southard, 9
Cole, Southworth, 23
Cole, W. N., 110, 120, 121
Cole, William, 127
Cole, William Ninde, 135, 144, 151
Coleman, ___, 66

Coleman, C. C., 68, 75, 137
Coleman, Cornelius C. 137
Coleman, Higby &, 108
Coleman, Kingman &, 78, 82
Coles, Marcus, 71
Collins, Amanda, 110
Collins, G., 134
Collins, Helen, 179
Collins, Orin, 85
Colt & Ledyard, 10
Colt Catherine, 62
Colt, Elizabeth, 78
Colt, J., 9, 59
Colt. J. S.. 65, 67, 127, 128
Colt, J. & S., 15
Colt, J. & J. S., 46
Colt, Joseph, 46, 62, 83, 128
Colt, Joseph Henry, 72
Colt, Joseph S., 45, 48, 55, 58 , 72
Colt, Judah, 128
Colt, Mary, 83
Colton, Amerila D., 147
Colvin, Anna S., 158
Colvin, John, 52, 62, 65, 72, 91
Colvin, John, Jr., 85
Comstock, Addison J., 27
Comstock, Daniel, 31
Comstock, Darius, 41
Comstock, Nathan, 46
Comstock, Ruby, 41
Conant, Mr., 144
Cone, Catherine, 178
Conklin, Frances R., 102
Conner, Daniel H., 88
Conner, Harriet, 59
Connet, Nancy, 15
Convention, political, 115
Cook, Adaline, 59
Cook, Halsey, 139
Cook, Julia Ann, 138
Cook, Lydia, 17
Cook, Lydia L., 174

Cook, Mary M, 139
Cook, Moses, 100
Cook, Stephen, 93
Cook, Williams &, 92, 93
Cooke, M., 141
Cooke, William H., 130
Cooley, H., 73
Coon, Eliza, 33
Coon, Elizabeth, 160
Coon, Ezra, 54
Coon, Samantha, 66
Cooper, E., 73
Cooper, Griffith, 154
Cooper, Griffith M. 160
Cooper, James Byron, 154
Cooper, Louisa, 87
Cooper, Rebecca M., 160
Cooper, Sarah, 58
Cooper, Silas, 38
Coppock, F., 54
Coppock, Frederick, 53, 55
Coppock, Julia Ann, 54
Coppock, W. R., 57, 63
Coppock, William R., 55, 61
Corbett, Celestia, 90
Corbin, Lynn, 20
Corey, Isaac, 56
Corey, Joseph, 98
Corey, L. B., 136
Corey, Maria Emeline, 94
Corning, Joseph W., 176
Corning, Joseph Henry, 176
Corning, Julia, 176
Cornwall, Andrew, 149
Cornwall, Ansel A., 124
Cornwell, Thomas, 124
Correll, John N., 74
Corwin, W. A., 14
Corwin, William, 64
Cory, Dennis, 19
Cory, Russell &, 144
Cosart, A. M. (Mrs.), 134
Cosart, Caroline, 116
Cosart, E. C., 129

Cosart, Enoch, 96
Costere, Mary, 55
Cottrell, Mary A., 165
Cottrell, Phebe Jane, 158
Counterfeiters, 172
Counterfiet money, 128
Cowan, Elisha, 24
Cowan, L., 26
Cowan, Luther, 12, 14, 30
Cowdrey, Dyer, 44
Cox, Electa, 151
Cox, Henry, 33
Cox, William, 151
Cragg, William, 152, 153
Craig, Elizabeth, 128
Cramer, Mary Jane, 47
Cramer, Philip G., 121
Crandall, A. P., 82, 97, 98, 150, 179
Crandall, Ann P., 150
Crandall, Daniel, 73, 103
Crandall, Eliza Clarinda, 175
Crandall, Emily, 177
Crandall, Ezra, 53
Crandall, Jacob R., 138
Crandall, Joseph, 177
Crandall, Joseph Daniel, 150
Crandall, Koziah, 128
Crandall, Miss, 134
Crandall, P. M., 127
Crandall, P. Milford, 144
Crandall, Perry &, 118
Crandall, Philip, 120
Crandall, Sherman &, 89, 144
Crandall, William, 55
Crane, George, 17, 62, 65, 72
Crane, Turner, 17
Crane, W. I., 119
Crane, Wheeler R., 80
Crane, Wheeler I., 108
Crane, Zebina, 157
Crater, Barbara, 94
Craw, Abigail, 55
Creig, Hilliard, 145

Cromwell, John W., 102
Crone, Henry S., 9
Crosby, Mary Ann, 40
Cross, David W., 130
Cross, John J., 149
Crothers, Burdette, 93
Crothers, C. A. (Miss), 178
Crowell, Calvin, 136
Crowell, Lucy, 132
Crowell, Solomon, 119
Crowell, Solomon, Sr., 136
Crowell, Solomon, Jr., 156
Crowl, John G., 90
Cruthers, Burdette,
Culver, Cooper, 96, 134
Culver, Cornelius B., 115
Culver, Eliza Ann, 109
Culver, Elizabeth, 151
Culver, George, 19, 43, 64, 129
Culver, George W., 121
Culver, Hannah, 115
Culver, Harriet, 158
Culver, James, 63, 67, 69, 73,
Culver, John, 169
Culver, Laura, 99
Culver, Lucretia, 156
Culver, Marietta, 169
Culver, Paul J., 163
Culver, Ruth, 32, 134
Culver, Stephen, 72, 145
Culver, Sylvannus, 68
Cumings, Horace, 156
Cumings, J. K., 111, 139
Cummings, John H., 89
Cummings, Chauncey, 124, 125. 132
Cummings, Horace, 119, 151
Cummings, J. K., 75, 84, 120
Cummings, J. K. & Co., 124, 132, 134, 140, 141
Cummings, Samuel P., 125
Cunningham, George, 178
Cunningham, Henry, 30

Curtis, Albert, 56
Curtis, Charles, 128
Curtis, Delight, 124
Curtis, Robert, 20
Curtis, Susanna, 17
Curtis, Treat &, 48
Cutter, Abdilla, 118
Cuyler & Aldrich, 138, 173
Cuyler & Godard, 94
Cuyler, Bayard &, 62
Cuyler, Eliza, 124
Cuyler, Elizabeth, 141
Cuyler, G. W., 68, 70, 72, 82, 89
Cuyler, Geo. W., 66
Cuyler, George, 60, 129
Cuyler, George W., 43, 51, 52, 53, 65, 67, 69, 73, 64, 80, 84, 91, 92, 98, 99, 100, 106, 113, 119, 120, 121
Cuyler, John L., 64
Cuyler, Mary Eliza, 124
Cuyler, Rev., 44
Cuyler, Rogers &, 173
Cuyler, Tucker &, 87
Cuyler, W. H., 114
Cuyler, William H., 9, 75, 78, 124, 166
Cuyler, William Howe, 10
Cuyler, Wm. H., 119
Daggett, A. K., 73
Daggett, Augustus, 66
Daggett, David P., 168
Daggett, Deborah Ann, 168
Daggett, Levi, 73, 91
Daggett, Lydia Amanda, 168
Daggett, O. E., 175
Daggett, Sarah, 36
Daggett. See Duggett, 175
Dailey, George, 57
Daily, Hannah, 123
Daily, John W., 141
DaLee, A. G. J., 168
Damon, ___, 92

Dana, Jacob A., 12, 15
Dancing school, 131
Daniels, Lyman I., 26, 30
Daniels, Nicholas, 178
Dart, Eliza, 66
Dart, Emma, 176
Dart, Jonathan, 66, 176
Dart, Jonathan & Co., 77
Dashnell, Romana, 93
Dates, Maria M., 145
Davenport, Ebenezer, 108, 152
Davenport, Edward C., 178
Davenport, Ephriam, 120
Davenport, John A., 19
Davenport, Lodema P., 133
Davenport, Louisa, 103
Davenport, Marium, 152
Davenport, Nathaniel, 15
David, Hannah, 68
David, Mr., 38
Davis, Ann E., 170
Davis, Caroline, 128
Davis, Charles, 64
Davis, Elihu, 144
Davis, Eliza S., 56
Davis, Henry, 48
Davis, Hetty, 99
Davis, James, 22, 99
Davis, Lucy Ann, 102
Davis, Maria Grace, 174
Davis, Mr., 47
Davis, Newton &,
Davis, Paul H., 102, 160
Davis, Thomas, 174
Dawley, Polly, 56
Day, Benjamin F., 64
Day, Betsey, 137
Day, Ezra P., 141
Day, Hiram T., 30
Day, Julietta S., 124
Day, Moses, 103
Day, Nathaniel, 137
Day, Nelson, 67
Dayton, Mary A., 174

Deaf mutes, 148
Deaf and Dumb, school, 80
Dean, Luther, 17
Dean, Sarah, 27
DeCamp, David, 121
Decker, Clarissa, 140
Decker, John S., 80
Decker, Julia, 77
Decker, Uri, 40
DeClair, Mrs., 176
Delamater & Loomis, 76
Delamater, J. D., 98
Delamater, J. J., 109, 113, 119
Delamater, Jacob J., 129
Delamater, John, 99
Delamater, Mr., 34
Delance, Laura A., 113
Delano, Israel, 75
Delano, Louisa, 99
Delano, Martha, 75
Delano, Mortimer F., 173
Delevan, William A., 100
Demick, Eliza, 16
Deming, Alfred James, 33
Deming, J. P. H., 147, 148
DeMunn, Catherine, 116
Dennis, Andrus, 155
Dennis, John P., 80
Dennis, Simeon, 103
Dennison, William H., 42
Dennison, Wm. H., 50
Denny, Elizabeth, 68
Denton, Eliza Jane, 97
Deo, Allen, 169
Devine, John, 85
Dewey, Anna, 127
Dewey, Elizabeth, 149
Dewey, Emeline, 146
Dewey, Jedidiah, 38, 149
Dewey, Rev., 175
DeWitt, Simeon, 16
DeWitt, Simon, 99
DeWitt, Susan, 16, 99

Dewy, Mr., 143
Dexter, Eliza, 67
Dexter, Eveline, 176
Dexter, Lydia, 168
Dexter, Sarah, 44
Dickerson, Lyman B., 58
Dickerson, Thomas, 117
Dickson, James, 87
Dike, F., 44
Dike, Flanders, 131
Dike. See also Dyke
Dillingham, Sophia, 21
Dillon, William, 174
Disbrow, Simon, 91
Ditton, John, 169
Ditton, Mary Ann, 169
Doane, Artemus, 21
Doane, Mary Elizabeth, 21
Dobbin, Charlotte, 68
Dodd, Mary W., 83
Dodge, A. F., 151
Dodge, Nehemiah, 10
Dolbeat, Rufus, 107
Doney, Peter, 99
Doolittle, Asher, 19
Doolittle, Hannah, 97
Doolittle, Nancy, 129
Doolittle, Rev., 82
Dorrin, John, 87
Doty, Asa A., 124
Doty, Mr., 169
Douglas, J. S., 35
Douglas, S. P. W., 129
Douglas, Williams &, 169
Douglass & Dunn, 46
Dow, Lorenzo, 44, 45, 83
Dow, Peggy, 83
Dow, Sarah M., 28
Dowd, Mary E., 178
Dowling, William L., 74
Downing, Ann Eliza, 164
Downing, George, 164, 165
Downing, Mary M., 164
Downing, Silas, 166
Downing, Thomas, 136
Downing, William L., 75
Downs, Wm. Theodore, 126
Dox, M. M. Co., 10
Doyle, Amanda, 41
Dozen, Charles, 107
Drake, Alinda, 108
Drake, Beecher &, 112
Drake, Benjamin, 169
Drake, Elijah, 89
Drake, Hannah, 57
Drake, Harriet, 137
Drake, Joshua, 62, 69, 138
Drake, Josiah, 135
Drake, Mary Ann, 139
Drake, Nelson, 134, 151
Drake, Percis, 13
Drake, Polly, 101
Drake, S. Cornelius, 174
Drake, W. & N., 133
Drake, William, 151
Drane, Casandra, 159
Drane, Stephen, 159
Draper, Silas (Mrs), 73
Driscoll, John, 129
Driscoll, Joshua, 28. 95
Drown, S., 14
Drum, Henry, 144
Drum, John W., 120
Dubois, Edward, 106
DuBois, Mrs., 19
Dudley, Charles E., 132
Dudley, Thomas J., 17
Duel, William, 116
Duer, Mary Ann, 97
Duer, Susan, 97
Duesler, Abraham, 43
Duffie, Dorothy, 127
Duggan, Delia C., 134
Duggan, Elizabeth, 95
Duggan, N., 93
Duggan, Nathaniel, 134
Dumond, Betsey M., 161
Dunbar, Margaret Jane, 177

Dunham, David, 53
Dunlop, Maria, 117
Dunn, Daniel, 147
Dunn, Jacob A., 23
Dunn, James, 46
Dunn, Martin, 118
Dunn, McIntyre &, 107
Dunning, J. D., 72
Dunning, J., 33
Dunning, Jeheil, 59
Dunning, Joseph, 142
Durand, Miss, 10
Durfee, Abel, 102
Durfee, Allen, 20
Durfee, Amanda, 38
Durfee, Ann, 47
Durfee, B. B., 131, 135
Durfee, Bailey, 106, 136
Durfee, Barton, 32
Durfee, Barzillai, 64
Durfee, C., 61
Durfee, Catharine, 29
Durfee, Charles, 40
Durfee, Clapp &, 75
Durfee, Edward, 11, 133
Durfee, Elihu, 36, 58, 89, 109
Durfee, George, 9
Durfee, Hotchkiss &, 77
Durfee, Isaac, 133
Durfee, Lemuel, 26, 44
Durfee, Lucina, 19
Durfee, Lucy, 102
Durfee, Maria Louisa, 150
Durfee, Marion Bailey, 57
Durfee, Mr, 38
Durfee, P., 74
Durfee, Permilla, 85
Durfee, Philip, 76
Durfee, Philo, 66, 69, 72, 90, 92, 150
Durfee, Philo D., 71
Durfee, Prudence, 176
Durfee, S. S., 64, 65, 168
Durfee, Samuel, 176

Durfee, Sarah, 45
Durfee, Sidney S., 66
Durfee, Square Beny, 66
Durfee, Stephen, 45, 57, 89, 98
Durfee, Susan, 142
Durfee, Susannah, 98, 141, 142
Durfee, Sydney S., 72, 74
Durfee, Sydney S. & Co., 96
Durfee, Townsend &., 145
Durfee, William, 85
Dusenbury, Emma Jane, 166
Dyke, Flanders, 54
Dyke, James, 54
Dyke, Samuel, 54
Dyke. See also Dike.
East Ridge, 82
Eastwood, Phebe Ann, 156
Eaton, H., 178
Eaton, Horace, 178, 179
Eddy & Elihu Clark, 77
Eddy, A. D., 39, 42
Eddy, Bathsheba, 17
Eddy, Clark & Co., 91
Eddy, Cyrenus C., 149
Eddy, David, 24, 39, 65, 78
Eddy, George P., 50, 78
Eddy, Hannah, 166
Eddy, Henry, 50
Eddy, Hiram E., 50
Eddy, Isaac, 89
Eddy, James B., 89
Eddy, Jane, 124
Eddy, Jesse, 150, 166
Eddy, Job H., 18
Eddy, John, 69
Eddy, Laban S., 81
Eddy, Lydia, 105
Eddy, Mary, 69
Eddy, Morton, 50
Eddy, Seth, 19
Edginton, Ann, 135
Edmonston, Eliza Ann, 165
Edmonston, John A., 165, 178

Edmondston, Lottie A., 178
Edmunds, E., 121
Edmunds, James, Jr., 55
Edmundson, Dorothy, 37
Edmundson, Thomas, 37
Edwards, I. O., 124
Edwards, Ira, 155
Eggerton, William, 160
Eggleston, Charles Payne, 56

Eggleston, D. J. S., 56
Eggleston, Dr., 44
Eggleston, Electa, 133
Eggleston, Henry Fenton, 132
Eggleston, J. S., 120, 127
Eggleston, Jane D., 140
Eggleston, Jonathan Silsby, 166
Eggleston, Jonathan S., 165
Eggleston, K. S., 75
Eggleston, Mary Ann, 68
Eggleston, Robinson &, 26
Eggleston, S., 125
Eggleston, T. N., 90
Eggleston, Thomas, 64, 89, 90
Elemendorf, A., 109, 111, 119
Ellison, George G., 57
Ellsworth, Levi, 59
Elmendorf, A., 113
Elmendorf, Samuel, 47
Elwood, J. L., 83
Ely & Avery, 152
Ely, Beckwith &, 81, 82, 197
Ely, Clark &, 75, 79
Ely, D. G.,, 99, 107, 114
Ely, David G., 81, 127, 150, 158
Ely, David G. O., 151
Ely, G. S., 75, 94
Ely, Giles S., 69
Ely, Hannah M. R., 169
Ely, Joseph N., 169
Ely, Mary E. T., 169
Ely, P. G., 61

Ely, Richard, 150
Ely, Ruth S., 161
Ely, William, 128
Empson, J. G. S., 72
Enos, Mrs. 155
Ensworth, Azel, 18, 27
Ensworth, O. Russell, 87
Ensworth, Sally, 18
Equestrian Co., 126
Erie Canal, 9, 11, 23, 41, 47, 80, 93
Errickson, Oren, 36
Essex Money, 118, 119
Estelow, Mr., 28
Estlow, Nathan, 21
Eustace, Rev., 47
Evans, A., 118, 122
Evans, A. E., 72
Evans, Naomi M., 46
Everingham, J. D., 9, 15, 22, 26, 95
Everingham, James D., 12
Everitt, Ann, 131
Everitt, Gertrude, 160
Everson, Bruce, 122, 132, 149, 163, 165
Everson, W. E., 122
Everson, W. E. & B., 121
Everson, William E., 149
Everts, Mary, 137
Eves, Reuben, 172
Failing, George, 56
Fairbanks, Elezear, 100
Fairbanks, Ira, 59, 118
Fairbanks, Lucinda, 118
Fairbanks, Phebe, 150
Fairbanks, Prudence C., 23
Fairbanks, Rufus P., 165
Fairbanks, Sarah, 59, 100
Faling, Daniel, 174
Faling, Mary Jane, 174
Farewell, Charles, 149
Farnham, Henry, 26
Farnham, Mr., 121

Farnham, William H,., 180
Farr, Clarinda, 81
Faulkner, Horton, 137
Feester, Mary, 145
Feller, Anna Christina, 170
Feller, John D., 170
Fenner, Jas., 73
Fenton, cashier, 133
Fenton, Catherine, 97
Fenton, E., 128
Fenton, F. S., 65
Fenton, Henry, 112
Fenton, J. B., 68, 106, 146
Fenton, J. H., 140
Fenton, J. S., 62, 67, 68, 73, 76, 77, 93, 107, 113, 114, 115, 126
Fenton, Joseph, 48, 76
Fenton, Joseph B., 116, 133
Fenton, Joseph, O., 52
Fenton, Joseph S., 48, 72, 89, 97, 100, 112, 119, 120
Fenton, Josiah J., 102
Fenton, Julia J., 89
Fenton, Lavina B., 93
Fenton, Loring, 52
Fenton, S., 126
Fenton, William M., 99
Fergy, Andrew, 122
Ferrin, Grandin &, 154
Ferrin, Jane Elizabeth, 163
Ferrin, Remus, 134, 139, 140, 150
Field & Robinson, 70
Field, James, 14, 15, 26, 38, 57
Field, James & Co., 41
Field, R. T. 83
Field, Solomon, 66
Fillmore, Adeline, 107
Fillmore, Hannah E.,125
Fillmore, Joseph F., 150
Fillmore, Luther, 24
Fillmore, Maria, 69

Fillmore, Williams &, 113
Filmore, Rev., 89
Finch, Caleb, 56
Finch, D. G., 65, 82
Finch, Daniel B., 69
Finch, Daniel D., 64, 80
Finch, Daniel G., 60, 75, 142, 118
Finch, Elizabeth, 118
Finch, Elsey Elizabeth, 80
Finch, Eugene, 64
Finch, G. G., 73
Finch's store, 68
Findley, Clarinda E., 168
Findley, Jones, 168
Finley, Alexander, 85
Finley, Lucina, 123
Finley, O'Neil &, 179
Fireworks, 79
Fish, Abram, 170
Fish, Chauncey, 158
Fish, Harriet G. J., 148
Fish, Harry, 89
Fish, Harry S., 174
Fish, Isaac, 154
Fish, Job, 27
Fish, Mary, 33
Fish, Mary E., 154
Fish, Mary M., 175
Fish, Polly Maria, 174
Fish, Stephen, 33
Fish, Thomas, 144
Fisher, Chastina A., 102
Fisher, George, 41
Fisher, Hannah, 41
Fisher, Howard, 154
Fisher, Matilda, 103
Fisher, N. W., 160
Fisher, Rev., 168
Fisk, Amasa, 164
Fisk, Ralph, 27
Fisk, Sarah A., 164
Fitch, Edward, 147
Fitch, Jabez G., 17

Fitch, William, 80
Fitts, Benjamin, 145
Fitzgerald, Elizabeth, 138
Fitzgerald, Evans, 173
Fitzsimmons, John, 94
Fitzsimmons, Margaret, 94
Flagler, Dorcas, 45
Fleming, John, 21
Fleming, John Jr., 9
Flint, Jeremiah, 128
Flint, Jonathan T., 146
Flower & Leach, 19
Flower, Alcymany, 165
Flower, Elisha, 150, 165
Flower, H. S, 171
Flower, Henry S., 158, 175
Flower, Martha A., 147
Fobes, E., 147
Fobes, Edson, 153, 161
Fobes, Jane A., 161
Fobes, Mary Ellen, 161
Folger, Charles J., 160
Folker, Sarah Hope, 176
Follett, Frederick, 29
Follett, Nathan, 17
Foot, Elisha, 79
Foot, Louisa, 159
Foote, R. S., 74, 126
Ford, Charles B., 93
Ford, Emily C., 90
Ford, James, 90
Ford, James W., 178
Ford, Morrison, 171
Ford, Nancy S., 118
Ford, Richard, 150, 159
Ford, Sarah, 58
Foreman, John W., 124
Foskett, Goodale, 88
Foskett, Mercy, 128
Fosman, James, 157
Foster, Ann Sophia, 10, 52
Foster, Burton, 66
Foster, C., 62, 70
Foster, Clapp & Durfee, 94

Foster, Cullen, 65, 178
Foster, Cyrus, 104, 126, 159
Foster, E. C., 62
Foster, Edwin S., 138
Foster, Emeline M., 159
Foster, J., 12
Foster, J. & Co., 12
Foster, Jeter, 10, 49, 52
Foster, Joel, 102
Foster, L., 61
Foster, Maria A., 104
Foster, Mary E., 178
Foster, Mary Jane, 126
Foster, Mason D., 108
Foster, Pliny, 141
Foster, R. H., 164
Foster, Reuben H., 177
Foster, Robert, 104
Foster, Rosetta, 177
Foster, Russell, 174
Foster, Samuel, 90
Foster, Sophia, 49
Foster, William, 158
Foster, Zenas (Mrs.), 98
Foster, Zenas, 22
Foundry, 121
Fowler, M. (Miss), 148
Fowler, William, 38
Fox, David S., 151
Francis, Annis H., 162
Francis, D. D., 179
Francis, J., 38, 63, 79
Francis, J. M., 159
Francis, John M., 169
Francis, Josiah, 91
Frankenberger, John, 38
Franklin, Bella, 31
Franklin, Sally, 16
Freeman, Benjamin, 177
Freeman, Gideon, 138
Freeman, Henry Wash. Sidney, 81
Freeman, Luther Tucker, 177
Freeman, Mahala P., 81

Freeman, William, 81
Freer, Peter, 22
Freer, Rachel, 22
Friedheim, J. & Co., 117
Frink, Eli, 41
Frisbee, Dr., 21
Frisbee, Salmon, 74
Frost, B., 133, 145
Fuller, Cyrus, 92
Fuller & Smith, 35
Gabriel, Louis, 67
Gage, Charlotte B., 174
Gage, George, 178
Gage, Nancy, 51
Gager, Maria, 36
Gaines, Sophronia, 82
Galen, 44
Galloway, A, 50
Galloway, A. R., 13, 15, 26
Galloway, Almond, 105
Galloway, Archer, 41, 57, 61, 70, 102
Galloway, Delia Ann, 170
Galloway, Emily, 123
Galloway, James, 128, 144
Galloway, John, 50 , 170
Galloway, John H., 123
Galloway, Julia L., 154
Galloway, Milo, 42
Galloway, Nancy, 144
Galloway, Russell, 109
Galloway, Sarah R., 60
Gallup, Aldrich &, 159
Gallup, Hiram, 80
Gallup, James, 162
Gannett, Abigail, 133
Gannett, Deborah, 34
Ganson, Harriet, 27
Ganson, James, 27
Ganson, John, 162
Gardener, Henry, 111
Gardiner, Eleanor, 178
Gardner, Amanda, 87
Gardner, Angeline, 74

Gardner, Belle, 179
Gardner, Cordelia, 89
Gardner, Eliza, 74
Gardner, Elizabeth, 68
Gardner, Grandin &, 91, 106
Gardner, Hannah A., 84
Gardner, Henry, 66, 72, 73, 75, 90, 92, 95, 106, 110, 113, 132
Gardner, Isaac, 89. 113, 119
Gardner, Isaac (Mrs.), 152
Gardner, Louisa, 87, 113
Gardner, Margaretta R., 132
Gardner, Mary, 36, 37, 103
Gardner, Sunderland P., 36, 37
Gardner, W. G., 87
Gardner, William, 74, 92,
Gardner, William G., 95
Gardner, William H., 140
Garlock, Artemas, 152
Garlock, Maria, 116
Gas, natural, 117
Gates & Thompson, 179
Gates, Eliza, 129
Gates, Higby &, 130
Gates, Jefferson, 53
Gates, Joseph W., 30
Gates, S. E., 129
Gavitt, Joseph, 88
Gay, John S., 150
Gear, Dorcas, 84
Gear, E. G., 42
Gear, Rev., 42, 45
George, Betsy, 55
Geralamon, Eliza Ann, 145
Gibbs, Joseph, 157, 168
Gibbs, Mary, 82
Gibbs, Sarah, 128
Giberson, Ann, 53
Giberson, Enoch, 167
Giberson, Jerusha, 167
Gibson, Caroline G., 153
Gibson, Mary, 102
Gibson, Mr., 110

Gifford, Isaac, 166
Gifford, Sarah Ann, 142
Gilbert, Frances Ann, 86
Gilbert, G. H., 86
Gilbert, Henry, 81 , 93
Gilbert, J. H., 33, 34, 82, 132, 152, 169
Gilbert, Joel Thayer, 169
GIlbert, John H., 36, 73, 79, 91, 92, 106, 168
Gilbert, Maj., 174
Gilbert, Marilla, 173
Gilbert, Mary Jane, 168
Gilbert, Mr., 76, 131, 156
Gilbert, Payne &, 45
Gilbert, Ruth, 82
Gilbert, Tucker &, 19, 22, 26, 33,
Gilbert, Wooster &, 22
Gildersleeve, J. S., 58
Giles, Chauncey, 114, 115, 137
Gillespie, Rev., 180
Gillett, John, 66
Giraud, Miss, 37
Gleason, Joseph, 39, 39
Gleason, Phebe, 47
Glimpse, Cornelius, 128
Glossender, Beecher &, 112
Glossender, David, 93, 163
Glover, Mary, 60
Glowacke, Mons., 86
Godard, Cuyler &, 94
Godard, E. P., 66, 69, 72, 73, 99, 103, 111, 113, 119
Godard, E. P. & Co., 89, 126
Godard, Edwin, 66
Godard, Eliza, 102
Godard, Festus, 92
Godard, L. O., 73, 92, 95
Godard, Lester O., 102
Godard, Lydia S., 104
Godard, M. J., 73, 102, 159
Godard, M. J. & Co., 126
Godard, Marcellus J., 97

Goddard, L. C., 176
Goddard, Mabel, 176
Goddard, S. O., 106
Goff, I. C., 132
Goff, Isaac, 121
Goff, Isaac C., 132
Goff, James, Jr., 128
Goff, Mary, 13
Gold, Benjamin R., 28
Gold, Harriet R., 28
Goldsmsith, ---, 81
Goldsmith, Abigail, 105
Goldsmsith, Ann, 96
Goldsmith, Benjamin D., 47
Goldsmith, Caroline M., 39
Goldsmith, David, 169
Goldsmsith, Emily W., 151
Goldsmith, F. A., 72, 76, 97, 98
Goldsmith, Festus, 105
Goldsmith, Festus A., 70, 91, 92, 120, 130, 142
Goldsmsith, Jane, 131
Goldsmith, Maria Antoinette, 172
Goldsmith, Mary, 120
Goldsmith, Ovid, 151
Goldsmith, Paul, 46, 55, 102, 177
Goldsmith, Temperance, 76
Goldsmith, Thomas, 131, 137
Goodell, Abisha, 152
Goodell, Morey, 99
Goodell, Richard, 26
Gooding, Lydia A., 30
Gooding, William, 30
Goodrich, Fanny, 127
Goodrich, J. W., 58
Goodrich, Jonas W., 151
Goodrich, Louisa M., 58
Goodrich, William F., 119
Goodwin, Adeline, 101
Gordon & Williams, 111
Gordon, Catherine, 163

Gordon, Delia M., 126
Gordon, E. H., 126
Gordon, John, 163
Gordon, Robert, 137
Gordon, Samuel C., 68
Gordon, Sarah Elizabeth, 180
Gordon, Sarah Isabelle, 174
Gordon, Susan Mary, 126
Gordon, W. W., 108, 112
Gordon, William Robert, 137
Gordon, William, 55
Gordon, William W., 126, 174, 180
Gorham, Nathaniel, 31
Gough, Mrs., 41
Graham, Frederick, 13
Gramesley, William S., 126, 134
Gramesly & Robinson, 134
Grandin, A. B., 65
Grandin & Ferrin, 154
Grandin & Gardner, 91, 106
Grandin & Thurber, 143, 150
Grandin, Andrew Jackson, 77
Grandin, B., 150
Grandin, Carlton Rogers, 109
Grandin, Daniel, 68
Grandin, E. B., 38, 45, 52, 62, 66, 68, 73, 75, 76, 109
Grandin, Egbert, 34
Grandin, Howard &, 50
Grandin, J., 9
Grandin, P., 13, 48, 50, 65, 67, 70, 75, 125
Grandin, Philip, 38, 40, 42, 52, 76, 82,
Grandin, Rachel, 68
Grandin, Rogers &, 69
Grandin, Sarah Marie, 125
Grandin, Thayer &, 60
Grandin, William, 115, 139
Grandin, William B., 165
Granger, Jane A., 155
Granger, John A., 42

Grannis, Eveline R., 170
Grant, E. T., 164
Graves, Aurelia, 174
Graves, Jane, 176
Graves, John, 135, 176
Grawbadger, Betsey Jane, 147
Gray, William H., 174
Green, Agnes, 138
Green, Byram, 54, 92, 121, 152
Green, Capt., 159
Green, Charles M., 141
Green, D. K., 167
Green, Eunice, 29
Green, Hannah, 38
Green, Harriet M., 121
Green, John N., 138
Green, Joseph, 92
Green, Louisa, 152
Green, Lucy, 54
Greenfield, Arah E., 23
Greenvault, Daniel, 104
Greenwood, William, 59
Gregg, John G., 16
Gregg, Louisa J., 101
Gregg, Lucinda C., 16
Gregg, Sarah, 12
Gregory, Benjamin T., 112
Gregory, Margaret, 83
Greig, Benjamin, 43
Grieve, Walter, 31, 32
Griffith, William, 42
Grinnell, Abel, 56
Griswold, Harmon, 100
Griswold, Louisa, 59
Griswold, William H., 40
Groesbeck, Myndert, 122
Groot, Edward H., 159
Grove, Catherine, 102
Grover, A. J., 91
Groves, John, 101, 102
Grow, Oliver, 98
Grundy, Felix, 132
Guion, Rev., 47
Gunsmith, 103

Gurley, Royal, 73
Gurney & Post, 74, 83, 89, 90
Gurney, Abram, 67
Gurney, Phebe, 104
Gurney, Thomas W., 89, 104
Guyuscutus, 175
Haddock, John H., 27
Haff, John P., 113
Hagaman, Catherine, 101
Hagerman, Abram, 140
Hahn, Thomas N., 160
Hahn, Valentine, 110
Haight, Lucina A., 92
Hakes, Jeremiah, 49
Hale, Charlotte, 93, 99
Hale, Ebenezer, 62
Hale, Gardner, 24
Hall, Amasa, 38, 103, 113, 117
Hall, Ambrose, 24, 46, 95, 147
Hall, Bailey, 11
Hall, Baily, 51
Hall, Caroline, 135
Hall, Hannah, 11
Hall, James 102, 139, 141
Hall, Jane, 139
Hall, Joel, 119
Hall, Laura Ann, 117
Hall, Lucy, 177
Hall, Mary, 102
Hall, Mary Ann, 38
Hall, Mary M., 95
Hall, Rebecca, 11, 51
Hall, Sally, 84
Hall, Sanford R., 58
Hall, Sarah W., 147
Hall, Susan, 165
Hall, Thomas E., 84
Hall, William L., 119
Hallett, Gitty M., 28
Hallett, J. W., 42
Hallett, Jacob, 28
Hallhimer, Margaret, 105
Hamilton, S., 15
Hammond, Betsey, 80

Hammond, Caroline E., 174
Hammond, Cynthia, 109
Hammond, E., 64
Hammond, Hart, 10
Hammond, Libeus, 109
Hammond, Mr. 161
Hammond, Polly, 53
Hammond, Rollin, 32
Handy, P. W., 82, 107, 120, 126, 127, 137
Handy, Peter W., 133
Handy, W. P., 114
Hanks, Levi, 85
Hanks, Philena, 18
Hanks, Waterman, 47
Hannah, D. T., 133
Hanner, C. M., 81
Hard, August, 97
Hard, Augustus, 78, 88
Hard, Burton, 88
Hard, L. W., 88
Harding, B., 91
Hare, Mariah, 33
Harlow, John M., 35, 75
Harmon, Delilah, 57
Harmon, Harvey, 37
Harmsley, Henrietta, 70
Harrington, D., 154
Harris, Abigail, 129
Harris, Barrett, 54
Harris, Chloe, 123
Harris, George W., 56
Harris, Hiram, 36
Harris, Isabella, 178
Harris, John, 53
Harris, Joseph, 95
Harris, Lucina, 34
Harris, Lucinda, 36, 95
Harris, Lucy, 18
Harris, Lydia, 15
Harris, Martin, 61, 136
Harris, Mary, 27
Harris, Naomi, 31
Harris, Peter, 129

Harris, Polly, 139
Harris, Seth, 46
Harris, Susan, 134
Harrison, George, 127
Harrison, Luman, 62, 63, 67
Harrison's Mill, 65
Harrison, President, 134
Harrison, Ruth Aramantha, 148
Harrison, William H., 134
Harrison, William R., 53
Hart, Abby L., 78
Hart, Adelia, 144
Hart, Ann Elizabeth, 99
Hart, Eliza, 20
Hart, George, 112
Hart, Harriet, 111
Hart, Heminway &, 174
Hart, Joel S., 17
Hart, Mary Ann, 22
Hart, Matilda, 112
Hart, Rodman, 137
Hart, Susan, 155
Hart, Truman, 65, 78, 89, 99, 100, 155
Hartman, Margaret, 138
Hartwell, O., 14
Harvey, Ashahel, 93
Harwood, Sophia, 14
Harwood, Webb, 32
Harwood, William, 21
Haskett, Jeremiah, 154
Hatch, George Whitfield, 40
Hatch, Israel, 77
Hathaway, Clapp, & Moore, 103
Hathaway, Clapp, &, 94, 108
Hathaway, Clemens, 106
Hathaway, Cynthia, 14
Hathaway, Ebenezer, 135, 163, 169
Hathaway, Elizabeth C., 51
Hathaway, G. A., 66
Hathaway, George, 77
Hathaway, George A., 73
Hathaway, J. C., 132

Hathaway, Josiah, 137
Hathaway, Loren, 55
Hathaway, Lucinda, 137
Hathaway, Luther E., 146
Hathaway, Mary Jane, 126
Hathaway, Rebecca, 135
Hathaway, S., 26
Hathaway, Salmon, 74, 86
Hathorn, Ann, 90
Haven, Eldridge, 105
Haven, Lovell &, 72
Havens, A. E., 73, 90, 105, 106
Havens, Aldrich &, 127, 138
Havens, Ann Maria, 69
Havens, Avery, 66
Havens, Avery E., 92, 107
Havens, E., 50, 73
Havens, Eldredge, 62, 76
Havens, Nancy, 50
Haver, Deborah P., 105
Hawes, Ann M., 178
Hawker, Elizabeth E., 151
Hawks, John, 53
Hawser, Lucretia, 59
Haxton, Betsey, 18
Hayden, Peter P. R., 36
Hayes, George E., 38
Hayes, Pliny, 63
Hayner, Kerzander, 117
Hayner, Peter, 117
Haynes, Charles G., 23
Haynes, John B., 162
Haywood, Asa, 166
Hayward, Elisha, 15
Hayward, J. D., 10, 21, 73, 105
Hayward, Stoughton, 139
Hayward, William D., 21
Haywood, Lucy, 166
Hazen, Elizabeth, 120
Heacox, Augustus, 91
Heartwell, O., 22
Heath, Francis, 173

Heath, Pamela, 104
Hecox, Cyrus, 62
Hedden, Aaron H., 148
Hedsall, Dorcas, 19
Hegeman, William, 165
Hemingway, Mr., 62
Hemingway, Silas, 44
Heminway & Hart, 174
Heminway, Albert G., 173
Heminway, T., 62, 65, 74, 76, 92, 104, 113, 114, 115, 119, 120,
Heminway, T. T., 121
Heminway, Truman, 35, 39, 41, 100, 106, 112, 132
Hendee, A., 41, 49, 73
Hendee, Alva, 141
Hendee, Ariel, 135
Hendee, D., 30
Hendee, Daniel, 39, 41, 45, 68
Hendee, Edwin A., 142
Hendee, Mary, 141
Hendee, Mary Ann, 45
Hendee, R. S., 79, 102, 152
Hendee, Richard S., 92
Henderson & Hibberd, 179
Henry Jessup, 48
Hepburn, Harriet Jane, 43
Hermans, J., 51
Hermans, James, 20
Herrick, George R., 152
Herrington, D., 176
Herrington, R., 177
Herrington, Rev., 177
Hersey, Charlotte, 156
Hewlett, Emery, 10, 51
Hewson, John, 146
Hibban, Mrs., 122
Hibbard, Ann, 91
Hibbard, Benjamin, 31
Hibbard, Noahdiah, 74
Hibbard, Simeon Orvil, 106
Hibberd, Alfred, 178
Hibberd, Henderson &, 179

Hibner, Sarah, 99
Hickey, James, 103
Hickey, Mathew, 123
Hickley, George, 94
Hickox, B. H., 24, 31, 59, 62, 63, 65, 73, 75, 78,
Hickox, Burton H., 10
Hickox, Rev., 29
Hicks, Angelica, 54
Hicks, D. C., 156
Hicks, Elias, 49
Hicks, Eliza, 106
Hicks, George, 117
Hicks, Joshua, 54, 58
Hicks, Orrin, 143
Higby & Coleman, 108
Higby & Gates, 130
Higby, G. C., 67
Higby, Gad C., 64
Higby, Hiram M., 139
Higby, Thomas B., 144
Higgins, David C., 64
Higgins, Rev., 16
Hildreth, Hollister &, 89
Hildreth, Mary N., 164
Hildreth, Phebe J., 134
Hildreth, Shadrach, 99
Hill, Abner, 44
Hill, Ann M., 129
Hill, Asa, 54
Hill, Benjamin, 28
Hill, Burissa, 169
Hill, Charles B., 145
Hill, Charlotte, 141
Hill, David, 28, 29, 53
Hill, Diane A., 68
Hill, Eli, 136
Hill, Ephriam, 59
Hill, Fanny, 56
Hill, Francis, 169
Hill, George W., 156
Hill, Hannah, 53
Hill, Hezekiah, 130
Hill, Ira, 56

Hill, James, 41, 59
Hill, Justus, 20
Hill, Keziah, 28
Hill, Milton, 34
Hill, P., 74
Hill, Parley, 66, 67
Hill, Philip, Jr. 62
Hill, Pratt &, 72
Hill, Rebecca, 35
Hill, S. G., 152
Hill, Thomas, 20
Hill, William, 38
Hillman, Mary, 53
Hills, Wilbert, 65
Hilman, Ann Maria, 131
Hinckley, Charles D., 90
Hine, Laura, 124
Hine, Mary, 148
Hine, Miss, 122
Hine, Phebe, 150
Hines, Paul, 128
Hiney, Anna Sophia, 151
Hiney, Garrett, H., 151
Hiney, Garrett Henry, 146
Hinman, Anna, 44
Hinman, Calista, 117
Hinman, Daniel Webster, 117
Hinman, Delia, 175
Hinman, E., 119, 145
Hinman, Elihu, 63, 117
Hinman, Eliza Ann, 131
Hinman, Harris, 44
Hinman, John, 93, 131
Hitchcock, James, 30
Hitchcock, Eliza Ann, 125
Hitchcock, Sarah, 30
Hoag, Ann, 133
Hoag, Hiram, 130
Hoag, James, 108
Hoag, Mary Ann, 70
Hoag, Matilda, 82
Hoag, Sarah, 94, 108
Hobart, John Henry, 55
Hobart, Rev., 42

Hodges, James, 85
Hodgkin, R. C., 86, 88
Hodson, John W., 135
Hoffman, Sophia, 95
Hoffman, Henry, 147
Hogoboom, George C., 161
Hogoboom, Robert, 161
Hohn, Catherine, 123
Hohn, Valentine, 123
Holcomb, Rhoda, 58
Holland, David, 43
Holland Land Co., 97
Holley, Byron, 36
Holley, Clarissa G., 45
Holley, Elizabeth D., 68
Holley, Horace, 36
Holley, John M., 85
Holley, Myron, 45, 133
Holling, Andrew, 176
Holling, James, 48
Holling, Julia Augusta, 176
Holling, Mary, 149
Hollister & Hildreth, 89
Hollister, Solomon D., 110
Holly, John M., 35
Holmes, D., 46
Holmes, John R., 17
Holmes, Peleg, 63
Holoday, Cornelius, 32
Holst, M., 127
Homan, B., 143
Homan, Benjamin, 72108
Homan, Daniel, 48
Homan, N., 75
Homas, Benj. E., 73
Homes, Myron, 127
Homes, Robert, 17, 38
Homes, Sarah, 20
Homes, William, 11, 52
Homes, William F., 56
Hooker, Mary Ann, 84
Hopkins, Edmond, 45
Hopkins, Edwin, 44
Hopkins, Emily H., 38

Hopkins, Joseph, 60
Hopkins, Josiah, 84
Hopkins, Stephen, 38, 64
Hopkinson, George, 61
Hopkinson, Jane, 109
Hornby, Allen, 173
Hornsby, J. D., 155
Horton, Allen W., 131, 139
Horton, Amy, 84
Horton, B. R., 139
Horton, Caleb, 64, 75
Horton, Col., 163, 168
Horton, Cynthia, 104
Horton, Francis, 43
Horton, Franklin, 136
Horton, Ira, 99
Horton, J., 61
Horton, James G., 70
Horton, James P., 39, 64
Horton, Joseph, 63
Horton, Maria, 70, 152
Horton, Mary, 32, 50
Horton, Mr., 113
Horton, Nathan, 84
Horton, Rev., 18
Horton, Samuel T., 104, 118, 152
Horton, William M., 169
Hosmer, Aaron, Jr., 155
Hotchkiss & Durfee, 77
Hotchkiss & Lake, 104
Hotchkiss, Chloe, 82
Hotchkiss, D. & Co., 118
Hotchkiss, D., 77, 98, 160, 162, 169
Hotchkiss, D. H., 139
Hotchkiss, David, 103, 128
Hotchkiss, Henry F., 151
Hotchkiss, Lemon, 32
Hotchkiss, Ralph N., 103
Hotchkiss, Rev., 38
Hotels, Aldrich's Inn, 88
Hotels, E. P. Lanes's (tavern), 99

Hotels, Asa Lilly's, 49, 74, 102
Hotels, Beacon Hill, 167, 173
Hotels, Boston, 138
Hotels, Bostwick, 121
Hotels, Bunker Hill, 35, 39, 41, 46, 51, 70, 81, 85, 116, 140, 135, 150, 152, 161, 165
Hotels, Eagle, 14, 22, 43, 46, 49, 51, 53, 54, 55, 63, 66, 67, 72, 75, 79, 80, 81, 85, 86, 91, 92, 95, 96, 98, 157
Hotels, Franklin House, 44, 57, 93, 109, 112, 148
Hotels, Horace Church's, 48, 50
Hotels, Higby's, 102
Hotels, Homans, 88
Hotels, Kingsley Miller's, 55
Hotels, Manchester House, 164
Hotels, Marion Springs House, 50, 57
Hotels, Nottingham & Martin, 144
Hotels, Nottingham's, 65, 145, 163, 179
Hotels, Palmyra, 22, 97, 108, 112, 114, 126, 128, 130, 170
Hotels, Powers, 41
Hotels, St. Johns, 30
Hotels, Sulphur Springs House, 63
Hotels, Temperance House, 154, 169
Hotels, Walworth House, 121
Hough, Richard, 48
Houghtaling, Levi, 67, 73
Houghton, Clarissa, 68
Houghton, Claudius V., 67
Houghton, Sheaver, 141
House, Elizabeth, 32
House, Jane, 167
House, Rev., 24, 27, 28
House, Spencer G., 152

Hout, D. D., 119
Hovey, Jonathan, 23
Howard & Grandin, 50
Howard, Cordelia, 49
Howard, Luther, 45, 52
Howard, Ruth Ann, 38
Howard, William, 100
Howe, Eliza, 39, 41
Howe, Jonah, 78
Howe, Mary Y., 42
Howell, Champion &, 40
Howell, Cynthia, 59
Howell, Epanetus, 57, 59, 66, 86, 92
Howell, Fanny, 141
Howell, Gilbert, 59, 129
Howell, James G., 66
Howell, Jane E., 68
Howell, Jonah, 12, 17, 59, 77, 90, 92
Howell, Margaret Ann, 127
Howell, Mariah, 61
Howell, Mrs., 17
Howell, N. W., 68
Howell, Nathaniel W., 141
Howell, P. R., 75, 108
Howell, W. M., 144
Howland, A. H., 127
Howland, Annie C., 85
Howland, David, 52, 59
Howland, Emily, 134
Howland, Henry H., 175
Howland, Isaac, 112
Howland, Lois P., 86
Howland, Lydia Elmira, 59
Howland, Maria, 16, 109
Howland, Mr., 40
Howland, Timothy, 116
Hoxie, B. T., 105
Hoxie, Benjamin T., 83
Hoxie's corner, 82
Hoyt & May, 68, 69, 111
Hoyt, D. D., 86, 89, 121, 124, 133, 163

Hoyt, David D., 78
Hoyt, Dr., 96
Hoyt, Sally, 148
Hoyt, William May, 124
Hoyt, William C., 121
Hubbard, Alfred, 105, 168
Hubbard, Charlotte, 83
Hubbard, Eveline, 100
Hubbard, H., 60
Hubbard, Rev., 38
Hubbard, Sarah Maria, 154
Hubbell, Dr., 119
Hubbell, James., 64, 73, 79, 113, 120, 151, 160, 174
Hubbell, L., 42, 51
Hubbell, Maria, 51
Hubbell, Sally, 160
Hudson, Charles, 22
Hudson, Lorenzo, 70
Hudson, Pliny, 141, 170
Hudson, Samuel, 170
Huestis, Alex C., 126
Huestis, Alex McG C., 128
Huggins, Almira R., 58
Huggins, Laura, 76
Huggins, Susan Sophia, 163
Huggins, Zadock, 58
Hughes, J. E., 154
Hughes, Miss, 154
Hughs, Stephen W., 26
Hulburt, Cynthia, 17
Hulbert, Silas, 13
Hull, Nathan, 161
Hullett, Joseph L., 59
Hulse, Ira, 129
Humphrey, James, 87
Hunt, Eliza C., 174
Hunt, Frances, 28
Hunt, Harriet Angeline, 156
Hunt, Lucius A., 134
Hunt, Montgomery, 28
Hunt, Susan. 80
Hunting Match Men, 65
Huntington, Jedidiah, 167

Huntington, Mary Jane, 128
Huntington, Samuel D., 12, 128, 131,
Huntington, Sarah, 167
Huntington, Welthy, 126
Huntoon, Abraham, 132
Hurd, L., 22, 26, 30, 73, 79,
Hurd, Lovell, 39, 69, 154
Hurd, Lovewell, 20
Hurd, Sally, 39
Hurd, Sally Ann, 154
Hurlburt, Charles, 83
Hurlburt, Francis, 52
Hurlburt, John W., 67
Hurlburt, Mary A., 113
Hurlburt, Rev., 29, 37
Hurlbut, Franklin, 32
Hurley, Catherine Heath, 74
Hurley, J. C., 74
Hurley, Maranda, 74
Hurley, Samuel, 74
Hurxthal, Frederick T., 121
Husker, Elizabeth, 172
Husker, William H., 172
Hussey, Jonathan S., 11
Hussey, Phebe Maria, 22
Hussey, William T., 11, 22, 65
Husted, Henry, 83
Hutchins, George, 125
Hutchins, Julius C., 50
Hutchinson, Julius C., 64
Hutchinson, L. F., 57
Hutchinson, Leonard P., 146
Hutchinson, Luther F., 142
Hutchinson, Polly, 142
Huxley, Lucinda, 173
Huxley, Thomas, 173
Huyck, Peter P., 172
Hyde & Lovett, 106, 134
Hyde, Christopher C., 104
Hyde, Henry, 70
Hyde, Joseph, 89, 91, 92
Hyde, Joseph S., 90
Hyde, Rosanna, 70
Hyde, Stephen, 81, 119, 120
Hyde, Wendell &, 50
Hyde, Widow, 31
Hyde, Williams, 47, 50, 67
Hyde, William & Co., 51, 69
Impson, Alanson, 115
Ingersol, Peter, 72
Ingersoll, William, 133
Inman, Calista, 63
Ireland, James, 29
Irons, Jeremiah, 41
Irwin, Laura Ann, 127
Irwin, William P., 153
Isaacs, Hannah, 142
J. E. & Co., 33
Jackaways, Elbert A., 129
Jacklin, James, 68
Jackson, Amasa, 42, 68
Jackson, Andrew, 38
Jackson, Aurelia F., 137
Jackson, C., 97
Jackson, Caroline, 98
Jackson, Catherine, 97
Jackson, Cornelia, 101
Jackson, Esther, 115
Jackson, Harriet, 42
Jackson, John F., 161
Jackson, Mr., 161
Jackson, R. C., 77, 91, 107, 112, 115,
Jackson, Rachel, 38
Jackson, Rebecca, 37
Jackson, S., 76, 101
Jackson, Sophia, 59
Jackson, Stillman, 46, 103, 106, 111, 173
Jackson, Timothy D., 98
Jackson, VanRensselear, 173
Jackson, William, 146
Jackways, Alantha, 135
Jackways, D. S., 22
Jackways, David S., 135
Jacobs, Caroline, 126, 128, 131

Jacobs, Miss, 130, 143
Jagger, Ann, 91
Jagger, Jeter, 118
Jagger, Paul, 37
Jarvis, W. F., 53, 158
Jarvis, William, 60
Jarvis, William F., 64, 67
Jefford, Esther, 19
Jenkins, Elizabeth A., 126
Jenks, Laura, 118
Jenner & Seely, 154
Jenner, James, 113
Jenner, James, 67, 97, 113, 145, 158
Jennings, James, 158, 162
Jennings, James M., 128
Jennings, Margaret, 37
Jennings, Samuel, 9
Jennings, Samuel C., 142
Jerolds, Phebe Ann, 35
Jerolemon. See Geralamon, 145
Jerome, Abram K., 124
Jerome, Frances Catherine, 74
Jerome, H., 49, 89
Jerome, H. K., 65, 67, 74, 90, 97, 111, 112, 143
Jerome, Hiram K., 14, 62, 72, 73, 141
Jerome, Isaac, 79
Jerome, K., 146
Jerome, Leonard W., 137
Jerome, Mary Sophia, 175
Jessup & Palmer's basin, 12
Jessup & Palmer, 33
Jessup, A., 141
Jessup, Albert, 67, 141
Jessup, Albert J., 125
Jessup, G. G., 57
Jessup, George, 52, 125
Jessup, George C., 115
Jessup, George G., 128, 141, 168
Jessup, George Post, 168
Jessup, H., 58

Jessup, Henry, 24, 65, 67, 71, 102, 125, 137, 141
Jessup, Henry, Jr., 137, 152
Jessup, Mary, 102, 137
Jessup, Miranda, 16
Jessup, Smith & Co., 62, 69
Jewell, Augusta, 157
Jewell, Ezra, 119
Jewell, Morris T., 22
Johnson, Barnet B., 131
Johnson, Betsey, 27
Johnson, Brian, 51
Johnson, Corrin G., 76
Johnson, Cynthia, 89
Johnson, David, 19, 130, 144
Johnson, David J., 89
Johnson, Davis, 99
Johnson, Deborah H., 164
Johnson, Eliza, 33
Johnson, Eliza O., 141
Johnson, Enoch, 168
Johnson, Frank & Co., 147
Johnson, Freelove, 74
Johnson, H. B., 166
Johnson, Harriet, 44, 144
Johnson, Hollis, 145
Johnson, Horatio N., 130
Johnson, J., 87, 129
Johnson, James. 145
Johnson, James H., 40
Johnson, Jerry, 135
Johnson, John, 41
Johnson, Joseph, 173
Johnson, Levi, 50
Johnson, Malinda, 145
Johnson, Marshall, 10
Johnson, Mary, 145, 148, 149
Johnson, Mary Ann, 52
Johnson, Nathaniel, 98
Johnson, Robert, 141
Johnson, Southwick &, 134
Johnson, Squire B., 123
Johnson, William, 122, 146
Johnson, William C. 145

Johnson, William R., 156
Johnston, Ann Maria, 175
Johnston, B. B., 167, 175, 179
Johnston, Barnet B., 175
Johnston, Caroline, 155
Johnston, Joseph, 20
Johnston, Robert, 155
Johnston. See Johnson, 131
Johnston, Truman, 175
Johnston, Truman Sylvester, 175
Johnston, William Clark, 150
Jones, Betsey S., 80
Jones, D. K., 12
Jones, Henry V., 95
Jones, J. F., 170
Jones, Richard (Mrs.), 89
Jones, Sarah E., 175
Jordan, Allen A., 153
Jordan, S. B., 118, 119
Jordan, Samuel W., 167
Jordan, Stephen P, 114
Jorry, Anthony, 49
Judson, Elizabeth, 143
Judson, Hannah, 160
Judson, Thomas, 70, 84
Kanouse, Peter, 52
Kean, Mary, 56
Keckel, Mary, 158
Kedder, Isaac, 18
Kedzia, John, 72
Keeler, David M., 113, 129
Keller, Jacob, 53
Kelley, Willis, 25
Kellogg, Ezekiel, 31
Kellogg, James H., 55
Kellogg, John, 95
Kellogg, Joseph, 101
Kellogg, Mary, 120
Kelly, Harriet, 70
Kennedy, John, 29
Kent, Elijah, 39, 65, 71
Kent, Elmira, 71
Kenyon, Daniel A., 156

Ketchum, Epinetus, 30
Ketchum, John, 104
Ketchum, Morgan C., 118
Kibbe, Simeon T., 14, 20
Kieth, Susannah, 129
Kieth, W. H., 145
King, Alanson, 58
King, David, 174
King, Earl, D., 24
King, George, 54
King, Henry, 134
King, Sylvia, 87
Kingman & Coleman, 78, 82
Kingman, Dexter, 25
Kingman, George G., 68
Kingman, M., 22, 54, 60, 66, 74, 79, 82, 87
Kingman, Mahlon, 30, 72
Kingsley, Achsah M., 98
Kingsley, E. C., 19, 22
Kingsley, Freelove, 162
Kingsley, Minerva, 134
Kinney, Alfrd B., 102
Kinney, D. F., 133, 155
Kinney, Darius F., 123. 161
Kinney, Duane Wing, 155
Kinney, Harriet, 155, 161
Kinney, Orville Dwight, 133
Kinsgsbury, Susan, 53
Kinsley, A. W. & Co., 47
Kinsley, Alonzo, 47
Kipp, Catherine, 111
Kipp, John L., 53
Kipp, Mary A., 53
Kirkland, Joseph, 35
Kirkland, Mary, 35
Klapp, E. M., 105
Klapp, Edmund M., 106
Klapp, Louisa H., 174
Knapp, Catherine, 139
Knapp, Elias, 139
Knapp, Linden, 18

Knapp, Seth, 68
Knapp, Uretta, 149
Knight, George, 135
Knolls, John B., 63
Knower, Benjamin, 103
Knower, Charles, 103
Knowles, Celestia A., 105
Knowles, J. L., 64
Knowles, Miss, 112
Knox, Edward, 134, 150
Lacey, Samuel S., 156
LaForge, Charles, 136
Lake, Abner F., 80
Lake, Hotchkiss &, 104
Laker, I., 98
Lakey, Abner, 165
Lakey, Abner F., 14, 45, 46, 67, 89, 107, 128, 137
Lakey, B. F., 143
Lakey, Caroline, 20
Lakey, Charlotte, 23
Lakey, Cynthia, 146
Lakey, Eliza S., 165
Lakey, Eunice, 137
Lakey, F, 119
Lakey, Franklin, 149
Lakey, Ira, 67
Lakey, James, 33
Lakey, Lucy, 45
Lakey, Mary, 170
Lakey, Mr., 97
Lakey, Thomas, 39, 50, 146, 162, 170
Lambert, Joseph D., 158
Lamberton, Mr., 113
Lambright, Rebecca, 62
Lamson, Butterfield & Walker, 161
Lamson, Mary E., 163
Lamson, N. K., 125, 142, 172
Lamson, Nathaniel K., 163
Lamson, William P., 151
Lancaster, Emma, 91
Lancaster, Mary Ann, 97

Landon, Climena, 149
Landon, Jarvis, 149
Lane, Betsey Ann, 136
Lane, Col. 143
Lane, E. P., 92, 99
Lane, Lydia Jane, 143
Langdon, Hiram, 37
Lansing, John A., 20
Lapham, Amy, 19
Lapham, Aretus, 103, 138
Lapham, Chloe, 21
Lapham, Elias H., 88
Lapham, Fidelia, 85
Lapham, Lydia, 104, 127
Lapham, Narcissa, 130
Lapham, Nelson, 84, 103, 136, 140
Lapham, William, 138
Lard, George, 100
Lasher & Cande, 10
Lathberry, John, 80
Lathrop, Harriet J., 130
Lathrop, Laura Louise, 53
Lathrop, Leonard E., 53
Latten, Wright, 155
Laver, Mary Ann, 53
Lawrence, A. B., 107
Lawrence, C. M. P. (Miss), 107
Lawrence, John, 111
Lawrence, Kemina D., 65
Lawrence, Mrs., 25
Lawrence, Sylvanus, 65
Lawton, Sarah, 37
Lazell, R. P., 22
Leach, Belinda, 48
Leach, Candice, 54
Leach, Flower &, 19
Leach, G. C., 52
Leach, Mary, 21
Leach, P. H., 107
Leach, P. K., 62
Leach, Payne, 127
Leach, Payne K., 114
Leach, Phineas, 122

Leblan, Primus, 112
Ledyard, Colt &, 10
Ledyard, Mary F., 85
Ledyard, S., 9, 12
Ledyard, Samuel, 85
Lee, Charles, 95
Lee, D. K., 155
Lee, Elizabeth M., 133
Lee, Eunice, 47
Lee, F. W., 40
Lee, Gideon, 137
Lee, Joshua, 95
Lee, Loraine P., 130
Lee, Perry B., 114
Lee, Reuben, 17
Lee, Rev., 151
Lee, Seth, 130,
Leech, Gurdon C., 46, 135
Leech, Payne K., 72
Leflin, Azor, 112
Leighton, Peter, 21
Lemmon, Miss, 106
Lemon, Dr., 121
Lemon, Mary, 152
Lemon, Rebeckah C., 159
Lemon, Richard, 152, 158, 166
Lemoreau, Sally, 56
LeMunion, Calista, 64
Lemunion, Priscilla, 64
Lemunyon, Nancy, 137
Leonard, ___, 136
Leonard & Linnell, 95, 103
Leonard, C, 119
Leonard, Charlotte, 117
Leonard, Cyrus, 112, 117, 134, 145
Leonard, Ischa, 132
Leonard, S., 33
Leonard, Uriah L., 159
Leslie, Edwin, 174
Lester, Hiram, 64
Lester, Ralph, 27
Letts, Ann, 31
Levens, Harriet, 30

Lewis, Amanda, 159
Lewis Charles N., 123
Lewis, Eliza, 175
Lewis, Eliza Ann, 104
Lewis, George Seymour, 179
Lewis, Henry, 94
Lewis, John, 163
Lewis, Joseph, 170
Lewis, Mary, 152
Lewis, Octavia J., 73
Lewis, Philena, 80
Lewis, Robert, 14
Lewis, Sally, 54
Lewis, Uriah, 80
Lewis, William, 29
Lilley, Asa, 10
Lilly, Asa, 49, 73, 102, 157
Lilly, Daniel T., 165
Lilly, Emily, 86
Lilly, Enoch, 134, 175
Lilly, Mary A. C., 56
Lily, Chloe, 134
Linell, E. & Co., 69
Linell, H., 159
Linn, Dr., 16
Linn, Susan, 16
Linnell, E. & Co., 70
Linnell, E., 66
Linnell, Elijah, 44, 65
Linnell, H., 61, 119, 121
Linnell, Haskell, 40, 47
Linnel, J., 33
Linnell, Leonard &, 95, 103
Linnell, Washington (Mrs.), 45
Lippincott, Joseph, 80, 87
Lippincott, Joseph F., 121
Liscom, George, 28
Littlejohn, L. J., 74
Livingston, Catharine G., 11, 52
Livingston, Gilbert, 11, 52
Lloyd, Cromwell, 12
Lobdell, Rebecca, 33
Lobdell, Sally, 31

Lockwood, Isaac, 170
Lockwood, Peter S., 169
Logan, John, 49
Loncost, Susannah, 11, 51
Loomis, Cornelia, 66
Loomis, Delamater &, 76
Loomis, H. N., 43, 55, 66, 72, 75, 79, 89, 98
Loomis, R. Maria, 164
Loomis, Riley, 164
Loomis, Robinson &, 82
Loop, Amos, 37
Lord, Catherine, 132
Lord, Josiah G., 146
Lord, Leonard, 166
Losee, Isaac, 59
Lothrop, Tucker &, 62
Loud, Cullen, 77
Louis, Prince, 13
Lovejoy, William C., 63
Lovell & Haven, 72
Lovell, Ann Maria, 42
Lovell, Charles, 59
Lovell, F. C., 79
Lovell, F. S., 106
Lovell, Gertrude, 62
Lovell, Ovid, 39, 42, 44, 48, 59, 62, 65, 67, 69, 72, 90
Lovell, Sidney, 173
Lovett, J. C., 106, 122, 119, 152, 168, 174
Lovett, James, 108
Lovett, Joseph C., 106, 113, 134
Lovett, Joseph Henry, 122
Lovett, Josephine, 168
Lovett, Lydia, 174
Low, Andrew G., 12, 25
Low, Cornelia, 44
Low, Sarah M., 28
Low, William B., 28
Luce, Caroline, 152
Luck, Edward, 59
Luck, William, 59

Lucky, Rev., 97
Lumbard, Betsy, 89
Lummis, William N., 39
Lund, Alfred, 159
Lund, Dr., 162
Lund, R., 149
Lunn, Samuel, 161
Lupkins, Henry, 64
Lupkins, Mr., 75
Lusk, Miss, 162
Lyon, Mary, 130
Lyon, Newton, 156
Lyon, Samuel, 155
Lyon, Silas S., 50
Lyon, Theodore, 172
Lyon, William, 2nd, 172
Lyons, Daniel, 29
M'Donald, Roderick, 33
M'Knight, Widow, 28
M'Umber, Ella, 33
M'Vie, Nathan, 19
Mabee, Israel, 103
Macedon Centre, 82
Macedon Furnace 89
Macomb, Alexander, 42
Macomb, Jane Eliza, 43
Macomb, John Navarre, 43
Macomb, Margaret, 42
Macomber, Marvin, 136
Macown, Sally, 105
Macown, James, 105
Mahan, Rev., 51
Mail schedule, 112
Main, Philura, 118
Malcomb, Deborah, 163
Mallary, Abigail, 26
Mallary, Azariah, 25
Mallory, Leah,, 101
Malona, Gilson, 174
Maltby, William, 94
Manchester, William H., 154
Mandeville, Austin, 138
Manley, L. D. C. (Miss), 156
Manning, E. N., 80

Marble, A. A., 178
Marble factory, 107
Marble, John, 132
Marcy, Cornelia L., 139
Marcy, Governor, 103
Marcy, W. L., 12
Marion Corners, 84
Markham, Anna, 129
Marsh, Dr., 143
Marsh, E. C., 64
Marsh, Elizabeth C., 64
Marsh, Frances, 143
Marsh, Valina, 48
Marshall, Ann, 68
Marshall, Erastus, 56
Martin, A. & Co., 87
Martin, Abraham, 73, 124
Martin, Alpheus, 40
Martin, George, 41
Martin, Harriet B., 94
Martin, Nottingham &, 123, 144, 153
Martin, Samuel G., 162
Martine, Heman, 127
Marvin, Capt., 38
Marvin, Mr., 44
Marvin, Ruth E., 81
Mason & Tuttle, 164
Mason, Eleanor, 128
Mason, Harriet, 174
Mason, James, 57, 70, 73
Mason, Jesse, 50
Mason, John, 67
Mason, John L., 92
Mason, Julia Ann, 92
Mason, Perry &, 49
Mason, Smith &, 19, 26
Massett, B. W. C., 111
Mathewson, George, 158
Mathewson, Henry, 135
Matson, Warren, 47
Matthewson, Artemus, 39
Mattison, Jacob, 137
Mattison, Seth, 38

Maxon, Harriet, 64
May, D. H., 159
May, Dr., 96
May, E., 78
May, Elezear, 170
May, Elezear Huntington, 124
May, Hoyt &, 68. 69, 111
May, Julia, 78
May, Mary, 36
May, Nancy, 95
May, William, 72, 106, 113, 115, 119, 124, 170
May, Wm., 74
Maynard, B., 81
Maynard, Charles, 139
Maynard, E., 82
McBane, C. A. (Mrs.), 175
McCarn, John, 142
McCarthy, Belinda, 58
McCarthy, James, 129
McCarty, John, 137
McCarty, Sarah M., 70
McCarty, Throop &, 153
McClary, Elizabeth, 42
McClave, Uriah, 122
McClave, Uriah S., 55
McCollum, Isaiah H., 174
McCollum, Joel, 42
McCollum, Nathaniel, 79
McCollum, Robert, 90
McCollum, Susan, 18
McCord, Andrew, 74
McCreery, Rebecca L., 162
McCumber, Mary, 115
McCumber, Susan H., 154
McDole, James, 55
McDonald, Margaret, 171
McDonald, S., 14, 27
McDowell, James, 59
McDuffee, Elizabeth, 117
McDuffee, Rebecca, 169
McEwen, Charles, 93, 97
McGraw, Aaron, 80
McGregor, John P., 172

McIlwain, James, 142
McIntyre & Dunn, 107
McIntyre, A., 9, 13, 14, 132, 148, 175
McIntyre, Alexander, 10, 72, 86, 166
McIntyre, Dewitt C., 169
McIntyre, Dr., 24
McIntyre, Isabella, 59
McKechnie, Robert, 121
McKeen, Marcellus, 138
McKeller, James, 154
McKinstry, P., 178
McKnight & Walton, 146
McKnight, Delia F., 148
McKnight, George H., 154
McKnight, James, 138
McKnutt, Archibald, 140
McKnutt, Sally, 140
McKnutt, William, Jr., 147
McLean, Julius, 140
McLean, William, 19
McLean, William A., 12, 14
McLouth, Lucinda, 117
McMellen, Sarah, 95
McMichael, Amanda, 74
McMichael, James, 75
McMichael, Joseph, 138
McNab, Andrew, 46
McNiel, David, 96
McNutt, Mary, 110
McOmber, Ann J., 164
McOmber, Orrin, 166
McUmber, Eleanor, 38
Mead, Isaac, 17
Mead, Judith, 108
Mead, Katharine, 49
Mead, Richard T., 103
Mead, Seales &, 155
Mead, Thomas W., 108
Meade, Henry M., 14
Meech & Woodward, 40, 49, 57, 67, 69
Meech, Horace, 15, 40

Meeker, Susan E., 131
Mellen, James, 28
Melvin, Alexander G. 159
Merrill, Andrew, 26
Merrill, Eliza Melvina, 116
Merrill, J. K., 105
Merrill, John, 156
Merrill, John H., 74
Merrill, John M., 116
Merrill, Rev., 23, 95
Merrill, Riley, 83
Merrill, Thaddeus, 156
Metcalf, D. W., 139
Metcalf, Wrolin K., 20
Middleton, George H., 166, 175
Middleton, Sarah, 166
Mighells, Elezear, 49
Mighells, Sally, 49
Miles, Clara, 67
Miles, Daniel, 44
Miles, Henry, 102
Millard & Allen, 140
Millard, Asabel, 73
Millard, Asahel, 101, 106, 112, 138, 168
Millard, Aurelia, 138, 168
Millard, Elizabeth Clinton, 138
Millard, Mary Ann, 101
Miller, Adeline, 52
Miller, Amasa O., 159
Miller, Benjamin, 30
Miller, Clarinda, 17
Miller, Cornelia S., 149
Miller, D. C., 25
Miller, Frances C., 172
Miller, Franklin G., 25
Miller, George R., 157
Miller, Harvey, 122
Miller, Hezekiah, 69, 92
Miller, John, 128
Miller, Jonas, 144
Miller, Joseph A., 103
Miller, K., 44, 73

Miller, Kingsley, 12, 55, 72, 172
Miller, Louisa, 103
Miller, Samuel, 132
Miller, Sophie, 178
Miller, T. C., 146, 152
Miller, Theodore V. R., 148
Miller, Thomas, 152
Miller, Thomas C., 158, 168
Millet, John, 150
Milliman, James, 74
Mills, Barnhart's, 134
Mills, Boyle's, 13
Mills, Cohn's, 149
Mills, Coon's, 149
Mills, Dowingsville, 171
Mills, flouring, 108, 146
Mills, Godard's, 134, 149, 153, 171
Mills, Jerome's, 151
Mills, Palmyra Steam, 118
Mills, Phebe Jane, 121
Mills, Red, 151
Mills, Sarah, 142
Mills, steam, 109, 114
Mills, Wayne County, 141, 146
Mills, Yellow, 41, 79, 103, 141, 152, 153, 171, 179
Miner, Amasa, 103
Miner, Chauncey, 140
Miner, Mary Ann, 21
Minor, James, 114
Minor, Maria, 114
Minshall, Elihu, 36
Mitchell, P., 36
Mitchell, Rhoda, 132
Mix, Mary Ann, 164
Mix, Thomas, 164
Monroe, George. 103
Monroe, Jeremiah, 149
Monroe, Seymour, 89
Moody, Jemima, 108
Moon, E. P., 43
Mooney, George E., 149

Moore, Catherine, 82
Moore, George, 49
Moore, Gilbert H., 103
Moore, Hannah Eliza, 142
Moore, Harriet B., 98
Moore, Harry S., 27
Moore, John, 82
Moore, Margaret, 82
Moore, Maria, 82
Moore, Maria H., 172
Moore, Martin, 82
Moore, Mary, 124
Moore, Peter, 126
Moore, Phineas, 121, 132, 148
Moore, Polly, 121, 132
Moore, Rev., 97
Moore, Sally, 132
Moore, Samuel, 55, 60, 84, 120
Moore, William, 124
More, Nelson W., 109
More, Peter V., 107. 108
Morehouse, Melissa, 40
Morehouse, Sarah, 121
Morely & Cole, 144
Morely, L., 56
Morey, Cornell, 178
Morey, William H., 82
Morgan, ____ , 67
Morgan, E. L., 88
Morgan, Eugene L, 86, 87, 88
Morgan, Jedidiah, 32
Morgan, Lucinda, 56
Morgan, Miss, 59
Morgan, Prudence, 62
Morgan, William, 56, 60
Morley & Toby, 135
Morley, F., 168
Morley, Frederick, 149
Morley, Joseph, 60
Morley, Luke, 58
Mormon, Book of, 49, 50
Mormon emigration, 61
Mormonism, 43, 118, 132
Mormons, 82, 100, 123, 136

Morrin, Adelaide, 142
Morris, Henry, 67
Morse, Amos, 123
Morse, Isaac, 61
Morse, LeGrand L., 40
Morse telegraph, 160
Morse, William, 81
Mosely, Leander P., 149
Mosely, Lois, 142
Moses, Eliza, 126
Moses, Martha, 139
Mosher, Stephen, 123
Mosier, Benjamin, 23
Moss, Daniel G., 27
Moss, Joseph, 62
Mott, Eliza, 129
Mott, Elizabeth, 42
Mott, J. M., 118
Mott, James M., 105
Mott, Jane A., 117
Mott, Mary Ann, 78
Mott, Samuel, 42, 93
Mower, Peter A., 66
Mumford, George H., 99
Munro, Dr., 104
Munroe, Mariam, 108
Munsell, Abigail, 70
Munsey, James, 126
Murdoch, Eliphalet, 84
Murray, Williams, 170
Myers, Harriet, 126
Myers, John J., 49, 83
Myers, Rev., 27
Myers, William, 115
Myers, William M., 106, 112
Myers, William M. M., 104
Myrick, A. T., 176
Myrick, Hannah, 176
Naftel, Joseph, 46
Naftel, Mary, 33
Nash, Adam, 145
Nash, William W., 54
Nearing, Misses, 139
Neele, Thomas, 96

Negroes, 93
Negro riot, 86
Nelson, Bloomy C., 26
Nelson, H., 44, 53
Nelson, Hannah, 168
Nelson, Henry, 54, 67
Nelson, J., 44
Nelson, Mr., 56
Nelson, Robert, 123
Netterville, J. W., 167
Nettleton, David, 165
Neward, George, 153
Newbury, Eliza Ann, 75
Newcomb, Wesley, 110
Newell, Chauncey, 25
Newell, John, 43
Newell, Laura Ann, 156
Newell, Mark, 170
Newland, George, 58, 79, 106, 107, 110, 125, 133
Newland, George Henry, 125
Newland, Margaret, 58
Newland, Mary, 58, 107
Newland, William G., 79
Newton & Davis, 78
Newton & Parshall, 135
Newton, Ann Eliza, 134
Newton, B., 93, 137
Newton, Betsey, 104
Newton, Butler, 134, 136, 154
Newton, George S., 154
Newton, Lucinda, 161
Nicholas, Benjamin, 21, 129
Nicholas, Mr., 94
Nichols, Charlotte, 131
Nichols, Clarissa, 17
Nichols, Pamelia, 60
Nichols, Samuel, 17
Nickerson, Eli, 174
Nickerson, Harriet, 94
Niles & Allen, 72, 77
Niles & Allyn, 84
Niles, Anne, 17
Niles, Frederick M., 91

Niles, H., 15, 17, 62, 70
Niles, Hiram, 52, 57, 59, 64, 66, 72, 73, 76, 91, 92, 112
Niles, Mr., 72
Niles, N., 69
Niles, Oliver, 84
Niles, Weed &, 42, 45
Nimo, Hezro, 152
Nims, Laura H., 133
Ninde, Eleanor, 149
Ninde, William, 149
Noah, M. M., 37
Noble, S., 14
Nobles, Lois, 166
Norcutt, Elizabeth, 29
Norman, George W., 93
Norrin, Dewitt C., 108
Norris, Abram, 104, 110, 115, 124
Norris, Diantha, 175
Norris, Mary Elizabeth, 115
Norris, Moses, 133
Norris, Samuel, 175
North & Pierson, 14
North, Charles, 62
North, H. M., 162
North, John E., 164
North, L., 69, 80
North, Linus, 21, 62
North, Mr., 95
North, Norris, 11, 52
North Rochester, 44
North, William Vial, 11, 52
Northrup, Eaton B., 138, 155
Northrup, Mary, 97
Northrup, R. K., 97
Norton, Almira, 96
Norton, Altha, 142
Norton, Ann, 62
Norton, Augustus, 54
Norton, B. R., 118
Norton, Benjamin R., 170
Norton, Frederick A., 54
Norton, James T., 178

Norton, Joseph A., 57, 62, 64
Nott, Serepta J., 128
Nottingham & Martin, 123, 153
Nottingham, Aaron C., 28
Nottingham, Henry, 126
Nottingham, J., 132
Nottingham, J. D., 22
Nottingham. Jeremiah, 42
Nottingham, John D., 15
Nottingham, Mr., 70
Nottingham, P. P., 175
Nottingham, W. P., 130, 153, 163
Nottingham, William P., 46, 72, 106, 112
Nottingham, Wm. P., 74
Nowton, B., 161
Noyes, Enoch, 132
Noyes, Selden, 40
Oaks, Thaddeus, 17
Occarina, Jacob, 22
Odell, Ira, 118
O'Hara, Margaret, 11, 51
O'Hara, William, 11, 51
Oliver, Elizabeth E., 160
Oliver, Gilbert, 143, 160
Oliver, William H., 20
Olmstead, Frances, 19
Olmstead, Jane, 141
Olmstead, Mary, 16
Olson, Oliver, 169
O'Neil & Finley, 179
O'Neil, Sophia Ann., 146
O'Rourke, Patrick, 25
Osband, Durfee, 21, 84
Osband, Gideon, 80
Osband, Marietta, 84, 125
Osband, Rowena L, 148
Osband, William, 125
Osband, Wilson, 148
Osborn, Chauncey, 105
Osborn, Pierce &, 132
Osborn, Sarah, 87
Osborn, Seleck, 32

Osborne, Caroline, 96
Osborne, Samuel W., 96
Osburn, Mr., 123
Ostrander, Tobias, 19
Ostrom, Maria,
Ostrom, S. Z., 59
Ottley, Capt., 44
Ottley, Mary, 44
Overnight, James, 33
Packard, Clark, 45
Packard, Ford, 21
Packard, John F., 16
Packard, Philander, 45
Packer, William S. 146
Paddie, James, 168
Paddock, Eleanor M., 169
Paddock, Eliza, 67
Paddock, Ira R., 143
Page, Caroline, 59
Page, Jane E., 173
Page, Peter, 173
Page, Terissa, 149
Paine, Harriet N., 173
Paine, William, 141
Palister, William, 163
Palmer, B. & C., 13
Palmer, Daniel, 97
Palmer, George, 24
Palmer, H., 125
Palmer, Henry F., 46
Palmer, James M., 137
Palmer, Jessup &, 12, 33
Palmer, Nathan, 166
Palmer, Nathaniel, 128
Palmer, Noah, Jr., 103
Palmer, O. H., 119, 123, 124, 130, 132, 142, 151
Palmer, Oliver H., 155
Palmer, P., 133, 136
Palmer, Patience, 18
Palmer, Permelia, 173
Palmer, Philip, 103, 108, 127
Palmer, Samuel, 71, 77, 85, 118

Palmer, Stuteley D., 175
Palmer, William, 40, 42, 104, 127
Palmeter, Matilda, 84
Palmyra Baths & Gardens, 72, 77
Palmyra Mfg. Co., 100, 114
Palmyra Springs, 153
Panker, Ira, 147
Parburt, George R., 109
Pardee, R. G., 150
Pardy, Chester, 132
Paris, Josiah D., 80
Park, H., 130
Parke, Moses, 66, 80
Parke, William, 19, 65, 67
Parke, William F., 126
Parke, Wm., 74
Parker, Alma, 42
Parker, Ann, 76
Parker, Augusta, 167
Parker, Benjamin, 165
Parker, Calvin, 58
Parker, Cynthia, 165
Parker, E., 134
Parker, Eldred, 140
Parker, Ira, 32
Parker, John, 63
Parker, John H., 170
Parker, Lucinda, 84
Parker, Lucy, 99
Parker, Perry, 130
Parker, Sylvester, 167
Parker, William, 65
Parks, Delphena S., 136
Parks, Hiram, 18
Parks, William, 83
Parmalee, Emma, 45
Parnell, P. A., 98
Parshall, E., 119
Parshall, Hendee, 152
Parshall, Israel, 153
Parshall, J., 64
Parshall, Mary, 158

Parshall, Nathan, 41, 64, 84, 97
Parshall, Newton &, 135
Parshall, Schuyler, 158
Parshall, Schuyler R., 122
Parsley, Thomas, 48
Parsons, S. C., 94
Parver, Ira, 19
Patch, Susan, 96
Patison, Catherine, 174
Patrick, J., 64
Patterson, Mungo, 143
Patterson, Thomas, 12
Pattison, George W., 114
Payne, Amanda M., 164
Payne, Allen, 164
Payne & Gilbert, 45
Payne, Ann, 30
Payne, Beers &, 121
Payne, C. T., 88
Payne, Charles T., 45, 71
Payne, Delia, 47
Payne, Franklin, 73
Payne, Gideon R., 88
Payne, Hannah Ann, 24
Payne, Hiram, 117, 128, 167
Payne, Joseph C., 73
Payne, Maria C., 158
Payne, Rhoda, 31
Payne, Thomas, 89
Pearsall, George, 157
Pearse, Jason, 158
Pease, James, 14
Pease, Samuel, 92
Pease, Thompson, 14
Peck, Calista D., 39
Peck, Cynthia, 37
Peckham, Dr., 24
Peckham, Henrietta L., 55
Peckham, James, 173
Peckham, Margaret, 71
Peckham, William, 71
Peckham, William A., 98
Peddie, J., 119

Peddie, James, 131, 155, 179
Peeler, Mariah, 44
Peer, Hannah P., 157
Pelham, Lucinda, 150
Pendergast & Tucker, 46
Pendergast, John G., 57
Pendergast, Stimpson &, 48
Pendle, Jane, 169
Pepper, Abraham, 168
Perine, Elizabeth H., 162
Perine, John A., 162
Perkins, Anna, 41
Perkins, Betsey, 81
Perkins, Calvin, 12
Perkins, Mary, 122
Perrine, Dr., 129
Perrine, Henry, 154
Perrine, Mrs., 129
Perrine, Peter, 166
Perrine, Sarah, 154
Perry & Crandall, 118
Perry & Mason, 49
Perry, Henry E., 47, 57, 67, 73
Perry, Louisa, 47
Perry, Phebe, 51
Perry Truman, 50
Perry Valentine, 133
Persons, Harriet, 47
Petrie, Capt., 145
Pettit, J. C., 130
Pettit, Jacob C., 145, 162
Pettit, S. Smith, 160
Pew, Sylvester, 151
Phelps, Ann, 100
Phelps, Arsena, 122
Phelps, Betsey Ann, 140
Phelps, Emily, 45
Phelps, H. R, 170
Phelps, Henry, 139
Phelps, J. D., 143
Phelps, J. S., 82
Phelps, Joseph August, 38
Phelps, Lester, 178

Phelps, Lyman Monroe, 156
Phelps, Minerva, 21
Phelps, Oliver, 31
Phelps, Paul, 101
Phelps, Philo, 146
Phelps, Sally M., 141
Phelps, Sarah A., 178
Phelps, Seth, 27
Phelps, Stephen, 45, 138
Phelps, W. W., 61
Philip, Daniel H., 92
Philips, Amanda, 125
Phillips, J. W., 127
Phillips, Lucy, 58
Phillips, Sarah L., 171
Picket, Harriet, 55
Pickett, William E., 120
Pierce & Osborn, 132
Pierce, Catharine, 66
Pierce, F., 75, 84
Pierce, Frances, 166
Pierce, Jane, 56
Pierce, Jeremiah N., 56
Pierce, John, 40, 164
Pierce, Lucy Ann, 161
Pierce, Mahala, 40
Pierce, Mr., 72
Pierce, Nathan, 17
Pierce, Thomas, 164
Piersoll, Rev., 152
Pierson, A., 18
Pierson, Martha, 35
Pierson, North &, 14
Piper, Asa, 86
Piper, Mr., 122
Pitts, Lucy, 56
Place, H. Niles, 100
Platt, A. E., 138
Platt, Rev., 176
Plumley, Matilda, 48
Polhamus, Daniel, 98
Polk, James K. L., 163
Pollitt, John, 123
Pollock, James, 165

Pomeroy, Achsa, 19
Pomeroy, Eliza, 171
Pomeroy, George E., 67, 69, 75, 79, 82, 94, 96
Pomeroy, Helen Augusta, 94
Pomeroy, Rachel B., 164
Pomeroy, Rev., 31, 44, 45
Pomeroy, Robert, 94, 171
Pomeroy, S., 20
Pond, Hubbard, 47
Pooley & Butterfield, 168
Pooley, Edward, 21
Pooley, George, 145, 154
Pooley, Maria, 143
Poor, John M., 59
Poor House, 136
Poppino, Daniel, 136
Porter, Caroline, 65
Porter, Catherine, 175
Porter, Chauncey, 51, 65, 99
Porter, Daniel, 65
Porter, Elizabeth Ann, 44
Porter, Latitia, 63
Porter, Norton, 28
Porter, Olive Ann, 51
Porter, Peter B., 63
Porter, Rev., 36
Porter, William, 13
Post, Elizabeth, 163
Post, Gurney &, 74, 83, 89
Post, Helen, 110
Post, Henry, 132
Post, J. W., 117
Post, L. W., 111, 118
Post, L. W. & Co., 102, 104
Post, Lyman, 172
Post, Lyman W., 112
Post, Mary J., 99
Post, Samuel H., 51, 163
Post, Stephen, 142
Post, Terry &, 126
Post, William S., 83, 90
Potter, Amelia, 156
Potter, Eliza, 41

Potter, Elizabeth N., 45
Potter, Jane, 11
Potter, Lucinda, 103
Potter, Nathaniel J., 45
Poucher, Charles, 135, 155, 164
Poucher, David, 175
Poucher, Harriet W., 155
Poucher, Mary, 155
Pound, Catharine, 37
Pound, Jesse, 78
Pound, Sarah, 57
Powell, Lucinda, 76
Powell, R., 76
Powell, Rev., 49, 55
Powell, Robert, 68
Power, Abiather, 39
Power, Moses, Jr., 80
Power, William P., 125
Powers, Calvin, 94
Powers, Gershom, 77
Powers, Harriet A., 125
Powers, Lydia A., 77
Powers, Peter, 166
Powers, Warren, 143
Pratt, A., 78
Pratt & Hill, 72
Pratt, Almond, 73, 76, 75
Pratt & White, 77, 75
Pratt, Cephlanett, 38
Pratt, Darius, 50
Pratt, David, 16
Pratt, Elkanah, 38
Pratt, Emeline, 71
Pratt, George, Jr., 130
Pratt, Jerusha, 60
Pratt, Mary, 71
Pratt, Sidney, 50
Prentice, Polly, 56
Prentiss, Azariah, 53
Prentiss, Susan, 137
Prentiss, Sylvia, 137
Preston, Tabitha H., 133
Price, Abigail, 54

Price, Benjamin, 54
Price, E., 164
Price, Ezekiel, 166
Price, Isaac, 163
Price, Mary, 104
Price, Susan Ann, 163
Prichard, James, 175
Prichard, Mary, 175
Priest, George, 135, 137
Prime, Julia, 158
Prime, William, 75
Prince, Black, 36
Proseus, Gertrude, 125
Provost, Augustine Palmer, 156
Provost, George W., 62
Pudney, Rebecca, 71
Pullman, Joseph, 47
Pullman, Louisa, 47
Purdy, A., 124
Purdy, Alexander, 79
Purdy, Amanda, 83
Purdy, Chester, 99
Purdy, Fay H., 135
Purdy. See also Pardy, 132
Putnam, Cornelius, 146
Putnam, Dorcas, 84
Putnam, H. L. (Miss), 115, 120
Putnam, Harriet L., 146
Putnam, Mary, 59
Putnam, Stephen, 84, 96
Quaife, Caroline, 173
Quance, Juliett, 165
Quance, King H., 165
Quimby, J. H., 86
Quimby, Jacob, 110
Quimby, Jacob H., 86
Quimby, Strong &, 86
Railroad, 80, 88, 89
Railroad meeting, 88
Railroad opened, 101
Raineer, Thomas, 32
Ramsdell, Gideon, 157
Ramsdell, Lydia, 55
Ramsdell, Mary D., 77

Ramsdell, Nathan, 70
Ramsdell, Stephen, 138
Rand, Electa, 11, 52
Rand, Samuel, 11, 52
Randall, B., 119
Randall, S. B., 152
Randall, Samuel, 77, 136, 145
Randall, Samuel B., 113, 136
Randolph, A. & Co., 12, 14
Randolph, Albert, 24
Randolph, Charlotte, 44
Ranny, Thomas S, 36
Ransom, J. L., 18
Rapelye, Susan, 39
Rawling, John,, 110
Rawson, Almira, 47
Rawson, Eveline, 86
Rawson, Philo (Milo) S., 126
Rawson, Philo S., 68
Rawson, Rebecca, 55
Ray, William, 29
Raynear, William, 100
Redfield, George, 92
Redfield, Mary, 67
Redmond, Peter, 41
Reed, Conrad, 17
Reed, Dr., 79
Reed, Francis, 10
Reed, Henry, 171
Reed, Hugh, 142
Reed, Martha Ann, 102
Reed, Mary H. E., 135
Reed, Mrs., 99
Reed, Nathaniel, 54
Reed, Peter, 131
Reed, Rhoda, 102
Reed, Royal, 135
Reed, Sarah, 147
Reed, Welcome, 133
Rees, Abigail, 57
Rees, Jane Eliza, 29
Reeves, Celina, 139

Reeves, Charles, 163

Reeves, Edwin, 146
Reeves, Elias, 152
Reeves, James, 88, 95
Reeves, L., 73
Reeves, Luther, 64, 113, 124, 139, 142
Reeves, Lyman, 64, 119, 138
Reeves, Mehitable, 88
Reeves, Mr., 53
Reeves, P., 40
Reeves, Philura, 131
Reeves, Zebulon, 98, 146
Reid, Jasper, 53
Reitz, George, 45
Reitz, T. & G., 45
Remington, Nancy, 16
Reyerson, John A., 67
Reynier, Lettis, 150
Reynolds, Abraham, 83
Reynolds, Isaac, 162
Reynolds, Melvina, 162
Reynon, Maria, 30
Rhude, Hiram, 13
Rice, A. E. (Mrs), 117
Rice, Adoniram J., 147
Rice, Almira, 56
Rice, Anna, 118
Rice, Arnold E., 116
Rice, Caroline, 118
Rice, Charles, 124
Rice, Fanny, 124
Rice, Harriet, 123
Rich, Hiram, 155
Rice, Josiah, 59
Rice, Julia Ann, 122
Rich, M., 155
Rich, Marvin, 50
Rich, Nelson, 84
Rice, Philander, 38
Rich, Sophia, 137
Rice, Sylvia, 152
Rice, William, 118, 123
Rice, Zalmon, 138, 160
Richard, Charles G., 130

Richard, Eliza A., 130
Richards, Charles G., 137
Richards, Dr., 88
Richards, Elder, 89
Richards, Robert Alsop, 137
Richards, William, 71
Richardson, I. J., 72
Richardson, Israel, 43
Richardson, Israel D., 12
Richardson, William P., 76
Richmond, Beers &, 89
Richmond, Silas, 147
Riggs, Sally, 55
Riker, George L., 154
Riker, John, 154
Riker, Mary T., 154
Ring, E. Ferdinand, 158
Ripley, Ann S., 147
Ripley, CLarissa L., 146
Ripley, Hiram L., 34
Ripper, Fanny, 146
Rising, Leonard R., 130
Risley, Marietta, 124
Ritter, M., 69, 75, 111
Ritter, Michael, 74
Robb, A., 93
Robbins, Buell &, 99, 107
Robbins, Loring G., 161
Robbins, Warren &, 107, 163
Roberts, E. J., 43
Roberts, Joseph Henry, 43
Roberts, Thomas, 39
Robertson, Eunice, 106
Robertson, Philo, 106
Robins, Jacob, 94
Robinson, A., 140
Robinson & Eggleston, 26
Robinson & Loomis, 82
Robinson, Bartlett, 102
Robinson, C., 43, 70, 131
Robinson, C. C., 75, 89
Robinson, Caius, 22, 24, 109
Robinson, Caius C., 45
Robinson, Chloe, 59
Robinson, Clarissa, 138
Robinson, Clark, 53, 62, 67, 72, 71, 75, 73, 81
Robinson, Clark &, 69
Robinson, E. D., 46, 64, 73
Robinson, Erasmus D., 39
Robinson, Eveline, 54
Robinson, Field &,
Robinson, Field &,
Robinson, Gain, 14, 26, 39, 45, 59, 62, 72, 79, 109, 166
Robinson, Gramesly &, 134
Robinson, Harriet, 97
Robinson, Harriet N., 143
Robinson, Helen E., 79
Robinson, James, 66, 93
Robinson, Jane, 32
Robinson, John, 127
Robinson, Lany, 48
Robinson, Lewis, 102
Robinson, Lydia, 159
Robinson, M. T. Rollin, 90
Robinson, Mabel, 102
Robinson, Mary, 151
Robinson, Morgan, 95
Robinson, Philo, 97, 115
Robinson, Richard P., 147
Robinson, Ruell W., 15
Robinson, Samuel D., 45
Robinson, Theron M., 138
Robinson, Walter, 141
Robinson, William, 50
Robson, Ann Maria, 30
Robson, Frances C., 136
Robson, J. R., 10
Roby, Nancy, 27
Rochester, Amanda, 58
Rochester, Nathaniel, 61
Rochester Theatrical Co., 145
Rochester, William B., 58
Rockefeller, Libbie, 178
Rockwell, Benjamin, 93
Rodney, W. G., 44
Roe, Stephen, 48

Rogers & Cuyler, 173
Rogers & Grandin, 69
Rogers & Scotten, 159
Rogers, Bartlett R., 48
Rogers Basin, 12
Rogers, Carlton, H., 154
Rogers, Celia L., 127
Rogers, Charles, 149
Rogers, Charles B., 142
Rogers, Charlotte, 149
Rogers, Cynthia, 107
Rogers, Cynthia Ann, 168
Rogers, David, 67, 127
Rogers, Dennis, 118
Rogers, Dennison, 83, 149
Rogers, Edwin E., 164, 176
Rogers, Elizabeth, 94
Rogers, F. D., 79
Rogers, Gen., 171
Rogers, H. W., 67
Rogers, Hamilton, 143
Rogers, Hannah, 77
Rogers, Hazard W., 64
Rogers, Isaac, 65, 89
Rogers, J. Clark, 152
Rogers, Jane, 146
Rogers, Jareb D., 107, 114, 168
Rogers, John, 154
Rogers, Lydia, 63
Rogers, Mary Jane, 149
Rogers, Mary A., 144
Rogers, Mary S., 143
Rogers, Prudence, 98
Rogers, Rodney A., 167
Rogers, Ryland J., 171
Rogers, Samuel, 50
Rogers, Sarah W., 154
Rogers, Shubal G., 144
Rogers, Stephen, 63
Rogers, T., 97, 152
Rogers, Thomas, 22, 35, 38, 42, 48, 95, 112

Rogers, Thomas, 2nd, 48, 49, 52, 62, 65, 67, 72, 82, 83
Rogers, William, 39, 75, 77
Rogers, William, Sr., 97
Rogers, William, Jr., 83, 84
Rogers, William, 3rd, 79
Rogers, William W., 110
Rolph, L. C. (Miss), 157
Rood, Elias, 178
Rood, Lucy, 108
Root, Mary A., 125
Root, Mary M., 122
Root, May S., 120
Rope factory, 100, 145
Rope walk, 58, 168
Rose, Caroline, 47
Rose, Charlotte, 126
Rose, Harriet, 69
Rose, John N., 43
Rose, Robert L., 18
Rosewarne, Georgianna Martha, 162
Rosewarne, John, 162
Rosman, Maria, 143
Rosman, Samuel I., 143
Ross, John J., 32
Ross, William, 26
Rossiter, D., 107
Rossiter, David, 114
Rossman, John, 117
Rowe, Catherine H., 78
Rowe, Epicratus, 78
Rowe, M., 16
Rowe, Rev., 40
Rowley, Hannah, 97
Rowley, Stephen, 16
Rowley, Sylvester, 139
Roy, See Ray, 29
Rucker, William L. & Co., 149
Rude, see Rhude, 13
Rumsey, C. B., 147
Rush, Daniel F., 97
Rushmore, Durant, 109
Rushmore, William, 139

Russ, Jeremiah, 79
Russell & Cory, 144
Russell, Caroline, 144
Russell, Daniel, 111, 174
Russell, Daniel R., 144
Russell, Hamlin G., 144
Russell, Jeremiah, 92
Russell, John, 142
Russell, Lucy, 174
Russell, M. B., 136
Russell, Moses B., 126
Russell, Polly, 89
Rutherford, Adam, 147
Rykard, Andrew M., 153
Sabins, S., 18
Sage, Sally, 33
Sager, Philip, 55
Salard, Sarah Ann, 152
Salisbury, A., 65, 69, 74, 132
Salisbury, Ambrose, 38, 39, 53, 55, 64, 92, 106, 113, 143, 145
Salisbury, Helen Mary, 145
Salley, Harriet M., 101
Salpaugh, Peter B., 102
Salsbury, Moses, 33
Sampson, George, 116
Sanders, C. W., 119
Sanford, A. C., 138
Sanford, Abel, 154
Sanford, Caroline, 95
Sanford, Dexter C., 176
Sanford, Emma M. 170
Sanford, George, 178
Sanford, Huron C., 176
Sanford, Isaac, 169
Sanford, Isaac R., 36, 170
Sanford, J. L., 131, 134, 138, 143, 144
Sanford, James H., 159
Sanford, James N., 151, 173
Sanford, Luther, 95, 176
Sanford, Luther, Jr., 134
Sanford, Maj., 71

Sanford, Melissa, 105
Sanford, Ruth, 176
Sanford, S., 121
Sanford, Samuel R., 163
Sanford, Stephen, 111, 120, 121, 125, 132
Saulpugh, Ann Jennet, 132
Saulpugh, Philip, 132
Saultenstall, Edward B., 90
Saunders, Enoch, 24
Saunders, John, 51
Saunders, Lorenzo, 79
Saunders, Randall B., 88
Sawtell, H. H., 128
Sawyer, A. P., 124
Sawyer, Daniel, 9, 130
Sawyer, Hooker, 144
Sawyer, Luke, 64
Sawyer, Norris, 155
Sawyer, Samuel W., 168
Sax, Ann, 98
Saxe, A., 178
Sayre, Jermiah, 158
Scantlin, S., 113, 130
Scantlin, William, 62
Scantling, Stephen, 87
Schermerhorn, Isaac M., 153
Schermerhorn, Jane C., 143
Schermerhorn, Morgan L., 78
School, Deaf and Dumb, 80
Scott, Alvah, 44
Scott, Ann, 31
Scott, Daniel O., 131
Scott, General., 133
Scott, John, 54
Scott, Winfield, 122
Scotten, Daniel, 162
Scotten, George, 127
Scotten, Rogers &, 159
Scovell, Cyntha R., 115
Scovell, Mariam. 151
Scovell, S., 10
Scovell, Seymour, 10, 115, 151

Scovill, Mary Jane, 142
Scranton, Edward, 31
Scudder, Sameul O., 175
Seales, & Mead, 155
Seaman, -. L., 149
Seaman & Thompson, 111, 116
Seaman, L. L., 116, 179
Seaman, Rebecca F., 152
Sears, Eliza Octavia, 136
Sears, James C., 59
Sears, John, 136
Seeley, C., 179
Seeley, James, 120, 127
Seeley, William S., 66
Seely, Jenner &, 154
Seelye, S. O., 159
Selby, Charity, 47
Selby, Harriet G., 110
Selby, Henrietta, 34
Selby, Ira, 43
Selby, Jared C., 22
Selby, Maria H., 107
Selby, Phebe Ann, 107
Selby, Sarah, 29
Selby, Satah Ann, 82
Selby, Stephen F., 164
Selden, David, 81
Selden, Nancy, 11
Seldon, Edward, 56
Seldon, Sibyl, 56
Sentell, John M., 144
Service, William, 53
Servis, Katherine, 59
Serviss, Nelson, 54
Severs, James McKnight, 135
Sexton & Butterfield, 95, 151
Sexton, J. K., 153, 159
Sexton, James K., 157
Sexton, Margaret, 61
Sexton, P., 18, 26, 65
Sexton, P. S., 132
Sexton, Pliny, 48, 52, 61, 62, 67, 72, 94, 104, 107, 114, 127, 152, 157

Sexton, Seymour &, 168
Sexton, Susan, 94
Seymour & Sexton, 168
Seymour, B. P., 153
Seymour, Bowman &, 127, 139
Seymour, Eli, 150, 167
Seymour, George, 79
Seymour, Martha, 168
Seymour, O., 18
Seymour, S. P., 153, 159
Seymour, Salome, 167
Seymour, Sidney S., 49
Seymour, Stephen P., 96
Sha, Elder, 23
Shaduck, Abraham, 65
Shannon, Richard Henry, 176
Shannon, William, 176
Shaver, Anna M., 165
Shaver, Joseph, 59
Shaver, Sally, 136
Shaw, Catharine, 43
Shaw, Elder, 17
Shaw, James, 124
Shaw, Miss, 99
Shaw, Noah, 75
Shear, Blaker, 156
Sheather, John, 92
Shedell, Richard A., 178
Sheets, Joseph, 86
Sheffield, Alice, 125
Sheffield, Bathsheba, 28
Sheffield, F. U., 39, 83, 88, 152
Sheffield, Frederick U., 31
Sheffield, John, 71
Sheffield, Nathan, 48
Sheffield, Paul, 105
Sheffield, Silas Stoddard, 88
Shekell, Ann, 44
Shekell, John, 44
Shekell, Samuel S., 44
Sheldon, Abraham C., 10
Sheldon, Margaret, 41
Sheldon, O. P., 10

Sheldon, R. H., 166
Sheldon, Samuel, 40
Shepard, E., 61
Shepard, Flora, 160
Shepard, Mr., 63
Shepardson, R., 10
Sheperdson, Ann Louisa, 92
Sheperdson, Lydia Ann., 66
Shephard, E., 62
Shepherd, Mary Ann, 36
Shepherdson, Nancy, 78
Sheppard, Erastus, 52
Sheppardson, Mrs. 59
Sherman & Crandall, 89, 144
Sherman, A., 82, 118, 179
Sherman, A. R., 179
Sherman, Alanson, 70, 80, 82, 88, 97, 106, 179
Sherman, Albert H., 121
Sherman, Augustus, 70
Sherman, Aurelia, 164
Sherman, Byram Green, 168
Sherman, Catherine, 155
Sherman, Charles B., 45
Sherman, D. H., 64
Sherman, David H., 48, 73, 75, 89
Sherman, Durfee A., 120, 121
Sherman, Edward, 169
Sherman, Gideon, 19
Sherman, Gilbert, 97
Sherman, J. Nelson, 126
Sherman, Jacob, 37, 119
Sherman, Jane, 97
Sherman, Jane Thompson, 147
Sherman, John F., 66
Sherman, John W., 60, 73
Sherman, Manson, 12, 14
Sherman, Mary Elvira, 106
Sherman, Nelson, 76
Sherman, Phineas L., 54
Sherman, Rhodes H., 128
Sherman, Roger, 57
Sherman, Ruth, 42, 60

Sherman, Samuel, 97
Sherman, Stephen, 40, 42, 60
Sherman, Susannah H., 121
Sherman, Warren, 50
Shermerhorn, Helen, 169
Sherwood, Isaac, 126
Shimer, J., 172
Shipwreck, 88
Shirts, Catherine, 89
Shirts, Sarah Jane, 81
Shoemaker, Marcia C., 174
Sholes, Elizabeth G., 43
Sholes, John, 43
Short, David, 140
Short, Georgianna, 130
Short, Leonard, 35
Short, Theodore, 35
Shove, Isaac, 150
Shove, Lydia P., 105
Shove, Sarah, 36
Shove, Sarah F. 36
Showers, James S., 34
Showers, Polly, 34
Shuler, Mathalane, 53
Shumway, G. M. H., 133
Shumway, G. R. H., 89, 90, 119, 170
Shumway, George R. H., 88, 168
Shumway, Mary Lindsley, 170
Shumway, Rev., 87, 89
Shupheldt, Jeremiah, 135
Shurtliff, Salome, 21
Sibley, Hannah, 60
Sibley, James, 60
Sibley, L. W., 16
Sibley, Maria, 29
Sibley, Mark H., 162
Sibley, Mary Ann, 31
Sibley, Mary Hopkins, 162
Sickles, J. F., 64
Sickles, Margaret, 36
Sickles, Myron, 101
Silk business, 128
Silk worms, 127

Simmons, Almira, 19
Simpson, Mary, 24
Sisson, Allen, 83
Sisson, Elisha, 159
Sisson, Thomas D. G., 157
Sisson, William, 157, 159
Siverson, William, 102
Skellinger, Sarah, 50
Skellenger, Stephen, 50
Skidmore, Delia, 116
Skinner, Asa, 50
Skinner, Matilda, 40, 42
Skinner, Nancy, 28
Slaughter, Mariah, 101
Sleigh ride, 117
Sloan, James, 68
Sloane, Douglas W., 94
Sloane, Harriet D., 94
Sloane, Maria, 83
Slocum, Joseph, 68
Smead, B. Franklin, 16
Smedley, Alonzo, 87
Smelt, William, 138
Smith & Champion, 12
Smith & Mason, 19, 26
Smith, Adeline E., 125
Smith, Adin B., 125
Smith, Alanson, 25
Smith, Albert G., 10,
Smith, Albert E., 51
Smith, Ammi C., 105
Smith, Ann, 167
Smith, Asa, 22
Smith, Asa B. 39
Smith, Barzillai, 167, 168
Smith, Benjamin F., 55
Smith, Betsey, 26, 48
Smith, Burrage, 46
Smith, C., 82
Smith, Capt., 159
Smith, Caroline, 127, 154, 156
Smith, Cephas, 67, 72, 151
Smith, Cyrus, 147
Smith, D. I., 19

Smith, D. K., 110
Smith, Daniel, 24
Smith, David, 39, 42, 55, 146
Smith, Delinda, 146
Smith, Denison, 60
Smith, Dennison, 25
Smith, Ebenezer, 158
Smith, Elijah,, 88
Smith, Eliza, 64
Smith, Eliza Ann, 169
Smith, Emily Maria, 121
Smith, Endoxura, 72
Smith, F., 10, 13, 14, 28, 21, 28, 32, 34, 38, 39, 62, 76, 119, 159
Smith, F. M., 79, 157
Smith, Frances A., 25
Smith, Frederick, 15, 20, 36, 37, 39, 64, 71, 73, 105, 111, 121, 148, 178,
Smith, Frederick, M., 146, 148
Smith, Freeman, 120
Smith, Fuller &, 35
Smith, George, 19, 26, 31, 95
Smith, George H., 125
Smith, George W., 173
Smith, H. F. & Co., 51
Smith, Henrietta, 151
Smith, Hiram, 32, 165
Smith, Hyrum, 161
Smith, Isaac L., 131
Smith, Isaac W., 143
Smith, Jacob, 111
Smith, Jane M., 169
Smith, Jarvis L., 39
Smith, Jesse R., 169
Smith, Jessup & Co., 62, 69
Smith, Joe, 100, 161
Smith, John, 9, 10, 117, 175
Smith, John, Jr., 52
Smith, Jonathan, 56
Smith, Jo[seph], 61, 136
Smith, Julia Ann, 175
Smith, L. C., 109, 134

Smith, Laura, 13
Smith, Louisa, 173
Smith, Lucina, 26
Smith, Lucinda D., 173
Smith, Lysander C., 151
Smith, Maria, 36, 37, 49, 168
Smith, Mary, 60, 62, 150
Smith, Mary Ann, 117
Smith, Mary B., 88
Smith, Nathan, 177
Smith, "Old Neighbor", 100
Smith, Olive, 19
Smith, Phebe, 110
Smith, Prudence, 170
Smith, R. W., 13, 61, 65, 70
Smith, Rachel, 85
Smith, Rev., 15, 21, 29
Smith, Robert W., 16, 91, 115, 120, 125, 141
Smith, Sally, 20, 177
Smith, Sarah A., 159
Smith, Shubael, 123
Smith, Sophia M., 126
Smith, Squire, 52
Smith, Thomas, 145
Smith, Uretta, 82
Smith, W., 37
Smith, W. H. A., 167
Smith, William, 150
Smith, William B., 123
Smith, William Henry, 152
Smock, Lucinda, 53
Smolten, John, 116
Smyth, Charles, 38
Smyth, Charles, Jr., 62
Snow, Mrs., 31
Snow, Sarah, 36
Snyder, Barbara, 62
Snyder, Henry, 94
Soda Springs, 153
Sodus, 82
Sodus Centre, 127
Soper, Ephriam, 163, 164
Soper, Miss, 57

Soper, Widow, 164
Soule, Freeman, 101
Soule, John, 38
Soules, Anthony, 62
Soules, Rufus, 70
Southard, Henry, 35
Southwick & Johnson, 134
Southwick & Thurber, 174
Southwick, C., 93
Southwick, Chad, 37
Southwick, Chade, 142
Southwick, W. H., 167
Southwick, William, 169
Southwick, William H., 119, 136
Southworth, Deborah, 97
Southworth, Fobes, 98
Southworth, Margaret, 96, 98
Southworth, Miss, 46
Sparhawk, E., 81
Sparhawk, Mary, 81
Sparhawk, Naomi, 37
Spear, A., 14, 124
Spear, Abigail, 80
Spear, Abraham, 24, 39, 48, 49, 52, 62, 72, 107, 114
Spear, Abram, 127
Spear, Alfred, 89
Spear, Charlotte, 160
Spear, Cordelia, 55
Spear, E. R., 49, 71, 74, 85
Spear, Emily,, 100
Spear, Erastus, 35
Spear, Erastus R., 76
Spear, Hannah A., 123
Spear, Harry, 157
Spear, Henry, 67
Spear, Irene, 49
Spear, Isaac, 67, 81
Spear, Jacob, 62
Spear, L., 61
Spear, Lemuel, 80, 98
Spear, Lemuel H., 112
Spear, Lorenzo, 86

Spear, Luther F., 168
Spear, Mary, 11
Spear, Mary A., 157
Spear, Philena, 124
Spear, Philetus B., 115
Spear, Ruth, 99
Spear, Stephen, 123
Spear, Stephen, 76, 118, 120, 135, 160
Spear, William, 94,
Spear, William R., 104
Spencer, Betsey, 114
Spencer, Clement Amos, 122
Spencer, Diana, 122
Spencer, E. M., 11
Spencer, George, 114
Spencer, Henry, 104, 106, 112, 122, 125
Spencer, Johannah, 122
Spencer, John C., 67, 71, 171
Spencer, Laura Catherine, 71
Spencer, Mary Natalie, 67
Spencer, N. E., 83
Spencer, Nelson E., 105
Spencer, O. Henry, 102
Sprague, Jonathan, 60, 62
Sprague, O. L., 178
Springer, Irena, 95
Springer, Richard, 127
Springer, Sarah, 127
Squires, Ezra, 44
St.John, Mrs. 14
St.John, S., 12, 14, 22
St.John, Solomon, 26, 33, 90
St.John, Thaddeus, 57
St.Lawrence, ---, 51
Stacy, Edwin, 152
Stacy, John, 127
Stacy, Sophia, 25
Stafford, Abraham, 58
Stafford, George, 37
Stafford, Lilly, 96
Stafford, Ward, 88
Stafford, William, 30

Stage, Railroad, 172
Stalp, Maria, 48
Stalp, Orella, 49
Stanbro, Josiah, 32
Stanbrough, Ira, 59
Stanbrough, James, 82
Stanley, Miss, 46
Stansell, Mary, 53
Stantial, Louise, 127
Stanton, A., 178
Stanton, C. S., 73
Starkes, Pamilla, 9
Starr, Albert J., 130
Starr, Jane E., 130
Staunton, Ann, 126
Staunton, William, 84, 89, 90
Stead, Thomas, 155
Stearns, Adaline, 58
Stearns, Erasmus, D., 133
Stearns, J., 63
Stearns, Joel, 55, 58, 60
Stearns, Joel, Jr., 82
Stearns, Lydia A., 108
Steele, David, 19
Steele, Frances Ann, 64
Steele, Harvey, 41
Steele, Rev., 15
Steele, William, 56
Sterling, H. P., 163
Sterling, Henry F., 166
Steven, Bushnell &, 12
Stevens, C. A. (Mrs.), 153
Stevens, Charles A., 152, 155
Stevens, Horatio, 27
Stevens, John A., 24
Stevens, John A., 31
Stevens, Mr., 55
Stevens, Phoebe, B., 24
Stevens, Rev., 27
Stevens, Ruth, 173
Stewart, Alexander, 79
Stewart, Cynthia, 36
Stewart, James, 75
Stewart, Joseph, 153

Stickney, Serepta, 177
Stiles, Hester Ann, 145
Stillman, Angelia B., 47
Stillman, Jared, 73
Stillman, Mary Ann, 66
Stillwell, Jacob, 57
Stilwell, Dr., 74
Stimpson & Pendergast, 48
Stimpson, Cynthia Ann, 82
Stimpson, Edwin B., 49
Stimpson, T. J., 12, 14
Stimpson, Thomas, 91
Stockton, B. B., 23, 29
Stockton, Benjamin, 15
Stockton, Benjamin B., 30
Stockton, Isaac, 127
Stockton, Rev., 13, 16, 20, 27, 32, 34
Stockton, Sarah H., 23
Stoddard, James S., 46
Stoddard, Bathsheba, 139
Stoddard, Calvin W., 103
Stoddard, E. V., 71
Stoddard, James S., 163
Stoddard, James A., 11
Stoddard, Lucy, 18
Stoddard, Lucy N., 31
Stoddard, Maria, 163
Stoddard, Mary Ann, 13
Stoddard, Nathan, 31
Stoddard, Silas, 139
Stoddard, Tabitha Frances, 139
Stoddard, Wait, 142
Stone, Bernice, 32
Stone, Edward G., 38
Stone, John, 177
Stone, L. D., 170
Stone, Lott, 64, 69, 73, 75
Stone, Sarah M., 173
Stone, Tammson A., 25
Stone, William, 25, 38
Storms, Jeremiah, 44
Stoudinger, Jacob, 30
Stout, Ellen, 165

Stout, Mary Ann, 129
Stout, Simon, V. W., 151
Stow, Joseph, 151
Stowell, A. W., 123
Stowell, Avery W., 113, 161
Stowell, Louisa, 170
Straight, Enoch, 146
Straight, Eunice, 97
Straight, Gardener, 93
Straight, Gardner, 92, 106
Straight, Nehemiah, 131
Stranahan, Farrand, 32
Straw, Liberty N., 58
Street, Emily Ann, 122
Streeter, Thomas J., 21
Strickland, Harley, 159
Strickland, Mary, 170
Strickland, Pamela, 130
Strickland, Sarah, 144
Strong & Quimby, 86
Strong, Cyrus, 48, 52
Strong, Delia, 53, 66
Strong, Julia Maria, 105
Strong, Lucius, 125
Strong, Rev., 21, 40
Strong, Silas, 66
Strong, T., 121
Strong, T. C., 10, 12
Strong, T. H., 80
Strong, T. R., 33, 43, 49, 52, 62, 66, 74, 75, 76, 82, 86, 89, 105, 119.
Strong, Theron , 106
Strong, Theron R., 70, 72, 75, 78, 89, 101, 104, 106, 140, 149
Strong, Theron P., 86
Stupplebeen, Jacob, 173
Styles, George, 69
Sullivan, ____, 75
Sullivan, James, 74
Sumner, James, 42
Sunderland, A. C. 46
Sutherland, C. J. & L., 65

Sutherland, Charles J., 78
Sutherland, Isaac, 29
Sutherland, Lemuel, 78
Sutherland, Reuben, 119
Sutherland, Sarah, 29
Sutton, Hannah, 18, 93
Sutton, J., 50
Sutton, Margaret, 156
Swan, Sybil A., 129
Sweet, Emily Ann, 122
Sweet, Emulous, 122
Sweet, Henry, 68
Sweet, Richard, 83
Sweeting, Rufus, 91
Sweezey, Rufus, 81
Swift, Asa R., 9,
Swift, Henry C., 98
Swift, John, 27
Swift, Mary, 98
Switzer, George, 151
Taber, B., 58 , 69, 79
Taber, Benjamin, 154
Taber, Benjamin Franklin, 163
Taber, Calista, 79
Taber, Gaylord, 60
Taber, Sally Ann, 69
Tabor, Deborah, 32
Tabor, Elizabeth, 177
Tabor, Abraham, 177
Tabor, B., 177.
Tabor, Sarah, 177
Taft, H. N., 139
Taft, Harriet J., 141
Taft, James T., 29
Taft, Mary, 14
Tague, Mrs., 11
Talbot, Runa H., 82
Tallent, R., 152
Tallmadge, John S., 24
Tannehill, James, 142
Tanner, A., 100, 101
Tanner, Alvenzo, 96
Tassell, James, 172
Tassell, Jane, 164

Taverns, E. P. Lane's, 99
Taverns, H. Church's, 50
Taverns, J. Baker's. 67
Taverns, L. U. Smith's, 141
Taverns, Lilly's Inn, 74, 85
Taylor, Eliphalet, 54
Taylor, Gen., 115
Taylor, George W., 126
Taylor, J. Orville, 92
Taylor, Mary, 55
Taylor, Nathaniel, 25
Teachout, Alonzo, 127
Teachout, Margaret, 29
Tedman, Alma, 104
Teller, J. V. C., 50, 66
Teller, W. J. & J. O., 25, 26
TenEyck & Fondey, 10
Terbuss, James, 75
Terrill, Chloe, 80
Terry & Post, 126
Terry, Ann, 18
Terry, C., 120
Terry, Constant, 34, 111, 113, 118, 140, 172
Terry, Ebenezer, 136
Terry, Jane, 107
Terry, Joshua M., 16
Terry, Lucy, 140
Terry, Mary, 162
Terwiliger, Alexander R., 159
Terwilliger, Martin, 137
Tharp, Emily, 49
Thatcher, Nancy, 138
Thayer & Co., 49,
Thayer & Grandin, 60
Thayer, Amasa, 78
Thayer, C. E., 43, 72, 73, 150
Thayer, Charles, 22, 104
Thayer, Charlotte Eaton, 153
Thayer, Chloe, 18
Thayer, Chloe P., 36
Thayer, Chris E., 75, 92
Thayer, Christopher D., 98
Thayer, Christopher E., 150

Thayer, Christopher F., 119
Thayer, Clarissa, 56, 95
Thayer, Delia Hart, 104
Thayer, Delia Marie, 124
Thayer, E. S., 127
Thayer, Edward S., 164
Thayer, Electa, 106
Thayer, Eliza, 81
Thayer, Elizabeth, 98, 115
Thayer, Franklin A., 166
Thayer, H. & C., 47
Thayer, H. P., 62, 63, 70, 73
Thayer, Hiram, 67
Thayer, Hiram P., 68, 75, 72, 92
Thayer, J. L., 10, 50, 47
Thayer, J. & L., 14, 26, 49, 69, 111, 128
Thayer, Jarvis L., 39, 75
Thayer, Joel, 11, 24, 36, 38, 42, 73, 84, 95, 130
Thayer, Joel E., 106
Thayer, John, 177
Thayer, L. & Co., 13
Thayer, Levi, 24, 35, 56, 64, 70, 73, 81, 86, 113, 115, 118, 121, 124, 153, 164, 166, 177
Thayer, Mary, 84
Thayer, Mary Ann, 104
Thayer, N., 13
Thayer, Nathan, 163
Thayer, Rhoda, 15
Thayer, Sally, 20, 78
Thayer, Smith, 98
Thayer, Susan, 30, 124, 177
Theatre, Franklin House, 112
Thespian Society, 122, 123, 124
Thomas, Eron N., 102
Thomas, J. J., 113
Thomas, Jane, 115
Thomas, Welthy Ann, 154
Thomas, Widow, 26

Thompson, Caleb, 104, 135, 148
Thompson, Charles, 31
Thompson, Charles A., 87
Thompson, Christina, 129
Thompson, Christopher C., 153
Thompson, Elijah, 165, 166
Thompson, Gates &, 179
Thompson, James, 29, 33
Thompson, Lucy G., 156
Thompson, Lydia Selina, 135
Thompson, Martha, 142
Thompson, Mary S., 124
Thompson, Samuel R., 123
Thompson, Seaman &, 111, 116
Thompson, Tripp &, 98
Thorn, Eber, 49
Thorn, Stephen, 56
Throckmorton, B., 125
Throop & McCarty, 153
Throop, Benj., Jr., 73
Throop, Benjamin, 83, 140
Throop, Benjamin T., Jr., 68
Throop, Eliza C., 139
Throop, Emily Mariah, 68
Throop, George B., 28
Throop, Horatio N., 85
Throop, N., 64
Throop, Nancy, 119
Throop, Rachel, 48
Throop, Rachel Brown, 140
Throop, Ruth, 84
Throop, Sarah C., 110
Throop, William H., 153, 155
Thurber, C. E., 168
Thurber, Grandin &, 143, 150
Thurber, Southwick &, 174
Thurston, Anna Maria, 131
Thurston, Isaac, 131
Tice, Abigail, 87
Tice, Elizabeth, 130
Tice, Hannah Louisa R., 137
Tice, John, H., 13
Tice, Lydia Ann, 140
Tice, Rhoda, 57, 58

Tiffany, A. R., 13, 33, 49, 55, 64, 65
Tiffany, Alexander, 46
Tiffany, Alexander R., 24
Tiffany, Edwin, 29, 169
Tiffany, Elizabeth, 24
Tiffany, Eunice, 169
Tiffany, Gardner, 62
Tiffany, George, 159
Tiffany, J. A., 66
Tiffany, L. H., 73, 119
Tiffany, Lyman, 79
Tiffany, Ruth, 135
Tilden, William B., 113, 141
Tillottson, L., 54
Tillotson, L., 60
Tingley, Catherine, 162
Tingley, D., 90, 134
Tingley, Daniel, 94, 158, 162, 163
Tingley, Emily, 150
Tingley, Sarah, 94, 158
Tinker, M. T., 158
Tinney, Hannah, 157
Tinney, Loretta, 116
Tippets, Caroline, 95
Tisdale, James, 16, 141
Tisdale, Sophronia, 141
Titus, Lucius B., 126
Tobey, A. B., 144
Toby, Morley &, 135
Todd, Alanson, 85, 135
Todd, Barbara Marie, 90
Todd, Jehiel, 52, 92
Todd, Margaret, 96
Tolford, William, 11
Tompkinson, Joseph, 72
Toohey, M., 12
Tooker, Charles K., 65
Tooker, Hiram H., 14
Torry, Charles W., 135
Torry, Roxy, 59
Tousley, A. M., 157
Tousley, Emily Frances, 157
Tousley, L. B., 157
Town, William, 30
Townsend & Co., 58
Townsend, & Durfee, 145
Townsend, E. S., 39, 65, 90
Townsend, E. S. & Co., 96
Townsend, Edward S., 96
Townsend, Edwin F., 120
Townsend farm, 137
Townsend, Harriet, 59
Townsend, J., 25
Townsend, Jesse, 75, 114
Townsend, Mr., 59
Townsend, W. F., 143
Towsley, Lorin B., 30
Tracy, Emeline N., 112
Transportation, railroad, 116
Transportation, stagecoach, 116
Transportation, steam, 112
Treat & Curtis, 48
Treat, H. H., 48
Treat, H. H. & Co., 41, 77
Trembly, Elizabeth, 55
Tripp & Thompson, 98
Tripp, John T., 129
Tripp, Mary Ann, 179
Tripp, Ruth, 118
Tripp, Timothy, 179
Troop, H. N., 36
Trowbridge, Hubbard, 176
Truax, Paulina, 151
True, Oliver, 19
True, Rev., 11
Trumbull, John, 61
Trumbull, M'Fingal, 61
Tubbs, David, 137
Tucker & Cuyler, 87
Tucker & Gilbert, 19, 22, 26, 33,
Tucker & Lothrop, 62
Tucker, A. W., 71, 132
Tucker, Abner, 96, 165
Tucker, Albigence W., 125

Tucker, Calvin, 149
Tucker, Edward Augustus,, 132
Tucker, Frances Ann, 60
Tucker, George, 10
Tucker, George A., 125
Tucker, James B., 165
Tucker, L., 65
Tucker, Lucy, 91
Tucker, Luther, 25, 37, 39,
    46, 60, 71, 81, 116
Tucker, Mary Alida, 176
Tucker, Mary S., 158
Tucker, P., 12, 15, 14, 18,
    38, 43, 52, 57, 62, 65, 70,
    74, 92, 111, 113, 115, 130,
    131, 140, 142, 148, 176
Tucker, Pendergast &, 46
Tucker, Pomeroy, 33, 58, 86,
    91, 111, 125, 133, 158
Tucker, Seth, 145
Tucker, W., 124
Tucker, W. L., 144
Tucker, William L., 140, 173
Tucker, Wm. L. & Co., 149
Tupper, Mary, 163
Turck, Margaret Ann, 123
Turner, Almira, 70
Turner, Alva W., 21
Turner, Amanda, 68
Turner, Caroline, 42
Turner, Chipman P., 94
Turner, Enoch, 42, 57, 62
Turner, Jonathan, 161
Turner, Laura, 9
Turner, Lois, 62
Turner, Melissa, 145
Turner, Mr., 142
Turner, Noah, 68
Turner, Orasmus, 83
Turner, Thomas, 134
Turner, Ursula, 70
Turner, William, Jr., 140, 148
Tuthill, David, 162
Tuttle, Daniel, 88, 91, 92

Tuttle, Marcus, 36
Tuttle, Mason &, 164
Tuttle, Myron J., 117
Tyler, A. S., 136
Tyler, Comfort, 36
Underhill, Caroline S., 130
Underhill, Mary Elizabeth, 43
Underhill, Mary Jane, 83
Underhill, P. P., 43
Vail, Israel, 87
VanAllen, Elizabeth, 76
VanAlstine, Daniel, 134
VanAlstine, Jacob, 80, 105,
    119
VanAlstine, Leonard, 134, 143
VanAlstine, Peter, 53, 85
VanAlstine, Thomas, 55
VanAlstine, William, 162
VanAlstyne, Leonard, 133
VanAlstyne, William, 156
VanBenschoten, Jacob, 11, 51
VanBenschoten, Rev., 178
VanBenthuysen, Obidiah R., 171
VanBuren Point, 94
VanCamp, ___, 154
VanCamp, Abraham I., 47
VanCamp, William, 156
Vanderhoof, David, 81
Vandine, Abram, 116
VanDoren, William J., 56
VanDruver, Azel, 24
VanDuesen, John, 173
VanDuesen, Nancy J., 16
VanDuser, Maria, 28
VanDuzer, Caleb, 26
VanDuzer, Isabel, 70
VanDuzer, Joseph, 95
VanDuzer, Mahala, 25
VanDyne, Peter, 67
VanHuzen, Caleb, 97, 114
VanKirk, John, 167
VanNess, Albert H., 175
VanOstrand, Jeremiah, 48
VanRensselaer, Jeremiah, 39

VanRensselaer, Jeremiah S., 40, 39
VanRensselaer, Sybella Adeline, 40
VanTassell, Barnabas, 54
VanWaggenen, Elizabeth K., 59
VanWagoner, Margaret, 90
Vanwickle, John, 48
VanWinkle, Miss, 22
Varick, Richard, 64
Vaughn, Stephen, 50
Vedder, Capt., 145, 159
Vedder, S. E., 167
Vine, Daniel, 134
Vine, Jesse, 133
Vine, John, 143
Voorhees, Amarilla, 177
Voorhees, William, 62
Vorse, Charles, 161
Vorse, John O., 130, 135, 163
Vorse, Lucretia, 161
Vosburg, Abraham, 159
Vosburgh, Abraham P., 33
Vosburgh, J. R., 159
Voter list, 86
Wade, C. B., 116
Wade, J. H., 119
Wade, Mary Helen, 138
Wadsworth, William, 12
Wait, Philena, 81
Wake, Jane, 152
Wakeman, Laura, 147
Wales, Arvine, 78
Wales, George, 135
Wales, Mary E., 135
Walker, Abraham, 104
Walker, Amos, 86
Walker, Eliza, 116
Walker, Elizabeth, 66
Walker, James, 177
Walker, James E., 120, 127, 151, 155
Walker, James S., 161
Walker, Robert, 27
Walker, Sarah J., 144
Wallace, Desdemona, 137
Walling, Mr., 123
Wallingford, Moss, 106
Wallis, Eliza, 135
Wallis, John, 85
Walrath Corners, 88
Walton, Louisa, 116
Walton, McKnight &, 146
Walton, William, 133
Ward, Artemus, 20
Ward, Daniel, 107
Ward, Harriet, 11, 51
Ward, John, 34
Ward, Levi, 100
Ward, Levi A., 11, 51
Ward, Marietta, 21
Ward, Ransom, 34
Ward, William P., 13
Warden, George I., 142
Ware, H. K., 105
Ware, Joseph K., 112
Ware, Mary, 112
Warner, Addison K., 66
Warner, Asenath, 49
Warner, David, 127
Warner, Elisha, 28
Warner, Eliza, 24
Warner, Henry, 21
Warner, Levi, 91
Warner, Lucinda, 19
Warner, Oren, 43
Warren & Robbins, 107, 163
Warren, John, 179
Warren, Joseph, 127
Warren, Laura Ann, 126
Warren, Nathaniel, 126, 127, 131, 161
Warren, Phebe, 122
Warren, Sarah, 37
Warson, Mary, 175
Warson, William, 175
Waters, Alvah, 30
Waters, M. Smith, 106

Waters, Maria, 45
Watson, G. W., 115
Watson, Thomas M., 144
Wayne Co., formation of, 82
Weaver, Catharine, 17
Webb, James, 156
Webster, Asher B., 97
Webster, Friend, 50
Weed & Niles, 42, 45
Weeks, Deborah, 111
Wells, Abigail A., 27
Wells, Albert, 151, 152, 164
Wells, H. G., 147
Wells, Hannah, 15
Wells, Helen H., 83
Wells, Henry, 36
Wells, Jenks, 33
Wells, Lucia, 34
Wells, Luke, 66
Wells, Maria, 63
Wells, Mary Ann, 165
Wells, Mehitable, 33
Wells, R. C., 138
Wells, R. G., 143, 144
Wells, Richard. 63
Wells, Rufus G., 165, 168
Welsh, William, 83
Wendell & Hyde, 50
Wentworth, A. H., 148
Wentworth, Edward D., 110
Wentworth, John, 164
Wentworth, Mary, 96
Wenzer, Dr., 170
Wert, Mr. 32

West, Edna J., 176
West, Mr., 71
West, P., 19, 49, 61, 69
West, P. & Co., 12
West, P. W. 93
West, Paulina, 59
West, Peletiah, 91, 97
Westcott, L., 19
Westcott, Leonard, 11, 24, 71

Westcott, Susan, 86
Westfall, Edward, 155
Westfall, Elizabeth, 162
Westfall, J., 155
Westfall, Jacob, 162
Westfall, James, 48,
Wheaton, Amanda Melvina, 27
Wheaton, Augustus, 21
Wheaton, Louisa, 21
Wheedon, Albert L., 179
Wheeler, A. G., 123
Wheeler, Albert G., 124
Wheeler, Capt., 145, 159
Wheeler, George, 171
Wheeler, John, 19
Wheeler, Robert B., 97
Wheeler, T., 167
Wheeler, William H., 106
Whelpley, Rev. 66, 83
Whelpley, Samuel, 70
Whipple, ____, 176
Whipple, Russell, 39. 64
Whipple, William H., 154
Whitcomb, Betsey, 21
White, Azuba, 25
White, C. W., 109, 111
White, Dr., 96
White, Elisha M., 144
White, F. (Miss), 114
White, Fanny A., 123
White, H. S., 51
White, Henry P., 90
White, Ira, 50, 58, 62, 72
White, Ira & Co., 75
White, J. O., 10
White, J. & O., 10
White, James, 15, 45, 65, 76,
  58, 65, 90
White, James & Co., 54
White, Jeremiah, 58
White, Marina, 13
White, Mary, 76
White, Mary Ann, 76
White, Nancy, 138

White, Pratt &, 75, 77
White, Rand, 18
White, Samuel, 117
White, Stacey, 93
White, William, 60, 62, 66, 69, 74, 75, 82,
White, Zuill &, 60, 69, 77
Whitely, William, 46
Whitfield, Elizabeth M., 146
Whiting, D., 135
Whiting, L. C., 147
Whiting, Orson, 147
Whiting, Rhoda Ann, 27
Whiting, Sarah, 126, 132
Whitman, John, 132
Whitmore, Moses B., 37
Whitmore, William, 146
Whitney, Jesse, 159
Whitney, John S., 37
Whitney, Lorenzo, 149
Whitney, Margaret, 33
Whitney, Mary Antoinette, 159
Whitney, Moses L, 124
Whitney, William E., 98
Wiants, H. S., 152
Wickham, Thomas, 39
Wicks, John, 94
Wiggins, Capt., 145
Wightman, J. C., 25
Wilber, John, 50
Wilber, Lucinthia, 44
Wilber, Samuel, 148
Wilbur, Isaac Underhill, 154
Wilbur, Phebe, 69
Wilbur, Sidney, 179
Wilcox & Bortles, 81, 83, 84
Wilcox, Ann, 16
Wilcox, George, 84
Wilcox, Hazard L., 116
Wilcox, Hiram, 18
Wilcox, Joseph,, 110
Wilcox, Lucy, 19
Wilcox, M. W., 66, 70, 72
Wilcox, Mary, 178

Wilcox, Mr., 125
Wilcox, R., 28
Wilcox, Thaddeus, 28
Wilcox, William, 38, 44, 46, 92
Wilcox, William S., 165
Wilcox, Wm., 74
Wilder, E. C., 179
Wilder, Erastus, 49
Wilezewski, Mons., 86
Wilkins, J., 30
Wilkins, Joseph, 21, 30
Wilkinson, Hiram, 147
Wilkinson, Kozia, 165
Wilkinson, Samuel C.,128
Willcox, Cynthia D., 72
Willcox, David, 141
Willcox, Diantha, 29
Willcox, H. R., 67, 93
Willcox, Hiram, 66
Willcox, Joseph, 40, 64
Willcox, Louisa, 60
Willcox, Lyman, 151
Willcox, M. W., 52, 61, 62, 64, 73, 75, 88, 106, 111
Willcox, Marlin W., 45
Willcox, Mr., 94, 111
Willcox, Mrs., 163
Willcox, Stephen, 25
Willcox, Sylvester, 161
Willcox, W. W., 43
Willcox, William, 20. 107, 113, 128
Willets, Henry, 177
Willets, Julia, 177
Willets, Stephen D., 177
Williams, A., 119
Williams & Co., 12, 22
Williams & Cook, 92, 93
Williams & Douglas, 169
Williams & Fillmore, 113
Williams & Williamson, 156
Williams, Alexander B., 70
Williams, Allyn, 47, 110, 121

Williams, Ann, 20
Williams, Butler &, 111, 120, 124
Williams, Button, M., 23
Williams, Chester, 29
Williams, Cornelia, 55
Williams, David, 64
Williams, Delia M., 55
Williams, Diana, 102
Williams, E., 92, 93, 140
Williams, Elbridge, 121, 169, 172
Williams, Eliza, 23
Wiiliams, F., 150
Williams, G. N., 24
Williams, George M., 52
Williams, George N, 16, 38, 48, 75, 115, 133, 157, 158, 160
Williams, H., 150, 161
Williams, H. B., 73, 158
Williams, H. G., 72
Williams, Helen P., 80
Williams, Homer, 76
Williams, Homer B., 75, 113
Williams, J. & Co. 89, 91, 92
Williams, James, 84, 87, 91
Williams, James D., 80
Williams, Jane, 169
Williams, John, 55, 78, 147
Williams, John, Jr, 94
Williams, M. W., 95
Williams, Margaret, 78
Williams, Margaretta, 156
Williams, Mary, 87, 157
Williams, Nathan T., 78
Williams, Platt, 176
Williams, R. M., 23
Williams, R. P., 164
Williams, R. S., 43, 62, 64, 66,
Williams, Richard M., 83
Williams, Richard S., 51, 80
Williams, saddlery, 129

Williams, Sarah, 59
Williams, Sarah E., 68
Williams, Selden, 126, 172
Williams, Seth, 86
Williams, Susan P., 83
Williams, tailor shop, 128
Williams, William A., 87
Williams, Z., 24, 74, 87, 89, 108, 110, 111
Williams, Zebulon, 25, 66, 106, 112
Williamson, Allyn, 166
Williamson, J. S., 135
Williamson, John, 166, 168
Williamson, William H., 168
Williamson, Williams &, 156
Williston, Amasa, 36
Williston, Rev., 22
Willits, Hiram, 104
Willits, Purdy M., 171
Willson, Delia, 144
Willson, James H., 134
Willson, Jared, 144, 175
Willson, Jered, 175
Willson, Lucy, 156
Wilson, Adoniram, 111
Wilson, Charity, 153
Wilson, David., 36, 153
Wilson, Gilbert, 132
Wilson, Henry P., 131, 153
Wilson, S. E., 121
Wilson, Samuel, 132, 135
Wilson, Samuel R., 157
Wilson, Samuel W., 119
Wilson, Stephen D., 171
Wilson, Wareham, 89
Winchester, Henry F., 171
Wing, Hiram, 67, 73
Wing, J. K., 146, 162
Wing, Sylvanis, 36
Winn, Elizabeth, 80
Winship, Joseph, 78, 86
Winship, Mary, 78
Winship, W., 82

Winslow, Calvin, 33
Winslow, Mr., 20
Winslow, Philander, 66
Winslow, Stephen, 170
Winslow, William, 26
Winters, Jack, 49
Winters, John C., 48
Witherall affair, 56
Withers, Mary Ann, 109
Withers, Mary Eliza, 109
Withers, Robert, 109, 151, 167
Wolcott, Laura, 96
Wolcott, Samuel, 43
Wolcott, Silvena, 106
Wood, Arba, 30
Wood, Charlotte E., 142
Wood, Daniel, 18
Wood, Isaac, 142
Wood, Phebe, 16
Wood, S., 170
Wood, Stepehn, 138
Woodbeck, Abraham, 97
Woodcock, David, 95
Woodruff, Amos, 41
Woodruff, Sally, 41
Woods, John, 110
Woods, Margaret, 110
Woodward & Co., 45, 57, 69, 75
Woodward, A. F., 57, 67, 69
Woodward, Arthur F., 72
Woodward, Eliza M., 97
Woodward, Elizabeth, 109
Woodward, F., 66
Woodward, Frances, 109
Woodward, J. M., 52, 57, 61
Woodward, Jabez, 40
Woodward, Jonas, 56
Woodward, Marianna Cornelia, 151
Woodward, Marvin, 123
Woodward, Meech &, 49, 69
Woodward, William, 97, 102, 109, 111, 147
Woodward, Wm., 119

Wooster & Gilbert, 22
Wooster, Albert, 165
Wooster, Anne, 153
Wooster, Charles W., 164
Wooster, L. N., 45
Wooster, Mrs., 165
Wooster, S. W., 108, 109
Worden, H., 40
Woren, John G., 86
woren. See also Warren
Wort, Mr., 32
Worth, C. B., 160
Worth, Susan R., 160
Wright, Benjamin, 114
Wright, Chauncey L., 59
Wright, Clark, 53, 65
Wright, Dr., 165
Wright, Joel, 45
Wright, Josiah, 41
Wright, Mary Ann, 114
Wright, Rev., 33, 37
Wright, Sally, 58
Wyborn, Lydia, 18
Wylie, William D., 104, 125
Wyman, Sally Ann, 130
Yoemans, Lucy, 123
Yoemans, Theron G., 108, 161
Yeomans, Vaniah, 58, 143
Yoemans, [Mr], 46
Young, Esther, 158
Young, John, 35
Young, Lydia, 157,
Young, Nelson D., 98
Young, Rebecca, 156
Young, Sarah, 96
Younglove, Aaron, 157
Zimmerman, Mr., 179
Zuill & White, 60, 69, 72, 77
Zuill, J. W. M., 72, 75
Zuill, John W. M., 73

www.ingramcontent.com/pod-product-compliance
Lightning Source LLC
Chambersburg PA
CBHW080430230426
43662CB00015B/2236